THE TWO GERMAN STATES AND EUROPEAN SECURITY

The Two German States and European Security

Edited by
F. Stephen Larrabee

Vice President and Director of Studies
Institute for East–West Security Studies

Foreword by Berthold Beitz

Preface by John Edwin Mroz

St. Martin's
Press
New York

in association with
THE INSTITUTE FOR
EAST–WEST
SECURITY STUDIES

© The Institute for East–West Security Studies, 1989

The Institute for East–West Security Studies does not take or encourage specific policy positions. It is committed to encouraging and facilitating the discussion of important issues of concern to East and West. The views expressed in this book do not necessarily reflect the opinions of the Board of Directors, the officers or the staff of the Institute.

First published in the United States of America in 1989

Printed in the United States of America

ISBN 0–312–02683–8 (hardcover)
ISBN 0–312–02820–2 (paperback)

Library of Congress Cataloging-in-Publication Data
The Two German states and European security / edited by F. Stephen Larrabee ; foreword by Berthold Beitz.
p.   cm.
"In association with the Institute for East–West Security Studies."
ISBN 0–312–02683–8 (hc) : $35.00; ISBN 0–312–02820–2 (pb)
1. German reunification question (1949–   ) 2. Europe—National security.   I. Larrabee, F. Stephen.
DD257.25.T89 1989   88–28313
943.087—dc19   CIP

Contents

v

List of Acronyms

ABM (Treaty)	Anti-Ballistic Missile (Treaty)
CDE	Conference on Disarmament in Europe
CDU	Christian Democratic Union (Christlich-Demokratische Union)
CMEA	Council on Mutual Economic Assistance
COCOM	Coordinating Committee for Multilateral Export Controls
CPSU	Communist Party of the Soviet Union
CSCE	Conference on Security and Cooperation in Europe
CSU	Christian Social Union (Christliche-Soziale Union)
DM	Deutschmark
EC	European Community
EEC	European Economic Community
FDP	Free Democratic Party
FRG	Federal Republic of Germany
GATT	General Agreement on Tariffs and Trade
GDR	German Democratic Republic
ICBM	Intercontinental Ballistic Missile
IGT	'Inner-German' Trade
INF	Intermediate-range Nuclear Forces
MBFR	Mutual and Balanced Force Reduction
NATO	North Atlantic Treaty Organization
PUWP	Polish United Workers Party
SDI	Strategic Defense Initiative
SED	Socialist Unity Party (Sozialistische Einheitspartei Deutschlands)
SPD	Social Democratic Party (Sozialdemokratische Partei Deutschlands)
START	Strategic Arms Reduction Talks
WEU	West European Union
WTO	Warsaw Treaty Organization

Notes on the Contributors

Dr Berthold Beitz is the Chairman of the Alfried Krupp von Bohlen und Halbach-Foundation in Essen and is the Honorary Chairman of the Board of Directors of the Institute for East–West Security Studies. A leading West German industrialist, Dr Beitz has been involved with oil, insurance and banking, and has played a key role in East–West trade. From 1953 to 1967 Dr Beitz was Chief Executive of Dr Alfried Krupp von Bohlen und Halbach. Among other posts, he is a Member of the Board of Trustees of the Max Grundig Foundation, a Member of the Supervisory Board of Dresdner Bank AG, and a Member of the Executive Board of the International Olympic Committee.

Amb. Jonathan Dean was deputy US negotiator for the 1971 quadripartite agreement on Berlin. Between 1973 and 1981, he was Deputy US Representative and then US Representative to the NATO–Warsaw Pact force reduction negotiations in Vienna. After leaving the Foreign Service in 1984, Ambassador Dean became Senior Arms Control Advisor of the Union of Concerned Scientists. He is the author of *Watershed in Europe* (Lexington, 1987) on the future of the NATO–Warsaw Pact military confrontation.

Dr Renata Fritsch-Bournazel is a Senior Research Associate at the Centre d'Etudes et de Recherches Internationales, Fondation Nationale des Sciences Politiques, Paris, and a Member of the Academic Advisory Committee of the Institute for East–West Security Studies. Her publications include *Rapallo: naissance d'un mythe. La politique de la peur dans la France du Bloc National* (Paris, 1974); *L'Union sovietique et les Allemagnes* (Paris, 1979); *Les Allemands au coeur de l'Europe* (Paris, 1983); and *Confronting the German Question: Germans on the East–West Divide* (Oxford, 1988).

Dr F. Stephen Larrabee is Vice President and Director of Studies of the Institute for East–West Security Studies. Formerly, Dr

Larrabee co-directed the Soviet and East European Research Program at the Johns Hopkins University School of Advanced International Studies, and was a visiting professor at Cornell University. From 1978 to 1981, he served on the US National Security Council staff as a specialist on Soviet–East European affairs and East–West political–military relations. He is the author most recently of 'Gorbachev and the Soviet Military', *Foreign Affairs* (Summer 1988) and 'Eastern Europe: A Generational Change', *Foreign Policy* (Spring 1988), and is currently working on a book-length study of Soviet policy toward the two German states.

Dr Anne-Marie LeGloannec is a research fellow at the Centre d'Etudes et de Relations Internationales of the Fondation Nationale des Sciences Politiques, Paris. A specialist on relations between the Federal Republic of Germany and the German Democratic Republic, she has been a Visiting Fellow at the Woodrow Wilson Center, Washington, DC (1985), and at the Institute for East–West Security Studies (1986). She is author of a book on the Berlin Wall, *Un mur a Berlin* (Brussels, 1985). She is currently working on a book that explores societal and governmental interrelations between the two German states.

Prof. Gert Leptin is a Professor of Economics at the Free University of Berlin's Eastern Europe Institute. He is a Member of the Executive Board of the Research Center for All-German Economic and Social Issues, Berlin (West), and was a Krupp Foundation Senior Associate at the Institute for East–West Security Studies in 1986. He has written several books and numerous articles on his special areas of interest, which include economic reform in Eastern Europe, problems of East–West trade (including security aspects) and the interplay between international economic relations and foreign policy interests.

Dr A. James McAdams is Assistant Professor of Politics at Princeton University, where he teaches courses in German, East European and Soviet politics. He holds a PhD from the University of California, Berkeley, and has been a Visiting Scholar at the Center for International Affairs, Harvard University. He is the author of *East Germany and Detente: Building Authority After the Wall* (Cambridge, 1985). During the 1987–8 academic year, he was in residence at the Research Institute of the German Society for Foreign Affairs, Bonn, and the Academy of Sciences, East Berlin, where he was completing a book on inter-German relations.

Prof. Gerd Meyer is affiliated with the Institute for Political Science of the University of Tubingen, West Germany. He is the author of *Strukturinterne und Umstrukturierende Neuerungen Dargestellt Am Beispiel der Forschung* (1982).

Prof. Dr sc. Juergen Nitz is head of a division at the GDR Institute of International Politics and Economics. His particular area of interest is the global economy and East–West economic relations, and he has published over 100 articles and five monographs on this subject. He is the GDR delegate to several international bodies, and in 1973 was appointed GDR representative to the International Council of East–West Cooperation in Vienna.

Prof. Dr Max Schmidt is the Director of the Institute for International Politics and Economics in the German Democratic Republic and a Member of the Board of Directors of the Institute for East–West Security Studies. He is also a Corresponding Member of the Academy of Sciences of the GDR, a Member of the Board of the GDR Committee for Research on Peace and Disarmament and Deputy Chairman of the National Committee of Political Science of the GDR.

Dr Gebhard Schweigler has been a research scholar at the Research Institute for International Affairs and Security of the Foundation for Science and Politics, Ebenhausen, since 1979. Previously he was a researcher at the Research Institute of the German Society for Foreign Affairs, Bonn, and at the Carnegie Endowment for International Peace, Washington, DC. Among his publications are *West German Foreign Policy: The Domestic Setting* (New York, 1984) and *Grundlagen der aussenpolitischen Orientierung der Bundesrepublik Deutschland* (Baden-Baden, 1985).

Dr William Richard Smyser, a former US Foreign Service Officer, is an expert on Germany and German–American relations. While in the Foreign Service, he served in both Berlin and Bonn. Dr Smyser is the author of *German–American Relations, The Defensive Option and Germany* and *Restive Partners*, books which deal with strategic, political and economic aspects of the relationship between the United States and the Federal Republic of Germany.

Mr Ryszard Wojna was a Polish press correspondent in the Middle East during the 1950s and in Bonn during the 1960s. He is the author of many books and essays on politics and history. Since 1976 Mr Wojna has been a member of the Polish Parliament (*Sejm*), and Deputy Chairman of its Foreign Affairs Committee. He also co-chairs the joint 'Polish Peoples Republic-Federal Republic of Germany Forum'.

Foreword

As Honorary Chairman of the Board of Directors of the Institute for East–West Security Studies I take great pride in the publication of this study on *The Two German States and European Security*.

This study appears at an important moment. After years of distrust and mutual recrimination, relations between the two German states have significantly improved in the last decade. Trade and human contact have visibly increased and the separation between the two states, which had begun to widen markedly in the 1960s, has been reduced. Perhaps most importantly, the German states have found a common interest in cooperating to secure peace. This common interest has been reflected in the oft-expressed commitment by the leaders of both sides that 'never again should a war arise from German soil'. At the same time both German states have come to have a deeper appreciation of the fact that, while they are divided by different political and social systems, they share a common history and culture.

One of the most important factors contributing to the improvement in the relations between the two German states has been an increased sense of self-confidence on the part of the GDR leadership. In the last decade the GDR has emerged as the strongest economic power among the USSR's Eastern bloc allies and its most important trading partner. Along with this economic resurgence has come a readiness to play a more active political role in East–West relations. This has been reflected in the GDR's strong support for a policy of *détente* and dialogue not only with the Federal Republic, but with the West in general, and a more active engagement on behalf of disarmament in Europe.

The GDR's more active and assertive role in East–West relations has been complemented by a strong consciousness of its own German, especially Prussian, roots. This has been reflected above all in the gradual rehabilitation of such historical figures as Scharnhorst, Clausewitz and Frederick the Great. It can also be seen in the restoration of important monuments and symbols of German culture in connection with the 750th anniversary celebration

xiii

of the founding of Berlin. The sense of pride and greater self-consciousness, both in social identity and in its German past, has in its own way contributed to easing the problems of separation and made the GDR leadership more willing to engage in an active dialogue with the Federal Republic.

Certain changes in attitude within the Federal Republic, particularly toward the idea of reunification, have also contributed to an easing of tensions. An increasing number of West Germans has come to recognize that reunification, if it is to occur at all, will only come as part of a long-term process and as a result of first overcoming the division of Europe itself. This has led to an important shift in West German policy. While not abandoning reunification as a long-term goal, successive West German governments have increasingly concentrated on reducing the burdens of separation through efforts to improve the conditions of Germans living in the GDR. This process has led to a significant increase in cooperation at a variety of levels, both governmental and individual, which has brought tangible improvements in the field of human contacts. In 1987 some three million East German citizens – over one million under retirement age – were allowed to visit the Federal Republic. This means that nearly one in five East German citizens were able to travel to the Federal Republic last year. The historic visit of East German party leader and Chairman of the State Council Erich Honecker to the Federal Republic in September 1987 was an important reflection of the increased desire for greater cooperation.

As one who has spent most of his professional life seeking to promote greater East–West cooperation, I take particular satisfaction in the inclusion in this volume of chapters by authors from the East. These chapters add a distinctive element to the book and are a concrete demonstration of the will of both East and West to work together to improve mutual cooperation and understanding. While many Western readers will not agree with all the points made, I am sure they will derive from these chapters an increased appreciation of the Eastern perspective. Such an appreciation is an important prerequisite for greater East–West cooperation. With the publication of this volume I believe that the Institute for East–West Security Studies has taken an important step toward furthering these goals.

Essen   BERTHOLD BEITZ

Preface

The future of the two German states, their relationship with each other and with the rest of Europe, is perhaps the central issue which will define the scope and nature of future cooperation between East and West in Europe. Since 1982 this issue has been a primary focus of the research, analysis and program activities of the Institute for East–West Security Studies. Recently, the Institute held its seventh annual conference, hosted by the government of the German Democratic Republic, in Potsdam. No city in Europe better symbolizes the legacies with which the continent has been grappling for the past forty years. The world is still living with the unresolved issues brought about by the Potsdam Conference of 1945.

The Institute's seventh annual conference focused on the future of East–West security relations. The role and behaviour of the two German states form one of the most critical issues affecting stability in East–West relations. Both states are bulwarks of their respective alliances, both possess the most productive economies in their respective parts of Europe, and both are strongly committed to achieving a new framework for relations between the countries of Europe. Both see the creation of a new and more cooperative relationship between the two parts of Europe as a prerequisite for the growth of long-term stable relations between the two German states.

Both the FRG and the GDR are conscious that their territory has the largest concentration of military forces ever seen in the world. Both host troops drawn from other nations in their respective alliances. This situation causes domestic tensions because of the visible presence of so many soldiers in a relatively small area. Both would like to see the level of military confrontation along their joint border reduced to the lowest possible level. To this end, they have been in the forefront of the disarmament negotiations in multilateral bodies, at the Mutual and Balanced Force Reduction (MBFR) talks, and in encouraging their respective superpowers to show pragmatism and flexibility in the negotiations concerning the reduction of both intermediate- and strategic-range nuclear weapons.

The GDR has made a number of proposals for nuclear-weapons-free and chemical-weapons-free zones which would embrace the territory of the two German states. West German Foreign Minister Hans-Dietrich Genscher has been forthright in seeking to shape NATO policy towards both current and possible future disarmament negotiations involving the two alliances. Leadership and policy changes in the USSR could further affect the range of possibilities for achieving arms-reduction agreements. As Mr Genscher said on 11 June 1988, in his speech at the Potsdam conference, 'Western policy must now recognize and use the historic opportunity presented by the Soviet Union's new thinking'.

In this volume, authors from East and West, including specialists from the two German states, analyze the German–German dialogue and explore the relationship of German–German affairs to East–West relations as a whole. As Berthold Beitz, Honorary Chairman of the Board of the Institute for East–West Security Studies, notes in his foreword, this study appears at an important moment of change in inter-German relations. F. Stephen Larrabee, Vice President and Director of Studies at the Institute, addresses this issue of change in his introduction. While the 'German Question' still remains an important feature of East–West relations, its nature has been transformed. Today the question is no longer one of reunification, but the character of the relationship between the two German states and its impact on European security. Renata Fritsch-Bournazel, Senior Research Associate at the National Foundation of Political Science in France and a member of the Institute's Academic Advisory Committee, discusses the historical importance of the German Question for European politics. A. James McAdams of Princeton University explores the changing leverage both states have in their relations in the 1980s. Max Schmidt, Director of the Institute for International Politics and Economics in the German Democratic Republic and a member of the IEWSS Board of Directors, reviews the current state of inter-German relations from an East German perspective. Soviet and American interests in German–German relations are carefully explored in the chapters by F. Stephen Larrabee and Richard Smyser, a former US Foreign Service Officer who is an expert on German–American relations. The arms-control dimension, in the wake of the INF Treaty and the eve of the Conventional Stability Talks, is studied by Jonathan Dean, Senior Arms Control Advisor to the Union of Concerned Scientists and former US Ambassador to the Mutual and Balanced Force Reduction talks. The larger European picture naturally includes the interests of countries bordering on the two German states: Ryszard Wojna, Deputy Chairman of the Polish Parliament's Foreign Affairs Committee, offers a stimulating presentation of Polish perceptions, while French views are examined by Anne-Marie LeGloannec, a Visiting Fellow at the Institute in 1986 and presently a Research Fellow at the National Foundation of Political Science in France.

Concentrating on the German–German relationship *per se*, Gebhard Schweigler of the Foundation for Science and Policy in Ebenhausen, FRG, presents an analysis of West German views of the German Democratic Republic and the issue of reunification, and Gerd Meyer of the University of Tuebingen's Institute for Political Science studies the motives behind Erich Honecker's continued postponements of a visit to Bonn in the early 1980s. Finally, two economists discuss the trade and economic aspects of the inter-German relationship from a West German perspective (Gert Leptin, a Krupp Foundation Senior Associate at the Institute for East–West Security Studies in 1986 and currently at the East European Institute of the Free University of Berlin) and an East German view (Juergen Nitz of the GDR Institute for International Politics and Economics).

This book is the first Institute study that we have chosen to publish with a commercial publishing house. It has been made possible by the dedicated work of the Institute staff. F. Stephen Larrabee, Vice President and Director of Studies at the Institute and a specialist on German affairs, conceived of the project and saw it through to completion. He would like to thank the Volkswagen Stiftung for its generous support of the research for his two chapters in this volume, and Heinrich Vogel, Director of the Bundesinstitut fuer ostwissenschaftliche und Internationale Studien, for providing a congenial atmosphere in which to conduct the research. Peter B. Kaufman, the Institute's Publications Officer, brought the manuscript through its various stages to publication. Mary Albon, Ian Cuthbertson, Heike Doerrenbaecher, Michael Gross, Larisa Iglitzin and Christopher Mattheisen contributed their talents in many ways. Thanks are also due to our dedicated publishing editors, Simon Winder and T.M. Farmiloe. Special appreciation is paid to the Ford Foundation and the John D. and Catherine T. MacArthur Foundation for making this publication possible.

As the Institute begins a major examination of East–West security issues for the 1990s, I am confident that the issues discussed in this volume will become increasingly important in the years to come.

JOHN EDWIN MROZ
President
Institute for East–West Security Studies
New York

1 From Reunification to Reassociation: New Dimensions of the German Question

F. Stephen Larrabee

In September 1987, after more than a six-year delay, East German leader Erich Honecker made a long-awaited visit to the Federal Republic. The visit – the first ever by a head of state of the GDR – was an historic event. Despite the fact that the FRG does not officially recognize the GDR as a foreign country, Honecker was accorded the honors of a visiting head of state. Thus the visit represented an important step – at least symbolically – in the GDR's quest for international recognition. At the same time, it symbolized the growing *rapprochement* between the two German states in recent years and prompted speculation in both East and West about a 'new German Question'.

It was probably inevitable that the visit should have provoked such speculation. Perhaps no issue in European politics has sparked as much emotion or controversy as the German issue. Historically, as Renata Fritsch-Bournazel points out in Chapter 2, the 'German Question' has been a central problem of European politics for several centuries. In the last three hundred years there has been no period when Germany has not to some degree formed an essential part of the European state system, either through formal alliance or through the more indirect execution of power.

Yet the idea of German national unity, either as part of the 'Greater Germany' of liberal ideals or Bismarck's Prussian-dominated 'Little Germany', was never universally accepted. Fear of German expansion and domination was a central feature of European politics throughout the nineteenth and twentieth centuries. Bismarck was able to dilute this fear by a series of complex alliances in which Germany was the cornerstone, as well as by ensuring that any change in the *status quo* did not upset the basic balance of power in central Europe. His successors, however, displayed neither his

1

diplomatic skill nor his clear sense of limits. Their effort to expand Germany's power led to two world wars – and finally to the country's partition in 1945.

In the postwar period the German question – the question of Germany's role and form – again became a burning issue as a result of the *de facto* partition of the country at the end of the Second World War and the failure of the four occupying powers to agree upon a final peace treaty determining Germany's political status and territorial boundaries. As a result, two separate German states, each with its own political system, each integrated into separate alliance systems, emerged after 1949. Over the next several decades the political *status quo* hardened; legally, however, it remained 'open' because of the lack of a formal peace treaty and because Bonn remained – and remains – committed to keeping it open under its constitution.

With the signing in the early 1970s of the Eastern treaties that regulated Bonn's relations with the Soviet Union and its Warsaw Pact allies, the German question lost much of its emotional and political impact. The treaties represented Bonn's acceptance of the postwar territorial *status quo* – one of the primary goals of postwar Soviet foreign policy. They paved the way for a normalization of relations with the Soviet Union and Eastern Europe, including the GDR. In effect, the treaties removed the German issue from the international political agenda which it had dominated for nearly thirty years. Or so it seemed.

I   THE RE-EMERGENCE OF THE GERMAN QUESTION

In the last few years, the German question has again emerged as an issue in East–West relations. On the one hand, the GDR's growing self-confidence in foreign policy, above all in relations with Bonn, has given the inter-German relationship a new dimension. Moreover, as Jonathan Dean points out in his chapter, this dialogue has now begun to touch upon, if only indirectly, important security issues. On the other, Bonn's commitment to deepening ties to the GDR has prompted concerns in the West about the long-term impact on the FRG's attachment to the Western alliance. These concerns were well illustrated by Italian Foreign Minister Giulio Andreotti's remarks in 1984 about the dangers of pan-Germanism. While undoubtedly exaggerated, his statement was a sharp reminder of the continued sensitivity of the German issue, even after forty years of partition.

The growing sense that '*etwas ist los in Deutschland*' – that important changes are taking place in both parts of Germany – suggests that it is time to take a more systematic and comprehensive look at the relations between the two German states. The essays in this volume, all by well-known specialists, attempt to do just that. They examine the changing relationship between the two German states and the implications of that relationship for European security and East–West relations more generally.

This volume is unique, moreover, in that it contains contributions from both West and East, including essays by authors from the two German states themselves. The German essays add an important dimension to the volume. They not only address some of the basic issues in sharp detail, but also indicate how much progress has been made in attenuating them. A decade ago a multinational collaborative volume such as this one on such a sensitive topic would have been practically unthinkable. Today it is possible because the will to overcome many of these basic differences on both sides has visibly grown, even if a number of complex and sensitive issues still remain unresolved.

While the essays in this volume reflect differing national and individual points of view, they all highlight the centrality of relations between the two German states for security and stability in Europe. Perhaps most important, they suggest that there is a need to re-examine the way we think about the German question and the relationship between the two German states. Changes have taken place over the last several decades in the policies of both states which have served to transform the German issue as it has traditionally been conceived. The old German question, as understood in the early postwar period, centered around the question of reunification. Yet changes in international politics, as well as in public attitudes in both the Federal Republic and the GDR, suggest that this issue has lost much, though not all, of its former relevance. The real issue today – the 'new German Question' – relates not to reunification but to the evolving modalities of inter-German *détente* and their implications for European security. It has two interrelated aspects: (i) how will changes in the policies of the two German states affect European security and (ii) how will changes in the postwar security order influence the policies of the two German states? It is to the nature and implications of this 'new German Question' that the essays in this volume are addressed.

II *DÉTENTE* AND THE GERMAN QUESTION

To note the re-emergence of the German issue in the early 1980s, however, begs the more fundamental question of why it has re-emerged now, and what it holds for the future. Does it represent, as the eminent historian Fritz Stern has suggested, a 'return of the repressed', the reappearance not only of concern for the 'other Germans', but of a brooding about German identity and destiny which has so often in the past led the Germans down the path of adventurism?[1] Or does the explanation lie elsewhere?

Probably there is no easy answer to this question. However, as the essays by Renata Fritsch-Bournazel, James McAdams and Gebhard Schweigler suggest, the deterioration of East–West relations at the end of the 1970s clearly was an important factor in the re-emergence of the German issue. The deterioration forced both German states to clarify their positions toward each other and decide how much they wished to maintain their previous investments. In the process both came to the conclusion that the investments were worth preserving, even at the cost of some friction with their respective superpowers.

The deterioration of East–West relations at the end of the 1970s, moreover, underscored the important linkage between inter-German *détente* and East–West relations generally. After the collapse of the negotiations on intermediate-range nuclear forces (INF) in 1983, both states tried not only to protect German–German *détente* from the general deterioration of East–West relations, but also to play a more independent role in preserving East–West *détente*. In the end, however, both had to recognize that the international environment set distinct limits on how far they could insulate their relationship from outside events.

The important linkage between inter-German *détente* and the international political climate – what Germans refer to as the '*Grosswetterlage*' – was well illustrated by the developments leading up to the Honecker visit to Bonn in September 1987. The visit was postponed several times – once in 1983 and again in 1984. While there were a number of contributing factors, some internal and some external, Soviet disenchantment with the timing of the visit clearly played an important role. The GDR's effort to pursue *détente* with Bonn ran counter to Moscow's effort to freeze East–West relations during this period and 'punish' Bonn for its willingness to accept the deployment of American missiles. By 1987, however, the situation had changed significantly. A new, more flexible Soviet leadership was actively seeking an improvement in East–West relations and the hard line toward Bonn and Washington had been replaced by a more conciliatory stance toward both countries. Thus the external conditions for the visit were auspicious, and both German states sought to exploit the improvement in the international climate to their own advantage.

The recognition of this important linkage has prompted both German states to play a more active role in promoting East–West *détente* and pushing both superpowers to improve their relations. For its part, Bonn has been the most outspoken advocate of East–West detente and arms control within NATO, largely because the success of its *Deutschlandpolitik* depends on the state of overall East–West relations. As developments in recent years have shown, without a stabilization of the international political climate, progress from the Federal Republic's side in German–German relations is likely to be slow at best.

The GDR has come to the same recognition. After the collapse of the INF talks in December 1983, the GDR, along with Hungary, emerged as one of the strongest proponents of East–West *détente* within the Eastern bloc. Honecker not only pursued his own policy of 'damage limitation' *vis-à-vis* Bonn, but gave strong backing to the Hungarian thesis that small and middle European powers can play a role in preserving *détente* in periods when relations between the superpowers are strained. The more assertive role played by the GDR during this period reflected East Berlin's growing stake not only in good relations with Bonn but in the stability and security of Europe generally.

In actual fact the two aspects are closely linked. A more peaceful and relaxed atmosphere is an important prerequisite for an intensification of relations between the two German states. Hence, as Max Schmidt points out in his chapter, the GDR has become one of the strongest proponents of the need for 'new thinking' in East–West relations, and has begun to play a more active role itself, particularly in the arms control and security area. One example has been its proposal for a chemical- and nuclear-weapons-free zone in central Europe. A more recent example is Honecker's proposal of January 1988 for the elimination of all tactical nuclear weapons from both German states. While these proposals are clearly consistent with Soviet policy goals, they also reflect a growing desire on the part of the GDR leadership to play a larger role in the East–West security debate and to make a contribution of its own.

To some extent, in fact, the GDR was out in front of the USSR regarding the need for 'new thinking' in foreign policy. Many of the ideas which Gorbachev is now espousing about the need for greater East–West *detente* were put forward by Honecker in 1983–84 in the wake of the INF missile crisis. Though ignored or rejected at that time by the Soviet leadership, they have since been embraced by Gorbachev. Indeed, Honecker can legitimately take satisfaction in seeing some of the ideas he advocated now being adopted, albeit for different reasons.

However, while the GDR has welcomed many of the new approaches to security pursued by the Soviet Union since Gorbachev's assumption of power, it has been more reserved about other aspects of his policy, especially his emphasis on the need for economic reform and *glasnost* (openness). The East German leadership has made clear that the reforms are fine for the Soviet Union, but that they are unnecessary in the GDR, whose economy has significantly outperformed Moscow's in recent years. As the SED's chief ideologist Kurt Hager bluntly put it in an interview in April 1987: Just because your neighbor papers his walls, does this mean you need to do the same thing?

To what extent this attitude can be maintained over the long run remains to be seen. The demonstrations in front of the Berlin Wall in the summer of 1987 by hundreds of East German youth as well as the more assertive stance adopted by the Evangelical church since the Honecker visit to Bonn highlight the difficulties of maintaining tight control over East German society in the face of growing pressures for change. Today, in effect, the GDR faces a dual challenge – one from within the bloc as a result of Gorbachev's reform program and one from outside as a result of the increased contacts with the West, above all Bonn. This presents the SED with an entirely new situation and the way the party manages to accommodate these dual pressures will have a major impact not only on the domestic situation within the GDR but on relations between the two German states as well.

III THE IMPACT OF THE INF ISSUE

It was the controversy over INF issue in the late 1970s and early 1980s, as much as any other factor, which really served as a catalyst for the re-emergence of the German issue. The INF issue underscored the important linkage between German–German *détente* and East–West *détente*. In the end, Honecker's statement that the former could not flourish in the face of a palisade of American missiles proved temporarily correct. But the brief effort by the two German states to prove the contrary in early 1984 highlighted how strong their mutual interest in *rapprochement* had become.

The INF controversy also had a strong domestic impact in both countries. In both it sparked wide-ranging domestic unrest and raised long-submerged questions of German 'national' interests. To be sure, the origins and motivations of the protest movements in each country were quite different. In the Federal Republic outside events played a much larger role, whereas in the GDR the non-official peace movement was largely a response to indigenous events.[2] Yet, as the missile controversy developed, these distinctions became blurred, and the peace issue itself became predominant. Moreover, the strong involvement of the Evangelical churches in both states in the peace movements gave the two protests a certain commonality. Thus the peace issue came to be a unifying force, tying both German states more tightly together. Both states increasingly began to stress their common responsibility for the preservation of peace.

At the same time, the INF controversy contributed to a broader questioning and search for alternatives that would more closely correspond to German 'national' interests. In the Federal Republic this was reflected in the emergence of a form of 'left-wing nationalism' which sought to link the national question with the peace issue. The German question was seen by the proponents of this view as being an instrument of peace for Europe. They argued that a withdrawal of the two German states from the military blocs would create a real *détente* zone and at the same time facilitate closer cooperation between the two German states. A confederation of the two German states would be conceivable as a stage in the process of attaining national unity.[3]

In the GDR the peace issue was by and large not linked with the national issue. However, Robert Havemann, the well-known dissident Marxist philosopher, did raise the issue in a letter to Soviet party leader Leonid Brezhnev in the fall of 1981 on the eve of Brezhnev's visit to the Federal Republic. The letter, which attracted support among a number of left-wing intellectuals in the FRG, called upon both superpowers to conclude a peace treaty and 'withdraw all occupation troops from both parts of Germany'.[4] In addition, Havemann's close friend, pastor Rainer Eppelmann, in a special appeal called for negotiations between the two German states for the removal of all nuclear weapons from German soil as a first step toward the creation of a nuclear-free zone in Europe.[5] While the statements from Havemann and Eppelmann were hardly representative of the views of the unofficial peace movement in the GDR as a whole, they nevertheless demonstrated the way in which the debate in the GDR began to transcend issues related purely to the GDR and spill over into a discussion of broader East–West issues.

Some members of the Green Party and the West German peace movement, on the other hand, spoke of a 'special German path', emphasizing the special role that both German states, particularly the Federal Republic, could play in promoting peace and *détente* in Europe. To achieve this goal, they advocated a withdrawal of the Federal Republic from NATO, the removal of all foreign troops from West German soil, and the recognition of the GDR under international law. The idea of a special German path (*Sonderweg*) is hardly new; it has deep roots in German history. Yet, as Kurt Sontheimer and others have pointed out, it is precisely this effort to pursue a 'special German path' that led the Germans to defeat and disaster in two world wars.[6] Others, like the West German journalist Peter Bender, called for a 'Europeanization of Europe'.[7] In Bender's view Europeans in East and West should decouple themselves from the two superpowers and establish a position of 'equidistance' between Washington and Moscow. Inevitably this would mean a weakening of both German states' ties to their respective alliances (though not necessarily their withdrawal).

It is perhaps not surprising that a related theme – the rediscovery of *Mitteleuropa* – also came into prominence during this period. The concept is vague, and means many things to many people. For many East Europeans, especially East European dissidents, it is used to underscore the cultural affinity of the countries of East Central Europe with the West and implies a certain 'distancing' from the Soviet Union. In the West German context, on the other hand, it has reflected a reawakening of the cultural interest in central and Eastern Europe. Historically, however, it has traditionally implied a certain distancing from the West.

The debate over *Mitteleuropa* and a German *Sonderweg* are linked to the larger question of national identity which has increasingly preoccupied West Germans in recent years.[8] To be sure, many of these issues would have emerged anyway as a new generation of West Germans came to maturity which had not experienced the deprivation of the early postwar period and which took for granted the prosperity and more relaxed East–West climate of the 1960s and 1970s. But the missile controversy acted as an important catalyst for the re-emergence of these issues and gave them greater resonance. The crisis tended to highlight the dependency of the Federal Republic on the United States as well as accentuate the tension between US and NATO goals on one hand and West German (and German) 'national' interests on the other. Hence much of the hostility was focused on the United States and NATO.

The missile crisis also highlighted the basic tension between Bonn's geographic position and its alliance membership. Politically the Federal Republic is tied to the West; geographically, it is a part of central Europe. The basic contradiction between these political and geographical realities, as Renata Fritsch-Bournazel points out, produces a certain tension. The Cold War tended to dampen this tension. In the face of what was perceived as an expansionist and hostile Soviet Union most Germans gave top priority to the Federal Republic's ties to the West, which they saw as the best guarantee of the FRG's security. At the same time the collapse of the Third Reich discredited German nationalism. For the next several decades most West Germans suppressed their national feelings and sought to channel them into a larger European entity. In effect, European integration and Americanization became surrogates for nationalism. By the late 1970s, however, the movement toward European integration had lost most of its momentum, and the United States no longer appeared to be the beacon of hope to a new generation of West German youth.

The missile crisis brought to the fore many of these sublimated feelings and energies. To a large extent these ideas reflect a disenchantment with the constraints imposed by the Federal Republic's alliance obligations and ties to the West. Many have deep roots in German history. Yet they all suffer from a fatal flaw: a tendency to overestimate the Federal Republic's room for maneuver. One of the main reasons for the initial success of the *Ostpolitik* – one which Chancellor Willy Brandt himself continuously stressed at the time – was Bonn's strong anchor in the West. It was precisely this anchor that made the *Ostpolitik* possible. A neutral Federal Republic would have been open to pressure from the East which would have made the pursuit of a vigorous, self-confident *Ostpolitik* difficult. Yet it is precisely this lesson which many of 'Brandt's children' seem to ignore or forget.

IV ALLIANCES IN TRANSITION

Part of the current disquiet and unease is also related to structural shifts within each alliance. In the early years of the alliances, both states had major constraints on their sovereignty and were largely dependent upon their respective superpowers for their existence and the achievement of their foreign policy goals. National goals were largely subordinated to alliance goals, which, in turn, were determined primarily by the two superpowers. When the goals of the superpowers shifted, the two German states had little choice but to fall in line with the policies of their patron.

This was as true for Bonn as for East Berlin. Thus, when Washington and Paris embarked upon *détente* in the 1960s, Bonn had little choice but to follow suit or risk diplomatic isolation. Bonn's *Ostpolitik* was not so much a matter of choice as of survival. As Josef Joffe has pointed out, for a country as sensitive to the specter of diplomatic isolation as the Federal Republic, *Ostpolitik* was a matter of staying in the Western mainstream rather than leaving it, of 'following rather than leading'.[9] The shift in US policy, in effect, forced Bonn to jettison Konrad Adenauer's linkage between *détente* and reunification. Rather than making reunification a precondition for *détente*, *détente* became a precondition for reunification. This opened the way for the signing of the Eastern treaties and the normalization of relations with Moscow and its East European allies, especially the GDR. Once it had joined the trek eastward, however, Bonn was reluctant to abandon the journey when US policy shifted to a more hardline stance in the late 1970s.

The same is true for the GDR. Initially the GDR was a reluctant proponent of *détente*. Once the Soviet Union had decided for reasons of its own to move toward a normalization of relations with Bonn, however, East Berlin had little choice but to fall in line. While Honecker's predecessor Walter Ulbricht initially resisted this process, his foot-dragging eventually cost him his job. But, as with the Federal Republic, once East Berlin had embraced *détente*, it was reluctant to return to the trenches of the Cold War when Soviet policy shifted after the collapse of the INF negotiations in late 1983.

A decade later, in a remarkable reversal of roles, it was East Berlin that was pushing a recalcitrant Moscow not to drop the reins of *détente*.

In addition, over the past fifteen years there has been a discernible shift in the role which each country plays in its respective alliance – and its relationship with its respective superpower. Once a client with little freedom of action, each has become the junior partner of its former patron and its most important ally. As a result, today each is less inclined to follow automatically the line laid down by its superpower, especially if this conflicts with more narrowly conceived 'national' interests.

This process of 'emancipation' has been most apparent in the case of the Federal Republic. Fifteen years ago it was common to refer to West Germany as an 'economic giant but a political dwarf'. Now the situation has changed considerably. Today Bonn has become both an economic *and* a political giant, albeit at times a reluctant one. Its economic muscle – in 1986 the FRG overtook the United States as the world's largest exporter – has inevitably given it greater political weight. Today it is without doubt the most powerful country – politically, economically and militarily – in Western Europe.

The invitation to West German Chancellor Helmut Schmidt to attend the Guadeloupe summit of the 'Big Four' Western powers (the United States, Britain, France and FRG) in 1979 was *de facto* recognition of this new status. So too was the appointment of Manfred Woerner, the former West German Defense Minister, as General Secretary of NATO. Yet adjusting to this new role has not been easy – for either side. In large part because of the legacy of the past, Bonn remains reluctant to assume a political role commensurate with its economic influence, a fact which from time to time has contributed to tensions with the United States. At the same time, the Federal Republic has gradually begun to develop a more autonomous foreign policy, especially toward the East.

Ironically *Ostpolitik* played an important part in this process of emancipation. For one thing it lightened the burdens of dependence. As long as Bonn refused to accept the territorial *status quo*, it was dependent on the Western allies to achieve its chief foreign policy goal (reunification). Once it reordered Adenauer's priorities and made *détente* a preprequisite for any long-term reunification, its room for maneuver was enlarged and it was no longer so dependent on its alliance partners to achieve its major foreign policy goals.

At the same time Bonn acquired new stakes in the East and in the process of East–West *détente*. The *Ostpolitik* brought important benefits – trade with the East, security for Berlin and above all, improved relations with the GDR. Having worked hard to acquire these benefits, Bonn has been reluctant simply to cast them overboard as US policy switched from *détente* to confrontation. This has served to create new fault lines in the alliance and in West German–US relations.

These strains were highly visible during the Carter years. The tensions between President Carter and Chancellor Schmidt reflected not simply differences of personality – though these clearly existed – but rather of national interests. As a global power, the United States can easily live without *détente*. Because of Berlin and the GDR, the FRG cannot. Hence, as US–Soviet relations soured, Bonn sought to insulate German–German *détente* from the fall-out of the deterioration. It also felt compelled to play a more active role in preserving or resurrecting East–West *détente*.

The differences with Washington have been more muted under Kohl, but they have by no means disappeared, as the initial cool reaction of the Kohl government to the INF agreement attests. In the end the Kohl government accepted the treaty – it really had little other choice – but the accord has stimulated West German fears of 'denuclearization' as well as revived old concerns about the dangers of 'singularization'. As a result the West German defense consensus has been further fragmented, and conservatives on the right have joined with radical arms controllers on the left to call for a removal of all tactical nuclear artillery from West German soil (the so called 'triple zero' solution), a move which many analysts felt would seriously undermine NATO's strategy of flexible response.

This does not mean, however, that the Federal Republic is about to become a 'wanderer between two worlds'. Fears of a drift toward neutralism or the threat of a 'new Rapallo' (a secret deal between Bonn and Moscow regarding reunification), which periodically surface every time Moscow casts a baleful eye at Bonn, are highly exaggerated, indeed absurd. As Richard Smyser makes clear in Chapter 9, the bonds that tie the Federal Republic to the United States and NATO are strong. Yet the desire and need to maintain a strong tie to the East – above all to the GDR – will continue to give Bonn a strong interest in promoting East–West *détente* and cooperation and make alliance coordination more complex and difficult.

To some extent the same process of adaptation and emancipation can be witnessed in the GDR as well. Once one of the most dependent of Moscow's 'satellites', in the last two decades the GDR has emerged as Moscow's most important political, economic and military ally in the Eastern bloc and its main source of high technology. The days when the GDR's leadership had to fear for its existence are long over. Today the GDR is one of the world's ten leading industrial powers. And while other East bloc countries have watched their economies steadily decline and their foreign debts rapidly increase, the GDR has recorded relatively high growth rates and developed a sizeable reserve of hard currency (thanks in no small part to several large credits from the FRG).

The GDR's economic performance, while not without its problems, has contributed to the emergence of a new self-confidence and assertiveness on the part of the GDR leadership. In recent years East Berlin has increasingly sought to exploit its growing importance within the Eastern bloc to expand its room for maneuver and pursue a foreign policy more closely attuned to its national interests. This more assertive policy has at times conflicted with Moscow's interests.

The most obvious example was Honecker's conscious effort to insulate German–German ties from the deterioration of superpower relations after the collapse of the INF talks in 1983. This effort ran directly counter to Moscow's desire to isolate and punish Bonn for its willingness to go forward with INF deployment and led to an unusual incident of open discord, discussed in detail by Gerd Meyer in Chapter 6 and my Chapter 8, over Honecker's visit to Bonn in the summer of 1984. While Honecker was eventually forced to postpone the visit, the fact that he held out so long is striking. Moreover, as Meyer and I point out, it would be wrong to see the decision to postpone the visit simply as an example of Honecker's bowing to Soviet pressure. Internal East German factors also played an important role, especially Honecker's desire to achieve an upgrading of the relationship and to promote a dialogue on arms control issues. Once it became clear that Bonn was unwilling to accommodate these interests, the proposed visit lost much of its initial appeal and Honecker decided to postpone the meeting.

There is a danger, however, in reading too much into this incident. The GDR is not about to sacrifice its bloc membership on the altar of German–German *détente* any more than Bonn is likely to cut its ties to the West in pursuit of *Ospolitik*. Both German states continue to see their primary allegiance as one to their respective blocs, and short of a major reordering of the political map of Europe – an unlikely prospect in the near future – this is likely to remain the case for some time to come.

V REASSOCIATION vs. REUNIFICATION

Both German states, however, maintain a strong interest in improved relations, as developments over the last several years have once again confirmed. The postponement of the Honecker visit in 1984 led to a brief cooling of relations. Since 1986, however, relations have once again begun to warm. Trade and cultural contacts have soared, as have visits by citizens of the two German states. In 1987 some three million East Germans – nearly one million of them under retirement age – visited the Federal Republic, a severalfold increase over previous years. In addition, in 1987 another 7 million West Germans visited the GDR. This increase in ties has served to lessen the estrangement and separation between the two German states.

At the same time, both states have developed a greater consciousness of their common historical roots. This, together with an increased consciousness of their national identity, has been reinforced by the proliferation of contacts between the two German states in recent years, which have given each state a stronger sense of the ties that bind them as well as the differences that separate them. Indeed, in the Federal Republic a dialectical process has taken place. On the one hand, the idea that all Germans should live in a national state has declined, while on the other there has been a growing awareness that there are strong cultural and historical ties between the two German states. As Richard Lowenthal has noted:

> Generally speaking, the longing for a return to a German national state, so natural to the generation that experienced the partition of Germany, has gradually faded first in the West and more recently in the East. At the same time, the awareness of being drawn together by a common history, including common cultural achievements and common horrors and sufferings, has revived, particularly in the West where the postwar generation has tended to turn away from it.[10]

This can be seen in the GDR as well, particularly in the effort to 'reinterpret' GDR history that has taken place in the last few years.[11] As a result of this effort, once-reviled figures such as Frederick the

Great, Clausewitz and Scharnhorst – not to mention Martin Luther – are now treated in a more positive light. Even Bismarck, once regarded as a 'reactionary Prussian Junker', has been partially rehabilitated, and is now praised as a far-sighted *Realpolitiker* for his pursuit of close ties to Russia.[12] East German historians have been encouraged to trace the GDR's historical roots much more deeply into 'German' history, putting less emphasis on the emergence of the GDR as a new nation after 1945, as was the case in the initial period after Honecker assumed power.

This growing national consciousness and concern with national identity in both German states should not be confused, however, with a desire for reunification. The majority of West Germans recognize that reunification is only possible, if at all, within a wider European framework. Moreover, as the polling data in Gebhard Schweigler's chapter illustrates, the belief that reunification is likely or possible has precipitously declined in the Federal Republic over the past two decades, particularly among the young.[13] Thus, while support for reunification as an abstract goal has remained strong, its operational significance in West German policy has significantly diminished. Instead Bonn has increasingly put emphasis on working with the GDR to manage and ease the division.

To a large extent, the emphasis has shifted from reunification to maintaining the 'unity of the nation'. Some West Germans, particularly the Greens, have even advocated changing the provision in the West German constitution obligating Bonn to promote reunification as a national goal. Others have begun to distinguish between overcoming partition and the idea of reunification. As West German President Richard von Weizsaecker has noted: 'Overcoming partition does not mean unification . . . for the former we will find understanding almost everywhere and for the latter almost nowhere. Most Europeans dislike the wall about as much as they do the idea of a large German state in central Europe.'[14]

In short, the real issue today, as James McAdams points out, is not reunification but 'reassociation', that is, the modalities and implications of inter-German *détente*. This process has taken on a new dynamic in the last few years, and both German states, albeit for different reasons, have developed a strong vested stake in its continuation and expansion. There is, moreover, a strong continuity over time and across party lines in Bonn's *Deutschlandpolitik*. While in opposition the CDU was highly critical of the SPD's policy toward the East and the GDR in particular. Once in power, however,

Helmut Kohl has pursued much the same policy. This highlights the degree to which *Deutschlandpolitik* has become a national priority in the Federal Republic.

How far the CDU's position has shifted since the early 1970s is reflected in the passages concerning *Deutschlandpolitik* in the position paper on foreign policy worked out by the internal party commission headed by CDU General Secretary Heiner Geissler, which was submitted for discussion and approval at the party conference in Wiesbaden in June 1988.[15] While the paper continues to hold out reunification as a long-term goal, it puts the main emphasis on the 'preservation of the German nation' through an easing of the current separation and a diminution of the East-West conflict. Moreover the paper clearly states that any resolution of the German Question can only be achieved in cooperation with the Federal Republic's neighbors in East and West.

This shift is well illustrated by the remarkable transformation of Franz Josef Strauss, the arch-conservative leader of the Christian Socialist Union (CSU), the Bavarian wing of the CDU, from hostile critic to ardent *Ostpolitiker*. Strauss not only helped to arrange the large 1 billion DM loan to the GDR in the summer of 1984, but has become a frequent traveller to Eastern Europe, including Moscow. His metamorphosis underscores the degree to which *Ostpolitik* and *Deutschlandpolitik* have become good domestic politics in the Federal Republic – whether in Bonn or Bavaria.

The GDR has also increasingly developed a strong vested stake in good ties with Bonn, especially in the economic area. The contributions to this volume by Gert Leptin and Juergen Nitz discuss the economic dimensions of the relationship. Both authors point to the way in which trade has served to stabilize relations between the two German states. Yet their perspectives are quite different. Whereas Leptin stresses the role that political factors have played in the development of trade, Nitz puts the emphasis on economic factors, arguing that politics and economy have been relatively independent of one another.

There can be little doubt that economic considerations have been a factor behind the GDR's interest in *détente* with Bonn. As Leptin points out, the GDR derives significant benefits from its economic relations with the FRG. Under a special provision of the Treaty of Rome, products from the GDR are considered part of 'inner-German trade' and are thus not subject to EEC customs duties. The GDR also benefits from an 850000 DM interest-free 'swing' credit, which has helped the GDR to build up its hard currency reserves, as well as from a series of special lump-sum payments for transit fees from the FRG to Berlin, the use of roads within the GDR, and the renewal and extension of access fees. All told, these transfers are estimated to amount to some 2.5 billion DM per year.

In particular inter-German trade has helped the GDR to cushion the impact of outside economic disturbances. In 1981–3, when the GDR faced a serious debt crisis, East Berlin made extensive use of the opportunities in inter-German trade to moderate its foreign trade and payments burden by shifting a part of its trade to inter-German trade, for which it did not have to pay hard currency. East Berlin also benefited from two large loans (1 billion DM and 950 million DM, respectively) guaranteed by the Federal Republic in 1983–4, which helped the GDR to restore its financial credibility and build up a strong cushion of hard currency reserves. Thus the real value of inter-German trade for the GDR is its ability to overcome bottlenecks by obtaining urgently needed goods that are in short supply without having to spend hard currency.[16] In return, East Berlin has been willing to make some limited concessions in the humanitarian area.

It would be misleading, however, to see the GDR's interest in improved ties with Bonn as solely economic. Political considerations also play an important role. For one thing, the special relationship with Bonn has given the GDR the opportunity to develop and articulate its own national interests more clearly. In addition, as in the FRG, *Deutschlandpolitik* is good domestic politics. Honecker's pursuit of better ties with Bonn has both helped to strengthen the SED's legitimacy and to increase his own personal popularity among the East German population. Both these factors suggest that the motivations behind the GDR's policy are more complex than is often assumed in the West.

James McAdams's chapter suggests, however, that the balance of power and interests between the two German states may be changing. The really important question today, in his view, is who wants inter-German *détente* most. And who is willing to pay the higher price for it. Bonn's strong vested stake in good ties with East Berlin, he argues, has given the GDR a degree of leverage it lacked a decade ago. At the same time, the SED leadership has become more confident in its ability to manage *détente* with Bonn and thus more willing to take risks.

Honecker's visit to Bonn in September 1987 highlights this point.

The visit itself did not lead to any dramatic breakthroughs. Indeed, as Jonathan Dean points out in Chapter 7, both sides consciously sought to keep expectations low in order not to burden the relationship unnecessarily and generate false hopes – or fears. In the end, however, Honecker's patience paid important political dividends. The visit resulted in a significant upgrading of the GDR's status. Although it was billed only as a 'working visit', Honecker was received by Chancellor Kohl and accorded all the honors of a head of state, whereas three years earlier there were disputes over protocol and even whether Honecker would be received in Bonn at all. Moreover this time he was able to come with Moscow's blessing – as a faithful ally rather than knight-errant.

Bonn, however, did not come away empty-handed. Besides the obvious domestic boon to Kohl's political fortunes, Bonn has achieved a number of important benefits in the humanitarian area. The number of East Germans allowed to travel to West Germany jumped from 60 000 in 1985 to nearly 500 000 in 1986. In 1987 the figure reached over three million. This means, in effect, that nearly one in five GDR citizens travelled to the Federal Republic in 1987 – a remarkable increase.

The key question is how far the GDR will be willing to moderate or abandon its policy of *Abgrenzung*, or 'demarcation' (limitation of contacts). To some extent the Honecker visit has raised hopes that may be difficult to fulfill. Indeed, the upsurge of dissent in its aftermath, which culminated in the arrests of some 100 political activists in January 1988 and the eventual expulsion of many of them to the Federal Republic, appears in part to be related to the hopes generated by the visit and underscores the potential dangers to social stability of any major opening to the West. The crucial issue is: To what extent can greater freedom of travel and expression be allowed without generating social pressures which may prove difficult to control?

These dilemmas are well illustrated by the internal debate within the SED over the joint document on ideology signed between the SED and SPD in August 1987.[17] Many in the West, especially in the Federal Republic, have criticized the document for blurring the traditional distinction between social democracy and communism. Yet in the long run the document may portend greater difficulties for the SED than the SPD. Several of the principal points – particularly the suggestion that 'imperialism' is capable of pursuing a peaceful policy, the moderation of the image of the enemy

(*Feindbild*) and the acknowledgement of the legitimacy of debate and discussion of internal developments – represent important ideological departures from traditional SED positions.

The publication of the joint document appears to have caused confusion among the rank-and-file members of the SED, long accustomed to see 'imperialism' as an implacable enemy, and stimulated heated debate within the party. In late October 1987, Kurt Hager, a member of the Politburo and the SED's chief ideologist, felt compelled to clarify the party's position – or at least the orthodox wing's interpretation of it. In a major article in the party paper *Neues Deutschland* Hager argued that imperialism was by no means peaceful by nature, but had to be forced to pursue a policy of peace and that there was no need to change the traditional perception of the enemy (*Feindbild*).[18] Hager's riposte appears to represent a counter-attack by the orthodox wing of the party and suggests that many of the theses contained in the document remain highly controversial.

VI THE SOVIET FACTOR

In the final analysis, however, the keys to any significant change in the relationship between the two German states lie in Moscow, not in Bonn or East Berlin. No far-reaching change or *rapprochement* can occur without the Kremlin's blessing. This gives Moscow a certain leverage over Bonn's policy as well as East Berlin's.

The USSR has traditionally regarded close cooperation between the two German states with skepticism and has sought to carefully control the degree of German–German interaction to ensure that it promotes rather than contradicts Soviet interests. As I point out in Chapter 8, however, Soviet policy has recently begun to change under Gorbachev. On the one hand, he has given Honecker more leeway to pursue the GDR's national interests, as the Honecker visit to Bonn in September 1987 illustrates. On the other, the post-INF policy of trying to punish and isolate Bonn has been replaced by an effort to woo the Federal Republic.

To a large extent this shift represents a tactical adjustment, an effort to jettison an outmoded policy inherited from his predecessors. Yet it may also presage a more fundamental shift in attitudes and generations which could have deeper implications over time. The old proponents of a policy of isolation and punishment are either dead (Chernenko, Ustinov) or have little influence on day-to-day foreign policy toward Bonn (Gromyko). Today there is a new leadership in the Kremlin which did not experience the Second World War at first hand and whose fear of German 'revanchism' is not as deep-seated as that of its predecessors. Moreover, some of the leading Soviet *Germanisti*, such as Valentin Falin, the former Ambassador to Bonn, now occupy influential posts as advisors to Gorbachev.

From time to time, in fact, there have been hints that Moscow might be rethinking its policy toward the Federal Republic. Some have even speculated that Gorbachev might make a dramatic gesture to solve the German problem, perhaps as part of a proposal for a 'Comprehensive Security System' in Europe. Even if not serious, such a proposal would cause considerable internal dissension in the Federal Republic, which Moscow might be able to exploit to its advantage.

The dangers of a new Rapallo, however, seem remote. For one thing, a united Germany would dominate Europe, particularly Eastern Europe. For another, there would be no guarantee that a united Germany would remain neutral. Last and most important, because a united Germany could only come about through free elections, this would require the Soviet Union to give up its influence over the GDR, which, as noted earlier, has become its most important ally.

Any effort to 'play to German card', moreover, would have serious repercussions in Eastern Europe, especially Poland. For Poland, as Ryszard Wojna underscores in Chapter 10, European security and Polish national security are closely linked to the German Question. 'Susceptibility to every manner of potential threat from the German side', as he notes, 'continues to be the most important point of reference in approaching the issue of national security in Polish foreign policy'. Having suffered terribly in two world wars at the hands of Germany, Poland remains profoundly suspicious of long-term West German goals, as well as calls for 'overcoming Yalta'. Most Poles, Wojna makes clear, see such calls as little more than a covert effort to overturn the postwar order in Europe and reopen the German Question. This, he argues, would present a grave danger to Poland's national security as well as peace in Europe generally.

For Poland, as for the GDR and Soviet Union, the German Question has been resolved once and for all. Peace and stability,

Wojna argues, must take precedence over self-determination. In the Polish view the Soviet Union and Western integration remain important constraints on the expansion of Bonn's power and on its ability to overturn the postwar order. Thus any hint of a radical shift in Soviet policy on the German issue would have serious consequences, not only for its policy toward the GDR, but also toward Poland.

Gorbachev has given clear evidence that he recognizes this fact. While he has been willing to allow greater interaction between the two German states, he has made clear that any *rapprochement* must be based upon acceptance of the 'reality' of the existence of two sovereign German states. In short, while Gorbachev may give Honecker somewhat greater leeway to improve relations with Bonn and may himself actively seek better ties to the FRG, he is unlikely to embrace or espouse any radical schemes which would lead to a fundamental restructuring of alliances or reunification of the two German states.

VII DOMESTIC CHANGE

Domestic changes, particularly the emergence of a new generation of leaders whose attitudes toward defense and security issues differ significantly from those of its predecessors, have also contributed to the unease about the directions in which relations between the two German states may move in the future. This is a problem throughout Europe, East and West, but because of the discontinuities in German history its impact in the Federal Republic has been and is likely to be particularly profound.

The initial postwar generation, the generation which founded and built the NATO alliance, came of political age during the Cold War. They were largely integrationist, anti-Soviet and pro-American. For them, as the West German writer Guenther Grass has noted, the United States was an *Ersatzvaterland* (a substitute fatherland). It represented a role model which substituted for their own lack of historical roots – roots which had been wiped out, physically and psychologically, by the destruction of the Hitler Reich.

This generation is now slowly passing from the political scene. It is being replaced by a new generation whose formative experience was not the Cold War but *détente*. This new generation, most of whom were born after 1950, associates the United States not with the Marshall Plan and the Berlin airlift but with Vietnam and Watergate. They display a strong adherence to what Stephen Szabo has termed 'post-materialist' values and life-styles.[19] This includes an antipathy toward technology and post-industrialist society, which they associate with the United States. While not pro-Soviet, many see little difference between the two superpowers.

The emergence of this new 'post-materialist' generation is beginning to have an impact not only on West German domestic politics but on foreign policy as well. The Green Party epitomizes this shift in values. In the security area it advocates a removal of all nuclear weapons from West German soil and Bonn's withdrawal from NATO. Some even favor a neutralization of both German states as part of a larger effort to foster closer ties between the two German states. While the Greens represent a distinct minority – less than 10 per cent of the population – they articulate sentiments and values of a much larger portion of the population.

At the same time there has been a gradual erosion of the consensus on defense and security policy that has been a hallmark of West German foreign policy since the late 1950s. Helmut Schmidt was the last true 'Atlanticist' of senior stature within the SPD. Since his resignation as chancellor in October 1982, the party has shifted increasingly to the left, especially on defense matters. While most leaders of the party still believe the Federal Republic should stay in NATO and that American troops should be stationed on West European soil, the SPD's policy has begun to diverge increasingly from that of its two main allies, Washington and Paris. On defense issues the SPD has favored strengthening of the European pillar of NATO and a greater emphasis on 'non-provocative defense'. In contrast to the position taken by the Kohl government and NATO, moreover, the SPD favors the removal of _all_ tactical nuclear artillery from West German soil.

In the foreign policy area the SPD has put emphasis on what it calls a 'second phase' of _Ostpolitik_. The basis of this new phase is a 'security partnership' with the Soviet Union and the East. As part of this effort the party has engaged in an intensive dialogue with the GDR on the creation of a chemical-weapons-free-zone in central Europe as well as initiated discussions with Poland and Czechoslovakia on the creation of a nuclear-weapons-free-zone in central Europe. In August 1987, moreover, the SED and SPD issued a joint declaration on the 'Principles of Ideological Coexistence', a highly controversial document which was criticized by some in the

Federal Republic, and even within the SPD itself, for blurring the historically important distinction between social democracy and communism.

To be sure, such initiatives can be dismissed as the efforts of a party out of power trying to gain votes and sharpen its political profile. Once in power it may well be that, as some argue, the SPD would temper many of its more far-reaching initiatives and move back toward the center. Yet the breakdown in the security consensus in the Federal Republic is worrying to many in the West. Indeed, as in the 1960s after the Berlin crisis, West German politics today shows signs of polarizing around two different tendencies, the 'Atlanticists' and the 'Europeanists' or 'Gaullists', with the former continuing to look to Washington for security and the latter looking to France as the leader of a strengthened 'second pillar of NATO'. As in the 1960s, these schools cut across party lines, though the Europeanists tend to be centered more in the SPD and the Atlanticists more in the CDU.

It is not only in the Federal Republic, however, that generational issues will have an important political impact. The GDR also faces an important generational change in the next few years, particularly within the top echelons of the party. The East German leadership is currently divided into two distinct groups: an older group, most of whom are in their early to mid-seventies, and a younger group, all in their fifties. The older group includes Honecker; Prime Minister Willi Stoph; President of the Volkskammer (Parliament) Horst Sindermann; Minister of State Security Erich Mueller (the oldest member of the Politburo); Deputy Prime Minister Alfred Neumann; Chairman of the Central Party Commission Erich Mueckenberger; Central Committee Secretary for Culture and Science Kurt Hager; and Central Committee Secretary for International Relations Hermann Axen.

The younger group is just beginning to move into positions of power. It includes Guenter Schabowski, head of the East Berlin Party District; Egon Krenz, Central Committee Secretary for Security; Guenter Mittag, Central Committee Secretary for Economics; Central Committee Secretary for Agitation and Propaganda Joachim Hermann; Central Committee Secretary for Party Organs Horst Dohlus; First Deputy Prime Minister Werner Krolikowski, and recent additions to the Politburo such as Werner Jarowinsky, Guenter Kleiber, Siegfried Lorenz, and Hans-Joachim Boehme. The orientation and political experience of this group differ significantly from those of the older generation. The younger men all joined the party right after the Second World War and came to political maturity at a time when the GDR's existence was no longer in question. While not necessarily more liberal, they are less fearful of the West and more willing to compete with it.

At the same time a new generation has grown up in the GDR that has never known at first hand a unified German state. Their formative political experience has come since the erection of the Wall. They have come of age at a time, moreover, when the ideological barriers *vis-à-vis* the Federal Republic have been breaking down and when expectations for a gradual liberalization are growing. As the growth of the peace and ecological movements in the GDR suggests, their group is willing to express their discontent more openly than their predecessors.

The emergence of the autonomous peace and ecological movements in the GDR should not be seen simply as a manifestation of a concern for peace and ecology; these movements are a reflection of a broader search for new values and an alternative life-style on the part of many young East Germans. In the past decade, the GDR has witnessed the growth of a 'counterculture' similar in many respects to that which has emerged in the FRG and many other Western industrialized societies.[20] In East Berlin, Leipzig, Dresden, and other large cities in the GDR, several tens of thousands of young people live a state of internal emigration. They reject both the old German/Prussian bourgeois values and the official socialist values promoted by the SED.

Many of these '*Aussteiger*' (dropouts) form the core of the political activist and dissident movement in the GDR. These activists and dissidents make up only a small portion of East German youth. Many of their concerns, however, are shared by a broader stratum of East German youth, which has formed the backbone of the peace and ecological movements in the GDR and has increasingly turned to the Evangelical church for support of their concerns. As a result the leadership of the Evangelical church has found itself under growing pressure from many among East German youth to speak out more forcefully on social and political issues and to act as an intermediary with the authorities on these issues.

The Evangelical church, however, should not be seen as a major oppositional force or an alternative power center. Its leaders are moderates who see themselves as heading a 'Church in Socialism', not an organization opposed to the state or system. They are concerned, moreover, to maintain and expand the important gains in status and autonomy which they have achieved in recent years. Nevertheless the more active role played by the church as an intermediary between the state and society, as well as the greater readiness of a large portion of East German youth to become more actively engaged in debate over political and social issues such as peace and ecology, is noteworthy and suggests an evolution of East German political life which bears watching.

VIII THE SECURITY DIMENSION

These domestic changes take on increased saliency because they interact with important changes in the security arena. The signing of an INF agreement and the probability that a strategic arms accord will be signed in the not too distant future have increased the prospects for a diminution and a restructuring of the military competition in Europe. Any restructuring of military capabilities in Europe, however, would have a direct impact on the two German states because they have the largest concentration of troops and artillery in Europe. Moreover a reduction of nuclear weapons poses special problems for the Federal Republic because Bonn depends on the US nuclear guarantee for its security.

Thus over the last several years security issues, especially arms control issues, have become more closely linked to the future of the postwar security order and the role both German states play in that order. At the same time, as Jonathan Dean points out in Chapter 7, both German states have begun to play a more active role in the arms control process and to articulate their own special interests in that process. In addition, both German states have increasingly begun to speak of their 'special responsibility' for preserving peace and stability in Europe.

The security dilemmas are most pronounced within the Western alliance, and particularly within the Federal Republic. Western policy, especially nuclear policy, is in a state of flux – some would say disarray – and disenchantment with American policy has visibly increased. Such nervousness, to be sure, is nothing new: it has periodically surfaced every time US–Soviet relations have begun to show signs of improvement. Three recent developments, however, have given these fears new prominence.

The first was President Reagan's March 1983 announcement of

the Strategic Defense Initiative, which was seen by many West Europeans, especially West Germans, as threatening to decouple US security from West European security through the creation of two unequal zones of security, one covered by a defensive shield (the United States) and the other (Western Europe) left uncovered. This revived West European fears that they would be left vulnerable to nuclear attack. The fears were particularly acute in the Federal Republic because the FRG is the ally most dependent on the American nuclear umbrella for its ultimate security. While the Reagan administration sought to calm these fears by assuring its allies that they too would be covered by any SDI-type 'bubble', these assurances were never regarded as terribly convincing.

A second important factor was President Reagan's willingness to move toward rapid denuclearization at the October 1986 Reykjavik summit by agreeing in principle to the elimination of all land-based intercontinental ballistic missiles, and all intermediate-range missiles – after little or no consultation with the NATO allies and very little consideration of the military implications of such a move, especially for Western Europe. Indeed, in part as a result of the strong reaction from the West European allies, the Reagan administration was eventually forced to modify its position and withdraw its proposal to eliminate all land-based ICBMs. By the time it did so, however, considerable political and psychological damage had already been done.

The third and perhaps most important factor contributing to this new unease was the 'double-zero' INF agreement eliminating all intermediate- and shorter-range missiles, signed at the Washington summit in December 1987. The agreement intensified West European fears of 'denuclearization', and has further weakened confidence in the American commitment to Europe. The reaction in West Germany was particularly sharp. While the Kohl government eventually came out in support of the agreement, it did so only after considerable debate and delay. The agreement has sparked a new fear regarding denuclearization, which could have an important long-term effect on West German attitudes toward security. In contrast to the past, moreover, these fears are shared by both the left and some prominent members of the right.

As a result of these three factors, new fears have arisen in Europe, and especially West Germany, about the future of nuclear deterrence and the American nuclear guarantee. The elimination of all intermediate- and shorter-range systems poses a special problem for the Federal Republic because it leaves NATO almost completely dependent on short-range tactical nuclear weapons for its defense. These weapons have ranges of less than 500 kilometers, and if fired would land primarily on West German soil, killing millions of West Germans. (As Volker Ruehe, a leading CDU defense expert, has put it: 'The shorter the range, the deader the Germans'.) This has given rise to renewed West German fears about the dangers of 'singularization'.

While to some extent these fears are a red herring (since in a European war all of Europe, not just the Federal Republic, would be affected), they nevertheless reflect a strong West German perception that Germany would be the battlefield in any conflict in Europe. Thus, in the aftermath of the INF agreement, pressure is likely to grow from both Moscow and Bonn to reduce sharply, perhaps even eliminate, tactical nuclear missiles in NATO's arsenal. The SPD, in fact, has already officially come out in favor of a 'triple-zero' solution. So have conservatives such as Alfred Dregger, who stunned many observers by warmly welcoming Honecker's January 1988 proposal for eliminating all tactical nuclear weapons from both German states.

However, West Germany's NATO allies, especially Britain and France and the United States, strongly favor modernization of NATO's tactical nuclear weapons, particularly the Lance ground-launched short-range missile, as agreed upon at the NATO meeting in Montebello in October 1983. The Kohl government, on the other hand, has expressed reservations about modernization, fearing that it would spark new protests similar to those that occurred after NATO's dual-track decision in 1979 regarding the deployment of cruise missiles and the Pershing II. Instead it has argued that no modernization should be undertaken until a new comprehensive defense concept has been worked out by NATO.

The issue of how to handle tactical nuclear weapons therefore could become a very explosive issue in the Federal Republic and within the alliance. Given domestic pressures in the Federal Republic, it will be much harder in the next phase of arms control to maintain the strong consensus among the major allied governments that marked the previous phase. The Federal Republic, moreover, is likely to be the focus of intensive Soviet lobbying since Bonn's interest in seeing a reduction of tactical nuclear weapons does not entirely coincide with that of other members of NATO. Hence the potential both for misunderstanding and friction within the alliance is likely to grow.

A fourth and related factor has added to this disquiet: the perception that the United States is losing interest in Europe and will inevitably be forced for budgetary if not for other reasons to reduce its commitment to Western Europe. This perception has been reinforced by calls from prominent American figures such as former Secretary of State Henry Kissinger and former National Security Advisor Zbigniew Brzezinski for a withdrawal of some US troops and aircraft currently stationed in Western Europe. Many West Europeans believe, moreover, that the mounting US budget deficit will compel some withdrawal of US troops.

Inevitably this perception has begun to have an impact on West German defense and security policy. One reflection of this has been the increasing military cooperation with France since 1982, discussed by Anne-Marie LeGloannec in Chapter 11. This cooperation has been a direct consequence of uncertainties created by Reykjavik and the INF agreement. For the Federal Republic, closer military ties represent a prudent hedge against any decrease in the American commitment as well as a means to draw France closer to NATO, while for France they represent an effort to bind the Federal Republic more closely to the West and prevent a feared drift toward neutralism. Both see the cooperation, moreover, as a means to strengthen the 'European pillar' of NATO.

The closer military cooperation with the Federal Republic is part of a larger shift in French military strategy away from the old Gaullist go-it-alone strategy toward greater cooperation with NATO. At the same time France has increasingly come to see its security as more closely linked with that of the Federal Republic. In an important speech in December 1987, for instance, Prime Minister Jacques Chirac stressed that, if the Federal Republic were attacked, the French response would be 'immediate and without reservation'.[21] Chirac's statement represents a reversal in his party's traditional position, which has previously stressed the independence of France. Both countries have also agreed to set up a joint brigade as well as a new bilateral Defense Council, which is seen as a possible nucleus for broader European defense cooperation at a later date.

The closer military cooperation with Bonn should be seen in conjunction with France's effort to strengthen the Western European Union (WEU) and as part of its wider effort to bolster the European pillar of NATO. In addition, France has quietly sought to increase military cooperation with Great Britain. In December 1987 the two countries announced plans for the joint development of a launched cruise missile. They have also set up joint procurement committees. These moves have in part been taken to offset what Paris feels is a general weakening of the American commitment to Europe.

While France and the Federal Republic continue to disagree on a number of issues, particularly on arms control, French policy has shown signs of softening since Mitterrand's reelection in May 1987, as France's willingness to participate in the upcoming bloc-to-bloc Conventional Stability Talks underscores. (France refused to take part in the previous NATO–WTO talks on Mutual and Balanced Force Reductions in Vienna, which the CST talks are designed to replace.) In part, the shift has been prompted by a desire to avoid isolation from its NATO allies. But the decision also reflects a concern that frustration over the slow pace of conventional arms control talks could weaken the Kohl government and strengthen neutralist sentiment in the Federal Republic.

Conventional arms control, in fact, is likely to become one of the key security issues in the next few years. Any major reduction of conventional forces in Europe, however, would have major implications for the postwar European order – and especially the two German states, since the bulk of the conventional forces of the two superpowers are located on their soil. This gives the two German states a strong interest in the outcome of the Conventional Stability Talks. At the same time a major withdrawal of US and Soviet troops from the continent could spark renewed fears about German nationalism among the Federal Republic's neighbors, and give the German issue new volatility.

Taken together these developments highlight the way in which security issues have begun to be linked more closely to the German Question, giving it a new dimension not present a decade ago. As noted at the outset, the real issue today is not reunification, though this still remains a residual issue, but how changes in the policies of the two German states may affect European security in the next decade, and in turn what impact changes in the postwar security order may have on the policies of the two German states and their role in their respective alliances. It is this question that forms the heart of the new German Question. And it is on this problem, rather than the highly theoretical and less politically relevant issue of reunification, that scholars and politicians should focus in the 1990s.

2 The Changing Nature of the German Question

Renata Fritsch-Bournazel

The 'German Question' has been a central problem of international relations in Europe since long before the end of the Second World War. Historically, the idea of German national unity was never universally accepted; it always posed problems. Arguments about the precise meaning of 'Germany' did not begin in 1945. For over three hundred years there has been no period when Germany has not to some degree formed an essential part of the European system of states, either through formal alliances or through the more indirect exertion of power. The German Question emerged as a wider European issue with the Peace of Westphalia in 1648, which gave an international legal framework to the Holy Roman Empire of the German Nation, a fragmented grouping of territories large and small, under varied sovereignty or foreign influence. A neutralized central Europe, without a focus of political power, remained a first principle for the preservation of peace until the beginning of the nineteenth century. At the Congress of Vienna in 1815, after the collapse of Napoleon's policy of European hegemony, the Great Powers again agreed on a rearrangement of German states in a new, looser grouping, the German Confederation, which they would guarantee.

After the disappointments of the revolutionary period of 1848–9, the German people in central Europe at last found the fulfillment of their hopes of national self-determination not in the Greater Germany of liberal ideals, based on popular sovereignty and the rights of man, but in the Prussian-dominated Reich of 'Little Germany' (without Austria). It is perhaps one of the tragedies of German history that unification was brought about through the Prussian 'revolution from above' and not the liberal 'revolution from below'. However, anyone looking at the historical facts must recognize that the national liberal movement faced opposition not only from reactionary forces within Germany, but from Europe as a whole. Indeed, the solution of 1871 represented a renunciation both of the romantic nationalist ideal and of the older historical concept of the German Empire. As the period which followed would show, any attempt to utilize either of these concepts, separately or together, as the model for a more widely-based political unity, met with opposition from neighboring countries in Europe.

In effect, the creation of this highly-populated 'Little German' empire introduced a major change in the European balance of power. Bismarck's answer to the Reich's vulnerable position in the middle of Europe was a prodigious accumulation of alliances that seemed contradictory, but were meant to keep all other powers perpetually off balance. The system he created for German security was a very complicated one, and in its complications were the seeds of future trouble. Bismarck's successors possessed neither his superior intellect nor his statesmanship to ensure that Germany would remain as Europe's diplomatic arbiter. The failure to renew the Reich's Reinsurance Treaty with Russia in 1890 marked the break. It eventually resulted in a Franco-Russian alliance directed exclusively against Germany and gave substance to the 'nightmare of coalitions' that had haunted Bismarck's era.

The success of the Bismarckian alliance system depended not only upon Germany's remaining the balancing partner in so many awkward triangles, but also upon convincing the rest of the world that Germany was indeed a 'sated power'. In Bismarck's view of the German interest, changes in the *status quo* were only possible if they did not fundamentally challenge the system and its equilibria. Holstein and others who guided Germany's destiny after 1890 introduced a different school of thought on its central European orientation. While Bismarck believed he had achieved the most that was possible, his successors thought that the Germans still had to secure their place in the sun. Wilhelmian Germany could not be an honest broker amid the dangers of the European state system, once its own dynamism constituted a basic source of danger.

The German 'thrust for world power' at the beginning of the twentieth century was out of phase, particularly in the East. The concept of a very large area of economic and political German predominance (Eastern Europe, the Balkans, Belgium, and much of Russia, plus overseas colonies and bases) that would make Germany the major power in Europe, globally equal to Great Britain and the United States, was historically comparable to earlier British and French expansionism. But such a concept was contrary to the rising principles of self-determination and, if successful, would have destroyed the European balance of power. Germany could only have achieved such predominance by suppressing central and Eastern European nationalism with military and police repression, which in the rest of Europe was no longer an appropriate measure.

The German government of 1914 disregarded the fact that, for all Germany's economic and military strength, the restrictions of its geographical position should have imposed self-restraint rather than military action leading to a war on two fronts. The European peace settlement agreed on at Versailles, however, in no way amounted to the annihilation of the vanquished country, as the large majority of Germans perceived it at the time. Rather, it left the German Reich still in existence, despite considerable territorial losses.

The year 1919 saw a new resurgence of the principle of the nation-state and of the democratic nationalist idea of self-determination of peoples. At the same time the need for a strategic barrier against Soviet Russia was felt both in Western Europe and in the United States. The logic of geography thus played a helpful role in the emergence of a democratic political system in Germany. However, the Weimar Republic's relationship with Western Europe and America was soon marred by the unexpressed threat of an alliance between the two pariahs of international relations, Germany and the Soviet Union. In the divided republic there was near consensus on the need to avoid siding with either East or West, or to take a stand except where economic interests were involved. Keeping the options open in this way was seen as the precondition for the future recovery of major power status.

Hitler's policy, in the final analysis, was an attempt to break out of Germany's role in the middle to achieve at last a dominant position in Europe and thereby to destroy the traditional system of European states. His lust for *Lebensraum* in the East was qualitatively different from Prussian expansionism and from the pan-German dreams of the First World War. Unlike them, Hitler's plan was organically linked with racism, particularly anti-Semitism, and replaced the German 'civilizing mission' with the enslavement of the Slavs. The untoward result of German aggressive imperialism was the Soviet Union's advance into the center of Europe. With this event Germany itself not only lost great areas of settlement but, more importantly, it forfeited its centuries-old economic and cultural role in central and Eastern Europe.

From the start the major powers who joined in coalition against Hitler agreed on what they were fighting against and what their goals should be. The first priority was to bring down Germany and to occupy it militarily, while at the same time liberating the occupied territories. A second aim was the abolition of National Socialism and the creation of conditions which would make it impossible for national expansionist policies to re-emerge in the future. On the other hand, discussion of the peace-time aims of the Western democracies and the Soviet Union was more contentious. The wartime alliance of Great Britain, the Soviet Union and the United States began to split apart at the moment when military victory was achieved and the factors dividing the allies again became apparent.

As the East–West conflict sharpened, so the differences in development between the occupied zones deepened the division of Germany, without any formal decision being taken. At the same time, the Cold War, which began in 1946–7, robbed Germany of its historical, central position as a European power. Instead, it found itself on the edge of two frontiers, as the line between the new, antagonistic power blocs coincided with that dividing the two German states. Increasingly, the major powers which dominated Europe strove to exploit the potential of that part of Germany within their own control and, whenever possible, to influence the Germany within their opponent's control, as part of their struggle for global supremacy.

The German problem thus became the central issue of the Cold War in Europe. In these circumstances, any attempt to counter the political, strategic, ideological and social splitting apart of the German people was doomed to failure. The division was maintained by the determination of the victorious powers not to give Germany up either to their opponents, or to German independent control; it never received legitimacy in international law, nor the assent of the German people. For the overwhelming majority of Europeans in East and West this freezing of the division of Germany was first and foremost a source of reassurance, if not of satisfaction – a factor for security and stability in a world where peace was without legal guarantees. Yet this was true only so long as the division of Europe was accepted as unalterable. As soon as the East Europeans – and eventually many West Europeans too – began to perceive the division of their continent into hostile military blocs under superpower domination as a serious hindrance to their personal freedom of movement, they had, sooner or later, to face the fact that the division of Germany had become the key issue in the political division of Europe.

While so far there appears to be no conceivable possibility of removing these two divisions, historically so closely linked, disquiet about the present pattern in Europe seems to have revived in recent years. This is to some extent attributable to the fact that foreign observers believe the German people – in both German states – to be exhibiting a degree of social unrest which revives traditional worries about the unpredictability of the Germans. Since the end of the 1970s there has in fact been much public reflection on Germany's position and role in Europe. The indications are increasing in the Federal Republic – and, in different ways, in the GDR as well – that many Germans are becoming conscious again of their peculiar historical, political and psychological place in the center of Europe.

In the fifth decade of the division, German viewpoints are affected as much by the changing international scene of the 1980s as by the lasting effects of postwar decision making. At the same time, the Germans' sense of their national and European identity is determined by factors which arise partly from developments specific to Germany, but which are comparable to similar developments in neighboring countries in both East and West. In the end, because Germany's fate is so closely tied to that of Europe, the division of Germany can conceivably be overcome only if the rift in Europe is healed first.

I THE GERMAN QUESTION REOPENED?

There are two sides to the German Question. On one side it forms part of the intellectual and political struggle between East and West for Europe's future; on the other it is part of Germany's history, and of a depressing everyday reality for the German people, especially in the GDR. For the Germans, the division of their country since the 1945–9 period has meant more than the mere loss of a unified state. More than anything else it has affected their national identity, that is, the sense of belonging of a people who, through common history and current interests, know themselves to be more closely bound to each other than to any other people. So it is no accident that the Germans' special historical, psychological and political position in the heart of the continent resurfaced in their consciousness at the moment when *détente* reduced the confrontation between East and West. This allowed Bonn to free itself from the self-imposed restraints of the 1950s in dealing with communist Eastern Europe and above all with East Germany. The wider room for maneuver brought about by *détente* in the 1970s, coupled with a growing awareness of its limitations – felt as painful restrictions by the Germans – led to new interest in questions of German national identity. The close interconnection between the Germans' political and legal status and the wider situation in Europe prompted a great deal of new thinking and writing, chiefly from 1980 onwards, through which various writers tried to prepare the way for the current divisions in Germany and Europe to be overcome, or at least reduced.

The Peace Movement and *Deutschlandpolitik*

Even a brief look at this debate makes it clear that the problems of Germany's future always have an international security dimension either for the Germans themselves or for their neighbors. In the first place, this is because the German Question is less the cause than the outcome of a number of wider problems, resulting from the uncertainties of the international situation at a time when neither *détente* nor Cold War predominates. East–West relations have worsened appreciably since the end of the 1970s and the system of security based on deterrence has, in the eyes of many Europeans, become distinctly less secure with the sudden acceleration of the arms race, chiefly in the area of nuclear weapons in Europe. Such a situation has caused not only growing frustration, but demands for a radical change of direction, an escape from the old pattern of alliances and, if possible, from any association with the global conflict between the superpowers.

The peace theme is a particularly explosive subject in political debate in Germany because it is tied up with so many unanswered questions, hopes and fears. In the light of the controversy over deploying nuclear missiles, the question of Germany's role in Europe is posed again with growing urgency. There were attempts in the early postwar years, too, to reject the reality of East–West conflict and to withdraw from its pressures. Further, this led to the idea that only a 'third way' between the two blocs then developing would offer German policy-makers any prospect of remaining independent and of preserving national unity. The situation in the immediate postwar period is not, of course, comparable with that of today's world, yet, despite all the differences, certain aspects of those arguments are clearly still relevant.

By far the most widespread argument associated with policies for Germany's future is that a war between East and West in Europe would pose particular danger to the German people, irrespective of whether it is waged with conventional or with nuclear weapons. In 1979 the exiled East German intellectual Rudolf Bahro wrote: 'This frontier between the two blocs and the concentration of destructive power on both sides of it – this is what in a crisis would turn our country, before any other in Europe, into a shooting range for the two superpowers . . . . This is the common danger shared by both German states.'[1]

The consciousness of a special vulnerability, manifested particularly in the peace movement, comes not only from apocalyptic fears of nuclear destruction. A further argument refers directly to the difficult legacy of German history in this century and from this draws a moral obligation to mobilize humanity to oppose nuclear weapons. This strand of the argument lay at the center of much of the discussion at the rally of the German Protestant churches in Hamburg in 1981, attended by nearly 120 000 people, most of them young people. Former General Gert Bastian, a leading figure in the peace movement who applied for early retirement from the West German army in 1980 as a protest against NATO's nuclear arms program, put it as follows: 'I believe that no country in the world, certainly not one in Europe, can be more conscious than the Germans are of their special responsibility for peace and for promoting such a step, a responsibility derived from history and from their own past errors and mistakes'.[2]

A third strand of argument in the peace debate which is relevant to the German issue is the much-quoted view of Pastor Albertz, that Germany is in fact still 'an occupied country' in both its parts, and that conflict and armaments are forced upon it by the former 'Occupation Powers'. Albertz voiced this opinion at the church rally in Hamburg in 1981, in a platform discussion with the then Chancellor Schmidt. And, in a letter to *Der Spiegel* magazine, Protestant theologian Hellmut Gollwitzer, discussing the stationing of Pershing II missiles on West German soil, stated: 'No German can accept this total subjugation of the interests of our people to alien interests, this giving up of our right to govern our own existence to a foreign government'.[3]

A Search for Identity

Discussions on West German defense policy, as part of the peace debate of the last few years, were clearly influenced by the difficult question of whether to accept or reject the decision to deploy intermediate-range missiles in Europe. Since the start of their deployment at the end of 1983 this theme has lost much of its power to activate people, even if the possibility remains that international security issues could again provide the focus for political protest movements. A further aspect, in the long run more central to the revival of the German Question in public debate since the 1970s, is some fresh thinking on German views of themselves in relation to other nations. In fact the rediscovery of their national problem stems only in part from preoccupation with the division of Germany and freedom of action in a situation of international tension. It is far more a symptom of a deeper uneasiness, arising both from changes in the international environment and from the alienating complexity of industrial society. As early as 1966 the philosopher Karl Jaspers identified elements of insecurity affecting German morale which seem very similar to the situation today: 'Some talk of a vacuum in our political consciousness. The fact is that we have no political goals which we feel deeply about. As a country, we still have no origins and no ideals, no consciousness of where we have come from, or where we are going in the future, hardly any sense of the present except the desire to live as private individuals in comfort and security'.[4]

A large number of recent books and articles makes clear that the questions about a German identity are being raised with growing insistence: What is Germany today? Germany's continuing history; the *Angst* of the Germans; the German neuroses; the insecure republic; the identity of the Germans; the search for Germany – all these phrases give snapshot pictures of a mood of mental unease which contrasts strangely with the everyday experience of stability and normality of the ordinary German citizen.

One might conclude from this that issues of Germany's future to a large extent provide a playground for political opportunists and sectarians, and that the renaissance of the German Question is found largely between the covers of books. This argument can certainly not be dismissed lightly, but the relationship between German self-questioning and concern in other countries is a good deal more complex. 'The explosive potential of this phenomenon', the West German authors of a recent study of foreign reactions noted, 'lies . . . in the fact that anxiety about the unpredictability of the Germans is being stirred up with such vigor, after three decades of calm. For this reason, the task cannot simply be to try to correct current prejudices, but rather to detect the many small pockets of fire behind the huge cloud of smoke'.[5]

Since the emergence in Europe of the modern nation-state, the creation of national identity has always had something to do with the drawing of boundaries. Thus, in the German nationalist movement, from its beginnings in the Napoleonic era, there was always a tendency to derive the German identity in the first place negatively, through the rejection of all things foreign. A connection was thus drawn between the basis of national identity and separateness from other people, by articulating strict criteria for being different. In the past this had far-reaching effects upon German political culture.

However, the Federal Republic made a fresh start after the catastrophe of the Third Reich, seeing as its most urgent task reconciliation with the West. Reversing the traditional process, people at first did not even want to be Germans any more, but simply Europeans. Behind this lay the extraordinary influence which the United States had upon the West Germans' search for identity. In the disaster of 1945 they lost their faith in themselves and put their trust almost unconditionally in those who had defeated and liberated them, who promised to protect them against the new communist danger, and who helped in their economic and political reconstruction. This historical background renders more readily understandable the anxiety of many foreign observers, who suspect that behind the search for a German identity lies a resurgence of anti-Western attitudes. 'By rediscovering its geography', a Parisian journalist has written, 'Germany is reviving the central European side of its character. This turns its back not only on imports from the USA's cultural "general stores", but also on its old, close friends, the French'.[6]

The problem here, though, may be more apparent than real, since it is precisely because a definition of identity based on nationality is so unattainable that there is now a chance of defining Germanness other than by separateness. Following the failure of Hitler's attempt at world power and the resultant division of Germany, the German problem today is defined for West Germany by the two basic facts of Western allegiance and a geopolitical place in the heart of Europe.

The basic contradictions between these two facts produce some tension. Through its obligations as part of the Atlantic alliance and the European Community, as well as through its Constitution, the Federal Republic belongs politically and socially to the circle of Western democracies. On the other hand, through its location in central Europe and as a result of division, it must reach understanding and compromise with neighbors in the East. Therefore, from the Germans' viewpoint, they have no sole and exclusive loyalty, but a varied pattern of allegiances. Political scientist Werner Weidenfeld has written in this respect that, 'in the future, too, the Germans will have to live with an identity which has many layers, corresponding to many different aspects of their communal life'.[7]

The Problem of Conflicting Goals

When the Federal Republic of Germany and the German Democratic Republic were founded in 1949, the German people could still hope that the Soviet Union would one day withdraw from central Europe and leave the way clear for a peace treaty. Since then the basic facts of the situation have altered considerably. Four decades after the end of the Second World War, there is no prospect in sight of overcoming the divisions of Europe and Germany, even though there are as good grounds now, as then, for refusing to accept the existing situation.

In the 1950s, international relations for West Germany meant, in practical terms, relations with the West. The series of agreements signed with the East European countries in the early 1970s, while certainly not loosening the older and more important ties with the West, did lay the groundwork for a new pattern of links with the East. For both Adenauer and Brandt, the Federal Republic had to adapt to external constraints, for the former in order to free itself from the situation of powerlessness in which it found itself, and for the latter in order to combat the diplomatic isolation which arose in the 1960s as a result of the relaxation of tension between East and West.

In the *détente* period, nearly all the countries of Europe, including the two German states, gained room for maneuver which they had not had previously. In contrast, in the ensuing period of renewed confrontation between the United States and the Soviet Union, European chances of achieving their own foreign policy goals have been reduced. This is especially painful for West Germany, which has an even stronger interest than its NATO partners in continuity in relations with the East. Whereas, for other Western countries, *Ostpolitik* forms merely an important part of a wider range of foreign policy options, it represents considerably more for the Federal Republic, since relations with the East are bound up with such central issues of national policy as concern over West Berlin and solidarity with the East Germans. Moreover, *détente* policies have an additional, concrete content for West Germany: improving human rights and freedom of movement, and developing economic relations with Eastern Europe.

Many observers of German affairs have appeared skeptical in recent times about the practical possibilities of balancing all the different components of West Germany's foreign policy, an exercise akin to keeping several balls in the air at the same time. In an influential article on 'the revival of the German Question', the French political expert Pierre Hassner notes that this juggling act 'is only an expression of the unique situation of West Germany, which makes it impossible for Bonn to commit itself completely to any of the three possible futures: Atlantic, West European, or central European'.[8]

Other authors frequently express the view that history has long ago rendered irreconcilable the twin goals put forward in the West German Constitution, which exhorts the German people to 'achieve the unity and freedom of Germany' and 'to serve world peace as an equal partner in a united Europe'. The Berlin political scientist Helmut Wagner asks:

> Does the achievement of Western European unity not mean the perpetual division of Germany? And the realization of German unity the perpetuation of European disunity? Logically, a United Europe which was not confined to Western Europe would end Germany's division. And surely German reunification (unless it was made conditional on non-integration in Europe) would not necessarily stand in the way of a United Europe. But is either proposition realistic?[9]

As these examples from the recent debate make clear, the term 'the German Question' covers a range of widely differing issues and expectations. It is rarely confined solely to Germany, nor is it exclusively a problem of the present day. Only by setting more recent events in the context of historical continuity is it possible to give a cautious answer on whether, in the 1980s, the German Question really is in the process of being reopened.

II THE FEDERAL REPUBLIC, THE GDR AND EAST–WEST RELATIONS

Through their membership in two very different alliances, the two German states give both focus and expression to the more comprehensive range of differences existing between East and West. As early as the late 1940s, and increasingly in the two decades which followed, it was evident that the Germans were among those who suffered most from Soviet–American confrontations. The Berlin blockade of 1948–9, Khrushchev's Berlin ultimatum of 1958, and the erection of the Berlin Wall in August 1961 had the greatest impact on the people living in these two countries; every renewal of East–West tensions in these years seriously affected the situation in Germany.

On the other hand, improvements in the climate of relations between Washington and Moscow also helped to make life in divided Germany easier. In 1963, following the Cuban missile crisis, agreements were reached between Bonn and East Berlin permitting travel by Berliners divided by the Wall. Again, after 1969, as *détente* facilitated a range of international agreements, it was the Germans who benefited first and foremost from these, notably the Quadripartite Agreement on Berlin and the Basic Treaty between Bonn and East Berlin, with its subsidiary agreements which regulated relations between the two states.

Throughout the whole postwar period, at least until the end of the 1960s, the political freedom of action for both German states proved to be highly dependent upon the current state of East–West relations. Neither Bonn nor East Berlin could pursue their own efforts if these ran counter to the current trend in those relations. Only in the 1980s is there a trend in relations between the two German states which appears to go against international relations generally, indicating a gradual widening of scope and greater flexibility in their mutual relations.

Precisely because of the deteriorating political climate after Afghanistan and deployment by the two superpowers of intermediate-range nuclear forces (INF), there were signs that Germans in both opposing camps were ready to maintain *détente* and to continue their former course of partial entente. Until the postponement of East German leader Erich Honecker's visit to the Federal Republic in September 1984, the GDR maintained its contacts with Bonn despite the evident disapproval of Moscow. Even after this, East Berlin has made it clear that it does not want to break off the contacts built up with Bonn – at least, not on those matters already under discussion.

When, in the autumn of 1982, the CDU/CSU returned to power after thirteen years in opposition, it adopted new approaches in several areas. To the surprise of many people, however, there was little change in its policy toward the GDR. Bearing in mind that the majority in the CDU/CSU since 1969 had continued to reject, in principle, the Eastern and inter-German treaties worked out by the Brandt–Scheel government, the policy pursued by the Kohl government signifies a change within Kohl's own party. At the same time, however, it reflects an astonishing degree of continuity with the *Deutschlandpolitik* of his Social Democratic–Liberal predecessors. Even in the more difficult international conditions of the early 1980s, the Kohl government succeeded in getting improvements in the practical approach and general attitude of the East German authorities towards frontier controls, and obtaining important improvements in the GDR's handling of applications for travel to the West. At the same time, by offering the East German leadership sizeable credits guaranteed by West German banks, as well as easing payment requirements in inter-German trade, the Federal Republic signalled its readiness to honor the concessions made on humanitarian questions.

The Shifting Limits on Freedom of Action in Times of Crisis

The emergence of a 'mini-*détente*' between the German states during a period of sharpened confrontation between the two leaders of their respective alliances raised for the first time the question of whether the relationship between the two states could develop quite independently of the overall international situation. Given the inflexible attitudes of the two superpowers in the wake of the Afghanistan crisis, demands were increasingly raised that the Germans should explore the scope for negotiation on their own and without necessarily being tied to their respective alliances.

One Bonn diplomat, discussing the chances of an independent foreign policy for the two German states emerging in the 1980s, noted Moscow's tendency to allow the GDR to contribute, within limits defined by the USSR, to the implementation of a common Eastern bloc policy. He went on to observe that 'The room for maneuver which the Federal Republic has in times of international tension is certainly a lot greater than that of the GDR, albeit still clearly limited. Even so, it has in the past usually been sufficient to allow West Germany to promote its own specific interests'.[10]

In a 1984 lecture at a German–American seminar held by the Konrad Adenauer Foundation in Washington, Heinrich Windelen, then Bonn Minister for Inner-German Relations, indicated why the Federal Republic ought to be interested in a widening of East Germany's freedom of action, stressing in particular the desire to achieve pragmatic results without 'harming the GDR or destabilizing it'. He underlined the FRG's recognition of political reality, stating that 'we see our responsibility as Germans and Europeans as being able to do what is possible and responsible today, in order to limit as far as we can East–West conflict in Germany and Europe, and to ensure the likelihood of change in the future'.[11]

The American Jonathan Dean, a diplomat who knows Germany well, takes the view that it is precisely in times of crisis that Bonn's *Deutschlandpolitik* represents a kind of 'burden sharing' that offers the United States more advantages than disadvantages, arguing that 'it reduces tension between the two German states in the area of the world's largest military confrontation; it promotes continued Soviet and East German restraint on West Berlin; and it stabilizes East Germany'. Despite the development of new West German priorities in the inter-German relationship which could preclude automatic acceptance by Bonn of Washington's stance on some East-West issues, Dean concludes that for overall Western policy, 'the compensating gain far outweighs this loss'.[12]

After the start of American missile deployment on West German soil in November 1983, informed public opinion was at first expecting a particularly difficult period in relations between the two German states. Shortly before the NATO weapons modernization plan was put into effect, Honecker had warned of a new 'Ice Age' in relations between the GDR and the FRG. He echoed the warning of the then Soviet party leader Yuri Andropov, who had cautioned that, after the missile stationing, the citizens of the two German states would be looking at each other through a palisade of missiles.

However the GDR conducted a surprisingly public debate with the Soviet Union, disregarding such dire prophecies, and stressing repeatedly the particular concern of all Germans for the preservation of peace, and hence their special responsibilities in regard to relations between the two German states. In a November 1983 speech before the 7th Plenum of the Central Committee of the SED, Honecker argued for a continuation of the dialogue between the two German states, and at the same time revealed the limits on his own freedom of action:

> We cannot overlook the fact that through this decision [on missile deployment] the whole system of European treaties, including the Treaty on the Bases of Relations between the GDR and the FRG, has suffered serious damage. We are for the limitation of this damage as far as possible . . . The GDR, as the first socialist state of workers and farmers on German soil, is firmly anchored in the Warsaw Pact and indissolubly allied to the Soviet Union. It is ready at all times to fulfill its alliance obligations.[13]

Characteristically, the expression 'damage limitation' met with considerable opposition in Moscow. In the context of an officially directed press campaign, widely held to represent serious criticism of the GDR's policy towards the Federal Republic, *Pravda* described such an attitude as hypocritical, though without associating this term with Honecker personally: 'Typically, they are trying in Bonn to base their current massive pressure upon the GDR on a kind of special mission of the two German states to "limit the damage" caused by the newest round of the arms race in Europe. This is truly the logic of hypocrisy! . . .'. *Pravda* concluded that this 'policy of hypocrisy' would further complicate the European situation.[14]

The Community of Responsibility Between the Two German States

The desire for peace can itself become a factor in creating strife, danger and instability in the nuclear age and in the context of the East–West confrontation. While there is no disputing that peace is the ultimate goal, the central question involves the content of that peace, and how it can be reached. In the northern hemisphere the freezing of international boundaries around the division of Germany and the split between the two political systems gives the Federal Republic and the GDR a special role in ensuring peace and security under the ever-present threat of international conflict.

Since the early 1970s this special role shared by the Germans in Europe has often been described by the expression 'community of responsibility'. Historian Rudolf von Thadden of Goettingen University, in a hearing before the Bundestag Committee for Inter-German Relations in 1981, reminded the Germans of both states of the origins of their division and of their responsibility for its consequences. Thadden spoke particularly of 'this community of responsibility of the Germans on days which we keep to commemorate the National Socialist tyranny and some of its specific after-effects'. As an example of this community, Thadden cited the 1979 announcement by the Protestant churches of both German states, on the occasion of the fortieth anniversary of the outbreak of the war, of a joint call for peace.[15]

In the context of the debate on the stationing of American intermediate-range missiles on West German territory, and the countermeasures threatened by the Soviet Union, the concept of a community of responsibility became a key phrase in statements by politicians in both German states, together with an expression used for the first time by Honecker in 1983, 'the coalition of reason'. When in October 1983 it became clear that the USSR was preparing to station additional medium-range missiles on East German territory, the official newspaper of the SED published a letter to Erich Honecker from the Lutheran parish church and graveyard supervisory board at Loschwitz, a part of Dresden:

> The idea fills us with horror, that the stationing of American nuclear missiles in Western Europe, which we all condemn, would be followed by reciprocal countermeasures on our territory and we and our children would have to live directly alongside nuclear missiles. We would like to offer you our support and at the same time to beg you most strongly to continue the dialogue between the two German states and to widen it, so that trust can grow as the basis for a partnership of peace and security: in your own words, "a coalition of reason".[16]

The printing of this letter was unusual, in that the East German government had hitherto always taken care that the armaments of Warsaw Pact states were not openly criticized. The cooling in the climate of world politics and the renewed arms race had led to the emergence of a relatively independent peace movement in the GDR, though naturally not numerically comparable to that in West Germany. The SED's tactic was to react with flexibility and tolerance toward gatherings of the 'spontaneous' peace movement held alongside the government-sponsored 'official' rallies, so long as they confined themselves to general demands for stopping the arms race and for disarmament. By the end of 1983, a certain amount of anxiety about the developing threat appears to have been generally shared, so that the letter from the local church undoubtedly expressed a widespread disquiet.

However the East German government's tolerance of the activities of the independent peace movement during the period of greatest controversy on the national security issue in the Federal Republic should also be seen in the light of Eastern efforts to suggest to the West Germans that they should have a permanent interest in *détente*. An inquiry conducted in Bonn about *rapprochement* between the two German states since the Soviet invasion of Afghanistan concluded that a policy of inter-German *détente* is clearly 'in the national interest' of both. According to the report, US–Soviet relations can affect relations negatively, in both the economic and political spheres. The GDR's priority is to maintain vital economic ties with the FRG to enhance its own domestic stability. On the other hand, the GDR strives to weaken FRG–US ties. The FRG, however, hopes to safeguard the existence of West Berlin, and strengthen inter-German ties on all fronts, thus preserving an overall German sense of identity.[17]

Prospects for greater political flexibility for the GDR appear closely related to the new course being pursued in the USSR. Soviet economists in particular consider that the measures for modernizing the economy which Gorbachev has announced since 1985 will fail to achieve their objective unless they are broadened to include the CMEA countries, and that the price to be paid would be some limited recognition of the national interests of member states. The landmark visit to the Federal Republic by the East German chief of state Erich Honecker in September 1987 laid a diplomatic foundation for what could become the most substantial improvement in inter-German relations since former Chancellor Willy Brandt's *Ostpolitik* policy in the early 1970s. However, in their policy towards the West, the SED leaders must continually take into account not only Soviet interests and sensitivities, but also the lasting distrust of some of their own immediate neighbors.

Occasional envious references in the Polish and Czechoslovak party press to the growing volume of trade between the two German states, or accusations of political blindness towards West German 'revisionism', are expressions of continuing skepticism and of doubts about East Berlin's political reliability. In the Soviet party press this undercurrent of suspicion was articulated in June 1985 in a leading article in *Pravda* by one O. Vladimirov, to which special significance was attributed, because the author was reputed to be Oleg Rakhmanin, then first deputy head of the International Relations Section of the Soviet Communist Party Central Committee. The author criticized 'nationalist tendencies' among certain socialist states, which he claimed 'undermine the unity and resolution of the socialist peoples and damage socialism as a whole, as well as each individual country'.[18]

With the resolution on *Deutschlandpolitik* adopted by the Bundestag on 9 February 1984 (with only the Green Party opposed), the concept of a shared German 'community of responsibility for peace and security in Europe' became a part of official policy in Bonn. A few months after the start of missile deployment, and in a period of severely limited dialogue between the superpowers (the Soviet Union had left the negotiating table in Geneva as a protest against NATO's determination to proceed with the deployment of American intermediate-range nuclear missiles on European soil), this document signalled the fact that polarization between the main West German political camps was decreasing and that the Kohl/Genscher government was trying to maintain continuity with the *Deutschlandpolitik* of its predecessors, in substance as well as in style.

On the basis of their shared history, the Federal Republic and the GDR do indeed have a special obligation to ensure that no additional tensions arise on German soil which would place an unnecessary burden on East–West relations. This 'community of responsibility' of the Germans in Europe nevertheless reaches its limits at the point where it touches on vital alliance interests or gives encouragement to the idea that the two German states could go their own way in defense policy. In an interview with German radio in Autumn 1984, the President of the Federal Republic, Richard von Weizsaecker, preferred to speak of the Germans' 'responsibility for the climate' of the East–West relationship. Noting that *détente* could not be introduced in central Europe if there is a serious deterioration in East–West relations, he stressed that it is thus also 'very greatly in the interests of relations between the Germans themselves that they do not make inappropriate attempts to pursue some special avenue of their own. So then, at bottom we always come back to recognizing the same thing: we form part of this overall climatic situation ourselves'.[19]

III THE RISKS AND OPPORTUNITIES OF A CENTRAL POSITION

Germany's position in the middle of Europe is not just a burden for the Germans; it is a continual problem for Europe. It has given rise to pressures and counter-pressures, longings, threats, anxieties, conflicts and wars. But it has also engendered cultural interchange, diversity of thought and the meeting of minds between Germans and their neighbors. Forty years after the end of the Second World War, Wolf Jobst Siedler, a Berlin writer and publisher, noted the change which has taken place in central Europe, as a result of the break-up of the Third Reich. The collapse of the Reich had prompted the Germans to turn to the West for the first time in their history. But, he pointed out, 'when the West won Germany for itself, it gave up the rest of Europe in return. It won only half of Europe, and not only in the geographical sense. The two European empires lost in wars this century were really the Eastern part of the West, and the Western part of the East'.[20]

The Tradition of *Mitteleuropa* Revisited

Sixty years after Friedrich Naumann's plea for a structured *Mitteleuropa*, in which the central powers, Germany and Austria, would be surrounded by their partners to the South and East, there is again much talk about the *Mitteleuropa* concept. Very varied motives are brought together in this discussion, among them geography, culture, and needs and desires which cross all boundaries. The repellent effect which the Soviet system exerts on its Western borders, along with the stronger consciousness of their own traditions and of differences in mentality and life-style, foster an urge for a relaxation of tensions, for opening up, which falls on fertile ground in many governments in the Warsaw Pact countries. When Czechs, Poles and Hungarians talk of the special character of *Mitteleuropa*, they most frequently mention the distance to the Soviet Far East, and emphasize what the nearest parts of the Soviet empire have in common with Europe. When people in the Federal Republic think about *Mitteleuropa*, there is on the one hand a reawakening of German cultural interest in central and Eastern Europe, which is in no way a rejection of the fundamental worth of Western civilization. At the same time, a concept of *Mitteleuropa* which has been refined in political discussion embraces a certain distancing from the West and hence it takes the *Ostpolitik* a stage further.

The Swiss journalist François Bondy takes a critical view of this, stressing the ambiguity of the concept of *Mitteleuropa*, which must both uphold its traditional political and cultural distinction from the East, while at the same time distancing itself from the West:

> One could say it would be only natural for each part of central Europe to want to distance itself from its 'protective power'. But this would be to forget the difference between a community imposed by force and an alliance freely entered into; the asymmetrical is represented as symmetrical, as if Western and Eastern Europe were both 'occupied' in similar fashion.[21]

Both Reich and nation-state came to an end in the Nazi defeat, the German catastrophe. A generation after 1945 the Germans are again beginning to ask about cause and direction in their history. The answers given in the immediate postwar period are no longer the only ones conceivable. Attempts to find a special path for Germany in Europe are stirring again. Questions about the German nation are linked with a new search for security in central Europe. The diplomat Henri Froment-Meurice, formerly French ambassador in Moscow and in Bonn, sees in this a challenge for French foreign policy: 'Germany is a house with two facades. The French have to get used to it and not worry themselves, if the Germans look ever more frequently through the windows facing East; but they must encourage them to use the Western side even more often, by leaving some large extra windows open. Foreign policy is a form of architecture'.[22]

The German Question has always been the question of where in Europe the Germans belong: looking westwards or wandering between East and West; recognizing their central geographical position or breaking out of it. This was the vital question for domestic as well as foreign policy in Bismarck's day. Despite all the breaks and discontinuities in German history in the last hundred years, the same questions were and are continually posed anew and require answers from responsible statesmen, in view of the continually changing pattern of international relations.

The setting aside of an active *Ostpolitik* during the Cold War was in one sense unavoidable, but in another sense temporary and provisional. The recognition that the Germans in their central position needed a long-term understanding with the East as well as their ties with the West is found as early as the mid-1950s in speeches by the first West German Chancellor. In many respects, the statement of policy which Adenauer made on 9 September 1955, on the occasion of his first (and only) visit to Moscow, already contains important elements of the *détente* concept of the 1970s:

> The highest good, which should be defended by every German, is peace . . . Every person in Germany knows that our country's geographical position would place us in special danger in the event of an armed conflict. In the shaping of our relations with the peoples of the Soviet Union, we wish [for ourselves]: peace, security, economic cooperation and the avoidance of tensions.[23]

German Questions – European Answers

What is the future of the German Question? Are there any practical prospects of development, or should one rather expect the establishment in the long term of that *status quo* which has taken shape in the years since the signing of the Basic Treaty between Bonn and East Berlin? Without doubt there is a serious contradiction between legitimate claims to self-determination and the realization of the currently unalterable nature of the postwar division of Germany. This strikes hardest at the Germans in the GDR, of whom more is demanded in terms of accepting the *status quo* than is the case with their fellow countrymen in the West. After more than a decade of efforts at normalization of relations between the two German states, hopes of more freedom and human rights for all Germans remain fragile. Yet at the same time there is no convincing alternative in sight to direct dialogue and limited cooperation between two systems of society which by their very nature are irreconcilable.

Nothing in this 'normalization' excludes the possibility for change in the global political scene, shifts in power relationships between East and West, new forms of conflict or cooperation, or far-reaching changes in politics and society. Still unchanged is the fact that the relationship between the two German states remains not merely limited by the global antagonism between the superpowers, but threatened by it. From this the conclusion can be drawn that, in the last resort, the special problems of Germany cannot be solved acceptably in isolation, but only within the context of a peace settlement for the whole of Europe.

The frontier which cuts through Berlin and Germany also runs through Europe; it divides the world. It follows that the two divisions, of Germany and of Europe, cannot be set off one against the other as in the power system of the nineteenth century, but can only be overcome together. Considered from the viewpoint that, as part of the global political confrontation since 1945, partitioning of countries has also been employed elsewhere as a diplomatic solution – one has only to think of Korea, Vietnam and Palestine – then this division appears in historical perspective as a new means of binding Germany into the whole European system of states, as often occurred in Germany's past. Germany's key role in Europe is to that extent nothing new, and Germany's neighbors have never ceased to see their own future as inseparably linked with that of the Germans. On the other hand, this insight into the conditions and limitations imposed by Europe upon German freedom of action also determined the decision of those who drafted the West German constitution, to couple the achievement of German unity and freedom with the creation of a United Europe, in the preamble to the Basic Law.

Thinking based upon historical categories and their experiences with the people of central Europe since the nineteenth century influenced the Allies in their planning during and after the Second World War and still to a great extent marks attitudes today in the countries surrounding Germany. It is true that the right of the Germans to national self-determination may not be contested in principle by the allies and partners of the FRG, yet there are all kinds of fears that a nation-state consisting of the whole of Germany could once again take on an order of magnitude critical for Europe, and so destabilize the European regional system of the postwar period.

These two facts mean that, for the solution of the Germans' national problem today, forms of organization have to be found which take appropriate account of their neighbors' security interests as well. In concrete terms, this means that all working concepts for solving the German problem must take as a starting point the basic preconditions of the international situation in order for it to become a reality; that not only must the Germans have the will to alter conditions in Europe's heartland, but they must be able to convince those around them that the model they propose as a solution would bring peace, security and other advantages to their neighbors too.

In a speech on the 'Day of German Unity' on 17 June 1967,

Chancellor Kiesinger, a Christian Democrat, put this basic dilemma as follows:

> Germany, a reunified Germany, would be of critically large size. It is too big not to have an effect on the balance of power, and too small to be able itself to hold the balance with the powers round about it . . . For this very reason, one can see the separate halves of Germany growing together only if this is firmly anchored in the process of overcoming the East–West conflict in Europe.[24]

He concluded that the most fruitful policy would be to promote inter-German *détente* at all levels.

For over forty years the connection between the German Question and the future organization of Europe has time and again provoked strong controversy and skeptical questioning, but also a wealth of working hypotheses, such as the unification of the whole of Europe for the peaceful overcoming of East–West tensions. Certainly that should not make one lose sight of the fact that the solution to European peace problems at the moment is nothing more than a vague vision, the practical realization of which seems just as far away as the dream of German unity. The opportunities and risks of a German foreign policy firmly grounded in Europe is the reality, and Germany must live with these contradictions.

3 The Origins of a New Inter-German Relationship*

A. James McAdams

I RETHINKING THE GERMAN QUESTION

Is there a new 'German Question' in Europe today? At one time, both the Germans themselves and their continental neighbors and superpower allies could agree that there were actually two points of uncertainty about Germany's postwar division. The first uncertainty lay in what future one might predict for the tenuous political experiments undertaken in 1949 by the liberal democratic Federal Republic of Germany and its socialist counterpart, the German Democratic Republic. The second uncertainty lay in what was to come of the division of Germany itself. Was the natural German condition one of unity? If so, did the two German states possess both the inclination and the wherewithal to press for national reunification?

Today, in contrast, most analysts would agree that these traditional ways of posing the German Question have become outdated. Most would contend that the FRG has managed to avoid the authoritarian temptations that observers once feared might lie beneath the surface of West German democracy. Similarly, many – although not all – analysts would agree that the GDR has been able to fashion a domestic consensus with its citizenry that few onlookers could have anticipated during the country's troubled first decade. A like fate appears to have beset the second question about Germany's future. Most German policy-makers and Western experts would now concede that real prospects for German reunification have steadily declined with the passage of time. Far from nearing any kind of national *rapprochement*, in fact, the two German states seem to have developed quite distinct political and social identities, which

---

* This is a substantially revised version of an essay which appeared under the title 'Inter-German Detente: A New Balance', in *Foreign Affairs* (Fall 1986), pp. 136–53.

themselves can be expected to work against any future chances of reunification.

If there is a German Question that Germans in both the FRG and the GDR now share about their future, however, it is about what has happened to the two states' interrelations during the time in which these distinct East and West German identities have been established. For, in contrast to the pessimistic predictions of most Western analysts, inter-German relations have soared during the 1980s: trade ties have been expanded, the GDR has been availed numerous new credit opportunities, and the leaders of both countries seem to have become taken with the need to exercise a calming influence on the competitive instincts of their superpower allies. What has not been well understood, however, is why inter-German ties have flourished at a time of rising East–West hostilities. Nor for that matter have Western experts found themselves in a strong position to anticipate what future directions relations between the FRG and the GDR might (or can) take.

In this chapter, I shall argue that if we want to understand why inter-German ties have prospered in the recent past and why, conversely, they may also encounter difficulties in the years to come, we need to view the evolution of East German–West German relations from a broad historical perspective. From this angle, there is good reason to think that the structure of the inter-German relationship itself has changed. For most of the two countries' history, the Federal Republic seemed to have every advantage in competing with its socialist rival. But with the emergence of a much stronger, more self-confident East German state, this advantage may now – a quarter of a century after the erection of the Berlin Wall – have slipped out of the West Germans' grasp. This shift brings us to the point where the bargaining relationship between East Berlin and Bonn can for the first time be characterized as symmetrical. That Bonn may at times have great advantages in inter-German negotiations will not surprise most observers. The new development is that, contrary to past truisms, the two countries' bargaining relationship may also occasionally shift in East Germany's favor.

Once this point is understood, it becomes easier to answer the question about why the two states have labored to preserve their special ties. But at the same time, this change in the inter-German balance also raises new questions about the ability of the formerly predominant power, West Germany, to continue realizing its traditional aims. Can the two German states continue to conduct their business on the basis of old trade-offs and concessions? Or, if the spirit of inter-German *détente* is to be kept alive, must each of the states now engage in a new level of discourse that will have consequences for its larger alliance commitments? To the extent that not only German interests but also alliance concerns are affected by the new inter-German relationship, the new German Question becomes an issue that may concern non-Germans as well.

The Immediate Postwar Period

For the first 20 years of their existence, the two German states essentially enjoyed a non-relationship. In their few interactions, the FRG held most of the advantages. Although it is generally taken for granted, the last word has yet to be written about why Bonn's position during this time was so much stronger than that of its communist counterpart. One of the factors was the more secure economic base of the West German state; another was the pervasive perception that its citizens had a higher standard of living than their fellow Germans in the East. But the greatest contribution to West Germany's strength and East Germany's weakness was the latter's direct association with the Soviet Union. The circumstances of the communist state's founding created the popular conviction that East Germany was little more than an artificial outpost of Soviet hegemony. As a consequence, Bonn hardly had to campaign for sole possession of the mantle of German sovereignty; in the eyes of most onlookers, in both the East and the West, it *was* Germany.

Accordingly, Bonn claimed an exclusive prerogative to represent German interests, refusing almost any official contact with East Berlin that might serve to legitimize the East German state. This policy not only prevented formal recognition of East Germany by any non-communist government, but it also meant that the country's leaders at the time, such as party chief Walter Ulbricht, were hard pressed to convince the East German population that a socialist German state was deserving of the same respect as West Germany. Even the erection of the Berlin Wall in 1961 failed to confirm the communist regime's claims to legitimacy.

Only later, however, would it become apparent that this barrier did provide the East Germans with one advantage over the West. Not only did the Wall keep the country's citizens confined to the East but, more important, it granted the communist leaders a dependable lever with which to control Western access to East German society. At the same time that it insulated the East German population from the corrupting 'swamp' of the West (to use Ulbricht's forceful image from the early 1960s), it also severely restricted the potential for influence that the stronger West German state had enjoyed in earlier years of open borders. This shift first became evident soon after the barrier's erection, when West Berlin government representatives sought to gain access to East Berlin for their zone's residents and encountered great difficulty. But only later, as West Germany's policy emphasis switched from isolating East Germany to influencing it, would East Berlin's advantage in controlling its borders become fully evident.

Background to *Ostpolitik*

It would probably be unfair to maintain that this turnaround in Bonn's *Ostpolitik* toward East Germany and the USSR came only with the accession to power of Willy Brandt's Social Democratic–Free Democratic coalition in 1969, as is commonly supposed. Even before that time, some leaders in the formerly predominant Christian Democratic Union had become aware that their policy of isolating East Germany had the unintended consequence of restricting West German access to the entire Eastern bloc. The inclusion of the Social Democrats in Kurt Georg Kiesinger's 'grand coalition' government in 1966 increased pressure in Bonn to develop a policy that would be more responsive to the needs and interests of fellow Germans in the East.

The stumbling block to any improvement in relations between the two German states was Bonn's insistence that it alone was entitled to represent German interests. This claim prevented movement on the German Question because it ran up against East Berlin's demands for recognition of its full sovereignty over East German territory and its jurisdiction over attendant issues like the status of Berlin and transit to and from the city. What made Brandt's response to this impasse so distinctive, however, was his government's success in devising a formula to revamp relations between East and West Germany that, for all intents and purposes, allowed Bonn to have its cake and eat it too.

According to the new formula, 'two German states in one nation', the Social Democratic regime conceded that the GDR should be considered a legitimate German state, and therefore deserving of *de facto* recognition. But at the same time the emphasis that Brandt's government placed on the existence of an overarching German nation underscored the 'special' character of any inter-German ties that would result. While Ulbricht was quick to reply that the Federal Republic had hardly met his regime's demands for full, *de jure* recognition, Bonn's implicit agreement to respect the territorial integrity of the East German state was sufficient to bring Soviet pressure for *détente* to bear upon East Berlin. The result was not simply Ulbricht's ouster in 1971, because of his outspoken opposition to the developments around him, but the eventual achievement of accords treating both the city of Berlin and relations between the two German states themselves.

West Germany was indisputably the major beneficiary of these agreements. In their Basic Treaty of 1972, for example, both German states agreed to exchange official representatives, but despite East Berlin's protestations, these were not to be full ambassadors. In the Four-Power Accord of 1971 on Berlin, Western access to the city was vouchsafed by Soviet guarantees. Not only did this step deny East German claims to full sovereignty over the city, but it also seemed to bring to an end the communist state's ability to interfere with the transit routes into West Berlin – long one of Ulbricht's favorite tactics. The West Germans' greatest gains, however, came in the area of expanded contacts with East Germany. The routinization of inter-German relations meant that a limited 'reunification' of the nation – in the form of restored contacts between long-separated families and friends – was now possible. These gains were matched by greater freedom for journalists, vast improvements in telecommunications and postal services, and even occasional visits between East and West German officials. In a symbolic if not also practical sense, this brought the two states back to the *status quo* that existed before 1961. A new era of at least partly opened borders seemed to signify that it would be that much easier for Bonn to give substance to its claims of inter-German commonality and, in effect, keep the German Question alive and open to debate.

Of course, East Germany also benefited from certain aspects of this process of inter-German accommodation. Bonn's acceptance of the country's existence was enough to break the logjam that had prevented the GDR's formal recognition by the non-communist world. This recognition brought with it countless economic advantages, and offered the leaders of East Germany unprecedented opportunities for making known their country's sovereignty on an international basis.

Nevertheless East Berlin's early reaction to these changes was never really as jubilant as one might have expected.[1] Far from celebrating their achievements, the East Germans' immediate response was defensive. When Honecker succeeded Ulbricht, no one in the leadership of the ruling Socialist Unity Party (SED) could have known for sure what the domestic consequences of even partly reopened borders might be. Would average East German citizens suddenly be reminded of all that they shared with their cousins in the West? And would that recognition inject new turbulence into the tranquility of East German society? Because of these uncertainties, East Germany's main efforts lay in redirecting its citizen's attention inward, through intensified ideological campaigns and such mundane activities as the construction of apartment buildings. Only later, when the success of such efforts could be adequately weighed, was it possible for East Berlin to turn its primary attention outward to take full advantage of new-found conditions.

After Afghanistan

The Soviet invasion of Afghanistan in 1979 was a turning point in East–West affairs, exacerbating the already deteriorating state of relations between the United States and the Soviet Union. But it had a far different effect upon the equally precarious set of understandings that had bound the German states together in the 1970s. In effect, the Afghanistan invasion forced all of the powers involved in East–West *détente* to clarify their interests to themselves and to weigh consciously the costs and benefits of a continuation of the foreign policy of the previous decade. While both German states deliberately undertook to shield their common relationship from the rising hostilities around them, this period of inter-German relations signalled something far more important than the continuation of business as usual. In a qualitative sense, the aftermath of the Afghanistan invasion showed that the structure of the relationship had changed, and that East Germany was now in a much stronger position than ever before.

At first the significance of this shift was not apparent to most observers. From Bonn's standpoint West German interests remained essentially unchanged and, accordingly, it made perfect sense for the Federal Republic to try to preserve a spirit of inter-German accommodation. But the new element that entered into play at this time was the recognition that Bonn's dependence upon *détente* had now become painfully acute. As the state that had gained the most from the regularization of relations with East Germany, did not West Germany also stand to lose the most with the onslaught of a new Cold War?

Few West Germans actually feared that their East German adversaries would use the new chill in inter-bloc relations as an excuse to renege on the inter-German agreements of the 1970s. But those accords, of course, had always been open to either favorable or unfavorable interpretation by their signatories; under adverse circumstances, Western journalists could find their coverage of stories impeded by excessive police scrutiny, visa applications could be delayed, and East German *émigrés* to the Federal Republic could find their requests for return visits to their homeland permanently obstructed. Perhaps most important, progress in the inter-German relationship had become largely taken for granted by the West German public. No West German politician wanted to be held responsible for its deterioration. As a result, decision-makers in Bonn were predictably concerned to assure continued Western access to the country and a semblance of continuity in the inter-German dialogue.

While growing international tensions clearly threatened West German interests, these difficulties put East Germany's leaders in a very different position. Events in Afghanistan and Poland could have allowed them the perfect opportunity to reject the relationship with the Federal Republic that they had regarded so ambivalently in the early 1970s. Such a step was easily consistent with prevailing Soviet policy at the time. But something seemed to have changed in the East Germans' calculation of their interests. Indeed, the crises of the early 1980s may have taught the East German leaders a lesson about their own progress in the decade following Ulbricht's ouster.

For one thing, by 1980 Honecker and his colleagues were no longer novices in the conduct of *détente*. Whereas they had once viewed the prospect of opening their country to the West with considerable uncertainty, they now had the advantage of knowing that East Germany had survived *détente* with its social order relatively unscathed. So long as a limited *détente* with West Germany served their state's interests, therefore, there was now no question that its disadvantageous aspects could be managed.

This may have been one of the reasons for the East Germans beginning at this time to reassess much of their own history and to attempt selectively to rehabilitate controversial figures from the German past, like Martin Luther and Frederick the Great. Whereas, in the early days of *détente*, the country's leaders had been so afraid of rekindling nationalist feeling among its citizens that many had been reluctant even to refer to the country's 'Germanness', the more recent attempts to synchronize the East German present with Germany's past suggested a new-found strength and self-assurance.

In addition to feeling more comfortable about invoking their national identity, East Germany's leaders could also see that, precisely because of *détente*, their country's bargaining position *vis-à-vis* the Federal Republic was strengthened. Unlike the situation in the old days, Bonn no longer enjoyed the luxury of simply choosing between ignoring or recognizing its neighbor; its commitments locked West Germany into the logic of inter-German *détente*. Correspondingly, because Bonn could no longer freely withdraw from this relationship, the old leverage that the West Germans had long exercised over East Germany was significantly reduced.

This shift in the two states' positions relative to one another could be seen quite clearly in the fall of 1980 when, in response to escalating tensions over Poland, East Berlin drastically increased the amount of currency that Westerners were required to change into East German marks when entering the GDR; in subsequent months, this move led to a dramatic decline in the number of West German visitors to the East. At first, Schmidt's government was indignant, announcing that it would not tolerate the new exchange requirement. Nevertheless the limitations on Bonn's room for maneuver quickly became apparent. When the West Germans hinted that an easing of the requirement might be a precondition to successful future negotiation of trade credits between the two countries, the East Germans effectively called their adversaries' bluff by feigning a total lack of interest in increasing the credits. As a result, over the next few years, Bonn was able to extract only the most limited concessions (for senior citizens, for children) on the exchange requirement issue. Even today, the strength of the East German economy means that West Germany's ability to apply economic pressure on its neighbor is not as great as it was in the past.

This is not to say, of course, that only the West Germans had strong reasons for sheltering the inter-German relationship from its turbulent surroundings. Had that been the case, East Berlin could simply have refused to participate in the process. However, East Germany's leaders had their own set of interests in continuing the dialogue, if only for purposes of self-legitimization. Hence the symmetry in the two states' bargaining relationship. So long as it could be shown that West Germany took the GDR seriously, the East Germans had every reason to favor further contacts. Thus Honecker went out of his way to welcome Chancellor Schmidt during the latter's visit to East Germany in late 1981, and to play up the appearance of, in his words, 'two independent German states' carrying on 'peaceful, good-neighborly relations according to international norms'. For his part, Schmidt was so concerned not to ruin the occasion that when martial law was imposed in Poland on the last day of his stay with the East German general secretary, he refrained from denouncing the action and merely joined Honecker in calling upon the Poles to solve their problems without outside interference.

II   INTER-GERMAN *DÉTENTE* AND THE HONECKER VISIT

The vested interests of both German states in *détente* help to explain why the two countries' leaders have consistently chosen to pursue something less than their maximal goals in structuring their relations. Although Bonn might wish to lay the foundation for an eventual reunification, it would, in retrospect, have been foolhardy to stress only the ideal goal of a single German nation, for such an uncompromising condition would make negotiations impossible for East Germany. Similarly, though East German leaders may frequently argue that there is no special German Question still to be discussed, their actions are often quite different from what their rhetoric about 'closing' the German Question might suggest. Somehow the leaders of the two German states have been able to avoid the classic 'prisoners' dilemma': a situation in which the temptation to win propaganda victories might have ultimately stalemated each state's chances of obtaining even its minimal goals.[2]

The primacy of such considerations has been nowhere more apparent than in the fluctuating policies of Helmut Kohl's coalition government. While Kohl's regime came to power promising to restore the issue of eventual German reunification to a central place in the Federal Republic's *Ostpolitik*, the new government in Bonn quickly found that there were distinct limits to the kind of discourse on the national question that East Berlin would tolerate. Then, too, as the new government participated in NATO's missile deployment schedule, it found popular support for the missile decision was contingent upon convincing the West German citizenry that inter-German *détente* would not be sacrificed in the process. In this case, ironically, the Christian Democrats were even more vulnerable to public pressure than the Social Democratic Party, since they operated under the electoral disadvantage of having once included among their numbers some of the greatest opponents of the inter-German agreements of the early 1970s.

For this reason, and because of the presence in the governing coalition of pro-*détente* members of the Free Democratic Party, Kohl's party has on several occasions been forced to qualify some of its hard-line stands. When the chancellor agreed in early 1985 to address a controversial organization of West German expellees from Silesia, he touched off an emotionally charged debate in both German states about the implications of such a move for the Federal Republic's recognition of postwar borders. Yet, when he finally met the Silesians in June 1985, Kohl's speech was punctuated with references to his government's respect for the territories of its eastern neighbors, much to the dismay of those in the West who had expected a far-reaching reassessment of West Germany's acceptance of the *status quo*.

The East Germans, too, have often gone beyond paying mere tribute to the virtues of *détente* in their efforts to sustain the rudiments of the bargaining process between the German states. In recent years, this has been evident in East Germany's de-emphasized demand for absolute recognition of its citizenship. Particularly since the Polish crisis, East Berlin has conspicuously toned down its old preconditions for good relations, to the point of requiring from Bonn only a basic 'respect' for what East German citizenship entails. Of course, this is still an important demand. But at least for the moment, the open-endedness of such a policy is sufficient to provide room for maneuver between the two sides.

Such restraint was also in evidence in 1986, when the East Germans agreed to impose new restrictions on the massive influx of South Asian and Middle Eastern asylum-seekers who were passing through East Berlin's Schoenefeld Airport on their way to a life of better economic fortunes in West Berlin. Throughout the previous year, the Western enclave, traditionally a haven for the oppressed, had become literally flooded with these refugees, but the East Germans had turned a deaf ear on demands that they come to West Berlin's assistance in controlling the foreign influx. Yet, when in late summer 1986 Bonn authorities were able to convince the GDR's leaders that the future of inter-German relations actually hung in the balance, East Berlin appeared to reconsider its options and then agreed to limit transit from its airport to only legitimate visa-carrying passengers.

Nevertheless it is only partly instructive to recognize that both German states have an interest in keeping up their favorable ties. However, if something really has changed in the nature of their relations, and if one wants to know how their relationship might develop in the future, the important question to ask is: who now wants inter-German *détente* the most? And which of the parties will be most willing to pay the price to assure that the two countries' relations will actually improve in coming years? These are, in fact, the new sorts of 'German Questions' which citizens of both the FRG and the GDR may be compelled to ask themselves in the future.

Bonn's undeniably strong interest in holding open channels of communication with East Germany and its citizens has seemed to make it more and more difficult to be tough with East Berlin and to impose preconditions upon a continuation of ties. The risks of offending the East German leadership and provoking countermeasures, such as a further tightening of the East German borders, have become too great. In contrast, East Berlin has shown itself to be unexpectedly skillful in reminding its adversary of the benefits of amicable relations; Bonn found this out in 1984 when over 30 000 East German citizens were allowed to emigrate to the West, quadrupling the previous year's numbers. True, the number of emigration permits granted in recent years has declined. But, at the same time, the West German government found that East Berlin could exhibit such flexibility in other, equally dramatic ways. In 1987, for example, East German citizens under the retirement age were allowed to make over one million short-term visits to the FRG. As a result, there has been an almost unanimous consensus generated among the major parties in the Federal Republic that nothing should be done to jeopardize such astonishing inter-German gains.

Of course, one should also be careful not to underestimate East Berlin's readiness to make its own sacrifices for healthy ties with the other German state. However complicated the role of economic interests in the GDR leadership's calculations, there can be no doubt that Honecker and his colleagues will always seek to exploit the credits, trade opportunities and access to Western technology availed through good relations with the FRG. Nor should one discount the vested interests which the SED itself has acquired in *détente*, simply as a result of allowing huge numbers of its citizens to travel to the West. By all accounts, Honecker has basked in the domestic popularity won through his pro-*détente* policy. But he must also recognize that once he has opened the door, however cautiously, to the West, he and his successors will have a hard time closing it without dashing the raised expectations of the East German populace.

Without a doubt, each of the German states would like to use the other's vested interests in the inter-German relationship as a way of raising the ante in their dialogue and forcing the other side to make concessions on key issues. This trend was quite evident in the mid-1980s behind-the-scenes bargaining revolving around Honecker's plans to visit the FRG. Much was made at the time about the Soviet role in forcing the postponement of the trip in September 1984. But it should also be recognized that the German states themselves may have contributed to the trip's failure, simply as a result of their own efforts to enhance their positions relative to each other.

Partly to make convincing to Moscow the case for a perpetuation of inter-German *détente*, the East Germans steadily lobbied Bonn for an upgrading of the content of the German–German dialogue to include issues that fully reflected the two states' 'special responsibility' for peace; the conclusion of a mutual renunciation-of-force pact was frequently mentioned. For their part, the West Germans, while clearly eager to have Honecker make the visit, also sought to exact maximum concessions from their counterparts, specifically on issues designed to emphasize the openness of the German question: Honecker could come to the FRG but he was not to be accorded the diplomatic recognition of comparable international heads of state, and it was not even clear that his visit could be held in Bonn. Naturally, when it became evident to both sides – at least by August 1984 – that the visit would not take place, each country's leaders rushed to save face. In a now famous remark, Alfred Dregger, the CDU's parliamentary leader, let it be known that the FRG's future did not depend on a Honecker visit; in like manner, the 72-year-old East German general secretary feigned patience in waiting for a time when his adversaries would choose to be more reasonable.

In retrospect, though, leaders of both German states did want the Honecker trip to take place, and in September 1987 it finally did occur. Honecker used the opportunity to demonstrate to the world, and particularly to his own citizenry, the equal sovereignty of a second German state. Similarly, Kohl and his fellow party members used the encounter to lecture their guest about inter-German commonalities and the need to address human rights issues in the GDR.

Yet, this time around, both sides unquestionably made key concessions for the visit to take place. The GDR's allowance of an unprecedented number of sub-retirement age visits to West Germany in 1987 was clearly part of this package. In addition, in the months leading up to the trip, East Berlin also made a number of symbolic gestures designed to lighten the German–German atmosphere: the country's death penalty was abolished, for example, and there was a noticeable reduction in the incidence of shooting on the inter-German border. Correspondingly, West German concessions were readily apparent in the first day of Honecker's trip. Although his presence in the FRG was officially classified as only a 'working visit', the East German leader did begin in the West German capital. And while in Bonn, he was treated (practically) like any other state guest. No one who witnessed the visit will be able to forget the spectacle of the West German and East German flags flying in tandem in front of the Federal Chancellery. Nor was Helmut Kohl able to hide his evident discomfiture at being forced to listen to the GDR's national hymn being played along with that of his own state.

Which side paid the most for the visit's successful outcome? The answer that one receives depends directly upon which German representatives one asks. Not surprisingly, neither the leaders of the GDR nor those of the FRG are willing to concede that they paid the most for the inter-German meeting, if only because, ironically, they have one thing in common: they both have to contend with large domestic constituencies who are always suspicious that GDR–FRG accommodation has gone too far. On the other hand, if one asks which German state had come the furthest with the achievement of the Honecker visit, it is hard to deny that the GDR stands out as the greater beneficiary from an historical perspective. To be sure, in its few years in office, the Kohl government has been able to achieve major gains in the inter-German relationship, many of which would have been regarded as highly idealistic in the early

days of the Basic Treaty. But in marked contrast, the prospect that
Bonn might stage an official reception for Erich Honecker, the man
who 'built' the Berlin Wall, was previously considered unthinkable.
No wonder, then, that East Berlin's confidence in its own abilities
– and particularly in its ability to drive hard bargains with any
negotiating partner – has been bolstered immeasurably.

III   THE GDR'S NEW PROFILE

Indeed, a visitor to East Berlin these days is immediately struck by
an air of quiet self-satisfaction among party officials that was not
present only a few years ago. After a lean period at the beginning
of the decade, the East German economy is growing at a perceptively
healthy rate and the government has simultaneously proved itself
to be adept at reducing the country's foreign debt. Even Soviet
General Secretary Mikhail Gorbachev, during his visit to the SED's
11th Party Congress in April 1986, found that the East German
leadership was not moved to engage in rounds of self-criticism and
calls for economic reform such as those heard elsewhere in the
Eastern bloc. Instead, the party congress proved to be a convenient
vehicle for charting the country's domestic accomplishments.
Honecker himself showed that this was hardly a time for modesty.
As he declared before his party's assembled delegates, the East
German social system may not 'yet [have] reached a state of
perfection', but it had made 'good headway'.
   Some Western analysts may have gone a little too far in interpreting
Honecker's markedly self-confident pose as an implicit challenge to
the new Soviet leader. Before the congress some observers had even
erred in the opposite direction, going so far as to predict Honecker's
removal as general secretary under pressure from the Soviet
leadership. But while there were no signs of serious conflict between
the East Germans and the Soviets at the meeting, it was hard to
deny that relations between the two countries had changed appreciably from the years when the East German state had been Moscow's
most subservient ally and had repeatedly found itself susceptible to
its patron's whim.
   For the Soviets, Honecker has become not merely a senior
statesman within the Warsaw Pact, but also the leader of the USSR's
most important ideological, economic and strategic ally. East
Germany epitomizes the successful construction of socialism outside

the Soviet Union's borders. In fifteen years in office, partly due to the success of his *Westpolitik*, Honecker has managed to build a level of domestic support for his regime that would have been unimaginable in the past. He has coupled this accomplishment with a firm grip on the SED leadership, even to the point, apparently, of designating his future successor: Egon Krenz, fifty-one, the former head (as was Honecker himself) of the Free German Youth organization. Moreover, however enviously the Soviets may at times regard their subordinates' manifest economic achievements, there can be little doubt that, if Moscow is to refashion its own economy under Gorbachev, the Soviets are likely to turn to the centralized East German model, and not, as so many Westerners believe, to the Hungarian reform experiments.

This does not mean that there will be no tensions in Soviet–East German relations. Gorbachev's calls for *glasnost*, or greater openness, in the conduct of public affairs have clearly ruffled the feathers of the more conservative members of the SED elite, who would rather see their policies and their prerogatives go unchallenged by mass opinion. Then, too, just as the cultivation of inter-German *détente* became an issue of controversy surrounding Honecker's planned visit to the Federal Republic in 1984, one can expect that further disputes over appropriate policy toward West Germany will occur in the future. Moscow's own policies, however, make it difficult to object to the continuation of strong ties between East Berlin and Bonn, no matter how ambivalently some observers in the Kremlin view any movement on the historically troublesome German Question. Despite growing Soviet skepticism about the USSR's ability to influence West German security policy, for example, Gorbachev has none the less attempted to hold open channels of communication to Bonn. To this end, the special relationship between the German states provides the Soviets with an unequalled degree of access to the West, an avenue that Moscow will be reluctant to imperil and that East Berlin, with the explicit support of allies like Hungary and Romania, is ready to exploit for its own purposes.

It is in this context that the Soviets themselves have begun to see that the new German Question in Europe is not only an issue of consequence for Bonn and East Berlin. To be sure, it is unlikely that the East Germans will ever go so far as to challenge Soviet authority within the socialist alliance – not deliberately, at any rate. Yet, this does not mean that the GDR's leaders always see this authority in black and white terms. For them, there is also a grey area of uncertainty in which their own interests obtain. And so long as East Berlin views the pursuit of these interests as not directly contrary to Moscow's aims, there will always be a degree of ambiguity in the coordination of Soviet and East German aims, which itself will occasionally become magnified by the uncertainties involved in the GDR's relationship with the FRG.

Such ambiguity was in evidence, for example, in late May 1986 when the East Germans cited West Berlin's counter-terrorist measures as a pretext to require Western diplomats to produce passports, not merely diplomatic identification cards, when crossing into East Berlin. This incident served to confirm what the GDR had always asserted about the Berlin Wall, that it marked an internationally recognized border, which itself demonstrated East Germany's legitimacy and the permanence of the inter-German divide. However, it was undoubtedly also a galling experience for the Soviets, who had no wish to see any disturbance in the delicate balance of understandings governing Berlin. Of course, the East Germans were ultimately unable to enforce the new passport requirement because of opposition from the city's Western occupying powers, France, the United Kingdom and the United States. But one wonders how important behind-the-scenes pressures from Moscow were as well. This time a major conflict between the GDR and the USSR was averted, unlike the situation in earlier years when Ulbricht had refused to go along with Soviet policy on Berlin. But the lesson remained the same: Soviet and East German interests, whether for or against the development of better relations with the West, were still uneasily synchronized.

Naturally, for Western observers, the passport episode also highlighted the uncertain state of the German–German relationship, if anything a far more precarious enterprise than the maintenance of stability in the Berlin question. What would happen should the East Germans choose in like fashion to raise the stakes in their relations with Bonn?

IV THE FUTURE OF INTER-GERMAN RELATIONS

No one, not even in East Germany, seriously expects Bonn to abandon its fundamental objectives, especially the pursuit of eventual national reunification. Rather, the real issue is *how* the West

Germans will choose to pursue their goals in the future. In this case, conditions may be propitious for the kind of rethinking of the country's Eastern policies that occurred under Willy Brandt's leadership. Who is to say that the two German states cannot finally choose to exchange real ambassadors? Or why should not the West German Bundestag have regular relations with the East German Volkskammer? The point is, some FRG politicians now assert, that if Bonn wants to encourage new levels of East German cooperation on any number of pressing issues, ranging from the lessening of border controls to the increase of emigration permits, West Germany's leaders may have no alternative but to begin thinking about a new phase in their country's policy towards the East.

Indeed, a debate about these questions has been under way for several years now within the leadership of the Social Democratic party, and was underscored when, amid a storm of Christian Democratic protest, the Bundestag's deputy opposition leader, Juergen Schmude, called for a revamping of the Federal Republic's constitution to provide for more realistic forms of German reunion. Similarly, in a November 1985 visit to East Berlin, the Saarland's Social Democratic premier, Oskar Lafontaine, expressed the opinion that the FRG would probably eventually have to recognize East German citizenship in the interest of facilitating inter-German travel. In early 1986, this controversy even extended into the ranks of the Christian Democratic Union, when the conservative state secretary for Inner-German Relations, Ottfried Hennig, proposed the abolition of a monitoring center in Salzgitter, which Bonn uses to record human rights violations on the German–German border, in exchange for East German guarantees not to shoot 'border-crossers'.

In effect this raises the new German Question from the perspective of the Atlantic alliance, that is, whether inter-German dialogue will remain limited to strictly German concerns or be extended to broader issues. One hears frequently from East German officials today that Kohl's governing coalition can scarcely afford to preach *détente* to the East while simultaneously subscribing to an American policy of 'armed escalation' and 'star wars'. If the Federal Republic is really interested in peace, it is said in the East, its leaders need to prove it by distancing themselves from the Reagan administration. Indeed, the idea of expanding the parameters of inter-German dialogue to include security questions has begun to win favor in some circles in West Germany, particularly in the Social Democratic Party, where prominent intellectuals and politicians have argued

that the discussion of such common concerns might at least help to
enhance the two countries' relationship. Not surprisingly, this
development has met with Soviet approval. Gorbachev spoke
favorably at the East German party congress in April 1986 about
discussions that have already taken place between the Social
Democratic Party and the East German SED concerning the
establishment of a chemical-weapons-free-zone in Europe. Notably,
not long thereafter the SED and the SPD reached agreement on a
similar accord, proposing the creation of a nuclear-weapons-
free corridor in central Europe. Most recently, and practically
simultaneous to the Honecker visit, the SED and the SPD also
issued a highly controversial discussion paper about their 'basic
values', in which the two parties articulated not only their points of
difference but also their areas of common agreement.

Naturally, no one can reliably predict just how open to compromise
the West Germans will choose to be in any of their future dealings
with East Berlin. Just as there are limits on the willingness of all
major West German parties to sacrifice their country's commitment
to national reunification, there seems also to be a general sense of
limits on the kinds of intercourse they are willing to entertain with
the Eastern bloc. Not only does this tacit understanding clearly
apply to a conservative Christian Democratic government, but the
majority of the Social Democratic Party's current leadership is
vocally opposed to taking any steps toward the East that might
impair the Federal Republic's responsibilities to the Western alliance.
Thus even the Social Democratic advocates of joint security talks
with East Germany have been careful to emphasize that they wish
only to facilitate discussion and exchange information, and not to
negotiate matters that are best left to NATO and the superpowers.
But which matters are properly left to NATO's custody? And which,
conversely, are legitimate matters of German concern? Here again,
as with the Soviet–East German case, the ambiguity of the US–West
German division of labor is enough to suggest that even such limited
discussions as those between the SPD and the SED will be a subject
of future controversy.

Of course the Federal Republic's openness to bargaining with
East Berlin will also depend upon how intensely West Germany's
future leaders feel the need to maintain close inter-German ties.
Surveys of younger West Germans suggest that the old spiritual and
psychological bonds that once held Germans together are now fading
with the passage of time; thus the coming generation of leaders may

feel less disposed to concern itself with the fortunes of distant relatives in East Germany. Ironically, this sort of generational change could produce a situation that might rebound to the East Germans' benefit but also change the nature of the present inter-German bargaining relationship by making it less predictable. The East German party leadership might find new governments in Bonn more open to a radical rethinking of their country's *Deutschlandpolitik*. Yet, if West Germany's stakes in the inter-German relationship also declined, the East Germans would then have to look for new levers for exerting pressure on the West.

Another development that might add a new dimension to inter-German negotiations would be a deterioration in East Germany's economic fortunes, an eventuality that some economists foresee happening in the next decade. Much of the current domestic stability of the communist state is directly attributable to its high rates of growth in the past five years. Should the East German economic upswing falter, East Berlin would not only be hard pressed to finance current rates of consumer spending, but might also find itself more dependent upon an infusion of additional credits from the Federal Republic. In this event, the West Germans might be able to drive tougher bargains in their negotiations with East Berlin, which would in turn reestablish a closer trade-off between the economic benefits that they can offer the East and the political concessions that they desire.

For the moment, however, we can hardly afford to underestimate the historical significance of the recent realignment of the inter-German relationship. We are witnessing a major shift in the old inter-German balance as future progress between the two states becomes more and more contingent on the interests and goodwill not only of Bonn but also of policy-makers in East Berlin. Since both sides have an interest in perpetuating the basic relationship and maintaining the inter-German accords of the early 1970s, at least the rudiments of inter-German *détente* will probably last long beyond the leadership of men like Helmut Kohl and Erich Honecker. The big question, though, that Germans on both sides of the national divide must be asking themselves is not about the maintenance of their countries' relations but instead about whether these same ties can be expected to develop beyond the level of their proponents' minimal expectations. Phrased in this manner, the German Question of the future need hardly be limited to the attention of officials in Bonn and East Berlin. Because any qualitative development of this relationship will never take place in a vacuum, we can be certain that any changes in mutual German understandings will also be of concern to each of the states' respective allies.

In this sense, it may be that the age-old German Question, far from being extinguished with the formation of the FRG and the GDR in 1949, lives on with us today. Indeed, because it is not German unity but instead the politics of national division and its consequences that have produced the new uncertainties in central Europe, it may even be appropriate to ask whether the German Question will ever be resolved.

4 German Questions or The Shrinking of Germany

Gebhard Schweigler

I THE REEMERGENCE OF THE GERMAN QUESTION

The German Question, seemingly dormant for many years, resurfaced with surprising vehemence during the early 1980s. The period of *détente* marked by West Germany's *Ostpolitik* appeared to have laid the German Question to rest, but it reemerged with the end of *détente* and the onset of a new Cold War that was characterized by renewed efforts on the part of the United States to contain the Soviet Union. The German Question, raised and repeatedly posed during the first Cold War, seemed to receive a new impetus as the second Cold War set in.

Of particular importance for the reemergence of the German Question was NATO's 'dual-track' decision of the late 1970s to deploy in Western Europe nuclear systems of intermediate range, designed to counter the threat stemming from the Soviet deployment of SS–20 missiles targeted against Western Europe. That decision aroused a storm of public protest in all countries faced with the imminent arrival of new nuclear missiles. In the Federal Republic of Germany, a fast-growing 'peace movement' sought to prevent the stationing of Pershing IIs and cruise missiles. The German Democratic Republic, surely under – possibly unneeded – pressure from the Soviet Union, attempted to influence the West German decision-making process by supporting the peace movement's activities and by threatening a breakdown of relations with West Germany if a 'palisade of missiles' were to be erected there. 'In the name of the German people' the East German leadership appealed to the 'shared responsibility of all Germans' to maintain peace in Europe, which was allegedly threatened by the INF deployment.[1]

These loud noises, with some long-suppressed overtones, fell on receptive ears among neighbors to the East and to the West, and of course in the United States and the Soviet Union as well.[2]

Here the German Question was being raised again in both its classical–historical and in its post-Second-World-War form: How reliable are the Germans, given their frustrated national aspirations? Can they be trusted not to seek reunification at all costs and in the process renounce their responsibilities for maintaining a peaceful *status quo* in the heart of Europe? Eighteen months after the Pershing IIs had begun to arrive in West Germany – an event that should at least have settled the question about West Germany's reliability as an ally of the West – the American columnist Joseph Kraft could still give voice to a sentiment that many others had uttered before him. In the midst of the furor surrounding President Reagan's visit to the Bitburg cemetery, he explained:

> But the visit to the cemetery does have a political logic. For the Germans are once again indulging themselves in fantasies about the national soul. They are tempted anew to balance East against West. They are likely again to react to frustration with another burst of the rage that yields revenge, destruction and immolation.[3]

It is ironic that such apprehensions about the Federal Republic's reliability arose at a time when the leftist SPD-led government under Chancellor Helmut Schmidt was being replaced by a conservative government under CDU Chancellor Helmut Kohl, for if nothing else that change of government in the middle of the INF controversy should have demonstrated West Germany's resolve. But the new government, whose leaders had once vehemently opposed the *Ostpolitik* pursued by the SPD/FDP coalition, found itself in a bind. Faced with the rise of a peace movement with uncertain public appeal, which argued that the much valued fruits of *Ostpolitik* might be snatched away if the government proceeded with INF deployment, it decided to counter that argument – and to prove it false – by continuing the previous government's *Ostpolitik* and thus adhering to a policy of regional *détente*, against American preferences at that. The Kohl government also felt it necessary to maintain good relations with the GDR in order to preempt some possibly dangerous nationalistic and neutralist appeals by the peace movement.[4] It therefore practiced continuity where many had expected a complete turnaround. And that fuelled additional suspicions: How strong must the desires for a solution of the Germany problem be when even a conservative government is forced, against its original intentions, to maintain close relations with East Germany? Italian Foreign Minister Andreotti vented widespread feelings when he expressed his misgivings about such 'pan-Germanism' and claimed that he preferred the existence of two German states (echoing the famous French *bon mot* about 'I like Germany so much that I prefer two').[5]

Andreotti's offhand remarks contributed mightily to the debate about the German Question. In the Federal Republic, some of the more conservative elements within the CDU/CSU–FDP coalition felt encouraged to voice their dissent regarding their government's policy of continuity, not because it was an exercise in 'pan-Germanism', as the Italian foreign minister had argued, but rather for the opposite reason – that it did not seek vigorously enough the reunification of Germany and the recovery of 'lost territories' in the East. Once again they complained that in the process of *détente* and *Ostpolitik*, the Federal Republic was giving up too many of its legal claims for dubious concessions regarding human rights. Thus the internal West German debate heated up considerably.

Interestingly enough, this debate – both in public discussion and published form[6] – eventually began to focus on the question whether the German Question might still be open or not. The official position is clear: The German Question is still open and will remain open until the time when 'a state of peace in Europe in which the German nation will regain its unity through free self-determination' has been achieved.[7] The official insistence on the openness of the German Question is not just self-explanatory, that is, the German Question is open as long as the West German government says it is open. The West German claims are based above all on legal considerations. Thus the Federal Republic's constitution, the Basic Law as adopted on 23 May 1949, speaks in its Preamble of the German people as 'animated by the resolve to preserve their national and political unity' and declares: 'The entire German people are called upon to achieve in free self-determination the unity and freedom of Germany'. These and other provisions in the Basic Law referring to the continued existence of the German nation have consistently been interpreted as a mandate for the Federal Republic to insist on the unity of Germany and to bring about its reunification.

It is not only constitutional law that speaks of one Germany and thus keeps the German Question open. International legal provisions arising from the Reich's unconditional surrender in 1945 and the subsequent disposition of Four-Power rights and responsiblities also point to the openness of the German Question. Of particular importance to the Federal Republic is the 'Convention on the

Relations between the Federal Republic of Germany and the Three
Powers' (the Paris Agreements of 1952/4, known in the Federal
Republic as the 'Germany Treaty'), in which the United States,
Great Britain and France retained all rights and responsibilities
pertaining to Germany as a whole, to Berlin, and to an eventual
peace treaty. In Article 7 these countries committed themselves to
cooperate with the Federal Republic in achieving by peaceful means
their 'common goal': a reunified Germany, constituted like the
Federal Republic and integrated into the European community. This
commitment presumably remains a binding one and thus tends to
keep the German Question open. Even the Soviet Union is seen to
be adhering to the concept of the continued existence of Germany
as a whole, in its insistence on retaining the 'hostile nations clause'
in the UN Charter, for instance, or in its acceptance of the 'Letter
on German Unity'. West German observers have noted with
considerable interest feeble East German efforts to refer to the
'group of Soviet forces in the GDR', and immediate Soviet insistence
on the proper term: 'group of Soviet forces in Germany'.[8]

Chancellor Kohl summarized the official West German position
in his annual 'State of the Nation' message, delivered on 27 February
1985, at the height of the debate about the German Question:

> By insisting that there is one German nationality we are taking
> account of our common past, of the continued existence of the
> German nation and of the fact that the German Question remains
> unresolved. The continued existence of Four-Power rights and
> responsibilities also constitutes an important element of inter-
> national law supporting the continued existence of a common
> German nationality.

Concerning critics of this position, he declared:

> Anyone who today, in an attitude of resignation and fatalism,
> draws a final line under the German Question is rejecting the
> right to self-determination and the realization of human rights.
> He denies any prospect of freedom for all Europeans in the
> future. And he has not understood history – neither its continuity,
> nor the manifold changes occurring on German soil at the heart
> of Europe.

> Nor can the German Question as a key European question be
> declared terminated by either politicians or historians. It has been
> one of the great questions of the shaping of Europe ever since

the system of European powers came into being centuries ago. It has always been and still is the question of how Germany is to be incorporated into Europe and how the Germans become integrated and assume or refuse their European responsibility . . .

By advancing the cause of European unification, we are, from a historical perspective, laying the groundwork for ultimately overcoming the division of our continent. The criteria by which our contribution will someday be measured are that we preserved the nation and our freedom and at the same time achieved a larger fatherland in Europe. We are not seeking an answer to the German Question single-handedly, nor by opposing our neighbors in East and West, nor by rejecting history.[9]

The official position regarding the openness of the German Question rests on foundations of constitutional and international law, evokes the right of self-determination, proclaims that 'German history will continue'[10] and seeks to combat 'the dangerous illusion that the present situation in Germany will historically last forever and remain so without endangering peace'.[11] Proponents of the idea that the German Question is, for all intents and purposes, closed base their arguments primarily on their perceptions of German and European realities (and concomitant requirements for peace). They simply see no chance that reunification could ever be achieved, given especially Soviet resistance to any such effort,[12] but also the reluctance of other European states to have the *status quo* in Europe changed so drastically. The longer the division of Germany lasts, they believe, the more acceptable it will eventually become to the Germans themselves. From this perspective, the German Question can no longer be considered open.

In the political debate within West Germany, this line of reasoning is most radically offered by the Green Party, the largely youth-based newcomer on the political scene since 1983. The Greens by and large reject all claims for reunification, plead for full diplomatic recognition of the GDR and consequently are in favor of doing away with West Germany's Ministry for Inner-German Relations or the 'Day of German Unity' as the national holiday (June 17, commemorating the unsuccessful uprising of East German workers in 1953).[13]

These extreme positions taken by the Greens are not shared by other parties in the Federal Republic. Still, it is interesting to note that some prominent members of the SPD, once in opposition, started voicing their belief that the German Question is indeed no longer open. Hans Apel, former Minister of Defense and then a candidate for mayor of Berlin (he lost decisively), was among the first to call the German Question dead, arousing considerable controversy in the process. Egon Bahr, once principal architect of the new *Ostpolitik*, argued that the German Question is indeed so wide open that it is simply beyond imagination how it could ever be closed. And Willy Brandt, Chancellor of the Federal Republic during the period of *détente* and recipient of the Nobel Peace Prize for his efforts, referred to hopes for reunification as 'a dream . . . which is over when you wake up'.[14] The SPD still shies away from supporting policies that might more definitely close the German Question. When, for instance, Klaus Boelling, once Chancellor Helmut Schmidt's spokesman and later his Permanent Representative in the GDR, suggested the elimination of the call for reunification in the Preamble of the Basic Law[15] – a theme later picked up by former Minister of Justice Juergen Schmude – the party leadership pointedly refused to go along and laid the matter to rest, for the time being anyway.[16]

Claiming an absolute priority of peace over reunification issues, the SPD instead went ahead to seek arms control agreements with its East German counterpart in such areas as nuclear-free zones and a ban on chemical weapons in Europe. Its hopes (apparently shared by the East German leadership) of arousing such widespread public approval in West Germany that it might be swept back into power are unlikely to be fulfilled, since security issues are no longer at the forefront of the public debate and the government was successful in characterizing such a 'side-show' as illegitimate. Widely expressed fears that such SPD–SED chumminess might portend early phases of closer inter-German relations leading to a stronger emphasis on reunification seem similarly misplaced. If anything, the SPD appears to be moving in the direction of solving the German Question, not by achieving reunification, but through opening the road to more normal relations with the GDR.

There are also some indications that the debate may eventually reach conservative circles as well. One of West Germany's most prominent historians, Golo Mann, frequently a spokesperson for conservative causes, told a startled CSU gathering in 1984 that he considered the West Germans' fatherland to be the Federal Republic, nothing more, certainly not a larger Germany which, he claimed,

Table 4.1 'With which of these statements would you agree: I The German Question is no longer open, we have to recognize that reunification is no longer possible; II The reunification of Germany must remain our political goal, however distant it may be'. (percentage of replies)

October 1984	Total	CDU/CSU	FDP	SPD	Greens
no longer open	40	30	34	48	61
remains goal	58	69	64	49	36

Source: *Der Spiegel*, 44/1984, p. 43.

could no longer be achieved. The subsequent debate, it was reported, revealed that 'the time of referring to the German Question in the style of comic-strip balloons is coming to an end even within the CSU'.[17]

The debate over the openness of the German Question involved West Germany's political elite more than the public at large. The public, in general fairly apathetic in regard to this question, showed itself somewhat divided when asked in a public opinion poll whether the German Question is still open (Table 4.1). The lack of public consensus, nowhere perceived as a troubling problem,[18] does hint at the possibility that the internal West German debate about the German Question will become more controversial yet. The German Question may indeed not be closed, but the political consensus that it is, in fact, still open is likely to become ever more fragile. It is important, therefore, to take a closer look at this evolving debate and at some of its possible outcomes.

II APPROACHES TO THE DEBATE

The debate about the German Question, both within West Germany as well as internationally, appears to be informed by two competing ways of thinking about things 'national', that is, nation, nationalism, national consciousness, national identity and other such terms, which, depending on usage and personal idiosyncracies, may or may not be used interchangeably. One might be called the 'natural' approach or paradigm. It sees a nation – and almost everything deriving from it – as something almost natural and therefore basically unchanging. Most of the fears that are shared outside Germany in regard to the German Question seem to reflect this 'natural' approach. Typically the argument runs as follows:

> The Germans – no longer dominated by feelings of war guilt, less mesmerized by the American ideal, distressed by the failure of Europe to become an alternative to divisive nationalisms – are *naturally* drawn to a growing preoccupation with the fate of their brethren living under an alien system. The notion that the destiny of a united Germany depends on a close relationship with Russia is not a new one in German political tradition. Frustration with the nation's division is giving it a new lease on life.[19]

German hopes regarding the continued existence of the German nation and the eventual achievement of reunification also appear to be based on the 'natural' approach. What else to call the firm belief in the forces of history that will, some day, deliver to Germany once again its national unity? These hopes, couched in terms of historical inevitability, constitute other countries' fears; both rely on an unstated belief in quasi-natural forces. Depending on one's perspective, these forces are either ennobling in nature, quietly at work until national destiny has been achieved, or they are lurking in the Germans' soul, ready to erupt once again in a rage of frustration 'that yields revenge, destruction and immolation'.[20]

Proponents of the notion that national – and nationalistic – attitudes are natural and therefore unchanging would, it appears, be hard-pressed to explain where exactly in nature such permanence is to be located. Are these attitudes genetically determined? Are they forever in the Germans' blood? Do they derive from unchanging external factors, such as the geographical location of the country?[21] To raise these questions is to point to the tenuousness of the 'natural' approach. Yet it has remained surprisingly strong.[22]

The competing approach to national questions might be termed the 'social model'. It recognizes that there is nothing necessarily natural about nations and that national attitudes are a social construct, not a natural phenomenon. Because national attitudes are formed as a result of social processes – through social communication[23] – they are themselves subject to change if and when the nature of social processes changes. The 'social model' does not deny the strong resilience of national attitudes, but rather than attributing it to natural forces it sees their strength grounded in social forces. When external conditions change – such as through the forceful division of a nation or even (as was the case with Austria) as the result of unfortunate experiences – social processes (here the patterns of social communication) are also subject to change, and so are corresponding attitudes. By the same token, attitudinal changes, once they have taken place, cannot be reversed (or revert as the result of underlying 'natural' forces) unless external conditions change as well.

From the perspective of the 'social model', nations are formed when a group of people develops a national consciousness or identity, that is, the belief that members of this group are in some way identical, and therefore different from other groups: that they do, in fact, form a nation. Nationalism is seen as the ideology of the nation-state, in its classical form as the drive for national self-determination in the context of a state, in its perverted form as claims for superiority of one nation-state over another. In general usage today, national consciousness – the conscious (and collective) recognition of being a member of a certain nation – is regarded as normal, indeed desirable, whereas nationalism – the claim to special privileges for one's nation – is considered to be a dangerous aberration.

In applying the perspectives of the 'social model' to the situation in postwar Germany, the real German Question becomes: What attitudinal changes have occurred as the result of the division of the country, and, in turn, what effects have attitudinal changes had on political realities? Or, put more simply: Does the German nation still exist? The following attempt to provide some answers to these questions will focus on the interrelationship between changing attitudes and processes of political adaptation. Given the nature of this chapter, this attempt cannot be as comprehensive and therefore as conclusive as any attempt at answering the German Question should ordinarily be.[24] Nevertheless it will become evident that the German Question is, in fact, gradually being closed.

III DEFINING GERMANY

The German Question, as has become obvious by now, can be asked in any number of ways. One useful starting point in the search for answers is to raise the very basic question: What is Germany? Again, the official answer is unambiguous: Germany is Germany as it existed in its borders as of 31 December 1937. According to this definition, then, Germany encompasses those areas beyond the Oder–Niesse Line (the present border between the GDR and Poland) that were once German but are now part of the Soviet Union and Poland. Most of the Germans living in Silesia, Pomerania and East Prussia either fled as the Red Army advanced or they were – often brutally – expropriated and expelled after the war had ended.

For many years thereafter West Germany refused to recognize the Oder–Niesse Line as the definitive border between Germany and Poland (the GDR had done so soon after it had come into existence in 1949). This policy of non-recognition was supported by West German public opinion, which into the early 1960s continued to hold on to the belief that these formerly Germany territories were still German, would one day become German again and should therefore not be given up as lost.[25] Gradually, however, that belief waned as the recognition set in that these territories were unlikely to be regained and that, in the meantime, Poles living there had begun to acquire rights of their own to remain there permanently (a point of view first given public prominence in 1965 by the Protestant church in Western Germany). In addition, the vague hope that recognition of the Oder–Niesse line might be traded for Soviet concessions regarding measures leading toward reunification also faded.

By the late 1960s attitudes in West Germany had changed considerably. These attitudinal changes laid the political foundations for the election of Willy Brandt as Chancellor and the subsequent intiation of a new *Ostpolitik*. Soon thereafter, in 1970, the Federal Republic concluded treaties with the Soviet Union and Poland in which it acknowledged the inviolability of present borders in Europe, thus in effect recognizing the Oder–Niesse Line as a definitive border of Germany. Formal legal recognition, however, was not extended, since, as the government maintained, under the postwar legal regime this could only be done in the context of a full-fledged peace treaty.

Barring such a peace treaty, however – and very few seriously expect that one will ever be concluded[26] – West Germany had, for all intents and purposes, recognized as final the loss of formerly German territories. Certainly the majority of West Germans felt that this was the case. For them Germany had in effect shrunk back to the Oder–Niesse Line.

The CDU/CSU, then in opposition, vehemently opposed the

Table 4.2   (Silesian functionary Hupka said) 'Silesia is the property of all Germans'. Do you agree or disagree? 'And should we reconcile ourselves to the present German–Polish border, the Oder–Niesse Line, or should we not?' (percentage of replies)

January 1985	Total	18–25	26–34	35–40	50–64	65+
disagree	65	79	69	68	55	59
reconcile	76	79	83	77	71	70

Source: *Der Spiegel*, 6/1985, pp. 93–4.

Moscow and Warsaw treaties, precisely because, so they argued, they amounted to a *de facto* recognition of the Oder–Niesse Line and thus to a renunciation of legal claims. Twelve years later, when the CDU/CSU returned to power, some elements within the party – particularly representatives of the various expellee organizations – still had not reconciled themselves to the validity of these treaties. The Kohl government, however, did not seek to question or change the treaties, as it continued its predecessor's *Ostpolitik*. (The presence of the FDP as a coalition partner, with, as foreign minister, Hans-Dietrich Genscher, who had previously engineered the collapse of the Schmidt government, may have been another important factor behind this continuity.)

The intra-party conflict finally broke into the open in 1984, when the Silesian expellee organization announced the slogan for its 1985 annual meeting: 'Silesia remains ours'. Chancellor Kohl, who had previously agreed to speak at the meeting, found himself under intense public and political pressure either to cancel his appearance or to have the Silesians (whose leading figures are CDU representatives) change their slogan. A compromise of sorts was reached eventually, when the Silesians dedicated their meeting to 'Silesia's future in a united Europe'. But a good deal of damage had already been done, as the episode fuelled East European charges of West German revanchism and contributed to doubts elsewhere about what the Germans might be up to.

In the end, however, the Silesia affair had a salutory effect, at least within West Germany itself. For one, it showed that the vast majority of West Germans in fact does not agree with the proposition that 'Silesia remains ours', but instead believes that these formerly German territories are definitely lost (Table 4.2). In the public's mind Germany quite obviously is no longer the Germany of 1937. In addition, it forced responsible members of the government and the ruling coalition to state with greater clarity that the Federal Republic would continue to abide by the treaties and would not actually seek to reclaim former German territories.

Due to its fears that a formal legal recognition of the Oder–Niesse Line might contribute to an unravelling of the whole postwar legal order, the Kohl government continued to insist that it could not and would not give up legal claims. But the political message was clear enough. Volker Ruehe, deputy whip and foreign policy spokesman of the CDU parliamentary faction, declared that, even if a peace treaty were ever to be achieved, the Eastern treaties would have a *'politische Bindungswirkung'* (that is, they would politically tie the Federal Republic's hands). Chancellor Kohl, in his 1985 'State of the Nation' message, made it as clear as he could under the circumstances:

> Turning to Poland, we repeat that we want further reconciliation and understanding. Today and for the future we reaffirm the Warsaw Treaty between the Federal Republic of Germany and the People's Republic of Poland which established 'the inviolability of borders and respect for the territorial integrity and sovereignty of all states in Europe within their present frontiers' as 'a basic condition for peace'. We, the Federal Republic of Germany and the People's Republic of Poland, have no territorial claims whatsoever on one another and will not make any in the future.[27]

And President Richard von Weizsaecker, in his remarkable speech to the Bundestag on 8 May 1985, pointed to West Germany's priority of humanitarian over legal considerations:

> The expellee's own homeland has meanwhile become a homeland for others. . . . Renouncing force today means giving them lasting security, unchallenged on political grounds, for their future in the place where fate drove them after the 8th of May 1945 and where they have been living in the decades since. It means placing the dictate of understanding above conflicting legal claims. That is the true, the human contribution to a peaceful order in Europe which we can provide.[28]

For most West Germans, as for most everybody else outside Poland, the question of the Oder–Niesse Line has long become irrelevant and boring.[29] All legal claims notwithstanding, the political facts have asserted themselves. The lengthy quotes presented above point out, in an exemplary fashion, how one element of the German Question that was once considered extremely important has in the meantime been answered.

IV   PERCEPTIONS OF THE DIVISION

In practical terms, Germany today is not the Germany of 1937 but rather, it now appears, the Germany of 1945. It is a Germany originally made up of four zones of occupation and, since 1949, of two newly founded states. By now, the goal of achieving the unity of the German nation has come to mean the reunification of the Federal Republic of Germany and the German Democratic Republic. But – to ask yet another German Question – what kind of nation might this be?

Initially the West German government maintained that Germany as a nation-state had not disappeared, despite the division of the country. Claiming the right to the sole representation of Germany as a whole, it was forced to deny the existence of the GDR, which – depending on the legal theory of one's choice – either did not exist, constituted a phenomenon unknown in international law, or was a rebellious part of Germany that had to be brought under the control of the legitimate government. For many years, therefore, West Germany refused to recognize the GDR or to have any official dealings with its government, while holding on to such remnants of national ties as a common team at the Olympic games.

The GDR, in turn, went through several phases in trying to define its own status. Originally it sought to compete with the Federal Republic by claiming that it rightfully represented all – or, in any case, the better part – of Germany.[30] Finding itself hopelessly outmaneuvered in that competition, the GDR later declared itself to be a separate German state and began to sever remaining ties to West Germany (including, by 1968, the common Olympic team: one area where the GDR won the competition). Eventually, however, the GDR announced that it was, in fact, a new nation-state, socialist in nature, that had nothing in common with the Federal Republic and little enough with Germany of the common past.

As time went by, West Germany was forced to change its approach to the GDR. Konrad Adenauer, the Federal Republic's first chancellor, might have hoped that by pursuing a 'policy of strength'

– which required the firm integration of West Germany in the Western alliance – the Soviet Union's hold on the GDR might eventually be loosened and reunification be achieved. By the early 1960s, with the building of the Wall in Berlin on 13 August 1961, such hopes had been dashed. The rebellious phenomenon had not disappeared or rejoined West Germany. On the contrary, the brutal closing of the border between East and West Germany demonstrated the GDR's capacity to protect its interests. Eventually the Wall would turn out to be a major factor behind the successful international build-up of the GDR.

The pursuit of legal claims having been proved fruitless, West Germans began to rethink the situation. Most of that thinking took place within the opposition party, the SPD, which began to look for a 'change through *rapprochement*', as Egon Bahr's famous slogan of 1963 put it. When the SPD, not least as a result of its new ideas, finally came to power in 1969, it was able to pursue corresponding policies. In its new *Ostpolitik* it struck a bargain of sorts with the Soviet Union and the GDR. In exchange for a less-than-formal recognition of the postwar *status quo* in Europe – including the existence of the GDR as a separate state – it secured unimpeded access to Berlin and gained East German concessions regarding the maintenance of human ties between East and West Germany.

In essence, the two sides made a bet. The East German leadership bet that even limited West German recognition of the GDR would help to undermine any remaining claims regarding the continued existence of the German nation and thus help consolidate the status of the GDR as a new nation-state in its own right. West Germany bet that improved human contacts across the border would help stem an ever deepening sense of national estrangement on both sides of the border and thus keep alive an all-German national consciousness as the essential precondition for eventual reunification.

The odds of this bet seemed to favor the GDR. A considerable number of public opinion polls taken in the Federal Republic at that time showed solid majorities in support of the treaties, but an astonishing disagreement with their alleged long-term objectives. Most West Germans felt that, after the conclusion of the treaties, reunification would no longer be possible. That, of course, was also the point raised rather vehemently by the opposition parties – to no avail. The GDR leadership could, therefore, expect that the processes of legal erosion and national estrangement would continue, if perhaps at a slower rate. In addition, it found itself in a position of being able to manipulate the rate of cross-border contacts through any number of devices, ranging from restricting hotel space to the imposition of a mandatory currency exchange for all visitors. The GDR also remained extremely restrictive concerning East German visitors to West Germany (with the exception of pensioners, whom it did not consider important, for both political and crassly material reasons).

The level of East–West German contacts did indeed increase quite dramatically after the conclusion of the Treaty on the Relations between the GDR and the Federal Republic.[31] But it never reached the level many proponents of this policy (and local bus operators) had hoped for; compared with West German travel to other neighboring countries (Austria in particular), the number of excursions to the GDR appears downright puny. Most West Germans, particularly that vast majority (some 70 per cent) without relatives or personal friends in the GDR, simply were not interested in travelling to the GDR. At the outset of his new *Ostpolitik*, Willy Brandt had coined the phrase: 'Nation is, when people see each other'. Measured against that standard, it has by now become evident that the German nation so defined is indeed in trouble.

The 'grand bargain' embodied in Brandt's *Ostpolitik* signalled not just a change in political tactics. It reflected – and then reconfirmed – significant underlying changes in West German attitudes towards the German Question. The protestations of the opposition parties at the time were quite to the point: the Federal Republic was politically moving away from its adherence to the German nation-state. In the process, West Germany's 'national' interest was being redefined. In the twenty years between 1949 and 1969, the Federal Republic's foreign policy was geared to protecting the all-German nation-state by refusing to recognize the GDR; the Hallstein Doctrine (according to which the Federal Republic broke off all relations with countries that recognized the GDR) was the most visible embodiment of that national interest. Now it became the national interest of the FRG to achieve an improvement in East German living conditions, in the hope that this might contribute to keeping alive a feeling of belonging together. The price for such improvements was semi-formal recognition of the GDR and thus a decisive step back from previous claims to the sole representation of all of Germany. Chancellor Brandt's slogan, first expressed in 1969, sought to capture the new realities: 'two states in one nation'.

V   TWO STATES, ONE NATION?

The formula of 'two states in one nation' reflected yet another step in the process of the shrinking of Germany. Certainly the underlying concept of nation itself had become less encompassing (a point underscored by the presence, since 1972, of two German states in the United Nations). In fact, the West Germans were now faced with still another German Question: What kind of nation could – indeed should – this nation be, now that the commonsensical definition of nation clearly no longer applied.

In their attempts to wrestle with this problem, West German politicians, intellectuals and scholars by and large pursued two different paths. One was, in effect, backward-oriented: a return to the beginnings of the German nation in the concept of the *Kulturnation*. In the eighteenth and nineteenth centuries a sense of German identity had developed, at least among the bourgeois elites of the day, around the conviction that the Germans shared a better or more highly refined culture than other people.[32] Now West German intellectuals once again began to argue that the Germans in East and West should make their common culture the source and focus of their national identity, not the unified state. In general, they no longer argue in terms of the superiority of German culture; they merely claim that it is their culture that sets Germans apart from other nations, which therefore should be the proper object of national identification.[33] After all, so their argument goes, all Germans read Goethe, like Bach, and admire Luther, not to mention the fact that they share a common history. Guenter Gaus, the Federal Republic's first Permanent Representative in the GDR, termed this concept, by way of recommendation, the *'entstaatlichte Nation'* – the nation without a state.[34]

There is a second definition of culture that does not rely on the – obviously elitist and possibly repulsive – notion of 'high culture', but refers instead to everyday behavior and value patterns. This anthropological definition of culture can also be applied to the concept of *Kulturnation*. According to this definition, the German nation continues to exist simply because Germans in East and West still talk, think and act alike. The knowledge that they are, in that sense, identical, and the value attached to it, can – or should – form the bases of national identity.

The application of either concept of *Kulturnation* to the German Question is, however, fraught with difficulties. There is, for one, the factual issue: Do East and West Germans indeed share 'high' and/or 'low' culture? Obviously they still speak the same language, although regional variations serve to identify most speakers as coming from either East or West Germany (and worries have been expressed for some time now that the Americanization of the West German language and the Russianization of the East German language may at some point contribute to a linguistic division as well). But do they still think and act alike? Observers of the German scene have long noted how different West Germans have become from East Germans, how little the typical modernized and American-ized West German appears to have in common with his still 'typically German' counterpart in the GDR. The experiences of East German refugees in West Germany have offered many hints that cultural commonalities can no longer be assumed, for which reason even this group of East Germans most interested in life in the West frequently faces difficult adjustment problems.[35]

Where obvious commonalities still exist, such as in certain (youth-based) subcultures, the question remains whether these are peculiarly German and thus a potential source for national identification or not, in fact, attributes of all modern industrialized societies. Among West Germans – especially the younger ones – the feeling that East Germans might be 'fellow-countrymen' has, in any case, gradually waned over the years (Table 4.3). And only a small number of them actually find the East Germans as a people[36] – their presumed fellow-countrymen – likeable (Table 4.4).[37] Not least because of this development, the German *Kulturnation* may well rest on rather shaky foundations.

The *Kulturnation* concept suffers from other problems as well. It is by no means evident, for instance, that for the broad masses of people the idea of a common culture, much less that of a 'high culture' (after all, who actually reads Goethe, listens to Bach and admires Luther?), is a sufficiently strong source of national identification. In the age of nationalism, national identity is everywhere focused on the nation-state: on its achievement or its existence. German history itself showed that the *Kulturnation* wanted the nation-state, which Bismarck finally brought about, if only 'with blood and iron'. It is very much to be doubted that Germans in East and West will satisfy their presumed need for national identity by making culture their source of identification while forgetting about the nation-state.

Conversely, if a national identity based on the idea of a

Table 4.3 'Imagine you are vacationing somewhere on the Black Sea. One day you meet another German. While talking with him you learn that he comes from the GDR. . . . Would you have the feeling that he is a fellow-countryman or would you feel no closer to him than to an Austrian?' (percentage of replies)

	7/1970	11/1975	11/1981	6/1983	10/1983
countryman	68	52	49	48	51
Austrian	20	29	30	31	32
undecided	12	19	21	21	17
10/1983 (by age group)		16–29	30–44	45–59	60+
countryman		37	47	54	68
Austrian		43	37	28	18
undecided		20	16	18	14

Source: Noelle-Neumann, 'Im Wartesaal der Geschichte', p. 142.

Table 4.4 'Which of these people do you find particularly likeable (*sympatisch*) or not likeable? (Choose only three please.)' (percentage of replies)

January 1983	likeable		not	
Austrian	52		6	
Swiss	47		5	
French	31		7	
Dutch	27		16	
People in the GDR	26		7	
Italian	15		24	
British	14		19	
Greek	13		7	
Czech	4		18	
Russian	4		37	
none	11		34	
(by age group)	16–29	30–44	45–59	60+
GDR people likeable	15	19	30	41
not likeable	8	9	6	4

Source: Noelle-Neumann, 'Im Wartesaal der Geschichte', p. 145.

Kulturnation actually were to take hold, the grave danger of German history repeating itself might arise. Would the Germans once again want a nation-state of their own, even 'with blood and iron'? And where to draw the borders? After all, *Kulturnation* borders, unlike state borders, are difficult to define. Are not the Austrians German too? The Swiss? German minorities in neighboring countries? Formerly German territories still characterized by the civilizing effects of German culture? Right-wing West German writing offers sufficient hints as to where this line of reasoning might lead.[38] For empirical as well as normative reasons, the attempt to define the German nation in terms of the *Kulturnation* does not appear to be a viable proposition.[39]

VI NATIONAL CONSCIOUSNESS AND ATTITUDES TOWARD REUNIFICATION

Partly in recognition of the conceptual and political difficulties involving the *Kulturnation*, some analysts followed a different path in trying to answer the question about the German nation with two states. They relied on the simplest definition of a nation, namely that of a people who believe that they are a nation. As long as the Germans in East and West still believe that they belong to one common nation, and especially as long as they profess to be in favor of eventual reunification, the German nation – despite the existence of two states – can still be said to exist, if only in the national consciousness of the Germans themselves. According to this definition, the German Question is reduced to a question about the Germans' national consciousness.

But does that all-German national consciousness in fact still exist? This is a seemingly simple question that unfortunately does not afford easy answers. Empirical data are not always available, especially not from the GDR, definitional problems abound, and contradictory interpretations are the rule.[40] Yet without doubt some attitudinal changes have occurred both in the Federal Republic and the GDR that tend at least to question the vibrant existence of an all-German national consciousness. A significant minority of West Germans, for instance, no longer believes that the people of both states form part of a single nation (Table 4.5). And when the question is put not in terms of people, but in terms of the two states, the changes that took place over the past decade can only

Table 4.5 'Today the Federal Republic of Germany and the GDR are two sovereign states. If you think of the people of the Federal Republic and the GDR, do you feel they are part of a single nation, or are they no longer part of a single nation?' (percentage of replies)

	September 1984
part of a single nation	59
no longer part of a single nation	37
undecided/no reply	4

Source: FRG Press and Information Office, *Bulletin*, 30 November 1984, p. 20.

Table 4.6 'Would you say that the GDR and the Federal Republic belong to one German nation?' (percentage of replies)

		1974	1984
one nation	total	70	42
	age 20–29 group	65	34
not one nation	total	29	53
	age 20–29 group	34	61

Source: EMNID, *Informationen*, March/April 1984, Table 1.

be called dramatic. At present, those believing that the two states belong to one nation are in the minority, and decisively so among the younger generations (Table 4.6). Of course, the replies to these questions do not reveal the kind of nation or concept of nation the respondents had in mind.[41]

The most important yardstick by which to measure the Germans' national consciousness has always been considered to be their position on the question of reunification. It is a stock part of West German rhetoric regarding the German Question that the German nation will exist as long as the Germans themselves desire the reunification of their nation. Depending on the wording of the question, that desire is either unbroken (Table 4.7) or somewhat in doubt, especially among the young generations (Table 4.8). Outright opposition to the goal of reunification is, in any case, still rather rare. From this perspective, then, the prevailing support for the achievement of reunification would seem to point to the continued

Table 4.7 'Are you personally in favor of the reunification of the two German states, against it or indifferent?' (percentage of replies)

	1978	1980	1984
in favor of reunification	79	77	80
against reunification	4	7	4
indifferent	16	15	16

Source: Forschungsgruppe Wahlen, 'ZDF-Politbarometer', January 1984, p. 37.

Table 4.8 'Would you like to see reunification come about, or is this not important for you?' (percentage of replies)

	1976	1981	16–29	30–44	45–59	60+
wish reunification	60	61	44	55	73	75
not important	36	32	51	38	20	19
undecided	4	7	6	7	7	6

Source: Noelle-Neumann, 'Im Wartesaal der Geschichte', p. 144.

existence of an all-German national consciousness.

While public support for the somewhat abstract goal of reunification has remained high, the expectation that it may actually be achieved has, since the mid-1960s, been rather low.[42] An overwhelming majority of the West German people considers reunification within the next thirty years as either unlikely or impossible (Table 4.9).

The growing gap in public attitudes between support for the goal of reunification and expectations regarding its achievement has resulted in some important political consequences. Unable to keep demanding something the achievement of which seems highly unlikely, the West German public has largely dropped the question of reunification from its political agenda.[43] Not only does it no longer appear in public opinion polls as one of the most important questions the government ought to deal with; it has also, in practice, disappeared from the government's agenda.

Compared to years past, reunification rhetoric is very subdued indeed. No political parties have made reunification their primary goal, no public rallies demonstrate urgent desires for reunification.

Table 4.9 'Germany has been divided for more than thirty years. Do you believe that the unification of the two German states into one single state within the next thirty years is certain, possible, unlikely, or wholly impossible?' (percentage of replies)

	1979	*1980*	*1984*
certain	4	2	2
possible	18	15	17
unlikely	51	51	52
impossible	27	31	29

Source: Forschungsgruppe Wahlen, 'ZDF-Politbarometer', January 1984, p. 35.

It has become an abstract goal, quite without current content or consequences, as far as the public at large is concerned. Most West Germans would probably accept reunification, if it somehow were to be dropped into their laps, but they no longer actively seek to achieve that goal; nor are they prepared to engage in any sacrifices for it. If reunification were somehow to be realized, it would have to be on West German terms (Table 4.10).

Of course, the Federal Republic is not entirely free in this regard. Not only do the three Western powers retain all rights pertaining to Germany as a whole; they also have obligated the Federal Republic – in Article 7 of the Paris Agreements – to seek the reunification of Germany only if a unified Germany were constituted like the Federal Republic and allied with the West. That restriction was never controversial, as the West German public fully endorsed it. The relatively large number of West Germans supporting a neutral mixture of the two German states most likely expresses its – generally rather vague – desire for a posture of neutrality[44] rather than an outright willingness to consider a reunified Germany unlike the Federal Republic.

Reunification always implied the pursuit of two goals: the restoration of the German nation-state and the achievement of freedom for the East Germans. At first the political and humanitarian goals were seen as one and the same and, therefore, indivisible: reunification would bring freedom, and reunification without freedom

Table 4.10 'There are different opinions concerning the question of what a reunified Germany should be like. We have written down some possibilities and would like to know with which of these you tend to agree.' (percentage of replies)

	1979	1984
A reunified Germany must under all circumstances be like the Federal Republic today and belong to the West.	63	62
A reunified Germany should represent a mixture of both German states. It should be neutral, belonging neither to the West nor to the East.	34	37
As far as I am concerned, a reunified Germany can be like the GDR and belong to the East.	2	1

Source: Forschungsgruppe Wahlen, 'ZDF-Politbarometer', January 1984, p. 36.

was inconceivable. But there was also a corollary: reunification must not be sacrificed for the freedom of East Germans. When the suggestion was first made in the late 1950s that freedom for the East Germans was more important than national reunification, public opinion showed itself quite opposed to that proposition, even though Konrad Adenauer and Franz Josef Strauss had hinted their support.[45] National attitudes still prevailed over humanitarian ones, as the West Germans' all-German national consciousness was still strong. In the course of the 1960s, however, attitudes began to change; these changes reached their political fruition with the new *Ostpolitik* in 1969.

By now the primacy of freedom over reunification is no longer questioned. The following quote by Heinrich Windelen, Minister for Inner-German Relations, reflects government thinking and reveals how far the CDU/CSU has come in acknowledging the validity of a position first only hinted at by Adenauer and Strauss in the late 1950s:

People have for a long time now been pondering how the German question can or should be solved following the disaster of this century. The prime objective need not be the restoration of a

unified nation-state if freedom and human dignity for all Germans
can be ensured by other means. Chancellor Kohl recently stated
in an interview with Swiss Television on 15 January 1984 '. . .
we also realize that the unity of our nation, a goal that we adhere
to . . . is only conceivable and feasible within a European
framework. There can be no return to the nation-state that existed
at the time of Otto von Bismarck'.[46]

The shift in political emphasis from the national goal of reunification to the humanitarian goal of freedom, or self-determination,
probably takes proper account of current East German realities.
While reliable data are missing, most observers of the GDR today
argue that the East Germans are, in fact, more interested in freedom
than in reunification (although they also appear more strongly
interested in reunification than do the West Germans, perhaps
simply because it would bring them freedom). There is also some
doubt on both sides – never fully explored, because the question
itself is so highly theoretical – as to whether the East Germans
would welcome or be able to live with the kind of freedom that
most West Germans have come to take for granted. The insistence on
freedom without reunification takes these doubts into consideration.

In the meantime, the Kohl government has taken the argument
in favor of freedom one step further. Realizing that the division of
Europe – and thus of Germany – can only be overcome through a
process of internal liberalization within the Soviet bloc and not
through any political moves the West might undertake, it now argues
that the Federal Republic would find any reunification of Germany
unacceptable that did not, at the same time, lead to freedom for
all East European countries, especially for Poland.[47]

By making reunification contingent, at least rhetorically, on the
achievement of freedom elsewhere in Eastern Europe, the West
German government is apparently trying to deal especially with
Polish sensitivities. For the fact remains that most of Germany's
neighbors to the East, but also to the West, remain deeply skeptical
about any designs regarding German reunification. A reunified
Germany in the heart of Europe, capable once again of mustering
its enormous political, economic and possibly military power,
continues to be an unsettling prospect.

Partly in response to such external reluctance, West German
governments have argued for a number of years now that the
German Question could only be solved in the context of the

unification of all of Europe, where borders would no longer matter. Scholars and intellectuals have jumped on the bandwagon by resurrecting the idea of a unified *Mitteleuropa* free of outside domination and capable of handling its own affairs.[48] But exactly how this is to be achieved – and, more important, what kind of entity a Germany so reunified would constitute – has rarely been spelled out.[49] By stressing freedom rather than national unity, the Kohl government may be trying to make this concept more palatable to other European countries, not all of which are likely to share the proposition that by working toward European unity they are also working toward the reunification of Germany.

While the Kohl government would certainly not admit as much, the shift from strictly national to humanitarian and indeed international concerns does seem to reflect a weakening desire for reunification and thus the gradual loss of an all-German national consciousness. Surely this reversal from previously held convictions is not just tactically motivated, as part of an effort to achieve the same goal by different means. Apparently the nature of the goal itself has changed, for the public as well as for its government. Largely unnoticed by the outside world, significant changes have taken place. More important yet, given political realities, these changes seem irreversible.

VII   AN EAST GERMAN IDENTITY

For most West Germans today, the idea of Germany as a nation-state has clearly receded. The formula of 'two states in one nation' itself is based on an increasingly hazy concept of what kind of nation this might be. Will this process of national erosion continue? And what might be the eventual outcome of further erosion: the development of two separate nation-states on German soil?

As far as the official position of the German Democratic Republic is concerned, that final answer to the German Question has already been achieved. The GDR, so it claims, represents an entirely new nation-state, whose citizens have also developed a new national consciousness. The connection with Germany is at best – and quite selectively – a historical one. Ethnically, the citizens of the GDR are Germans; in every other respect, however, they are not 'German': that is the official line today.

The GDR fought long and hard for recognition as a separate

nation-state. It scored its big breakthrough in 1972 with the successful 'grand bargain' of *Ostpolitik*. But full-scale recognition by the Federal Republic of its status as a new nation-state has so far eluded its grasp. For reasons outlined earlier, West Germany continues to deny the GDR such recognition. The two German states, for instance, do not exchange ambassadors, but rather 'permanent representatives' (a practice the GDR has sought unsuccessfully to change).

The largest remaining stumbling block in the way of full recognition is West German acceptance of a separate East German citizenship. It is a complex issue. The GDR needs such acceptance not only in order to secure full recognition, but also in order to prevent its citizens from gaining automatic 'German' citizenship in the Federal Republic. West Germany, however, cannot accept a separate East German citizenship, because to do so would, at the present time, be against constitutional strictures, symbolize the final division of Germany, prevent East Germans from exercising their rights as 'German' citizens and – for all of these reasons – amount to too large a concession to the GDR.

Over the long term, the GDR probably holds the better cards in this serious game. It can make a plausible case (though for obvious reasons it does not do so publicly) that it cannot agree to a relaxation of travel restrictions on its own population unless the Federal Republic accepts a separate GDR citizenship; otherwise it stands to lose a sizeable portion of its people were they allowed to travel abroad. The West German shift away from national towards humanitarian concerns tends to imply eventual recognition of GDR citizenship, if only to gain easier cross-border travel. The outlines of the next 'grand bargain' thus seem predetermined. A domestic debate within West Germany over this question has already begun. But it will be some time before this bargain can actually be struck. The Federal Republic would first have to cope with its constitutional dilemmas. It would also have to come to terms with the problem of then having to admit – or turn back in case of non-qualification – East German refugees as seekers of political asylum rather than, as is now the case, as German citizens.

East German claims to separate nation-statehood might be more convincing if it could be shown conclusively that the East Germans themselves have developed a corresponding national consciousness, focused on the GDR and not on the idea of one German nation. At present such proof is not available and unlikely to be forthcoming.

Many observers of the East German scene find themselves in a bind. On the one hand, they see the GDR as more 'German' than the Federal Republic and its people more strongly interested in reunification. On the other hand, they are also forced to note the development among East Germans of a set of attitudes they find difficult to characterize: loyalty to their state, a sense of identification with their state, a growing state-consciousness, a GDR-feeling, a GDR-consciousness, a consciousness of self, a self-assertiveness.[50] Rudolf Bahro, for instance, one of the most prominent refugees in recent years, made this rather typical observation:

> You find that workers will grouse and swear about conditions when they are in their factory, but when some well-heeled uncle arrives on a visit from West Germany, they stand up for the GDR and point out all the good things about it, all the disadvantages they had to overcome after 1945, and so on. Although the state's demands for loyalty are widely resented, I would say that in normal, crisis-free times there is a sufficiently high degree of loyalty to assure the country's stability . . . The increase in international recognition has certainly boosted the sense of loyalty to the state.[51]

Most GDR-watchers are by now prepared to agree with the argument that the East Germans have, in fact, developed 'a basic stock of behavioral patterns, attitudes and values, which is characteristic only for them and different from that in the Federal Republic'.[52] They remain reluctant to see in such a development the emergence of a separate East German national consciousness or even national identity, but are nevertheless forced to conclude, albeit with some verbal dexterity: 'It is not least due to the fact that the Federal Republic of Germany as the Federal Republic has gained in identity that, with internal consequence, the *Selbstbewusstsein* of the GDR society has come to show more definite contours'.[53]

Whatever the exact label may be, East German attitudes apparently have changed over the years in the direction of closer identification with the GDR. This is particularly obvious in one area of great importance to the GDR, namely East German athletic prowess. These changes may not amount to a full-fledged separate national consciousness. But they do appear to represent a set of attitudes that contributes to strengthening the GDR internally and thus, over the longer run, to a deepening of the division of Germany.

VIII   WEST GERMAN VIEWS

In strong contrast to the GDR, the Federal Republic never sought to engage in efforts at developing as a separate nation-state. On the contrary, all official efforts were – and continue to be – geared to maintaining an all-German national consciousness among West Germans. This was a difficult enterprise from the start. For one thing, owing to the painfully obvious excesses of German nationalism during the Hitler period, postwar governments in West Germany felt it necessary to play down all displays of nationalism. National symbols – the flag, the national anthem, a national holiday – were therefore scarcely in evidence, contributing to a lack of effective attachment to the idea of the one German nation.[54] Furthermore, feelings of guilt and shame over what Germany had done led to efforts at dissociating oneself from Germany; early identification with the ideal of a united Europe was one consequence that rivalled continued emotional attachment to Germany.

The biggest problem, however, was the build-up of the Federal Republic as a new state, firmly integrated into the West politically, economically and militarily. While historians are still debating the question whether Adenauer himself really wanted reunification, or did not, in fact, stealthily seek to build up a new nation-state centered in his native Rhineland, the eventual outcome of that policy is by now beyond doubt. The Federal Republic, conceived as a provisional entity until reunification was achieved, has today become a very stable fixture on the European landscape. The SPD foresaw this development when the momentous decision in favor of rearmament and membership in NATO had to be made during the early 1950s, for which reason it vehemently opposed those measures. In retrospect, its argument that these steps would negate any chances of reunification appear quite correct.[55]

The problem faced throughout these years by the Federal Republic was how to instill a sense of loyalty into the newly established democratic institutions, while at the same time maintaining that these might only be provisional. Or, put differently, how to create what Germans call a *Staatsbewusstsein*, a state-consciousness, focused on the Federal Republic, without endangering an all-German national consciousness (a concept relying on the traditional German distinction between state and nation). One solution to this continuing problem turned out to be merely definitional, evident in the attempts to redefine nature and content of the German nation and the West

Table 4.11 'Suppose there were a TV program with the title 'The German nation yesterday' (in a parallel survey: 'The German nation today'). Could you tell me, according to this list, what is meant by "German nation" in this case?' (percentage of replies)

November 1981	yesterday	today
Federal Republic	6	43
Federal Republic and GDR	20	32
Federal Republic, GDR and		
former German territories	52	12
all German-language areas	14	7
impossible to say	8	6

Source: Noelle-Neumann, *Jahrbuch 1983*, p. 197.

German state. As outlined above, however, these definitional changes reflect underlying attitudinal changes and thus do not, in fact, constitute a real solution to this dilemma.

For many years, worried observers of the West German political scene claimed that the West Germans had not developed a sufficiently strong sense of identification with the Federal Republic and its institutions. Precisely in order to safeguard freedom and democracy, they argued for deliberate efforts to instill a stronger sense of identity with the Federal Republic, for – as it eventually came to be known – a *Verfassungspatriotismus* ('constitutional patriotism').[56] While it is probably true that the West Germans' identification with their state is somewhat more sober than might be the case elsewhere, it does not, in fact, seem underdeveloped. By now the West Germans' support for their state is nowhere in doubt. The political, economic and social institutions of the Federal Republic enjoy as much legitimacy as do such institutions in other European countries.[57] Everything considered, West Germans solidly identify with their state.

Not only do they identify with their state; they increasingly identify their state as 'Germany'. This is one of the more remarkable, yet widely unnoticed, developments of recent years.[58] It offers a strong hint that, in the minds of most West Germans, Germany has finally shrunk to the Federal Republic. This is evident not only in public opinion polls that refer to the German nation 'yesterday' and 'today' (Table 4.11), or to the personal meaning of the term 'Germany'

Table 4.12 'When people talk about "Germany", what does it mean to you?' (percentage of replies)

	1979	1984
Federal Republic of Germany	57	57
Federal Republic and GDR	27	27
Former German *Reich*	11	8
no definite meaning	5	8

Source: Forschungsgruppe Wahlen, 'ZDF-Politbarometer', January 1984, p. 34.

(Table 4.12), but also in everyday usage. Certainly most non-Germans today mean only the Federal Republic when they speak of Germany. The same is true for the West Germans, especially in such an emotionally charged context as sports.

In terms of their definition of what Germany is, most West Germans appear to have excluded the East Germans from that definition.[59] Certainly most West Germans have very little interest in and knowledge of East German affairs, a cognitive deficit long viewed with alarm by West German authorities (whose campaigns to foster such interest and instill knowledge have, however, met with little success). Even more so, West Germans do not identify with things East German in any meaningful way. GDR athletic successes in international competition, for instance, are not a source of satisfaction – and thus identification – in the Federal Republic.[60] Cognitively as well affectively, it would appear, Germany for most West Germans has shrunk to the Federal Republic. It has now become the source of national identification for most West Germans. Their *Staatsbewusstsein* gradually seems to be supplemented, as Karl Dietrich Bracher has noted, by a *Nationalbewusstsein* as well (if, in fact, this typically German distinction is an empirically valid one, something placed in doubt by some of the poll data quoted earlier).[61] West Germany does not face, as he argues, the challenge of being a 'post-national democracy'; rather, it is a democracy in the process of becoming a normal nation-state.

For the German Democratic Republic this development, though

possibly welcome, is not without problems. In most simple terms, the appropriation of the term 'German' by the West Germans is likely to force the GDR into searching for possible alternatives to identifying itself. In the early 1970s, when the GDR sought to distance itself from the Federal Republic and its all-German claims, the GDR took a first step in that direction. Not only did it stop singing its own national anthem (with its reference to 'Germany, united fatherland'), it also eliminated the word 'German' from a number of official terms. Apparently, however, it had taken that first step without thinking about the second one: If no longer German, then what? As a result, this campaign came to a halt, and the GDR is still the 'German Democratic Republic', just as the ruling party is still the 'Socialist Unity Party of Germany'. But the GDR is not yet off the hook. And a suspicious mind may begin to wonder whether the rehabilitation of Prussia – a process that began at the very time the GDR had to call off its campaign of eliminating the term 'German' – is indeed a return to the fold of historical Germany, as many West German observers claim,[62] or not rather an attempt at laying the groundwork for an eventual renaming of the GDR. Could we, some day, be faced with a 'People's Republic of Prussia'?

Developments in East and West Germany have always tended to influence each other. Such an ultimate step by the GDR – a highly speculative thought at the present time – would have repercussions in the Federal Republic as well. It would probably contribute further to the West Germans' own sense of a separate national identity. To what extent such an identity already exists is still a controversial question in West Germany.[63] Not all observers interpret these and other data, as well as the political activities themselves, in the way they have been interpreted here. Admittedly, the West Germans' own national consciousness may not quite be fully developed in all aspects. Yet, forced by events and political as well as psychological necessities, they appear to have set off down that road. It is difficult to imagine that they would – or could – reverse direction. Attitudes of this kind, central to an individual's sense of identity, are not easily changed. Nor can one envisage a set of external events that might stimulate a drastic change of attitudes. The development of separate national identities is thus likely to continue. In the process, the German Question will become ever more closed.

IX PROSPECTS FOR THE FUTURE

The political repercussions of this process of national separation should not be too dramatic. For the fact is that, as described above, these gradual changes in attitudes pertaining to the German Question have already resulted in significant political changes. The lifting of the Hallstein Doctrine, the new *Ostpolitik* of the 1970s, and the insistence of the Kohl government on the primacy of freedom are the political manifestations of changing national attitudes. In turn, these political adaptations – which also include such seemingly banal efforts as the build-up of Bonn (soon to house a 'Museum of the History of the Federal Republic'!) or East Berlin (with its 'Palace of the Republic'!) into representative capitals – are likely to contribute to further attitudinal changes.

As a result of these developments, both the Federal Republic and the German Democratic Republic have gained a considerable measure of political room for maneuver. Where they were once tied down by their interests in protecting legal claims to reunification, they are now free to deal more openly with the outside world as well as with each other. Their definition of 'national interests' has changed. Increasingly, these refer to strictly West German or East German interests, not to all-German interests. With their own *Selbstbewusstsein* they have gained more self-confidence; their policies, as a result, have become more self-assertive. This is evident in the way both the Federal Republic and the GDR have begun to seek more influence with, if not to say independence from, their respective superpowers. It is not a dramatic development, as it has been going on for some time now. Nor is it likely to become drastically more evident in the future, since both countries remain tied into the discipline of their alliances. Thus, while the increase in national self-assertiveness may make alliance relations somewhat more difficult, the alliance structures themselves are not in danger.

Relations between the GDR and the Federal Republic will also not undergo significant changes. The more both sides have shed what might be termed their national ballast, the more they have sought to engage in 'good-neighborly' relations. It is, after all, normal for neighboring states and their inhabitants to trade with each other, to deal with each other, to visit each other. The relative increase in such contacts over the past years does not necessarily reflect a resurgence of all-German national concerns, as some observers hope and others fear. Rather, they symbolize the gradual emergence of normalcy. If, in the end, such normalcy were to lead to an 'Austrian solution' of the German Question, where the Federal Republic and the GDR relate to each other as they now do with Austria, most Germans in East and West would consider this to be an optimal – and final – answer to the German Question.

5 The Two German States and European Security

Max Schmidt

I INTRODUCTION

Europe continues to be a centrally situated region of great relevance to the destiny of the world at large. The question today is: Where are we heading – toward a fundamental improvement in the international atmosphere and the safeguarding of peace or toward still more confrontation and insecurity?

Posing the question this way, with the focus on Europe, does not invalidate the fact that the central axis of international relations is between the USSR and the United States. The orientation of that axis is shaped decisively by Europe, the continent that acts as an important abutment for the central axis. European security is good for both the United States and the USSR; conversely, the process of European security and cooperation has proved to depend strongly on the quality of relations between the two superpowers.

Inside Europe a substantive role is played by the relationship between the two German states, the Federal Republic of Germany and the German Democratic Republic. The quality of their relations – be they relaxed or tense – is important to the political atmosphere in Europe and beyond, determining whether international relations are characterized by reason and stability, or unrest and insecurity. Evidence for this view can be seen in the entire course of postwar history and is reinforced today by the present situation in Europe and the GDR–FRG relationship. This chapter is an attempt to clarify the nature of this relationship as it is viewed from the perspective of the GDR.

II SAFEGUARDING PEACE: A CHALLENGE TO EUROPE AND THE WORLD

An intriguing theme employed by the German poet and playwright Bertolt Brecht is applicable to any consideration of Europe and to

106

the policies pursued by the two German states:

> Three wars were fought by the great city of Carthage. The city
> was still powerful after the first and was still habitable after the
> second but no longer retrievable after the third.

While the nations of North America have been spared in this
century from suffering the experience of modern warfare on their
own territories, Europe has had to live under the burden of two
world wars, both unleashed by the rulers of the former German
'Reich' and fought primarily in Europe. Furthermore, today the
states and peoples of the European continent are 'doomed', at the
risk of annihilation, to break the vicious circle of war and peace
that they have faced for centuries. They must now assume a genuine
commitment to eternal peace, despite the fact that they find
themselves facing each other in the form of two antagonistic social
systems and the two most powerful military alliances in human
history, NATO and the WTO. In this context, the continuity in the
GDR's foreign policy was fully reflected at the XIth Congress of
the Socialist Unity Party of Germany (SED) in April 1986, when
the political line of earlier SED congresses was reaffirmed and
continued by underlining the following priority for all international
activities of the SED and the GDR: to work persistently for joint
action of all the world's forces for peace, common sense, and realism
for effective steps toward arms limitation and disarmament with the
aim of avoiding nuclear war, preventing an arms race in outer space,
getting rid of nuclear weapons and overcoming confrontation through
interstate cooperation. At the same time, a new element was added
to that continuity, as an anti-war posture was clearly emphasized as
a priority in the GDR's international orientation. Oskar Fischer,
the GDR Foreign Minister, made this clear: 'To our Party and our
country the safeguarding of peace is the overriding challenge of the
present time'. This clearly emphasizes the GDR's priorities. Peace-
making supersedes all other issues and political goals, which stems
from our most recent evaluation of the world situation. This
evaluation concludes that there is a need both for new political
thinking and for a fresh approach to political action by all states, if
the survival and continued progress of human civilization are to be
ensured.

At this point a brief outline of the GDR's assessment of
developments in the world today is in order. Politically, the world
scene is no longer determined merely by the existence of over 150

states of varied political, military, economic and social groupings, each with diverse and even contradictory interests. Rather, the world today is most strongly influenced by the nuclear and space ages. The variety of phenomena and processes has occasionally obscured one issue of fundamental importance: the world, with all of its diversity and contradictions, is one whole, the common house of all mankind which cannot be exchanged for another abode and which is threatened in many ways. Furthermore, these are threats by which all states and peoples are equally endangered.

There can be no doubt that the nuclear threat is the most serious of all dangers. The existence of nuclear weapons of mass destruction, with their unprecedented numbers and capabilities, rules out any chance of survival for mankind in the event of a third world war. Hence, safeguarding world peace has become the indispensable prerequisite for man's continued existence and for any social progress.

In East–West relations, accordingly, one is compelled toward the conclusion that peaceful coexistence between both systems has become the only reasonable and even feasible form of the inter-systemic competition. A military clash resulting from that competition would favor neither side but would lead instead to the downfall of both sides.

The political alternative of 'peace or war' did exist in earlier centuries, and under certain circumstances policy-makers could opt for war to advance specific interests. That alternative has ceased to exist in the nuclear age. Now, with the potential danger of a nuclear exchange or of military conflict that might escalate into nuclear war, the alternative is simply 'peace or death'. Therefore, nuclear war must be prevented at any cost. This is objectively in the interest of all states and peoples.

Viewed from this perspective, the unabated arms race has continued to pose a threat no less dangerous to mankind. It has given rise to military technologies that aggravate the danger of war, and in its socioeconomic consequences is comparable to a war of attrition even without a single shot being fired. It is absorbing financial, material and intellectual resources that are urgently needed to come to grips with a number of pressing global problems. These problems have progressively sharpened and will, if unsolved, endanger the natural and social conditions for the very existence of human civilization.

The current momentum of the arms race is taking us to an entirely new situation: systems of weapons are invented which relentlessly shorten the time available for human decision-making. The human and political right to thought and judgment is transferred to computers and other hardware. Yet such hardware – even when repeatedly tested – may occasionally fail. This has been clearly demonstrated by both the explosion of the US space shuttle *Challenger* in January 1986 and the Soviet nuclear power plant disaster at Chernobyl in April 1986. But with the weapons systems of today and tomorrow, the 'occasional' breakdown will inevitably turn out to be a 'once-and-for-all' breakdown of mankind.

Global problems include underdevelopment and the deepening poverty of a majority of the human race in developing countries; progressive destruction of the environment; and exhaustion of traditional mineral and energy resources. A solution to any of these problems would be far beyond the capability of one single country or group of countries, even the most advanced. Management of such problems depends on at least two conditions – stable world peace and a halt to the arms race and effective steps towards disarmament. In the absence of this, any attempt at a solution would be illusory, owing to the implacable economic obstacles involved.

The situation of the world today, with the interconnection and interdependence of all these problems, represents a challenge to the human species and its interest in survival, a challenge cutting across all social, political, ideological, ethnic and other differences which separate states and nations and even make some of them opponents to each other.

This interest in survival, however, cannot be addressed unless it is perceived by policy-makers of all sides as something superior to existing contradictions and unless political action is adjusted to that perception. Applied to the East–West relationship, the main axis of international relations today, this means that those who are opponents in terms of social systems will remain opposed to each other and will continue their inter-system competition; at the same time, they will have to initiate complex and intensive cooperation to secure the conditions for man's survival. For all intents and purposes, objective conditions have emerged under which the competition between capitalism and socialism can take place solely in the form of peaceful rivalry.

The reality of our time is a fundamental challenge to political thought and action in East and West, North and South. A new approach is required, one which proceeds from the perception of a coherent world, and which overcomes the fixation on the fragmented and antagonistic character of this world's numerous components. It is essential, in the words of Erich Honecker, Chairman of the GDR State Council, 'to learn the art of handling each other and of getting along with each other'. This is valid for the world as a whole, and it is even more urgent for Europe. There are several major elements and orientations necessary for political thinking and action which are in keeping with the demands of the nuclear-space age, yet they are not necessarily being put into practice.

There have been quite a few states that continue to believe in the ancient Roman motto '*Si vis pacem para bellum*', that is, 'If you desire peace, prepare for war.' To follow such a motto today would be suicidal, since under the conditions of nuclear overkill any further build-up in the arms race would eventually increase the probability of destruction even for the side that builds up first. Peace can no longer be 'obtained' by an arms build-up. More weapons do not provide more security. Even very large military potentials are no guarantee for security in our time. There is no place where this is more clearly demonstrated than the line between NATO and the WTO. They face each other armed to the teeth. In a conflict, this arms build-up would not provide security to either side, but rather would assure mutual destruction.

The relationship between war and politics has undergone a radical change in the nuclear age, and so has Clausewitz's dictum of war as a continuation of politics. The use of nuclear weapons cannot be an instrument of rational policy; such use would rather signal an end to rational policy. Hence the substance of several conventional notions in political and military terminology has become outdated in the nuclear age, as it can no longer be placed in any logical relation to objective reality. Take, for example, the notion of victory, which has always been the objective of war. In a thermonuclear war there will be neither winners nor losers, as was confirmed by Mikhail Gorbachev and Ronald Reagan in their joint statement at the Geneva summit of November 1985.

There can be no military–technological solution to the East–West peace issue. This is clearly borne out by the trends in the nuclear arms race, ranging from nuclear fission and fusion weapons through intercontinental launching systems and multiple warheads to the present tendency toward offensive space weapons. Any qualitative leap in arms technology in recent decades has had unfavorable consequences for political action and room for maneuver in the case of crisis or even war. We now find ourselves on a threshold beyond which, due to the reduction of early-warning periods to less than ten minutes, political decision-making could be fully replaced by 'automatic' technological processes. Man, now dependent on computers, would cease to be the master of his own destiny. Hence neither side can draw any political or other advantage from a continuation of the arms race.

The danger of war can be eliminated only by political means, by limiting and removing the entire spectrum of instruments of warfare with particular emphasis on weapons of mass destruction. Every attempt made in the nuclear age to neutralize weapons by new weapons has failed to remove feelings of insecurity. Rather, such attempts have taken us to the present high level of East–West military confrontation. Thus the predominant trend of the past – according to which anything that was technically possible would eventually be deployed – must cease if the problem is to be solved.

State security, traditionally defined as a national issue, as security from or against others, is no longer obtainable for any state acting on its own. Security today can be created only as a joint, inter-system process on the basis of political cooperation and even more against the background of arms limitation and disarmament. East–West interdependence for mutual annihilation has taken us into a situation in which both sides are objectively interconnected by a security partnership, whether they like it or not.

To change political thinking and action to such new principles is certainly not easy for either side, since it will be necessary to depart from traditional attitudes which have matured over centuries. While the difficulties implied in such a change must not be underestimated, it would be wrong to consider them insurmountable. I would rather subscribe to the words of the literary critic Walter Benjamin, who once said, 'How awfully simple is this world, if you test it to find out whether it deserves to be destroyed.'

III RELATIONS BETWEEN THE TWO GERMAN STATES: THE SECURITY ASPECT

The above assessment of the present world situation and resulting conclusions may be enlarged by additional, specific references to the actual situation of the GDR and FRG as European states and as countries located along the demarcation line between the two social systems and between NATO and the WTO.

First, history shows that during the early postwar decades GDR–FRG relations were a source of permanent insecurity and even presented a temporary danger of war in Europe. Hard factual evidence has been produced to the effect that major political circles in the Federal Republic were not ready, over decades, to accept the very existence of the GDR and were trying by all means to wipe the GDR off the map. The following statement was made in the early 1950s by Clemens von Brentano, later Foreign Minister of the FRG: 'We shall take every possible and even ultimate action, I repeat every possible and ultimate, to regain the Soviet occupation zone' (his disparaging term for the GDR).[1] The wide-ranging plans prepared for that purpose are a matter of record and include economic embargo, diplomatic blockade, subversive activities and even preparations for military action. However, the worst did not happen, thanks to the persistent peace policy pursued by the GDR and its socialist allies as well as, on the Western side, the level-headedness displayed by the United States, France and the United Kingdom, which in critical situations did not allow themselves to get involved in a shooting war against the Warsaw Treaty Organization for the purpose of revising the outcome of the Second World War. There must be no return to such a state of affairs.

Second, the role of peace-making is predominant for another, even weightier reason. German history has been burdened by the responsibility for having unleashed two world wars. The GDR has a particular obligation from that burden, to ensure that never again shall war be unleashed from German soil and that never again shall death and destruction be inflicted upon other nations.

Finally, with the very nature of modern weapons and the amount of armaments possessed by NATO and the WTO, military conflict in central Europe would not leave the slightest chance of survival to the GDR and FRG. No scenario of military conflict in central Europe is conceivable in which the two German states continue to exist as functioning industrial societies. Within the context of these insights the following concept was reaffirmed by the XIth Congress of the SED: 'Safeguarding peace was and continues to be the decisive issue for relations between the German Democratic Republic and the Federal Republic of Germany.' It is the GDR's established view that relations between the two German states ought to be developed to the point where they not only impose no burden on international developments but rather help to determine and improve them.

There is another political aspect of fundamental importance to GDR–FRG relations which is closely associated with the issue of safeguarding peace: both countries must see that stability and security are not upset in Europe. This primarily implies unconditional recognition of the European realities that emerged after the Second World War. Part of that reality is the existence of two sovereign, independent German states with opposing social systems and affiliated with different alliances. The GDR-FRG state frontier is another element of that reality, just as all other postwar state frontiers are throughout Europe.

The great importance of these realities to peace and security in Europe and the positive impact of their recognition upon further political developments in East–West relations were again clearly demonstrated in the past year. The date 13 August 1986 marked the twenty-fifth anniversary of the day when the GDR closed its West Berlin frontier, which previously had been open and exposed. Many loopholes were sealed which had been used by the West to upset internal developments in the GDR. The GDR was at last in a position to stabilize its own independent development and to put an end to illusions in the FRG about the GDR's incorporation. The incident – terminologically reduced to 'Wall building' in bourgeois circles in the West – entailed far-reaching political and economic consequences which eventually proved to be favorable by all realistic accounts. True, the 'Wall' is not a beautiful structure (can any security installation be beautiful?), but it was necessary. It will continue to be necessary, as long as dreams are dreamt of an 'elimination' of the GDR. It will continue to be necessary until a European system of security and cooperation is established and until the GDR, in its own right in terms of international law, will be fully accepted as the criterion of all its international relations. The eventually positive effect of a safeguarded GDR state frontier was conceded by Otto Graf Lambsdorff, former Economics Minister of the FRG and one of the leaders of the Free Democratic Party, when he made the following points in a leading West German magazine:

Can it really be disputed that the phase of *détente* in Germany began only after [the Wall's] construction? . . . For it was in the shadow cast by the wall that gradually a new policy began to grow . . . Agreements became possible between the Allies and the Soviet Union on Berlin. German agreements were achieved on humanitarian issues and visits. Tough bargaining helped the two German states to gradually obtain agreements on issues relating to the economy, environment and, finally, cultural exchange.[2]

Recognition of reality, then, is the point of departure and the foundation for good relations between the two German states and is the basis on which a certain amount of consensus can be achieved between the two governments. This was unambiguously underscored on 12 March 1985, in a joint policy statement made by Erich Honecker, Chairman of the GDR State Council, and FRG Chancellor Helmut Kohl. The GDR continues to attribute great importance to this statement, which reads as follows:

> Inviolability of frontiers and respect for territorial integrity and sovereignty of all states in Europe within their present frontiers are basic conditions for peace. War must never again be unleashed but peace must originate from German soil.

> Both parties are committed to taking efforts on the basis of the Basic Principles Treaty to develop and build normal relations of good neighborliness between the German Democratic Republic and the Federal Republic of Germany to the benefit of peace and stability in Europe.[3]

Such an approach is fully in keeping with both the requirements of our time as well as with the spirit and letter of the Treaty on Basic Principles of Relations between the two German states signed in 1972.

It cannot be overlooked, however, that the attitude taken by the FRG government has not been free of contradictions, with a gap between words and deeds. The 1985 government agreement on the involvement of the FRG in the SDI program, in my opinion, goes against its duty of keeping the peace.

Against such a background, it is not sufficient to confine one's own posture to mere contemplation and a verbal commitment to peace policies. The challenge today more than ever before is for the active implementation of everyone's public commitment to peace. That is the only practicable way to take a consistent approach to realizing the declared intention of the governments of both German states, namely, 'to make peace with ever fewer weapons'.

An additional obligation toward that end is implied in Article V of the 1972 Basic Principles Treaty between both German states. It reads as follows:

> Both states shall support efforts towards arms limitation and disarmament, particularly in the context of nuclear weapons and other means of mass destruction, for the purpose of achieving general and complete disarmament under effective international control and conducive to international security.

The GDR, in pursuit of its own policy, has honored this obligation in a sophisticated way, both by its active involvement in the coordinated peace and disarmament policies of the Warsaw Pact countries and by its own specific contributions.

The GDR emphasizes five major issues of arms limitation and disarmament. First, the GDR supports the December 1987 treaty between the United States and the Soviet Union eliminating all intermediate-range nuclear weapons. This is a decisive step toward the lowering of nuclear confrontation in Europe. This step is the greater because, in the course of a zero option, the Soviet Union will also withdraw from the GDR and Czechoslovakia those intermediate-range systems (with ranges between 500 km and 1000 km) which were deployed in both countries, beginning in 1983, as a countermeasure to NATO INF missile deployment. Such steps have at last brought about a breakthrough toward disarmament and as such have considerable effects on other areas. The GDR also supports the Soviet proposal for a complete elimination of all shorter-range missiles (with ranges below 500 km). The GDR has also responded positively to a proposal by the Palme Commission to establish a zone free of nuclear forces in central Europe and has expanded the idea by offering its entire territory, provided that a similar gesture is made by the FRG.

Second, an international convention on a ban on chemical weapons, in the GDR's perspective, could be ready for signing in the near future. The subject, according to experts, has been 'negotiated to the point of accomplishment'. We welcome the USSR's statement according to which chemical-weapon production has been stopped and construction has been started of a plant to destroy existing stock. An international Pugwash Symposium held in the GDR in 1987 clearly demonstrated that no insoluble problems exist in verifying compliance with such a convention by the relevant sectors of the civilian chemical industry.

Third, a reduction by 50 per cent of strategic nuclear weapons of the US and USSR might be achieved in Geneva, on the basis of the *rapprochement* of positions set out at Reykjavik, provided that the ABM Treaty is not only preserved but its regime strictly observed and an arms race in outer space thus averted. Otherwise all efforts for strategic disarmament might turn out to be futile. Although a START agreement was not signed at the May–June 1988 Moscow summit, the momentum has not been lost, and a treaty is still likely to be concluded in the near future.

Fourth, while US insistence on nuclear tests prevented their discontinuation, despite repeated extension of the Soviet moratorium, the GDR remains, together with the USSR, a staunch advocate of a nuclear test-ban treaty. This would substantially help contain the qualitative arms race.

Finally, on 11 June 1986, the GDR together with the other members of the Warsaw Treaty submitted a far-reaching proposal to reduce conventional forces and armaments in Europe (the 'Budapest Appeal'). Armed forces – from the Atlantic to the Urals – should be reduced, according to that proposal, by half a million men on either side by the early 1990s, with emphasis on those components particularly suitable for surprise attacks (units close to frontiers, tactical airforce units). Dismantling of theater nuclear weapons and systems on either side could be discussed and settled in the same context.

The GDR is making specific additional contributions of its own, evidenced by the following examples. In a letter by Erich Honecker to Helmut Kohl in early March 1987, the GDR again suggested, in the spirit of responsibility for peace, that envoys of both governments should meet and discuss what the GDR and FRG could do to take advantage of the historic chance which is a result of the Soviet proposal of a zero option on medium-range missiles. The GDR is very interested in such a solution, since in the context of countermeasures to NATO missile deployment, nuclear weapons were stationed for the first time on GDR territory.

Continuous and achievement-oriented political dialogue is considered by the GDR as a substantial element in all efforts to prevent war in Europe. Such dialogue had been pursued and intensified by the GDR with all political forces in Western countries that are prepared to respond now or in the future. Specific initiatives by which security can be improved along the sensitive line between East and West, that is, between the two German states, are integral components of this dialogue. For example, extensive efforts have been made for years by the GDR to set up in central Europe a zone free of chemical weapons. In April 1988 the SED, the Czechoslovakian Communist Party and the SPD issued a joint statement which sought to build on their 1985 joint proposal for creating a chemical-weapons-free zone in Europe. These proposals are being put forward by the GDR with the dual objective of consolidating regional security in central Europe and stimulating action towards a more comprehensive solution to the problem. The FRG government, unfortunately, has so far evaded all offers made by the GDR in the field of security.

The SED has started talks with the SPD in the FRG on these issues in order to demonstrate what would be achievable with good will and a willingness to compromise on both sides. Preliminary results have been recorded from these talks. A joint expert committee of both political parties submitted to the public a framework for a draft agreement on a zone free of chemical weapons in the summer of 1985. Included in the draft were solutions to all aspects involved, among them wide-ranging measures of verification, such as on-site inspection.

Late in 1986, working groups of both parties drafted proposals for a nuclear-free corridor along the NATO-WTO demarcation line in central Europe. That initiative is of extraordinary importance, since it would establish a major link between nuclear and conventional disarmament. An area of 150 km on either side of that line would be cleared not only of *all* nuclear weapons but also of those systems, such as heavy artillery, capable of firing both nuclear and conventional charges. Roughly 92 to 95 per cent of all artillery would be involved. The governments of the GDR and Czechoslovakia have formally proposed to the government of the FRG to enter into negotiations at government level, and are awaiting a reply.

It is the assumption of the GDR that the two German states bear responsibility for military measures relating to their own territories and military forces. Their reciprocal relations cannot be kept free of these issues by referring to the rights and responsibilities of the big powers. The very fact of the GDR's and FRG's involvement in opposing alliances does not mean that there is no need or room for an active pursuit of specific objectives of peace. There are, in fact, possibilities for action at various levels, proceeding from both countries' firm integration in their respective alliances – which must not be questioned on either side – and for activities which are paralleled in the other German state, both within the alliances and between both states. This is increasingly understood by growing numbers of politically committed and active people and researchers in the FRG.

The GDR does not insist in a narrow-minded and self-righteous manner on having all its own proposals completely accepted. The GDR has never thought that the philosopher's stone originated in this country. The proposals made by the GDR are rather a reflection of its policies of dialogue for peace, disarmament and cooperation. The GDR will continue to believe in dialogue and will take advantage of any chance for helping to bring about a change for the better in the international situation and will continue to contribute appropriate ideas and suggestions for European and worldwide discussion. This is our interpretation of the linkage between international and our own interests. Such an attitude, by our own definition, should include the willingness to listen to the other side and to familiarize oneself with the other side's interests, in order to find on such a basis compromise and consensus for reduction of the physical danger of war as well as for arms limitation and disarmament in the heart of Europe and beyond. That is what is meant in the GDR by thought and action in terms of a broad coalition of common sense and realism for peace.

IV EXISTENCE AND COEXISTENCE OF TWO GERMAN STATES: AN ELEMENT AND CONSTANT OF EUROPEAN STABILITY AND PEACE

The two states of the GDR and FRG have been in existence since 1949. The FRG, as is generally known, was founded before the GDR. The Constitution of the FRG came into effect on 23 May 1949. The GDR was established on 7 October 1949. The proclamation of the Federal Republic of Germany reflected the political determination of its ruling circles in that period of history to divide Germany. Konrad Adenauer, later to become the first chancellor of the FRG, was quoted as saying 'Full control over half of Germany rather than half control over the whole'. He made that statement in the pre-FRG period, when restoration of bourgeois society appeared to be increasingly difficult and eventually impossible throughout the postwar remnant of the former German 'Reich'.

Incorporation of the FRG into the political and military alliance of NATO (1954–5), the subsequent formation of the Warsaw Treaty, with the GDR as one of its founding members, and decades of diametrically opposed social developments in the two German states have made the existence of the GDR and FRG an irreversible fact and a constant of the European postwar system. Today, the very existence of the two German states and their affiliation with different alliances are components of stability and are part of the international balance of forces, that is, security, in Europe.

That is the point of departure from which one ought to proceed and from which the GDR, and to some extent the FRG, does proceed. However, this has not always been the case in the past. The political leaders of the FRG long refused to accept the outcome of the Second World War and the postwar developments. Rather, they worked for revisions which, in plain language, would have modified the postwar European frontiers at the expense of the FRG's eastern neighbors. The FRG defended the fiction of 'the continued existence of the German "Reich" within the frontiers of 1937', an illusion supported even today by substantial right-wing conservative forces in the CDU/CSU. It was from that fabrication that the claim was derived for the 'reunification of Germany'. In fact this claim had not even been based on an assumption of equality but had always been a desire to incorporate the GDR (plus certain regions of Czechoslovakia, Poland and the USSR) and to eliminate those countries' political and social systems. Efforts were made by the FRG, up to the second half of the 1960s, to enforce that claim by a policy of international isolation of the GDR and proclamation of its 'non-existence' and by presenting the FRG as the only legitimate German state.

That situation was changed only in the early 1970s, when the FRG decided to recognize the *status quo* in Europe (though not with all of its consequences) and to have that recognition laid down in international law, after its foreign policy principles had begun to backfire in Europe and had isolated it as a Cold War fossil even from its own NATO allies. A formally binding legal basis for the postwar system and national frontiers in Europe was established at last; it has five constitutent elements. First, there are the Treaties of Moscow, Warsaw, and Prague between the FRG and the states concerned; and second, there is the Quadripartite Agreement (the USSR, United States, France and the United Kingdom) on Berlin (West). The Treaty on Basic Principles of Relations between the GDR and FRG is the third element. Its purpose is to make a positive contribution to *détente* and security in Europe and to developing normal, good-neighborly relations, as well as providing for both sides' commitment, now and in the future, to the inviolability of the frontier they have in common and to unrestricted respect for their territorial integrity. Both sides shall assume that the territorial authority of either state shall be confined to its own territory, and shall respect each other's independence and authority with regard to internal and external affairs. Admission of both German states to the United Nations is the fourth element, and the last is the Helsinki Final Act, resulting from the Conference on Security and Cooperation in Europe and signed by the heads of all European states (except Albania) as well as of the United States and Canada.

A German problem or even an 'open' German problem no longer exists. History has bypassed it. The people of the GDR have exercised their right to self-determination and have opted for socialist development.'German reunification' is out of the question for the overwhelming majority of the GDR population and, for that mattter, for the majority of FRG citizens as well. As Ronald Asmus, an experienced analyst of German affairs for Radio Free Europe/Radio Liberty in Munich, has pointed out, 'The reestablishment of a Bismarckian national state is more remote than ever before'.[4] An accurate insight.

So, since the 'German problem' as a 'political problem' is something which was decided long ago by history, it can hardly be formulated in an unambiguous way today, not even by its defenders. Yet, even when formulated, it remains highly disputable and, paradoxically, unanswerable even for partisans. There is a state of confusion in which reality is understood, on the one hand, and denied, on the other, as may be concluded, for example, from a statement made by Wolfgang Schaeuble, Minister of the Federal Chancellor's Office, according to whom 'the division of Germany . . . was only provisional', while at the same time 'factual change was not on the agenda for the foreseeable future . . .'.[5]

Many of those trying to square the political circle may find themselves in the doldrums, similar to Heinrich Heine, the German poet who wrote in his Paris exile: 'Thinking of Germany in a sleepless night, gives me no peace but only plight'.Yet Heine's causes for concern and for deep sighing were quite different from those of certain FRG 'Germany policy thinkers' today or their like-minded colleagues elsewhere who cannot stop dreaming.

These issues are perceived by the GDR not only in their national but also in their all-European and even global aspects. In this respect one point can be made crystal clear: The existence of two German states is a fact with which the Germans themselves and other nations in East and West can live – and they have all been living with it through four decades, much better off and safer than they ever were at the time of the former German 'Reich'! That 'Reich' had brought other nations nothing but ruin, and it is, therefore, fortunate for them all that it perished once and for all in the flames of the Second World War. The present territorial *status quo* in Europe is both a prerequisite and foundation for adding content to the network of European conventions and for establishing the order of peace in our continent. The leading circles of the Federal Republic, too, are absolutely aware that no one in any of the countries neighboring the two German states, not even among their NATO allies, can be won over for change in terms of German reunification.

In early summer 1986, a reconnaissance tour of sorts was made through the GDR by a team of journalists from *Die Zeit*, a renowned weekly magazine published in Hamburg. The group was headed by Theo Sommer, editor-in-chief, and Countess Maria Doenhoff, the publisher. They published a series of articles about the GDR, which concluded on 15 August 1986, with a summary account written by Theo Sommer. Here are some remarkable extracts:

> The two German states' affiliation to their respective alliances is one of their substantial foundations. The Federal Republic is integrated into NATO, and the GDR into the Warsaw Pact. This will continue to be the case in the foreseeable future, and attempts to change it would make little sense . . . Giulio Andreotti, Italy's Foreign Minister, has publicly said what many thought to themselves but had preferred not to say in public: 'There are two German states now, and there should be two in the future'. . . . Re-unification may be a dream to us, but it would certainly be a nightmare to most of our neighbors. They are aware that re-composition of the two German states would mean the largest conceivable distortion of the East–West balance and would thus introduce into the equation of world politics an unknown variable causing displeasure to most people, or even anxiety.[3]

The concept, after all, that there is no sane alternative today to peaceful coexistence among states of different social systems is fully applicable to the two German states. The conditions in international law for such coexistence on an equal footing include renunciation of force, inviolability of frontiers, respect for sovereignty and territorial integrity, and abstention from interference in other countries' internal affairs. These have been explicitly codified in both the Charter of the United Nations and the Helsinki Final Act. These principles are, at the same time, the very basis for the consistent policy of peaceful coexistence which is generally pursued by the GDR towards all countries that differ from it on the basis of social system, whether Japan, France, Italy, the US, Sweden, the FRG or any other Western country.

GDR–FRG relations, pursued with persistence on the basis of these principles, can be a factor of growing stability in Europe as well as of reliability and predictability; also, taken as a whole, they can have a beneficial impact on people in both states. While the two states have mutually congenial interests, political determination is also required. Today we can proceed from and build on a considerable body of accomplishments in GDR–FRG relations which ought to be preserved, broadened and strengthened.

V   RESOLUTION OF UNRESOLVED ISSUES

The substance of overall relations among states may be evaluated by different criteria. Some weight should be given to the extent to which these relations have contributed to bilateral or regional and international security and on the specific benefits to people in the countries involved. A retrospective review of the past fifteen years of GDR–FRG relations, that is, from the date of the Basic Principles Treaty, justifies the following conclusions.

The first of these achievements relates to the fact that the general improvement of relations and the removal or mitigation of earlier contentious issues have helped to defuse a dangerous hotbed of tension in East–West relations and have made life in Europe palpably safer. This has been largely attributable to the fact that both the GDR and FRG, in a bilateral process of learning at times painful to one side or the other, have succeeded in objectifying ways in which to deal with each other.

A network of agreements has been woven and considerably expanded between the GDR and FRG since the early 1970s, with direct, favorable effects on the everyday life of citizens of both states. The progress achieved through these agreements and numerous subsequent implementation clauses has been tangible in a very real sense. Those using transit routes between the FRG and West Berlin through the GDR or frontier-crossing postal and telecommunications services and facilities at different levels, all draw specific benefit from the above agreements. In all these areas today there are far fewer irregularities than used to be the case fifteen or even ten years ago. A cultural exchange agreement which came into effect in early May 1986 as well as agreements on protection of the environment and scientific–technological cooperation have further normalized relations.

Each of these formal agreements has considerably eased the life of many people in both German states, and all of them have contributed strongly to the development of inter-human relations proper. Mutual flows of visitors, GDR citizens travelling into the FRG in connection with family affairs, and similar developments are part of a strong and steadily rising trend. Youth group exchange programs are growing. 1.8 million GDR citizens travelled to the FRG in 1986, while 3.6 million West German citizens travelled to the GDR. Assistance has been rendered to thousands of people in the complex tasks of reuniting families, a legacy of Germany's postwar division, the effects of which are still felt today. In the context of family reunion activities, almost 40 000 GDR citizens moved permanently to the FRG in 1984, and another 25 000 by June 1985. In the view of the GDR, this is a humanitarian dimension directly related to all-European security, since efforts for comprehensive security are facilitated by an atmosphere in which humanitarian issues of interstate relations, like military, political and economic issues, are tackled and resolved by agreement. At the same time, this helps prevent progress in one area from being held hostage to progress in another.

Economic relations, finally, rank high in GDR–FRG relations. In this context, some points have to be made for clarification (see Chapter 13 by Juergen Nitz) since one-sided views have quite often been publicized in Western countries. First of all, the GDR today is a modern industrial state and ranks among the top ten worldwide. The GDR has established its own basis for a microelectronic industry. Between 1981 and 1985 hard work caused the national income of the GDR to grow annually by 4.5 per cent on average, a figure which compares well internationally. Similar national income growth rates, between four and five per cent per annum, are planned in the forthcoming years. Economic developments in 1986 show that this goal is realistic, since 4.3 per cent was already being achieved.

The national economy of the GDR is characterized by one of the highest foreign trade intensities world-wide – more than 40 per cent of its national income is derived from foreign trade. Hence a high degree of stability in foreign trade relations is imperative. The same conclusion applies to the GDR's economic relations with the FRG. These are, at the same time, weighty factors for stability and linkage of interests in the relationship between both states. Despite certain problems economic relations have developed favorably. GDR–FRG trade grew from 4 500 million DM in 1970 to 16 500 million in 1985. This has been a reflection of clear-cut economic interests on both sides and of the rejection of all trade-war concepts in favor of agreeable overall political relations.

Finally, it must be pointed out that, counter to views which state that the GDR has enjoyed 'substantial economic benefits' in the form of various subsidies and payments by the FRG, the GDR does not receive any subsidies. Rather, the GDR is paid for services, including use of its transit routes, railroads, waterways, post and telephone, water and power supply as well as waste disposal for West Berlin. Nor is the 'swing' a no-interest credit as such, but rather a FRG government act to promote its own small and medium-size enterprises and keep them competitive in GDR trade. To the GDR the absence of interest payments is offset by the amount of money annually transferred by the GDR to FRG citizens from the latters' accounts in GDR banks (from inheritance, for example). In addition, the GDR is a reliable, predictable, equal partner in trade and other economic exchange.

Overall relations between the GDR and FRG have taken a path of positive development, when measured by the original points of departure. Nevertheless, these conditions should not be idealized. On important issues relations are still very far from comprehensive normalization and are far from having reached standards comparable to those typical of relations between either German state and third countries. The causes relate to some difficulties in coming to terms with the burdens of the past. Some major interests of the GDR are at stake, including full recognition of the existence of GDR citizenship, settlement of the Elbe border between the two German states, and dissolution of what is called the Central Record Authority in Salzgitter. These are policy issues in GDR–FRG relations, and are of importance to normalization.

All these problems have resulted from the FRG's continuing refusal to fully recognize the GDR under international law, a refusal not only by declaration but by political practice. In the final analysis, this attitude is aimed not only against the GDR, but against the territorial *status quo* in Europe and is thus a potential danger to stability and peace. A solution to these problems is urgent, not because of the demands made by the GDR, but because the FRG is lagging somewhat behind developments in international law and should catch up for the benefit of Europe as a whole.

These problems deserve a brief examination. First, the fictitious idea of the 'continued existence of the German "Reich" within the frontiers of 1937' has prompted the Federal Republic, from the very beginning of its own existence, to proclaim the continued existence of 'one single German citizenship' and to infer in a presumptuous manner that this citizenship is identical with the citizenship of the FRG. The substantial political intention concealed behind that fabrication is the denial of the existence of an independent GDR citizenship. The FRG claims citizenship for the entire population of the GDR (as well as for all individuals who are considered ethnic Germans and have their residences in regions which had been part of the German 'Reich' but have become Czechoslovak, Polish and Soviet territories). Whenever and wherever possible, all these people are treated as FRG citizens.

GDR citizenship does exist, with or without the consent of the FRG government. The FRG is required to respect fully GDR citizenship, which ought to end the treatment of GDR citizens that would be considered intolerable insults by any state. GDR travel documents held by GDR visitors in the FRG are withdrawn and invalidated by FRG authorities. FRG passports are issued to GDR citizens by FRG diplomatic missions in third countries. Extradition of GDR citizens wanted in the GDR for legal offenses but who have fled to the FRG is refused as a matter of principle, with the excuse being that they are 'Germans' and thus citizens of the FRG. Such disrespect for GDR citizenship actually prevents further normalization of relations between the two states, including work on humanitarian issues.

Second, the frontier stretch along the Elbe River is another case in which attempts have been made by certain political forces in the FRG to prevent solutions to problems that are ripe for settlement. Precisely 10 per cent of the GDR–FRG state frontier is in dispute (as the rest has long been settled by agreement) and has been subject to negotiation for more than a decade. The Elbe River had been the point of contact of the former Soviet and British occupation zones. Documents held by the allies, as well as their practice, suggest that the frontier had been on the mid-line of the river. The GDR has proposed to find a settlement in keeping with former allied practice and in agreement with customary practice in international law, that is, to mark the center line throughout as the formal frontier line. The FRG has rejected this up to now, demanding that most of the frontier stretch should be marked on the eastern bank of the Elbe River, that is, on the GDR side.

Third, the Central Record Authority of the State Law Enforcement Agencies in Salzgitter is not only an elaborate name for an administrative body. Established in 1961, it is a unique 'jewel' in the world that seems to originate from a collection of curios or rather politico-legal absurdities. Its very existence is a blatant violation of clauses in the Basic Principles Treaty between the two German states, according to which either side's territorial authority shall be restricted to its own territory. The Salzgitter Authority demonstrates that, in this respect, the FRG continues to treat the GDR as home territory, in an attempt to expand its own jurisdiction into and over the GDR. The Salzgitter Authority has been established for the purpose of collecting evidence against GDR citizens who committed offenses against FRG law on the territory of the GDR. Such 'offenders' are to be brought to FRG justice, whenever an opportunity arises. Circumstances of this kind may perhaps go beyond a non-German's imagination. Let us try to illustrate the problem with an artifically created example: Salzgitter is comparable to the hypothetical existence in Canada of an authority to investigate the practice of US customs officers for compliance with Canadian law. 'Offenses' would then entail legal investigation procedures against the US citizens concerned who, in the case of entry into Canada, would be brought to court. Should such citizens dare to travel to any other country, Canadian authorities would be entitled to demand their extradition. Between 1961 and early 1984, 31 000 legal cases were prepared in Salzgitter against GDR citizens. Theo Sommer, referred to earlier, stated that these demands should be 'negotiable'.

VI CONCLUSION: BUILDING GDR–FRG RELATIONS THROUGH PRINCIPLES OF NEW APPROACH

The relationship between the GDR and FRG constitutes a major component in the struggle for peaceful coexistence, European security, and *détente*. It is here, along the demarcation line between NATO and the Warsaw Pact, that inter-German relations exemplify the direct interaction of socialism and imperialism. The importance of relations between the two German states, therefore, reaches far beyond the bilateral level. This was very clearly shown during the official visit to the FRG made by Erich Honecker, SED General Secretary and Chairman of the GDR Council of State.

The first official visit ever made to the Federal Republic of Germany, 7–11 September 1987, by Erich Honecker was an outstanding political event of truly historic dimensions. As far as the importance of developments between the two German states is concerned, the official visit was the major highlight since the Basic Principles Treaty was concluded between the GDR and FRG in 1972.

Fundamental importance should be attributed to the Joint Communiqué issued during the visit, on 8 September 1987. Together with the 1972 Basic Principles Treaty and the Joint Statement by Erich Honecker and Helmut Kohl of 12 March 1985, it actually provides the platform for the strengthening of relations between the GDR and the FRG.

To make an active contribution to the safeguarding of peace and *détente* in the heart of Europe, right along the vulnerable dividing line between NATO and the Warsaw Pact, was the most important objective of the visit. That purpose was fully accomplished, and this is a victory for common sense and realism. Both sides emphasized in the Joint Communiqué that the relationship between the two states must continue to be a stabilizing factor for constructive East–West relations. That relationship should provide positive momentum for peaceful cooperation and dialogue in Europe and beyond. Considering the key role played by the FRG and GDR for peace in Europe by virtue of their outstanding positions in the Western alliance and NATO as well as in the Warsaw Pact, the above consensus may be interpreted as a striking result of the talks in Bonn, which will, no doubt, have an impact on other states as well.

During the talks, consensus was reached on the fact that contradictory views, resulting from different social orders and affiliation to different alliances, must not be allowed to be obstacles to cooperation against the danger of nuclear war. Security of one side presupposes security of the other. Neither side can have peace solely for itself. It was against this background that the value of negotiations on effective measures of arms control and disarmament at all levels was stressed in the Joint Communiqué. Particular importance should be attributed, in this context, to the consensus reached in Bonn on specific issues such as a zero-zero option, chemical weapons, a nuclear test ban and 50 per cent reductions of strategic weapons in conjunction with the strengthening of the ABM Treaty regime.

Honecker's official visit, with all its protocol-related aspects, has underscored for the international public the independence and equal status of both German states, their sovereignty, and the nature of relations between them, based on international law. An overwhelming majority of international commentaries share this assessment of the visit.

Each of the two German states possesses and claims its own values and advantages. Each, at the same time, has been adding its own weight to the construction of the 'European house'. These are the political and international–legal realities of today.

Additional steps could be taken toward the normalization of bilateral relations on the basis of the reciprocal recognition of each state's independence and existence in its own right. Here a new element has been introduced into the relationship. It is noteworthy that the two foreign ministers of the GDR and the FRG at their first meeting ever in a German state agreed that disarmament consultations would be regularly held between them or their deputies or other authorized envoys. Consensus was also reached on the existence of direct correlations between the two German states' responsibilities for peace and their mutual political respect, as well as with their economic, technological–scientific, ecological, cultural and humanitarian cooperation. Concrete progress and agreements have been achieved on all these issues.

In sum, an overall assessment of developments demonstrates that relations between the GDR and the FRG have grown in a positive way since the early seventies. Developments have been neither problem-free nor straightforward. On the contrary. Yet even this is evidence that balancing and adjusting interests and compromise solutions between East and West is possible, provided that positive approaches are taken and the political will exists on both sides. GDR–FRG relations have thus been reshaped in a way that has proved to be of substantial benefit to security in Europe and to the everyday life of citizens in both German states. This is a sound platform for further progress toward normalized relations among states of different social systems. Past experience with German–German relations has shown that this would be entirely conducive to the consolidation of all-European security.

6 The GDR's *Deutschlandpolitik* in the Early 1980s: Bloc Integration and the Search for Autonomy

Gerd Meyer

I INTRODUCTION

The GDR's security and foreign policy, including its *Deutschland-politik*, has to be analyzed within the context of hegemonic Soviet global strategies – either cooperative or confrontational – for maintaining peace, power and influence, world-wide and in Europe. The GDR's *Deutschlandpolitik* is a central and very sensitive part of the overall European policy of the Warsaw Pact countries. It is under close watch by the superpowers, and more or less supported by the smaller countries whose own interests are not always in accordance with those of the GDR. The GDR's *Deutschlandpolitik* can only make a positive contribution to the autonomy of its system in so far as the goals and interests, the strategy and tactics of the Eastern alliance are accepted in general. It enhances the autonomy and the legitimacy of its political system the most, perhaps, when it follows a line of *détente* and dialogue: that of fruitful cooperation and visible advantages for its citizens, of an independent standing in pressing for rapid progress in disarmament and in arms control negotiations, of reluctance to increase the defense budget or the GDR's burden within the Warsaw Pact, and of avoiding excessive hostile propaganda and internal repression.

The historical process of the division of Germany after 1945 resulted in the foundation of two German states and, later on, in the institutionalized division of a nation. Since 1945, the political and socioeconomic order which developed under Soviet occupation in the Eastern zone has been challenged on the grounds that it lacked legitimacy and autonomy. In the 1950s and 1960s the GDR

built up 'socialism in a half of the country'; its internal structures
and foreign relations were publicly questioned and often attacked,
both from inside and especially from outside the country. Is not the
GDR, observers asked, simply a satellite of the Soviet Union? Is it
not essentially based on military power and violence, dominated,
suppressed and even exploited by 'big brother', enjoying neither
real sovereignty nor true autonomy? Since the 1960s, there has been
a question as to whether the GDR functioned merely as a junior
partner to the USSR in achieving its questionable foreign policy
goals, for example in the armaments race, in its world revolutionary
aspirations, and joining in political and military interventions in
other socialist countries. The authoritarian, often ruthless 'socialist
transformation of society', the introduction of 'the Soviet model'
against the will of the majority – with its lack of 'free elections',
political repression, its hundreds of thousand of refugees since 1945,
severe restrictions on travelling, freedom of speech and information
and, finally, with the ultimate symbol of the Wall in Berlin – all
these and many other elements in the GDR's society gave reason
to question the autonomy and legitimacy claimed in its ideology and
propaganda.[1] It is a main characteristic of the GDR's *Deutschlandpolitik* that, from its beginning, it had to meet these challenges of the
system's autonomy and legitimacy – by defense or by attack, by
compensation or by justification, by *détente* and dialogue or
by dogmatic 'delimitation' (*Abgrenzung*), by cooperation or by
confrontation. Today, peace and the system's stability are the two
top priorities of the GDR's leadership, maintaining a difficult balance
between policies that either stabilize and enhance or destabilize and
diminish the system's autonomy and legitimacy. Indeed, that
legitimacy has grown gradually over the years, but is still somewhat
shaky in some major respects.

For more than twenty years the GDR tried in vain to achieve
international recognition outside the 'socialist camp' as a sovereign
state, on equal terms with West Germany, and with a leadership
that is respected in the international arena. In the 1950s and the
1960s, the GDR was very sensitive (and sometimes still is today)
about all questions related to its isolation or recognition, to the
prestige and protocol accorded to its leaders, and to the neglect
shown, especially by Western countries. In all these areas West
Germany's interests and its restrictive definitions of legitimate
relations with the GDR have influenced the West. This discrimination
lasted for more than two decades, and only came to an end in the

early seventies with the 'Basic Treaty' (*Grundlagenvertrag*) between the two German states. The GDR has gained respect in terms of economic performance, sports and culture, and because of its relative stability and growing importance within the Soviet bloc. The isolation ended with the full membership of both German states in the UN, and since then there has been a slow but steady growth in the prestige of its leadership and the performance of its political management in general. During the last ten years in particular, the GDR has gained limited but growing room for maneuver and initiative in its *Deutschlandpolitik*. All major moves in this field still need the consent of Moscow. However there no longer exists a relationship of simple subordination by a satellite regime. The pattern of how the GDR's *Deutschlandpolitik* is made appears to be changing gradually, developing into a close consultation between a clearly dominant, but responsive senior partner and an absolutely loyal, but more self-conscious and independently-minded junior partner with a clear sense of its own interests. This, in turn, enhances the opportunities to increase the system's legitimacy.

In its relationship with West Germany, the GDR acts as an equal partner, rejecting any discrimination and claiming full respect for its specific interests as a sovereign state, rather than as 'the other part of Germany' that is due 'to return to the mainland'.

At least since the early 1970s, the SED has formally renounced any interest in reunification. The GDR's current *Deutschlandpolitik*, in contrast to its policy in the first two decades, no longer develops any proposals for a formal (con) federation, an institutionalized unity or even a *rapprochement* between the two German states that is designed to lead to 'reunification'. (Casual suggestions that a reunified Germany could be acceptable 'on the basis of a socialist order', an order which would presumably be similar to that of the GDR and be introduced in West Germany, are not regarded here as serious proposals that could be realized, that is, negotiated and accepted by East and West, at least not in the foreseeable future.) The GDR accepts the *status quo* and basically does not want to overcome the division of Germany. The GDR's policy tries to combine two principles, the first being that 'day and night cannot be unified', and the second focusing on the many practical steps toward cooperation that are in the interests of the citizens of both German states. This approach neglects certain feelings of East German and, to a lesser extent, West German citizens who think 'that we are still Germans and Germans still belong together'. But the SED's approach is also accompanied by the hope of many GDR citizens that better relations between the two German states, 'an opening up' or 'liberalization' of its political system, can be achieved by an intelligent and careful handling of delicate questions by both German governments. In this regard, since the 1970s, the GDR's *Deutschlandpolitik* has stimulated mixed or ambivalent reactions in the GDR itself, with an ambiguous balance of positive and negative elements for enhancing the regime's legitimacy. In the early 1980s, an increasingly critical and concerned semi-public discussion developed, particularly among the better educated and young, about the GDR's (and the USSR's) security and foreign policies. Questions were raised about the GDR's role in the arms race and in the Eastern bloc as a loyal follower of the Soviet Union; further questions arose about the growing militarization of society. The Protestant Church and a small peace movement were (and still are, to a certain extent) the main organized exponents of such positions.

In the early 1980s, the GDR found itself in a situation where differences over the Soviet Union's management of East–West problems, especially in its security policy, became stronger because they endangered the GDR's policy of *détente* with West Germany and with Western Europe in general. In order to highlight the GDR's difficulties in maintaining a balance between a policy of loyalty – or perhaps even obedience – towards the USSR and the Eastern bloc on the one hand, and a policy of searching for more autonomy and special benefits for itself, on the other, this chapter will focus on an analysis of events that led to the postponement of the visit of the SED's General Secretary Erich Honecker to West Germany in the fall of 1984. This 'moment of crystallization' in inter-German and international relations contains some insights into understanding the specific character as well as lasting structural problems of the GDR's attempt to gain more autonomy (and legitimacy) by a more cooperative approach, and to use it to develop a 'special relationship' with the Federal Republic. Furthermore, such an analysis illuminates the reasons behind Honecker's decision to visit the FRG in September 1987.

The following analysis is based chiefly on a careful study of official statements, newspaper reports, some recent literature and informal discussions in the East and West.[2] It does not rely extensively on detailed documentation (which in any case is easily accessible) since this would only overload an attempt to provide a coherent study. This chapter should not be understood as a systematic or strictly empirical analysis of the GDR's autonomy in its foreign policy. It is less descriptive than interpretative in looking at the relative achievements of the GDR in one problem area. It should be read as a preliminary assessment of a complex situation.

II AUTONOMY IN DIALOGUE AND COOPERATION? THE GDR'S *DEUTSCHLANDPOLITIK* IN 1984

The GDR's *Deutschlandpolitik* in the years 1983–4 must be seen, above all, against the background of the deterioration of East–West relations, primarily between the two superpowers. After the breakdown of the Geneva intermediate-range nuclear forces talks and the deployment of missiles by both European military alliances in Germany, European relations reached a stalemate, characterized by growing confrontation and a lack of substantial dialogue. This characterization remained accurate at least until the late fall of 1984.

On the other hand, relations between the two German states developed remarkably well – at first quite independently of international tensions, primarily determined by the 'national interest' and pressures of domestic politics of the two states to continue a 'policy of dialogue and *détente*'. There was an obvious contrast between the 'top level' of East–West relations and the way inter-German relations developed, culminating in the preparations for a visit of the SED's General Secretary and Head of the State Council of the GDR, Erich Honecker, to West Germany, scheduled for the end of September 1984. But in a sudden move, on 4 September, Dr Ewald Moldt, head of the East German Mission in Bonn, announced that the visit had been 'postponed' for an indefinite period. Dr Moldt and, later, East Germany's leading party daily, *Neues Deutschland*, linked this decision to the fact that West German politicians and the conservative Springer press had made declarations that were 'unseemly', 'detrimental' to the visit, and 'absolutely unusual in relations between sovereign states'.[3] The public in both East and West Germany were surprised by the postponement and questioned what lay behind these accusations; indeed, these accusations seemed of only secondary importance and presumably served as a diplomatic pretext. Why had such a long-planned and long-awaited visit, which could only have served to improve East–West relations, been cancelled? The reasons for the decision were undoubtedly much more complex than the official explanation.

Factors Behind the Postponement

The development of relations between the two German states depends heavily on the state of relations between the two super-powers. Since the fall of 1983, the Soviet Union had taken a hard line toward the West and had carefully monitored the relations of its allies with the Western countries. In late summer 1984, when the final decision on Honecker's visit had to be made, the Soviet leadership was still pursuing a confrontational rather than cooperative approach to US–Soviet relations. It therefore opposed any uncoordinated, 'undisciplined' overture by its smaller European allies that could – if only implicitly – conflict with its own harsher line.

'Moscow's Veto': Foreign Policy Interests and Leadership Struggles

Like most observers in the West, as well as some East German officials in informal and indirect statements,[4] I would argue that the *predominant* factor behind the postponement of Honecker's visit was intensifying pressure on the GDR by the Soviet Union, amounting to a *de facto* veto that clearly gave first priority to the global foreign policy interests of the Soviet Union in contrast to those of the GDR. The Soviet Union wanted to make very clear that it was willing to grant only a limited, secondary and basically instrumental role to both German states in European and global conflict-resolution.

First, a look at the message to East Germany is in order. The Soviet Union was not willing to allow East Germany to pursue a *détente* policy whose development the USSR could not control, particularly since it did not appear to square with the prevailing confrontational pattern of Soviet foreign policy. First of all, the Soviets assessed East Germany's *Deutschlandpolitik* in terms of its potential for weakening West Germany's allegiance to the West and especially to the policies of the Reagan administration. At that moment it did not appear that closer ties between the two German states would have had such an effect. Secondly, they assessed the moves of the GDR leadership in terms of the risk of growing political and economic autonomy for the GDR. From this perspective, too, the Kremlin was opposed to East Germany's rather rapid development of closer bilateral ties with the Federal Republic of Germany (FRG), relatively independently of the Soviet Union and the Council for Mutual Economic Assistance (CMEA). On 30 March 1984, the Czechoslovak party organ *Rudé Právo* reinforced this line by warning against tendencies of 'particularism', 'opportunism' and 'separatism' in the foreign policy of fellow parties who sought 'momentous national or unilateral financial advantages', and wanted 'to demonstrate some sort of independent course' in their foreign policy, deviating 'from the line agreed upon by the community of socialist states'.

In the Soviet view, the GDR, hitherto its most loyal and probably its most strategically critical and economically advanced ally in the Eastern bloc, was about to maneuver itself into a dangerous political and economic situation by means of its special, even unique, relationship with the FRG. Informally, but also publicly, in an unprecedented press campaign, the Soviet leadership, or at least a significant part of it, clearly indicated to the GDR that it regarded closer economic ties with the FRG as a threat to East German sovereignty and to internal stability. Favorable West German offers of a new 950 million DM credit to the GDR in July 1984, presumably in exchange for a substantial easing of travel restrictions between the two German states, were denounced by the Soviet Party organ *Pravda* as 'revanchist solicitations' that sought to undermine the GDR's socialist order by the influx of dangerous political and ideological ideas.

The Soviet intervention was aimed not only at East Germany, but also represented an important message to West Germany and NATO. Moscow wanted to make it clear that West Germany could not continue its policy of partial East–West *détente* in this crucial region of central Europe, particularly during a period of critical tension in East–West security matters. In the Soviet view, further *rapprochement* between the German states was contingent on greater West German sensitivity to Soviet security interests and on less support for American policies, especially those in the field of 'offensive security policy' and disarmament negotiations. The Soviets sought to demonstrate that there is only limited space for the smaller allies of the United States to pursue an independent foreign policy toward Eastern Europe through economic rewards and sanctions or, as in the case of the FRG, through an appeal to national sentiments as well.

The Soviet campaign against West German 'revanchism' must be seen in the context of this overall confrontational policy toward the West. Numerous attacks since late 1983 contained three basic reproaches:

1. The FRG wants to regain its prewar might, to recover lost territories, to restore the German *Reich* to its borders of 1937 (or even beyond), to restore a powerful nation-state in the heart of Europe under the label of the 'legitimate reunification of the German nation'.
2. Neo-fascist groups in the FRG have grown in numbers, public exposure and influence.
3. The FRG uses 'economic levers' such as credits to undermine the stability of the communist states.

Clearly these are, above all, propagandistic charges meriting no serious consideration. The old formula of 'revanchism' serves as justification for the Soviet Union's policy of confrontation and the GDR's old policy of *Abgrenzung*, of 'delimitation' of the socialist system from the imperialist capitalist order of the FRG. On the other hand, this campaign reflected genuine fears in Eastern Europe and the Soviet Union of a united Germany in the heart of Europe, a potential threat to the security of all its neighbors. Such fears are still strong. They are fully understandable in the light of these countries' devastating experience of German Fascism.

The message to the two German states was clear. First, the Soviet Union sought to reassert its superpower prerogative to determine the overall character of East–West relations in accordance with its own interests. Second, the Soviet leadership was insisting that it also has a decisive role and, in case of conflict, the final say in defining the amount of maneuvering room that its allies, with the possible exception of Rumania, had. The USSR would determine the degree of autonomy allotted to them – and hence, to a considerable extent, also to their Western counterparts – in inter-bloc as well as intra-bloc relations. This is supported by Moscow's subsequent veto of the visit of Bulgarian leader, Todor Zhivkov, to Bonn, scheduled to take place shortly after Honecker's visit in October. (By contrast, Rumania's Ceausescu actually did go to Bonn in mid-October.)

In 1984, the Soviet Union would not allow the two German states to ignore the grave deterioration of superpower relations that followed the collapse of the Geneva talks; it would 'only tolerate a policy of *détente* of its own timing and design'.[5] Probably the Soviets were slow to recognize that the GDR, Hungary and Bulgaria had a different understanding of what a continued policy of limited cooperation and *détente* meant under these conditions. Behind these differences lies the issue – as Ilse Spittmann put it – of 'whether East–West relations are primarily at the disposal of the big powers and should be frozen by Soviet decree until the American follow-up deployment is withdrawn, or whether *détente* is the achievement of all European nations and should be revived by a network of bilateral contacts and national initiatives demanded and pursued by the GDR and Hungary'.[6]

One other factor underlying Soviet resistance to Honecker's visit should be mentioned: the leadership struggles within the Soviet Politburo. There is some scattered evidence that the Soviet veto of Honecker's visit probably represented some sort of uneasy compromise in an unstable balance of power between two schools of thought competing under a relatively weak CPSU general secretary.[4] The two seemed to have differed on policy options toward the West in the spring and summer of 1984, and in particular over the amount of leeway to be granted to the GDR in its development of closer relations with West Germany. There is said to have been a group of 'hard-liners' (Gromyko, Ustinov and Romanov), arguing more for strict discipline in the bloc, and against too close and independent economic ties with the West, and a group of moderates (Tikhonov, Gorbachev and, to a lesser extent, the then general secretary of the CPSU, Chernenko) arguing instead for a cautious relaxation of tension with the West, for fostering favorable conditions to resume disarmament talks, and in favor of profitable East–West trade and technology transfer. The compromise, probably worked out in the absence of Chernenko but with his support, would halt the process of East–West German or central European *détente*, ensure bloc discipline on the eve of the upcoming renewal of the Warsaw Pact in 1985, and provide a more solid basis for a carefully coordinated resumption of disarmament negotiations after the presidential elections in the United States. At the same time, the compromise would allow for controllable and prudent contacts between the central European states, particularly the German states.

The GDR's *Deutschlandpolitik*: Unforeseen Constraints in the Search for More Autonomy

In the last months of 1983, the GDR declared that it wanted to 'limit the damage' of the breakdown of the Geneva INF talks and the military build-up in Europe that followed.[8] Moscow was anxious to link any progress in East–West relations to progress in disarmament talks, and to penalize all US allies who agreed to the deployment of Pershing II and cruise missiles. East Berlin wanted no such strict linkage, so as to be able to continue the improvement of its relations with West Germany. It advocated a policy of constructive European dialogue, *détente*, and cooperation with the open or tacit consent of the two superpowers. The GDR called for a 'partnership of responsibility' (*Verantwortungsgemeinschaft*), and a 'coalition of reason' (*Koalition der Vernunft*) between the two German states to help safeguard peace, security and cooperation in Europe.

While the GDR wanted to achieve a certain degree of autonomy in its relations with the Federal Republic, it conceived of this within the framework of the Eastern bloc. It saw such a policy as not being in basic opposition to the interests of the other East European countries and the Soviet Union, but rather, at least partially, in accord with them. The GDR also wanted to be accepted at last as a serious and important political actor in Europe. An important aim of the visit was to enhance the standing and legitimacy of the GDR, its political system and leadership and, equally important, Honecker himself.

And indeed, for about one year, the GDR leadership made important political progress and significant economic gains in relations with West Germany.[9] The agreements and achievements of this period are numerous. For example, in June 1983, a 1 billion DM credit, unrelated to trade or direct investment, was granted to the GDR by a consortium of West German banks. In return, the GDR made only minor concessions on some travel and border regulations, hardly a genuine *quid pro quo*.

In the autumn of 1983, a new postal treaty was signed, increasing the compensatory payments of the FRG for excess services by the GDR. An agreement was reached on the cleaning up of a small border river, and negotiations between the two German states on several other issues were resumed or begun, including environmental problems and cultural exchanges.

In December 1983, quite unexpectedly, a hitherto unresolved

problem of great legal and financial complexity was settled after only a few weeks of negotiation: the operating rights for the West Berlin elevated railway were ceded to the West Berlin authorities, thus saving the GDR an estimated annual hard currency deficit of 80–140 million DM. Furthermore, in 1984, negotiations between the GDR and the *Volkswagenwerk* led to the signing of a 600 million DM long-term investment deal.

In the first four months of 1984, the GDR allowed the legal emigration of an estimated 30 000 citizens. (An estimated 400 000–500 000 more applications for legal emigration were then still pending.) The GDR's motivation for allowing the emigration is still not quite clear. Was it in return for the credit of 1983? Did the GDR want to rid itself of a potential source of discontent? Or did it let them go because of new sums paid by the FRG?

Finally, in late July 1984, the GDR obtained another 950 million DM credit in exchange for a substantial relaxation of border regulations. The Soviet Union carefully followed and sometimes cautiously criticized the progress in inter-German relations, but never intervened to block it. However, in late summer 1984, this skepticism escalated into a veto of further *rapprochement* that not only placed a limit on the GDR's autonomy, but also raised questions about the wisdom of the latter's inter-bloc diplomacy.

Honecker's search for more autonomy may have been based on an inaccurate assessment of the attitude of the Soviet leadership. In early July, after talks with Chernenko in June, the East German leader was still intent on his visit. Obviously, at that time he felt he still had the Kremlin's backing or tacit consent for the Bonn trip. Then Chernenko fell ill and Gromyko's line appears to have gained more influence in the decision-making process.

Some Eastern diplomats have suggested that Honecker refused to go to Moscow once again to get final approval because he felt the only appropriate partner for discussions with him was the then ailing secretary general of the CPSU, not the minister of foreign affairs. Honecker was probably afraid that Gromyko would be strongly opposed to the trip or even attempt to veto it. However, he could not be sure whether the gains of such a visit would be worth the risk of serious conflict with Moscow. This undoubtedly weakened Honecker's position and in August, when Soviet pressure increased, Honecker finally postponed the visit.

Honecker clearly did not want to run the risk of an open clash with the Soviet Union or the strong displeasure of an important faction within the Soviet Politburo. Apparently the GDR did not anticipate such strong resistance to the visit within the Soviet leadership. Some observers have questioned whether the GDR had been too optimistic, too bold, moving too quickly and independently, by failing to keep the Soviet leadership fully informed on details of procedure and substance, underestimating the early warnings, and failing to convince the Soviet leaders of the potentially desirable outcome of the visit. There may be some truth in these speculations, but there is simply not enough evidence to permit a definite or even more precise judgement of their veracity.

These considerations suggest that the GDR probably under-estimated the constraints on its search for more political autonomy and more independently managed economic relations with West Germany.

The precise limits on the political and economic autonomy of the Eastern European countries in their relations with their Western counterparts have never been clearly defined; indeed, in recent years, they have become even more uncertain and controversial.[10] Hence the risks and gains involved in the GDR's efforts to achieve more autonomy in this area were and are difficult to calculate in advance. The unanticipated forced postponement of Honecker's visit may simply have been one step in an uncertain learning process.

The FRG's *Deutschlandpolitik*: Shortcomings of Diplomacy and Leadership

The quality of relations between the two German states depends primarily, but not exclusively, on the quality of the relations between the two superpowers. In fact, over the last two decades, inter-German relations have become increasingly a matter of autonomous bargaining between the FRG and the GDR. Accordingly, not only the USSR and GDR but also the FRG must be seen as having a share of the responsibility for the postponement. For two reasons, Honecker's visit was more difficult to present to the Soviet Union as a desirable step that would bring substantial gains for the GDR and the entire Eastern bloc. First, the West German government offered too little too late in areas of primary importance to the East. The FRG presumably could have gained more by more strategic bargaining with the GDR and by making a number of concessions that were indeed quite possible. Second, the West German government and leading representatives of its majority party, the CDU, contributed in public statements to fears about its long-range intentions. In some respects, as a result of pressures from inside and outside the country, the FRG's diplomatic and public preparations for the visit did not display sufficient professionalism or effective leadership. While the FRG's responsibility for the postponement of the visit was not the most important reason, the impact of these factors also should not be underestimated and deserve to be discussed in greater detail.

First, the GDR wanted to use Honecker's visit to discuss questions of European security, disarmament and arms control, and the possible common contribution of the two German states to the solution of these problems. The basis of such efforts had been laid earlier by the mutually agreed-upon formulas of a 'community of responsibility for peace' to ensure that 'war will never again originate on German soil'. More precisely, the GDR wanted to discuss existing proposals for a nuclear- and chemical-weapons-free zone in central Europe, a pledge of renunciation of force between the two alliances, and joint German initiatives at the Stockholm Conference for Confidence-Building Measures and Disarmament in Europe.

The FRG's conservative–liberal coalition government, however, did not feel it was in a position to initiate proposals for breaking the deadlock in the then stagnating or suspended international negotiations on disarmament and arms control, because they viewed the primary responsibility for these negotiations as lying with the superpowers. The FRG government did not want to take any steps that could bring it into conflict with the United States or NATO. It wanted to limit itself to negotiating procedures that had a serious chance of being accepted by all European countries and the two superpowers. Therefore Foreign Minister Genscher proposed to discuss only an initiative by the two German states for a pledge of renunciation of force by NATO and the Warsaw Pact.[11]

Second, the GDR was handicapped in defending Honecker's visit to the Soviet leadership and all hardliners and skeptics in the East by Chancellor Kohl's statement early in the summer of 1984, which indicated that while he was ready to *discuss* the four major and long-standing demands of the GDR, he expected no serious *results*. The four demands in question had been outlined in a speech by Honecker on 13 October 1980, in Gera:

1. the transformation of the permanent missions of both states into embassies with all the rights and prerogatives provided by

international law;
2. recognition, or more recently, respect of GDR citizenship by the FRG;
3. the abolition of the office for registration of criminal offenses and violation of human rights, committed by GDR authorities, especially by border officials; and
4. an agreement fixing the disputed common border in the middle of the Elbe River, rather than on its north-eastern shore, as demanded by the FRG.

The prior refusal of the FRG to consider any concession at all in these areas seems to have discouraged the GDR from substantive bargaining on the four demands during the preparations of a joint communiqué, at least until shortly before 4 September. One or two of the four appear to have been discussed in some form on the morning immediately after the cancellation of the visit, but by then it was obviously too late.[12]

Other issues, such as environmental problems, cultural exchange, scientific and technical cooperation, and postal matters, while certainly of importance to both sides, did not promise the kind of substantial gains for the GDR that would have helped to convince skeptics in some Eastern bloc capitals of the necessity of the visit at that particular moment.

Third, the government of the FRG, particularly the leading representatives of the two majority parties, the CDU and the CSU, contributed considerably to concern, irritation, and even fears in Eastern Europe over too close a *rapprochement* between the two German states. In particular, they argued that the German Question 'is still open', that the division of Germany (and the whole of Europe) is unnatural and illegitimate, and that it is the natural right of the German nation to seek national reunification in freedom, peace and self-determination. The FRG officially acknowledges the 'real state of affairs' and the existing borders in Europe and has no revisionist territorial claims. However, Chancellor Kohl in some of his own speeches and public appearances created the impression that the West German government still aims or should aim at peaceful revision of the borders in the East, especially Poland's western frontier; and he did not openly oppose two of his ministers, Friedrich Zimmermann and Heinrich Windelen, or other right-wing conservatives who stated this explicitly. References to the German borders of 1937 (or even earlier) 'which could only be fixed in a final peace treaty' and were, until then, 'open to peaceful revision', as well as statements about the rights of the German minority in Poland, nourished fear and charges of West German 'revisionism' and 'revanchism' in the East, particularly in Poland.

In addition, delicate aspects of the visit and its protocol were publicly discussed by CDU/CSU 'hardliners' in a way that significantly irritated the GDR and its leadership on a sensitive issue – their prestige and their anxiety over their former status as a second-class actor in the international arena. The statements also had potentially harmful implications for Honecker's personal prestige. The GDR seemed especially offended by the remark of Alfred Dregger, floor leader of the governing party, that 'West Germany's future does not depend on whether Mr Honecker pays us the honor of a visit'.

The CDU leadership under Chancellor Kohl probably underestimated the amount of resistance to inter-German *rapprochement* by the ideologically oriented national-conservative right wing of the CDU/CSU. In the tradition of Adenauer and on formally correct legal positions, they attempted to disturb and to hinder Honecker's visit and were opposed to a policy of compromise with the 'undemocratic SED regime'. Their objections, rhetoric, and maneuvering were probably not taken seriously enough in the preparatory stages of the visit. The CDU leadership had not built up enough support for its policy, and was unable to ensure discipline in its own ranks.

Bonn's handling of the protocol issues also probably seriously irritated the GDR leadership. In Bonn's view, the head of the State Council of the GDR neither could nor should be received and treated as a head of state equal to any other foreign visitor of this rank and status. Chancellor Kohl did not want to meet him in Bonn. There was a serious public discussion over whether the FRG's president (Bundespraesident) and the president of the Parliament (Bundestag) should meet Honecker in their official residences. Certainly the visit of the most powerful representative of this important central European power was not to be treated on equal terms in the official protocol with a state visit of prime importance (for example, with the Bundeswehr honor guard playing the two national anthems on arrival). All these points of protocol and public respect were of high political, symbolic and psychological importance to the GDR leadership, not only in 1984, but also three years later, when Honecker's visit finally took place this time with a substantial increase in status. During his visit to the Federal Republic in 1987

Honecker was treated as a *de facto* international head of state, that is, with all the special honors and symbols of international diplomatic protocol for such a VIP visit. This equality in public protocol and internationally visible respect was a major concession by Bonn, and was regarded by the GDR as a substantial political gain for which it was ready to make concessions in other fields, such as travel and communication restrictions.

Finally, for better or worse, the FRG's coalition government did not (and still does not) have a systematic long-range concept of *Ost-* and *Deutschlandpolitik*, defining the future role of the two German states in European, East–West, or global international relations. The long-term goals, and the steps necessary to achieve them, are far from clear, and hence cannot be explained to the public or made acceptable to West Germany's partners in the East and West. There is thus reason to doubt whether, on the whole, the FRG made all necessary efforts to convey, in a credible fashion, that the principles of a peaceful and cooperative *Ost-* and *Deutschlandpolitik* of the 1970s remain unchanged and that the concerns of the Soviet Union and its allies are still being taken into consideration.

For several Eastern European countries, above all the Soviet Union and Poland, German reunification and possible border revisions are definitely not on the agenda. West German rhetoric regarding the 'openness' of the German Question contributed substantially to suspicion in the East as to the 'real' goals of Bonn's *Ostpolitik*. This was particularly true in the light of US statements questioning Yalta and the 'illegitimate division of Europe'. The FRG should have made it clear that better personal contacts, an easing of travel restrictions, the solution of practical matters, intensified dialogue and economic cooperation between the two German states would not endanger the stability of the GDR or the balance of power in Europe.

These observations seem to justify the initial conclusion that, in some important aspects, the FRG government and particularly the CDU/CSU were not up to the demanding task of this delicate diplomatic situation. At the same time, however, the shortcomings of the West German actors were clearly not the primary cause of the cancellation.

**The Search for Autonomy Continued: The GDR's *Deutschlandpolitik*
and its Interest in *Détente***

After the cancellation of Honecker's visit in 1984, inter-German
relations recovered slowly but firmly from the momentary setback.
With the takeover of Mikhail Gorbachev as new CPSU general
secretary, a gradual but substantial change in Soviet foreign and
security policy took place, especially towards the West. On the key
question of disarmament, that change was rapid. On the one hand,
the Soviet Union managed to instill greater discipline within its own
camp.[13] On the other hand, the debate on the degree of autonomy
of the smaller central European WTO states went on.[14] The GDR
got enough leeway to continue its policy of *détente* and dialogue.
Among the more important milestones of this development, the
following stand out: the visit to the FRG of the President of the
Volkskammer, Horst Sindermann, in February 1986; the agreements
with the SPD on zones free of chemical and nuclear weapons in
central Europe in 1985 and 1986; the agreement on cultural
exchanges in spring 1986; an increase in travel permits related to
'urgent family affairs' for East German citizens below the age of
retirement (approximately 500 000 in 1986 and more than 1 million
in 1987); and – an innovation – partnership agreements between
cities in the two German states. The most remarkable event is, of
course, Erich Honecker's visit to West Germany in September 1987,
which we cannot analyze here in greater detail because of the limited
scope of this study. If the underlying factors of this development
are studied, it is clear that in both Eastern and Western Europe,
especially within the two German states, there is a permanent and
vital interest in the continuation (or revival) of *détente* in Europe
through dialogue, cooperation, and verifiable agreements negotiated
on equal terms. At least in West Germany, pressures have been
and continue to be so strong that a setback like the postponement
of Honecker's visit did not preclude a policy of 'controlled and
reasonable cooperation' in fields of common interest, such as support
and limited initiatives for substantial progress in disarmament
and arms control negotiations; intensified inter-German economic
cooperation; efforts to improve living conditions; and, most difficult,
the freedom of movement for East German citizens. Such activities
imply or even consciously aim at more political and economic
autonomy for the two German states, albeit under the conditions
peculiar to each of them within the framework of their respective

alliances.

In general, one can say that the key factor among pressures for *détente* is the growing economic and political costs of the arms race, and increasing doubts about whether new weapons systems really create greater security or, on the contrary, make the situation more critical. Peace movements in many European countries have articulated widespread fears of an increased probability of war and have influenced general attitudes on basic security questions, especially among the young and well educated. Urgent economic, social and environmental needs as well as considerable pressure resulted in strong support, though in varying degrees, by most of the European members of NATO and the WTO for a policy of *détente* and international agreements to curb the arms race.

But a full exposition of this thesis would require a much more complex analysis and argumentation that is beyond the scope and aim of this chapter. The focus of the discussion here will be much narrower: to define the particular interests of the two German states in *détente* – particularly of the GDR, which has often been overlooked as an individual actor in more globally-oriented perceptions of European politics.

The GDR's interest in *détente* reflects a number of military, political and economic concerns. In recent years Germany has increasingly emerged as a likely battleground in any future global war or even in a so-called limited nuclear or conventional war between East and West. Hence the lessening of tensions and the slowing down or even the avoidance of a greater military build-up is as much a genuine interest of the GDR as it is of the Federal Republic. For both, disarmament and cooperation are certainly more promising than the deployment of more weapons.

The GDR, moreover, also has strong economic interests in increasing trade with West Germany in order to obtain more hard currency and important advanced technology and equipment; it also has an interest in lowering its defense budget so as to be able to pay for its ambitious economic, social and housing programs, which improve the standard of living of its population and are crucial to ensuring the legitimacy and stability of its system. Let us look more closely at the structure of those interests. (See also Chapters 12 and 13.) First of all, half of the GDR's trade with non-socialist countries is now conducted with West Germany, representing a relative decline in the share of most other countries. (There has also been some growth in the shares of Japan and Austria, but at a much lower rate.) West German trade amounts to 10 per cent of East Germany's overall foreign trade, 40 per cent of which is conducted with the USSR. However, by an amendment to the Treaties of Rome that created the European Economic Community in 1957, inter-German trade is not considered to be international trade. As a result, the GDR is the only CMEA country enjoying direct access, free of tariffs and duties, to West German and, indirectly, other EEC markets.

Inter-German trade is conducted under extraordinarily favorable conditions for East Germany: it is based on a one-to-one exchange rate (on the basis of so-called 'clearing units'), and both sides have agreed to make available to each other an interest-free line of credit of up to 600 million DM (subject to change from time to time). Until now, these arrangements have been of real benefit only to the GDR. Further, the GDR receives more than 1 billion DM annually from the FRG's federal, state, and West Berlin budgets as compensation for a broad spectrum of services. In addition, it receives another estimated 1.5 billion DM in the form of private payments, for example, visa fees and obligatory amounts of currency exchange for private visitors from the West, gifts by private persons, and charitable donations, especially those of the Protestant Churches to their fellow Christians in the East. To this can be added an estimated 700 million DM in profit from internal sales in 'intershop' hard currency stores.

The GDR, like many other East European countries, has considerable debt management problems. Estimates range between $9 and 11 billion in the late 1970s and early 1980s, and approximately $7 billion in the mid-1980s, a considerable proportion of which is in the form of short-term credits. About half of the total debt is owed to West German creditors. Nonetheless, the GDR has managed thus far to get along quite well and is regarded internationally as a relatively reliable credit risk.[15]

Finally, the Soviet Union is no longer the powerful and reliable trading partner that it once was, offering 'unlimited' reserves of raw materials for relatively low prices fixed on a long-term basis. The USSR no longer buys large quantities of all kinds of consumer goods, with little regard for their quality. It has been forced to raise the price and ration the supply of its energy and raw materials, and to ask CMEA countries to make up any resulting shortages through purchases on the capitalist world market.

Therefore the GDR, probably more than any other East European country, has little choice but to orient certain key sectors of its economy increasingly toward Western markets. Only there can it buy many needed commodities. To obtain them it must often sell locally produced goods that many of its own citizens and other Eastern Europeans would be only too happy to buy. At the same time, the difficulties of the capitalist world economy, along with the nearly insoluble debt problems of Eastern Europe, have also had a strong impact on East Germany's economy.

The GDR's economy is thus faced with multiple pressures: to produce high-quality export goods for Western markets in order to pay its debts and to buy more advanced technology; to satisfy its own highly demanding domestic consumer market; and to fulfill its obligations to the CMEA and the Warsaw Pact, particularly toward the Soviet Union. The latter obligation carries with it the heavy additional financial burden of sharing in the Soviets' world-wide military and economic aid programs, the arms build-up in Europe and special subsidies to the ailing Polish economy.

As a result, the GDR has an extremely strong interest in reducing the costs of the arms race and extending trade with West Germany, in order to make gains that can permit it to pay for its own ambitious economic and social programs. We may indeed conclude that the GDR's interest in continued regional *détente* and its policies towards West Germany are determined to a greater degree by domestic political considerations than are those of the FRG.

First, there are the pressing needs of its advanced economy to increase productivity and to maintain economic stability and relative prosperity. The GDR must struggle to maintain its standard of living, the highest in Eastern Europe, which has been a crucial factor underlying the stability of its political system. This is particularly necessary, given the general lack of democratic freedom, for securing the legitimacy of its political order and ruling bureaucracy. The GDR leadership, moreover, has to meet the rising economic expectations of its population, aroused by constant comparison to West Germany. There is a very strong challenge to the legitimacy of the system, of its rationality, efficiency and viability, provided by the everyday shortcomings of the economy, particularly in the consumer sphere. The impact of these daily frustrations on public morale should not be underestimated. At the same time, there is a growing concern, particularly among the young, about environmental issues. This fairly recent concern, however cautiously expressed, calls into question the entire mode of industrial production and the consumer model of socialism that the GDR stands for.

In fact, Honecker's visit and the general attempt to continue a policy of *détente* and economic cooperation were *also* (not primarily) motivated by the GDR leadership's desire to enhance its own internal and international acceptance, and consequently, the legitimacy of its political system. It sought to achieve this goal by continued economic gains and by enhancing its international prestige. The GDR leadership wanted thereby to present itself as efficient and credible representatives of the interests of the GDR population. More concretely, it wanted to increase its popularity by an improvement in inter-German relations with positive practical results for the population (such as an easing of travel restrictions, cultural exchange and environmental cooperation). On the whole the GDR leadership would have gained by a 'negative legitimation', demonstrating some autonomy towards the unpopular 'big brother'. At the same time, however, these steps had to have at least tacit Soviet consent, and the GDR had to remain an attractive economic partner in the East.

Likewise the GDR leadership wanted to gain support and internal stability by assuaging the doubts of 'hard liners' in the party leadership on the one hand, as well as the fears of the churches, the peace movement and young people on the other. Last but not least, Honecker sought to enhance his personal prestige by becoming the first chief of the East German state and party to make an official state visit to the FRG.

Despite the fact that the long-term interests, general orientation, and world-view of the two German states are strongly contradictory, their short- and middle-range interests show some remarkable mutuality – a fact which served as the basis for a relatively successful *Deutschlandpolitik* of both German states.

III THE GDR'S SEARCH FOR AUTONOMY IN THE 1980s: TRENDS AND PROBLEMS

The GDR's *Deutschlandpolitik* in 1983–4 was, until the postponement of Honecker's visit, well on its way to enhancing the legitimacy of the political system. It included:

(a) highly profitable economic cooperation, especially in the commercial and financial field; growing acceptance as a borrower by Western banks and creditors, and even by conservative Western politicians (such as Franz Josef Strauss);

(b) strong support for its demand for progress in disarmament talks and for its leadership's 'non-enthusiasm' for the deployment of new missiles;

(c) tolerance, though within limits, of a small but active peace movement and an intensifying semi-public discussion on security policy, travel restrictions and many other aspects of GDR society, mainly sheltered and carried out by the Protestant Church;

(d) permission to let approximately 30 000 persons emigrate to West Germany; and

(e) the rather popular plan of Honecker's visit to the West, with some hope for practical results for the improvement of inter-German relations, travel and, indirectly, living conditions for GDR citizens.

The GDR conducted an active and fairly successful *Deutschlandpolitik* that was characterized by a remarkable degree of dynamism and a certain independence, in contrast to the restrictive tendencies of confrontation in East–West relations. The GDR indeed exploited its limited room for maneuver, in a situation of a rather weak and presumably 'split' Soviet leadership, with a hitherto unknown degree of autonomy. It was exactly this active use of its autonomy that presented opportunities to enhance the system's legitimacy – and to diminish it severely when, as it happened, the 'veto from Moscow' became dramatically visible to the public in the two German states, in Europe and world-wide. However, what may look like a short 'phase of aberration' could be interpreted as a beginning of the manifestation of structural problems of the Eastern bloc by public communication in the press and in visible diplomatic interactions. These problems lie in defining the role and the degree of autonomy for the smaller East European allies of the Soviet Union in their domestic and in their foreign and security policies – particularly the special case of the GDR's *Deutschlandpolitik*.

The decisive question for the future of *détente* between the two German states is the relationship between the GDR and the Soviet Union. In this unequal partnership, the unquestionable fact of Soviet supremacy served as a check on the seeming differences in the approach of the two countries not only to inter-German *détente*, but also to their domestic policies. The CPSU general secretary's reform policies are a serious challenge to the GDR in many respects. In foreign and security policies there seems to be complete agreement between the USSR and the GDR; the GDR strongly supports all of Gorbachev's disarmament initiatives and has added some proposals for confidence-building measures and arms control in central Europe.[16] With the acceleration of disarmament talks and the signing of a treaty between the two superpowers on the elimination of middle-range and short-range nuclear weapons ('double-zero solution'), the Soviet Union now seems to be ready to further improve relations with the FRG as well. This is evidenced by the intensification of official diplomatic exchanges on a high level since the federal elections in January 1987 and a general easing of tension between East and West. In the field of *Deutschlandpolitik* there was not only the visit of the West German President Richard von Weizsaecker in July 1987, but also Erich Honecker's visit to West Germany in early September 1987. Yet, in May and June 1987, the Soviet Union made it quite clear once again that it would not allow any GDR move to change the status of Berlin by opposing an official visit by Erich Honecker to West Berlin or a visit by Mayor Eberhard Diepgen to the Eastern part of the city to celebrate jointly its 750-year anniversary. Prior agreement seemed to have been attained by the German negotiators, with the approval or toleration by the three Western allies responsible for Berlin.

A much more serious challenge to the GDR's internal stability, a totally new pattern of relating to the Soviet model of 'developed socialism', is presented by Gorbachev's sweeping reform policies, especially in the political and cultural spheres of public life. The GDR is under strong external and internal pressure to undertake similar reforms. The SED has so far reacted to this pressure by stressing the principle that each socialist nation is independent, equal and sovereign; that each party and each government must decide on its own how best to care for the nation's future, and to determine the development of socialism according to the specific conditions of the country. The SED has proudly pointed out that, especially in its economic and social policies, it had already achieved many or most of the targets for which the CPSU has just begun to strive.[17] This is the answer of the GDR's 'conservative reformism' to the 'radical reformism' of Gorbachev's blueprints for the future. For the first time, the Soviet Union seems to be 'more progressive' than the GDR which, in turn, has to defend itself not against Soviet traditionalism, against its anti-democratic and interventionist domestic and intra-bloc policies, but against a thorough and critical public discussion of necessary reforms of its political system, and hence, virtually of all spheres of public life. Up to this point the Soviet Union has granted autonomy to the GDR *not* to follow its policies of '*glasnost*' and '*perestroika*' and the GDR leadership has made 'negative' use of its autonomy in order to stabilize the *status quo* by waiting, and by rejecting quick reform moves, not verbally in the open but *de facto*, perhaps with clandestine feelings of superiority, anxiety and skepticisim. The SED clearly wants to keep tight control over any 'dangerous' public discussions on political and cultural reforms, not to mention organized activities in this direction.

The interest of the two party leaderships converge here: both are interested in the stability of the GDR's internal order, whatever may be the best way to achieve it. As long as this kind of political and military stability and integration is guaranteed, the CPSU leadership seems to be ready to grant greater leeway to the smaller East European states to undertake limited political, economic, social and cultural reforms. A new pattern of Soviet hegemony seems to be emerging. The CPSU refrains from a general and operative 'monopoly of truth' except for fundamental political and ideological questions, and concentrates on safeguarding the essentials of Soviet foreign policy interests in order to overcome its own domestic problems. The CPSU seems to be trying to make its foreign and security policies more pragmatic in order to lessen the burdens from outside and to fight, above all, for a comprehensive economic reform, for innovations in science and technology, for a substantial improvement of the standard of living of the population and, last but not least, for more 'socialist democracy'. Therefore, from a Soviet perspective, the GDR's contribution to the achievement of these goals is of prime importance. The GDR's relative autonomy and its *Deutschlandpolitik* now seem to be no longer subordinated to a confrontational approach to East–West relations (as in 1983–4), but much more to the spirit and practical efforts of carefully controlled but continuously intensified cooperation, as demonstrated during Honecker's visit and its results in 1987.

We may conclude then that there is, as a structural precondition, a basic convergence of interests and policies in the foreign relations of the USSR and the GDR. But there is also a certain divergence of interests, as Wolfgang Pfeiler has recently pointed out.[18] These divergences may increase in the future if Gorbachev's reform policy is effective and successful. Here is a virtual structural conflict on the future of socialism which may develop a dynamic of its own that cannot easily be controlled by the GDR; on the other hand, this potential conflict may drive the GDR back to a very traditional and conservative line which would probably be joined by some other East European states.

But, in the long run, the GDR's interests do seem seriously to run counter to those of the Soviet Union and its East European allies (even if there is no *perestroika*, or restructuring, in the GDR). A prosperous, viable and strong East Germany with a stable and growing economy, with access to sources of modern technology, and an enhanced capacity to produce high-quality goods and develop its own advanced technologies would better contribute to the Eastern bloc's economic and military needs; further, such a GDR would no doubt enjoy greater political stability, thus safeguarding socialism at one of its most vulnerable points of confrontation with the West. Likewise East Germany's augmented prestige as an important and serious partner in international relations would certainly be a stabilizing political factor in the Eastern bloc, above all for the Soviet Union. East Germany could also play the role of a secondary spokesman and agent of the Soviet Union's foreign and security policy by virtue of its special relationship with West Germany.

On the other hand, such striving for more autonomy is obviously troubling to the Soviet Union, as it challenges the notion of bloc integration under Soviet supremacy. At least in the short run, the strict limitation of the autonomy of the small central European states represents only one type of 'solution' to the Soviet Union's alliance problems. However the pressure for autonomy is structurally based and growing stronger; thus, in the long run, inflexibility and the exercise of veto power are not real solutions, as they can create even more friction and become increasingly costly to implement. Ultimately, the contradictions within the East bloc are probably manageable, if not solvable, by conceding more autonomy to the East European states, both in their domestic and European foreign policies. Over time, the Soviet Union can only gain by giving more leeway on all questions that do not touch the substance of the alliance and its socialist premises, and are more or less exclusively related to the more narrow national interests of the individual East European states. The USSR could, in its short- and middle-term management of the relations between the two German states, limit itself to general control over the structural limits of the process.

Despite differences in structural conditions, much the same could be said of West German autonomy *vis-à-vis* the United States. A moderately more independent role for West Germany, especially in

Ost- and *Deutschlandpolitik*, as well as in disarmament and foreign policy, would enhance the Western alliance's capacity to solve East–West problems. As long as the risks and gains of certain policy options cannot be precisely determined, the West German position that trade and cooperation with the East should not and, in the long run, cannot be effectively and reasonably used as a political weapon, should be finally accepted by the Western allies. Furthermore, attempts to destabilize the socialist systems of Eastern Europe will probably result in less change and liberalization than hoped for.

Looking at the interests of the two German states from the perspective of the international system, one can conclude that, in the long run at least, the interests of the two German states in their *Deutschlandpolitik* are not in conflict with the interests of their neighbors or the two superpowers. This is the case so long as the latter, particularly the USSR, are willing to grant more political and economic autonomy to their German allies within the existing framework of alliances and the maintenance of the division of Germany for the foreseeable future.

Certainly neither the European neighbors of the FRG and the GDR nor the two superpowers have a serious interest in the reunification of the two German states in the near future. A realistic West German and GDR *Deutschlandpolitik* requires the practical acceptance of the division of the nation and its political organization into two states as the basis for all further planning and practical progress in the relations between the two German states. For the foreseeable future, German reunification cannot be an operative goal for West German (or GDR) *Deutschlandpolitik* – and, in fact, it is not, despite all the rhetoric and wishful thinking that can sometimes be heard in the Federal Republic. German reunification would have as a precondition, among other things, a profound change in the existing balance of power in Europe and in the internal structures of both societies. The vast majority of the West German population actually does not care very much about or believe in the possibility of German unification, and none of its neighbors, afraid of a strong reunited Germany, would support such a step.

Indeed the two German states are so deeply integrated in their alliances, and their internal orders have developed in such opposite ways that one could argue the following: chances for a rapid or substantial increase of the political and economic autonomy of the GDR, a close *rapprochement* between the two German states, German reunification, or a revival of pan-German nationalism are so small that fearful speculation about a substantial weakening of alliances should be dismissed in East and West. Furthermore the same applies to a neutralization or Finlandization of Germany, or a new German nationalism that could spiral out of control or be bluntly anti-Soviet or anti-American. Such speculation overlooks or underestimates the structural barriers to such developments – not to mention the lack of support, on the governmental as well as the popular level. East as well as West German intentions, initiatives, bilateral agreements and internal political discussions have been grossly distorted by those who seem to suggest that some sort of national foreign policy coalition, economic marriage or political confederation is in the making.

The most probable development in relations between the two German states will be a continued policy of dialogue and limited economic and other cooperation closely monitored by the two superpowers and the two states' European neighbors. The strong pressures for *détente* in East and West, the change in the CPSU leadership and Soviet domestic and foreign policies, and particularly the economic needs of the WTO countries sooner or later will lead to a resumption of *détente* in central Europe. Thus, on the one hand, the GDR is obliged to be and will remain a reliable and attractive partner for the Soviet Union; on the other hand, the GDR, like other East European countries, and perhaps in cooperation with others, will need to attain greater autonomy in the formulation of its foreign and domestic policy.

7 Changing Security Dimensions of the Inter-German Relationship

Jonathan Dean

The 'Gorbachev era' and the improvement in East–West relations associated with it have not changed the basic political facts of the European situation: the division of Germany into two separate states and the continued incorporation of these states into opposing military alliances, NATO and the Warsaw Pact, is regarded by most governments in both alliances as the precondition for military and political stability in Europe.

True, the three Western wartime allies – France, the United Kingdom and the United States – undertook a contractual obligation in the 1954 Bonn Convention to promote the reunification of Germany, but this commitment does not alter the political facts. Even the West German government, while insisting that the ultimate possibility of self-determination must be kept open for the population of the German Democratic Republic (GDR), also insists that any chance of realizing this possibility is distant in time and that the security of the Federal Republic of Germany (FRG) can be assured only by continued West German membership in the NATO alliance. At this time, majority public opinion in the Federal Republic supports the position of the West German government, although this support could shift if the West German public thought other possibilities were real and would assure the current level of economic well-being, political freedom and security in the FRG.

For its part, the government of the GDR insists that the existence of the GDR as a separate state is permanent and that it has every intention of continuing GDR membership in the Warsaw Treaty Organization. At present, only a portion of the GDR population, whose size cannot be measured given the authoritarian nature of the GDR system, but which is probably considerable, actively desires a change in the *status quo*, and then only under conditions where at least current standards of living and security can be assured. The forces supporting continuation of the *status quo* of division of Germany and membership of the two German states in opposing alliances are very strong.

Yet, since their mutual acceptance as separate states in the '*Grundlagenvertrag*', or Basic Treaty of December 1972, the Federal Republic and the GDR, in each case pushed by strong domestic public opinion, have entered into a complex relationship whose increasing scope and intensity has caused considerable concern in both East and West.

To allies of the two German states who have these worries, no aspect of the inter-German relationship is more sensitive – because apparently so directly related to possible change in the *status quo* in Europe – than the possibility of inter-German collaboration on security and arms control issues. Starting from timid beginnings in the early 1970s, the security dialogue between the two German states has intensified with the emergence of the reform-minded Gorbachev leadership in the USSR.

The policies of the two German states already overlap on an increasing number of arms control and security issues. The circumstances surrounding conclusion of the December 1987 INF Treaty have brought strong support in the Federal Republic for negotiated reduction of tactical-range nuclear weapons, vigorously seconded by coordinated East German and Soviet pressures for the 'third zero' and total elimination of nuclear weapons from Europe. The next five years may bring conclusion and implementation of a US–Soviet accord on reduction of strategic nuclear weapons, a second Stockholm-type agreement on confidence-building measures covering NATO and Warsaw Pact armed forces, a NATO–Warsaw Pact agreement to reduce these forces in the Atlantic-to-the-Urals area and, possibly, a world-wide prohibition on production and storage of chemical weapons affecting Europe. Such developments could well intensify the inter-German dialogue on security and arms control issues.

This chapter examines the possible extent of such intensification, its implications for the inter-German relationship, for the security policies of the two German states, and for the relationship of the two German states with their respective alliances. For non-German observers in the West, the question is whether the prospect of this expanding inter-German dialogue should elicit the picture of two small boys playing with matches near a gasoline tank – the image often held by conservatives worried about expansion of Soviet influence in Europe – or whether it should be regarded as a useful potential resource in lessening the NATO–Warsaw Pact military confrontation.

I THE 'GROUND RULES' OF THE INTER-GERMAN SECURITY RELATIONSHIP

During his fifteen-year leadership of West German politics, Chancellor Konrad Adenauer gave clear priority to integration of the newly-founded Federal Republic of Germany into NATO and Western Europe over efforts to reunify Germany, an issue which he considered mainly the responsibility of the Western allies and the USSR. Under Adenauer, West German policy posited the prior dissolution of the German Democratic Republic and the reunification of Germany as a precondition for East–West arms control agreements. As the dominant Western power of the postwar period, the United States was in basic agreement with Adenauer's fundamental policy and supported his approach to arms control. For the United States, the pattern of German unity as a precondition was broken only when the shock of the Cuban missile crisis led to the conclusion of the Limited Test Ban Treaty and the emergence of bilateral US–Soviet talks on nuclear arms.

For the first five years of the GDR's existence as a separate state, from 1949 to 1955, the Soviet Union implied a willingness to trade off independence of the GDR if the Western allies relinquished their intention to rearm West Germany. During this period, the GDR had no independent arms-control or foreign policy of its own. After 1955, when the FRG entered the NATO alliance and West German armed forces were established and the GDR became a member of the Warsaw Pact with armed forces of its own, the GDR sought to use its support for arms control projects and initiatives as a lever to gain admission into international organizations and to establish its independent existence. Again and again the GDR suggested arms control proposals for the two German states as a means of gaining its acceptance by West Germany and its NATO allies as a separate German state (rather than as 'the Soviet zone of occupation' or 'the so-called German Democratic Republic', as Western politicians then referred to it).[1]

These efforts were rejected. Repeated meetings of Four Power

Foreign Ministers on the German Question failed to bring results. The Soviet Union used force to put down the Hungarian revolt and later the 'Prague Spring', and supported the erection of the Berlin Wall. The GDR was recognized as an independent state by an increasing number of countries of the Third World. The United States and other NATO allies of the FRG seemed incapable of preventing these developments. As a consequence, in the late 1960s, West German policy changed in the direction of accepting the existence of a second German state and of attempting through that acceptance to bring about step-by-step practical improvements in the situation of the East German population.

The first specific result for GDR–FRG relations of the Federal Republic's new *Ostpolitik* was the May 1972 Transport Agreement containing procedures for implementing the 1971 Quadripartite Agreement on Berlin as regards unimpeded civilian access to the western sectors of Berlin and the opening up of visits to East Berlin and the GDR. The second result, in December 1972, was the *Grundlagenvertrag* between the Federal Republic of Germany and the German Democratic Republic, in which the two states recognize each other as separate. The Treaty's accompanying documents provided for membership of both German states in the United Nations. When this took place, France, the United Kingdom and the United States, together with other NATO states, recognized the GDR as an autonomous state.

After a spurt of exaggerated hopes in the FRG for the rapid development of FRG–GDR relations subsided in the mid-1970s, the inter-German relationship took on a prosaic character. It focused on agreements covering the environment, water pollution, air pollution, communicable diseases of livestock, and on negotiations on transportation and postal matters designed to improve the lot of Berliners and East Germans.

None the less, Article 5 of the *Grundlagenvertrag* did provide that the two German states would contribute to security and cooperation in Europe, support efforts to reduce armed forces and arsenals in Europe (a reference to the then-pending negotiations on Mutual and Balanced Force Reductions [MBFR]) and support efforts aimed at arms control and disarmament, especially as regards nuclear weapons and other weapons of mass destruction. An oral agreement which forms part of the Treaty states that 'both governments have agreed, in the course of normalizing the relations between the Federal Republic of Germany and the German Democratic Republic, to consult on issues of mutual interest, especially those which are important for securing peace in Europe'.[2]

This brief statement was a modest basis for a modest beginning. In the decade following conclusion of the *Grundlagenvertrag*, inter-German discussions of security issues were formal and limited, restricted mainly to periodic contacts between Dr Friedrich Ruth, the Federal German commissioner for arms control, and a working level East German official, Ernst Krabatsch, contacts which focused on review of widely known information on the ongoing US–Soviet SALT talks and on the Vienna MBFR talks in which both German states were participating. For the most part, discussions of the latter topic did not go beyond a formal exchange of comments on the Vienna talks, which replicated comments exchanged at the negotiation site between the two German negotiators.

There was good reason for this reticence. Both German governments knew the ground rules for their relationship and especially for discussion of security issues directly affecting the interests of their alliances and of their major allies. Each government would stay firmly based in its own alliance, rigorously avoiding the slightest appearance of departing from agreed positions of the respective alliances. By common understanding, alliance status of each government is never discussed between them.

When raising general political issues with the Soviet Union or discussing their own inter-German policy with their allies or even at home in the FRG, West German leaders unfailingly declare that they are speaking as loyal and unshakeable members of the NATO alliance. Typically, West German President Richard von Weizsaecker, speaking during his visit to Moscow in July 1987, told Soviet leaders that 'the Federal Republic of Germany' was 'a steadfast and reliable member of the Atlantic alliance'. Chancellor Helmut Kohl, in making his annual State of the Nation report on inter-German developments to the Bundestag in October 1987, stated at the outset of his speech that progress in inter-German relations had been possible only through the Federal Republic's 'unequivocally stating its loyalty to the Western community of values, by cohesion and the closest coordination in the alliance'.[3] In his speech welcoming East German leader Erich Honecker to Bonn on 7 September 1987, Chancellor Kohl said, 'The Germans have learned to assess their possibilities and limitations realistically. These possibilities and limitations are determined by the incompatibility of the political systems of the two states and their membership of different alliances. The Atlantic alliance, a community with common values and common security interest, remains the immutable foundation of the policy of the Federal Republic of Germany'.[4]

Honecker makes similar statements about the GDR's loyal membership in the Warsaw Treaty Organization and periodically repeats the formula that socialism and capitalism (that is the GDR and the FRG) cannot share common ground; they are, as he said during his September 1987 trip to Bonn, as compatible as 'fire and water', and there is nothing to unite between the two German states.

II ADDING THE SECURITY DIMENSION TO THE INTER-GERMAN RELATIONSHIP

But more dramatic developments for the inter-German relationship were in store as the first decade after the Basic Treaty elapsed. Meeting General Secretary Honecker in Werbellin in the GDR in December 1981, just at the time of the East–West crisis over martial law in Poland, West German Chancellor Helmut Schmidt elicited many questions in other NATO countries by playing down the significance of these Polish developments. Instead, the two German leaders agreed on the first version of a frequently repeated pledge that war would never again emanate from German soil. In October 1982, after the defection of the Free Democrats from the Schmidt coalition, a coalition with the Christian Democrats brought a CDU/FDP government under Helmut Kohl to power. The Western allies were surprised and upset to see this government, dominated by a party whose majority had voted against the Brandt–Schmidt *Ostpolitik*, take up the relationship with the GDR and develop it still further.

In late November 1983, just after the West German Bundestag took its final vote to deploy the new American medium-range missiles and the Soviets walked out of the INF talks in Geneva, Honecker made explicit in a speech to the Central Committee of the Socialist Unity Party of the GDR his determination to maintain the inter-German relationship despite the missile deployment. Only a few months later, as mutual accusations of sabotaging the INF talks were flying between Washington and Moscow, and the Soviets were deploying new nuclear missiles in the GDR as an answer to deployment of American GLCMs and Pershing IIs, Honecker met

Jonathan Dean

Chancellor Kohl at Andropov's funeral in Moscow. The two leaders agreed that, in times of international tension, both German states had a specific responsibility to nurture peace and East–West understanding. Honecker expressed his dissatisfaction over forward deployment in the GDR of the new Soviet 'devil's machines'. A year later, in March 1985, Honecker and Chancellor Kohl met at the Chernenko funeral in Moscow, and again pledged to work together to assure that no war would ever again emanate from German soil.[5]

This repeated, striking evidence of the tenacity of the inter-German relationship in the face of pressures for maximum alliance solidarity with their respective great powers caused the allies of both German states to sense that something new was afoot in the inter-German relationship. Nervousness about change in the status of the two German states caused many to misinterpret these developments, despite vigorous denials by the leaders of both German states, as a slide toward neutralism and moves toward reunification. Provoked by considerations of this kind, in a January 1983 speech to the West German Bundestag President Mitterrand of France went so far as to support deployment – unusual for the head of a government not formally involved in NATO's 1979 two-track decision to deploy new American INF missiles and negotiate on reductions of Soviet INF systems.[6] In actuality, what these concerned observers were witnessing was the addition of a security dimension to the existing inter-German relationship.

Prior to the dramatic denouement of the INF deployment dispute in 1983–4, the inter-German dialogue was motivated mainly by the interest of the West German public and political leadership in improving the situation of their fellow Germans and in keeping the door open for ultimate resolution of the German unity issues; by East German interest in receiving the economic concessions the FRG was willing to make to achieve these objectives; and by the desire of the East German population to expand contacts with West Germans.

Although doubts have been expressed about the durability of these motives, especially as regards attitudes of younger Germans on both sides, it is probable that, even in the form just described, they were lasting on both sides. But after the INF talks broke down in 1983, the public in both German states saw the possible end of East–West arms control and the beginning of a new period of East–West tension which could culminate in conflict on German soil. These active apprehensions were diminished as the political leaders of both German states joined in an effort to protect the inter-German relationship with a pledge that not war, but peace, would come from German soil.

With these statements, very strongly supported by public opinion in both parts of Germany, the pursuit of national German interests in the inter-German relationship became transmuted and broadened to include the pursuit of peace: actions to strengthen the inter-German relationship became at the same time German contributions to peace in the world, a contribution which all Germans were obligated by their historical past to make and which because of their situation only they could make. As the 1986 annual report of the Federal German Ministry of Inner-German Relations puts it, 'Improved inner-German relations are at the same time a contribution to peace'.[7] Tapping the peace dimension broadened and deepened the sustaining motivation of the inter-German relationship on the part of the public and political leaders in both German states in a way which appears enduring.

There are sound reasons why the two German states would wish to have some cooperation on security and arms control issues. Both German states have a more direct, if not a stronger, interest than other European states in acting to prevent war. They share common knowledge of how Nazi Germany unleashed the Second World War and of the devastation and death which the war brought to Germans as well as to all of Europe. The bulk of foreign troops in the huge East–West military confrontation in Europe which emerged in the postwar period are deployed on their territories; their populations would suffer most directly in the event of conflict in Europe, when the armies of each would be called on to shoot down their countrymen. As the two German governments see it, they are firmly imbedded in their respective alliances to hold to a minimum their capacity to initiate conflict, but they would at the same time be primary victims of conventional, chemical or nuclear war. Both German states are non-nuclear states and neither has chemical weapons of its own. Both have a common interest in promoting good relations between Washington and Moscow, perhaps by helping to resolve some of the issues which divide the two great powers. In the light of the decline in American and Soviet power relative to Western, and even Eastern, Europe, they are less concerned than were Chancellor Adenauer and the former East German leader Walter Ulbricht over possible domination of Europe through excessively close cooperation between the two great powers. At the same time, they are more concerned than those two leaders about their degree of dependence on the two great powers.

In theory, this broad parallelism of security interests could be furthered by deliberately intensifying the scope of discussion of arms control and security issues between officials of the two governments. Without presuming a right to negotiate on behalf of their respective alliances, they could go beyond reporting new developments to each other to exploring alternative solutions to stalemated problems and to reporting back these possibilities to their respective alliances. They could identify aspects of the East–West military confrontation which are now being discussed by the alliances, such as a NATO–Warsaw Pact risk-reduction center, and do some preliminary exploratory work on them. Wilhelm Bruns of the Friedrich Ebert Foundation, which is supported by the opposition Social Democratic Party, has suggested that the two German states might consider negotiating mutual restrictions on their arms sales and transfers to Third-World countries; develop a common program to eliminate some continuing 'enemy-image' elements in their official, political statements, public media and schoolbooks; conduct an analysis of each other's armed forces and those of their allies to identify force elements considered especially threatening and report them to alliance members; to advance mutual understanding of each other's military budgets (still carefully held secret in the GDR), with an ultimate view of reducing them; and consider forming a joint security commission in which these and similar topics could be dealt with at a suitably high political level.[8]

Yet the drawbacks of such common endeavors are as clear as their potential gains. Questions have been raised in discussion of this topic in the FRG as to the validity of the GDR government as a partner in discussion of security issues. It is argued that Moscow would not provide the GDR much latitude of its own. The only subjects it would be permitted to raise would be those approved by Moscow, so that Moscow would, in effect, be obtaining a second, perhaps somewhat more effective, channel for its viewpoints. The charge is also made that inter-German agreement with the GDR does not bind the USSR, which has the advantage of sounding out the West Germans without commitment of its own. The counter-argument by German proponents of the security dialogue – most of them, like Dr Bruns, on the opposition political left – is that experience shows a developing if still limited degree of national independence in the positions of individual Warsaw Pact states; that it is in the Western interest to encourage this development; and that the GDR–USSR consultations which accompany inter-German contacts provide West Germany and its NATO allies with an additional voice in Moscow.

Both these criticisms and the responses to them appear to have some substance; which element is most important depends on the individual issue under discussion. Far less ambiguous, however, is the risk that intensified inter-German discussion of security issues could cause dangerous suspicions on the part of the alliance partners of the two German states – especially but not at all exclusively the great powers – that their respective German allies could be drifting away from alliance links or, less dramatically, might undermine alliance policies in their enthusiasm for reaching agreement with one another.

Among political parties in the FRG, the Christian Democrats have been the most cautious about expanding the inter-German relationship to include security issues and arms control. As the party of Chancellor Kohl, with primary responsibility for the policy of the West German government, the CDU/CSU is the West German party hitherto most interested in maintaining and protecting the relationship with the United States. Moreover the CDU/CSU is the most conservative of the German political parties in both domestic and East–West policy. There is an important faction in the party, sometimes called the '*Stahlhelm*' group (in analogy to a right-wing veterans' organization of the Weimar period), which remains highly skeptical of Chancellor Kohl's continuation of the Social Democratic policy of developing the relationship with the GDR and acts as a brake on government activities in this field.

Reflecting the concerns of conservative CDU/CSU members over the destructive potential of the inter-German relationship, at the end of 1985, Heinrich Windelen, then Federal Minister for Inner-German Relations in the Kohl government, devoted a thoughtful speech to defining the contributions which inter-German relations could make to peace in Europe. Attempting to discourage efforts by the Social Democrat opposition to expand the inter-German security dialogue, Windelen warned that any impression of special German deals or unpredictability of German policy would trigger suspicion in East and West. Therefore measures to preserve the peace through armed forces were exclusively a topic for internal decision in each alliance. The two German states could contribute to the peace process by promoting increased respect for human rights and by personal and cultural exchanges (and, by inference, by staying as far as possible from defense issues and arms control). Neither German state should attempt to test the loyalty of the other to its alliance. 'Elbow room for steady development of inner-German relations is only possible if the respective loyalty of both states to their respective alliances is exposed to no doubts whatever'. Such issues as corridors free of chemical or nuclear weapons should be handled between the superpowers whose business they are. The proper business of inter-German relations was to contribute to the solution of humanitarian problems.[9]

Because they conform to evident life-and-death interests of the two German governments, we should accept as genuine statements by the leaders of both that in pursuing the inter-German relationship they do not have the slightest desire or intention to leave their respective alliances. For Erich Honecker and his fellow leaders of the communist Socialist Unity Party, only continued Soviet political and military support protects their government from eventual dissolution. The GDR government is making some progress in eliciting positive loyalty from the East German population, yet the attractions of the West German system, reported by the millions of East and West Germans who visit the other German state (a total of perhaps ten million in 1987) and by television screens through most of the GDR, are simply too strong for the GDR system to become self-sustaining. Similarly, the stark rejection by FRG leaders of any role for West Germany as 'a wanderer between East and West' as fatal for the survival of the FRG, with its present standards of security, economic well-being and personal liberties, is also both rational and genuine.

There have in fact been several instances where either the GDR or the FRG have been held back from intensification of the inter-German discussion, either directly by their allies or out of consideration for the views of those allies. In 1981 West German Foreign Minister Hans-Dietrich Genscher made an effort to interest the GDR in a dialogue on military confidence-building measures. But this was still in the Brezhnev era, and the GDR, apparently apprehensive over the possibility of adverse Soviet reaction, failed to respond.[10] In preparation for the Honecker visit to Bonn, then planned for September 1984, GDR officials raised for possible discussion between Honecker and Kohl the renunciation of force and a corridor free of chemical weapons, but FRG officials rejected those points as too sensitive.[11]

The Honecker visit, planned for September 1984, was itself called off when sharp attacks in the Soviet press in July and August 1984 suggested that East German leaders were trading off political concessions in return for cash payments from the FRG (a not inaccurate characterization of those aspects of inter-German relations which concern improving conditions of life for the East German population). In actuality, the main reason why Honecker was discouraged in 1984 from making the first visit ever by a leader of the GDR to the Federal Republic was that an intensification of *détente* between the two German states would have been too inconsistent with the Soviet effort of the time to blame the United States and FRG as those chiefly responsible for the collapse of the INF talks. Similarly, when, during the 1984–6 Conference on Security and Confidence-Building Measures in Europe (CDE), West German Foreign Minister Genscher raised the idea of advancing the Western position by discussing a possible commitment on non-use of force with his East German colleagues, he was informed that the United States and other alliance partners considered it far preferable to focus all aspects of the Stockholm negotiations at the negotiation site.

On the credit side of the ledger, growing mutual understanding and acceptance of FRG and GDR officials engaged in multilateral negotiation on European security issues, while deliberately played down by both sides to avoid suspicion from their allies, has proved increasingly helpful in bringing about an outcome. At the outset of the Vienna MBFR talks in 1973, relations between representatives of the two German states were strained and distant. But, by the end of the 1970s, they had developed into a useful working relationship. The relationship had developed still further by the time the Stockholm Conference on Security- and Confidence-Building Measures in Europe was held between 1984 and 1986. To judge from comments by non-German negotiators on both sides and from the informal comments by both FRG and GDR negotiators, the working relationship was close and made a measurable contribution to the positive outcome of that conference.[12]

III   SOCIAL DEMOCRATIC INITIATIVES FOR INTER-GERMAN COOPERATION ON SECURITY AND ARMS CONTROL ISSUES

In 1984, the opposition West German Social Democratic Party (SPD) began a series of working consultations with the East German Socialist Unity Party (SED), motivated by their stinging election defeat by Chancellor Helmut Kohl in March 1983; the breakdown of the US–Soviet Geneva arms control talks in November 1983 over the INF issue; strong Social Democratic suspicions of the Reagan administration as excessively militant toward the Soviet Union; and the real commitment of the Social Democrats to an active relationship with the GDR. Surprised and disgruntled by the alacrity and energy with which the Kohl government had taken up the inter-German relationship pioneered by the Social Democrats under Chancellors Willy Brandt and Helmut Schmidt, the Social Democrats wanted to show they could go a step further than the latecomer Christian Democrats. The Social Democrats also wanted to exploit strong anti-chemical and anti-nuclear sentiment in the FRG. Finally, they were motivated by a desire to get the arms control process moving again after the INF breakdown.

In early 1982, the Independent Commission on Disarmament and Security Issues convened by Swedish Prime Minister Olaf Palme proposed a chemical-weapons-free zone in Europe, beginning with central Europe.[13] In the spring of 1984, Egon Bahr, the West German Social Democratic leader who had been the trail-blazing negotiator of Brandt's *Ostpolitik* and also the West German member of the Palme Commission, persuaded his colleagues in the SPD leadership to take initiative with Honecker to establish a common working group of senior members of the SPD and SED to work out the practical details of such a zone.

The Soviet Union was consulted by the SED and agreed to the project. The most prominent members of the working group were Bahr and Hermann Axen, a member of the SED Politburo. Up to January 1987, when General Secretary Gorbachev stated that the Soviet Union had ceased production of chemical weapons, the USSR had never publicly admitted possession of these weapons and it still maintains the claim that it has none stored outside the USSR. Consequently, from the Soviet viewpoint, the SPD/SED project would be aimed only at the United States which had known chemical weapons stocks in Federal Germany and which was then engaged in a difficult effort to gain Congressional agreement to produce new binary chemical weapons.

In June 1985, the SPD/SED working group reported that agreement had been reached on a framework agreement for eliminating chemical weapons from the territory of the FRG, the Benelux countries, the GDR, Poland and Czechoslovakia (the countries whose territories composed the reduction area used in the MBFR talks). The participating states would obligate themselves neither to produce nor obtain chemical weapons, nor to permit their stationing or transit in their territory. States possessing chemical weapons would commit themselves to respect the zone. The framework agreement contained provision for obligatory on-site inspection by an international commission which, however, lacked implementing measures.

The members of the SPD/SED working group made the tactical error of presenting their work as a quasi-official framework agreement drawn up in treaty language with a preamble and provision for duration and review of the agreement. This permitted the Kohl government with some justice to criticize the SPD for arrogating to itself negotiating authority which could be exercised only by the West German government. The West German government and other NATO governments also criticized the framework agreement as undermining official governmental efforts to agree on a world-wide prohibition of production or storage of chemical weapons in the United Nations Disarmament Conference in Geneva.

SPD spokesmen pointed out that those talks were not at the time making progress (much progress has been made since). They argued that the SPD motive was to take action in a European area where the great powers had failed to act and did not appear interested in acting; to give an impulse to the Geneva talks by suggesting a workable verification system; and that regional agreements were easier to achieve than world-wide ones and once achieved would stimulate a world-wide agreement while serving as a model for disengagement zones in Europe.[14]

The proposal had a mixed reception in West Germany and failed to elicit the hoped-for public support, perhaps because the US–Soviet nuclear arms talks in Geneva had been resumed in March 1985. None the less the draft may have played some role in bringing about the informal understanding between President Reagan and

Chancellor Kohl a year later in May 1986 that the aging stock of American chemical weapons stored in Germany would be removed by 1992, when binary weapons would be ready for storage in the United States and transport to Europe in the event of crisis.

The SPD/SED working group continued its work and in October 1986 reported an agreed proposal for a corridor in central Europe from which nuclear weapons would be removed. As with its proposal for a corridor free of chemical weapons, the working group was fleshing out a proposal made earlier by the Palme Commission. Its report, now called 'Principles for a Corridor Free of Nuclear Weapons in Central Europe' rather than a framework agreement, provides for a corridor of about 150 kilometers on the territory of the FRG on one side and of the GDR and Czechoslovakia on the other, for a total width of 300 kilometers, from which all capable delivery vehicles, including dual-capable vehicles which could deliver nuclear warheads, and all nuclear warheads, including nuclear mines, are to be removed. Verification would be by a permanent international commission which would carry out inspection within a period to be specified if grounds for previously submitted complaints had not been resolved.[15]

Social Democratic participants claimed that the bulk of Warsaw Pact tactical missiles and nuclear-capable aircraft were inside the Eastern portion of the suggested zone and would have to be moved back, while no NATO missiles and few nuclear-capable aircraft were in the zone. When Warsaw Pact missiles and aircraft were moved back, US nuclear missiles deployed in the FRG would be out of range of preemptive Warsaw Pact attack, and crisis stability would be enhanced. The authors insisted that the two German states will remain participants in their respective alliances for the foreseeable future and that a separate German–German arrangement would not meet German security interests, but that the SPD/SED initiative was intended to encourage the two German governments to develop similar ideas within their respective alliances.[16]

All NATO governments rejected this concept on the grounds that, if implemented, it would cause US nuclear weapons to be removed from FRG territory and make unworkable NATO's strategy of nuclear deterrence through flexible response. The proposal has received continuing vigorous support from the USSR and all other members of the Warsaw Pact. But once again, the SPD/SED initiative was overtaken by new developments – rapid movement to conclude the INF Treaty and the emergence of proposals to negotiate reduction or diminution of air-launched and tactical ground-launched nuclear weapons. The impact on West German and Western European opinion was again mixed, this time mainly because the INF talks were at last showing real promise as the result of important Soviet concessions to the agreed NATO position. The proposal did not save the Social Democrats from a second severe election drubbing at the hands of Chancellor Kohl and the Christian Democrats at the beginning of 1987.

A third product of SPD/SED discussion, a paper on 'Conflicting Ideologies and Common Security' developed between the Commission for Basic Values of the SPD and the Academy of Social Sciences attached to the SED, published in August 1987, is directed less to military security and arms control than to establishing a set of suggested rules for competition between pluralistic and Marxist–Leninist societies. Although the understanding is not enforceable in any way, nor does it have any mechanism to apply it inside the GDR, it does represent considerable success on the part of the SPD discussants in achieving the agreement of their SED colleagues to a joint document for publication in the GDR which contains a good description of Western pluralist society and which, if taken seriously, would legitimize internal criticism in the GDR.

The SPD/SED joint working group on arms control and security met again at the end of January 1987, again expressed its support for establishment of a nuclear-free corridor in Europe, and announced that it would next be submitting suggestions on how to establish mutual incapacity for offense under conditions of sufficient capacity for defense. Apparently the intention is to revive the chemical- and nuclear-free zone proposals and, by the end of 1988, to work out the details of a disengagement zone in central Europe from which all armored and air forces and missiles would be removed.

The original intention here appears to have been to move into a more general discussion and endorsement of the ideas on non-provocative defense or alternative defense developed by the anti-nuclear left in the FRG and endorsed in general terms by the Gorbachev leadership during 1987. But this project was preempted by a February 1988 joint declaration from a working group composed of the FRG Social Democrats and the communist Polish United Workers Party, also established in 1984. The SPD/PUWP declaration advocates eliminating offensive components of NATO and Warsaw Pact forces 'including the existing disparities and asymmetries', so that neither alliance is able to launch a surprise attack. This objective would be carried out through radical cuts in tactical nuclear weapons, tanks, combat aircraft, tactical-range rockets and missiles, artillery, and armed helicopters. The size and frequency of ground and air exercises is also to be restricted.

Apparently the Jaruzelski government insisted to Moscow that it should be given the lead in efforts of individual Warsaw Pact states to push force reductions and confidence-building measures and Moscow agreed, braking the GDR's desire to press forward in this area. If these indications are borne out, they evidence an increasingly frequent jockeying for position among individual East European members of the Warsaw Pact to obtain a name or identity of their own in East–West arms control, an indirect reflection of public interest in this subject in East European countries.

In addition to frictions with other members of the Warsaw Pact, the SPD/SED security dialogue has not been without its problems for the SED leadership. Old-line SED conservatives have apparently repeatedly asked what the SED will gain from making concessions on arms control to the out-of-power Social Democrats, who have no present prospect of leading the FRG government. None the less, after a slow start in the inter-German security dialogue before advent of the more flexible Gorbachev leadership in the Soviet Union, the GDR leadership seems attracted by the possibility of a role as favored emissary of the Warsaw Pact with the FRG government (as distinguished from the SPD), to which no other non-Soviet Warsaw Pact state can aspire and which so thoroughly meets the desires of the East German population.

Critics in the Kohl government continue to fault these collaborative activities of the Social Democrats with the SED as undermining Western negotiating positions as well as the official government-to-government discussion of security issues. At the same time, as intended by the Social Democrats, the stream of SPD/SED proposals has drawn attention to the relative absence of content in those official contacts and has brought pressure to bear on the West German government to do more.

Indeed the political dynamic involved is more important than the content of the SPD–SED discussions thus far on security and arms control issues. Often this dynamic begins with a Social Democratic initiative in the inter-German dialogue which elicits some attention and support from the West German public and especially from the media. The SPD initiative then frequently elicits some support from the small Free Democratic Party of Foreign Minister Genscher, which itself plays a vital role in the coalition with Chancellor Kohl's Christian Democrats. The Christian Democratic leadership has to balance its desire to appeal to West German public opinion with sensitivity to alliance suspicions of inter-German dealings on security issues and the pressures of its own conservative faction.

In a second part of the loop, the GDR, influenced both by the West German Social Democrats or on occasion by the USSR, attempts to press the West German government to move on the same project. (As we shall comment further below, pressures are also brought to bear on the GDR government by its own population as part of the process.)

Despite vigorous rejection by the Kohl government of SPD/SED projects like corridors free of chemical and nuclear weapons, in the long term these pressures push both German states in the direction of common positions. For example, on a non-defense issue, several years ago the SPD picked up and supported long-standing GDR efforts to establish contacts between the West German Bundestag and the East German Volkskammer. This project was long rejected by the Christian Democrats, who argued that meetings between the two chambers would degrade the status of the democratic Bundestag while unjustifiably raising the standing of the undemocratic Volkskammer. But in early 1988, Heiner Geissler, General Secretary of the Christian Democratic Union, indicated that the CDU might agree to an exchange of visits between Bundestag and Volkskammer.[17]

On a more defense-related subject, in the early 1980s, individuals and groups sympathetic to the SPD developed the ideas of non-provocative defense, already mentioned above. These concepts were vigorously rejected by the Kohl government and the CDU (and, at the time, by the GDR), but were picked up in Moscow by the new Gorbachev leadership and also by Free Democrats in the FRG. They were given honorable mention by West German President Richard von Weizsaecker, a prominent CDU liberal, during the 1987 Honecker visit to Bonn and have now been picked up by the GDR as the subject of the next SPD/SED working group. Despite its insistence that Warsaw Pact forces must relinquish their '*Invasionsfaehigkeit*', or offensive capability, in forthcoming NATO–Warsaw Pact force reduction talks, the Kohl government still rejects the non-provocative defense concept. But, if the established dynamics of the inter-German dialogue on security issues remain applicable, it seems clear that a good deal more will be heard on this subject, which is so directly related to the security interests of the two German states and their allies.[18]

In describing the dynamics of the expanding inter-German discussion of security and arms control, it is important to note that consultations with the GDR on security and arms control by NATO governments other than the FRG have been increasing, both from the viewpoint of high-level visits in both directions between the GDR and France, Italy and the United Kingdom, and as regards discussion of arms control by officials. US negotiators on START, INF, MBFR and the Stockholm confidence-building negotiations visit East Berlin for consultations as a matter of routine, with the support of the Federal Republic, to ensure that the GDR is not solely dependent on the USSR for information on these topics.

IV THE HONECKER VISIT TO BONN – DISCUSSION OF SECURITY AND ARMS CONTROL

Given its role as the scene of the main public demonstrations against deployment of American INF missiles, it was perhaps ironically appropriate that the FRG should also be the site of the last dramatic controversy of the INF negotiations, the controversy surrounding elimination of ground-based missiles between 1000- and 500-kilometer range and specifically of the Pershing 1A missiles held by the West German Luftwaffe.

Chancellor Kohl's abrupt decision of August 1987 to destroy the West German Pershing 1As on completion of destruction of US and Soviet INF missiles was taken without advance warning to other FRG coalition leaders or alliance members. But it not only opened the way to conclusion of the INF Treaty itself, but also to the long-postponed visit to Bonn of SED General Secretary Erich Honecker. (In addition to being General Secretary of the SED, Honecker is Chairman of the GDR's State Council, or cabinet.)

The Honecker visit to the Federal Republic took place on 7 to 11 September 1987. It was well prepared by both sides and included twelve hours of discussion between Honecker and Kohl. Its meticulously scheduled and smooth, unemotional course seems to have summarized and symbolized the current state of inter-German relations rather than to have produced dramatic new breakthroughs in any aspect of the relationship. The absence of drama was deliberate in both governments, highly conscious of the sense of risks which would arise in the non-German world from important new understandings during this first visit to Bonn of the political leader of East Germany. In fact it was quite clear that both governments, perhaps the FRG more than the GDR, decided not to use the Honecker visit for the purpose which it might have served – some progress on security and arms control issues – precisely because of international interest. Some observers have expressed disappointment at the lack of arms control content in the visit.[19]

In a meeting on 8 September 1987, during the Honecker visit, Foreign Ministers Genscher and Oskar Fischer spoke of combined initiatives of the two German states in the arms control area, but this point is not mentioned in the official communiqué of the visit and no initiatives were agreed on.[20] As indicated by the text of the joint communiqué issued at the end of the visit, Honecker did raise the proposal for chemical- and nuclear-free corridors in the two German states but received a negative response from his FRG interlocutors. Chancellor Kohl asked for the Berlin Wall to come down (as did President Reagan in a Berlin visit in July 1987), but Honecker apparently did not respond to this point in any way.

However, the joint communiqué shows that the visit did mark a fairly broad spectrum of agreement on arms control issues. The two leaders agreed that arms control negotiations should produce a stable balance of forces at the lowest possible level, accompanied by the elimination of disparities and effectively verifiable reductions, 'on the basis of equality and parity', an endorsement of this important principle. Both agreed to seek to exercise constructive influence on the bilateral negotiations between the United States and the Soviet Union, and endorsed the then-pending INF agreement. Chancellor Kohl argued for reduction of short-range nuclear missiles to low equal ceilings in conjunction with the establishment of conventional equilibrium and the global elimination of chemical weapons. (With his phrase 'in conjunction with', Chancellor Kohl seemed to be stretching views of other NATO countries that further nuclear reductions should follow after results from negotiations on conventional and chemical reductions have been achieved.) Both leaders expressed their support for the January 1985 formula negotiated between US Secretary of State George Shultz and then Soviet Foreign Minister Andrei Gromyko – that the US–Soviet arms control talks should be resumed on the basis of the objective of preventing an arms race in space and terminating it on earth (a formula no longer heard from the American administration) – which opened the way to resumption of the Geneva talks. Both German leaders backed a 50 per cent reduction of strategic nuclear weapons and 'expressed their support for the ABM Treaty' (again, a theme not often heard from US officials), as well as for the earliest possible agreement on an adequately verifiable nuclear test ban.

Kohl and Honecker also supported early agreement on a mandate for conventional disarmament in Europe from the Atlantic to the Urals, but presented 'divergent viewpoints on regional agreements in the fields of nuclear arms and chemical weapons'. The joint communiqué closes with a statement that consultations between the disarmament commissioners of the two governments have become a firm part of their political dialogue and welcomed the continuation of these consultations.[21]

The many common motivations of the two German governments to collaborate with one another on arms control have been described earlier. As the joint communiqué of the Honecker visit makes clear, the actual policies of the two governments on arms control overlap on an increasing number of issues: support for the September 1986 Stockholm Document on confidence-building measures and for the continuation of the Stockholm talks; for a comprehensive nuclear test ban; and for a parity outcome at reduced levels in the pending Atlantic-to-the-Urals force reduction talks. More recently, leaders of both German states have independently criticized the Reagan administration for holding back on the conclusion of a treaty prohibiting production and storage of chemical weapons. In fact, on the issues of maintaining the ABM Treaty, reduction of short-range nuclear missiles, and willingness in principle to reduce NATO as well as Warsaw Pact conventional armaments in the Atlantic-to-the-Urals talks, the West German position is somewhat closer to that of the GDR than it is to that of the United States, France or the United Kingdom.

In the aftermath of the Honecker visit, Josef Holik, the present West German commissioner for arms control, was received by GDR Foreign Minister Fischer (December 1987), a definite upgrading of the level of these discussions. Holik's usual discussion partner is now Deputy Foreign Minister Kurt Nier, which also marks an elevation of the level of these talks.

Together with Soviet leaders, Honecker is vigorously acting to maintain the post-INF appetite in broad segments of the West German public, from right to left, to get rid of all nuclear weapons. In a December 1987 letter to Chancellor Kohl following up his visit,

Honecker pushed for reduction of tactical nuclear weapons and replied to a question publicly raised by Kohl as to whether the GDR and its allies would forego modernizing some short-range weapons systems. Honecker said he was consulting on this with Warsaw Pact allies. The outcome would depend on the reciprocal willingness of the FRG to refrain from modernization. This might 'lead to the elimination of asymmetries in disarmament right up to further zero options'.[22] In his New Year's address to the GDR public, Honecker once again pressed for complete elimination of nuclear weapons of range under 500 kilometers.[23] Alfred Dregger, leader of the CDU Bundestag caucus, publicly welcomed Honecker's suggestion to reduce short-range nuclear missiles, although Dregger made clear that he had in mind reduction, not elimination, of the missiles on the basis of a minimum number agreed by NATO and negotiated by the superpowers, the position also taken by Chancellor Kohl.

Honecker again pressed for the idea of eliminating short-range nuclear missiles in a mid-January meeting with Johannes Rau, Minister President of North Rhine Westphalia and now a Deputy Chairman of the SPD. In this meeting, Honecker also supported the Soviet Union's theme on the building of 'a common European home'. The concept appears to be a Soviet effort to exploit West European interest in a closer relationship between Eastern and Western Europe. For Germans, this is a generalized, broader version of their view of a developing inter-German relationship.

V   COMING DECADES – HOW FAR WILL THE INTER-GERMAN SECURITY DIALOGUE DEVELOP?

Assuming the continuation of a cooperative Soviet arms control position for at least the next five years, that period may bring a US–Soviet agreement on strategic nuclear reductions, a further agreement of the 1986 Stockholm type on East–West confidence-building measures, initial results from the Atlantic-to-the-Urals force reduction talks, and a possible world-wide chemical weapons agreement. What effect would such developments have on the inter-German relationship and on the security policies of the two German states?

One clear result would be a further – and not unjustified – decline in the West German perception of the Soviet Union and its Warsaw

Pact allies as an immediate threat to the security of the FRG. A sharp decline in that perception has already taken place, as indicated by the statement of Franz Josef Strauss, the most conservative of West German political leaders, after returning from a talk with General Secretary Gorbachev at the end of 1987, that nothing was further from Gorbachev's mind than war.

Hopes on the European left – and fears among Western conservatives – of some Soviet proposal for the reunification of Germany under conditions of military neutrality and withdrawal from military alliances have increased as Europeans have observed the flexibility of the Gorbachev leadership in arms control and in domestic Soviet affairs. This possibility does not impress seasoned FRG political leaders like Chancellor Kohl, who repeatedly declares, as he did in his latest 'State of the Nation Report' on the status of inter-German relations, already referred to here, that German reunification 'is not now on the agenda of world history'. This statement closely reflects the attitude of an overwhelming majority in the West German public. *The Economist* of 6 June 1987 cites a recent Emnid poll in West Germany: 81 per cent of the respondents said they wanted German reunification, but only 8 per cent considered it possible in the next decade.

But in the context of expanding East–West arms control agreements, more than the customary third of the West German public might find a neutrality guaranteed by the United States and by a visibly more cooperative Soviet Union a not-impossible price to pay for genuine self-determination for the East German population. Bundestag member Eduard Lintner, a Bavarian conservative who chairs the Bundestag committee on inter-German relations, states that he has opinion polls which show that 82 per cent of West Germans would accept reunification with neutrality.[24]

But polls of this kind do not provide an accurate assessment of West German opinion because they posit improbable conditions for changes in the status of Germany. Nearly all NATO governments, including that of the United States, would consider NATO without the FRG to be unworkable and German unity under conditions of neutrality a dangerous risk. They would not back such a concept. As regards the Soviet view, General Secretary Gorbachev told West German President Weizsaecker during the latter's July 1987 visit to Moscow that the German Question was no longer open. If 'someone' none the less wanted to go another way and seek to reverse this fact, he said, there would be 'serious consequences'.[25]

Even in the situation of significant further improvement in East–West relations posited for the present enquiry, it remains almost inconceivable that the Soviet Union would allow the withdrawal of the GDR from the Warsaw Pact. And, without the most explicit guarantees from the United States and other major NATO governments for the security of this new Germany, assurances which would not be forthcoming, most Germans would not have the slightest interest in a neutrality solution. Even if West Germans should think the East–West situation so drastically improved as to take some risks in the security field, they show no readiness whatever to hazard their present economic well-being and political freedoms unless the Soviet Union were prepared to assure the population of East Germany political and economic freedoms equal to those enjoyed by the FRG – in other words, to accept the elimination of Marxism–Leninism from the GDR, as well as to permit the GDR to withdraw from the Warsaw Pact. Any real possibility of such an outcome will have to await the advent of a non-communist Gorbachev. Before sacrifices like these would be acceptable to it, the Soviet system would have to have evolved to a point where it had itself relinquished its Marxist–Leninist system.

VI OTHER RISKS OF THE INTER-GERMAN DIALOGUE

There will be no German reunification while the Soviet system remains intact, and both German states will remain in their respective alliances even under conditions of improved East–West relations. But other developments are possible in the conditions under examination here.

One distant but more than theoretical possibility is that, under the impact of improving East–West relations and under continuing pressure from the West German government, political parties and its own population, the East German government may gradually lose control over developments and over its population. For Honecker and his successors, communism and capitalism will remain as fire and water; in 1987 and early 1988, they showed their distrust of *glasnost* and of economic restructuring by cracking down on dissenters and the Lutheran church in the GDR and by refusing to publish in full some of Gorbachev's speeches. Yet GDR leaders may have an increasingly difficult time with the hitherto highly disciplined East German population when that population is encouraged from both sides – from the West and from the East – to urge more flexibility and openness on the GDR government. This may particularly be so if the GDR population comes to think, in part because of Soviet willingness to cut Soviet forces in the GDR, that it can afford to take the initiative in pressing for more concessions. The relevance of these comments is clear: widespread public unrest in East Germany and inability of the GDR government to control it are among the increasingly limited circumstances which could ignite a NATO–Warsaw Pact conflict.

The West German role is already of cardinal importance in coping constructively with this possibility. With their large payments to East Germany for road, rail, telephone and postal charges, with their actions opening the way for millions of personal visits in each direction and for millions of parcels and hard currency remittances to East Germany, West German policy toward the GDR is now making a signal contribution to Western security by decreasing public dissatisfaction while improving the situation of the average East German.

The capacity of the FRG to continue this valuable role depends on the understanding or, at the least, skeptical toleration of its allies. Yet all aspects of the German–German relationship are viewed with suspicion by those in the West who have an exaggerated assessment of the possibility of a genuine FRG drift away from NATO. In December 1986, statements of then Assistant Secretary of Defense Richard Perle, that Bonn should reduce subsidies to East Germany which were diminishing needed FRG expenditures for defense,[26] illustrated the widespread ignorance of the significance of West German expenditure for Western security, or reflected a view that a more militant FRG attitude combined with higher risks of conflict were preferable to the present trend. It would be contrary to Western interests if the FRG's timid and limited security dialogue with the GDR were to elicit so much suspicion from its allies as to impede the operation of these more long-standing 'humanitarian' aspects of the relationship.

The inter-German dialogue on security issues has thus far produced only modest results, results that in the next decade are not likely to represent more than an increment to the existing East–West discussion of arms control. However it is highly likely that, despite obstacles, the dialogue will not only continue but will both broaden and intensify.

The interest of the two German states in a continuing build-down of the East–West military confrontation in Europe seems stronger and more persistent than that of any of the other participants in the confrontation. By intensive exploration and discussion of the details of confrontation, the two German states may resolve old deadlocks and turn up new approaches. Since neither Moscow nor Washington has a monopoly on ingenuity and common sense, benefits for both alliances could arise from intensification of the inter-German dialogue. The allies of the Federal Republic thus have a choice between continuing to indulge their suspicions about the inter-German dialogue on security and arms control issues at some cost in relations with the Federal Germans, inhibiting but not blocking the dialogue, or benefiting from that dialogue.

8 The View from Moscow
F. Stephen Larrabee

For the Soviet Union, the German Question – the question of Germany's place and role in Europe – has been the paramount problem of European politics in the postwar period. Soviet concerns are understandable, given the geography and history of the USSR. An unconstrained and resurgent Germany started two world wars. Having fought a costly and destructive war which it did not start, the Soviet Union, one of the four major powers with responsibility for the fate of postwar Germany, insisted at the close of the Second World War – and continues to insist today – that resolution of the German Problem must take into consideration Soviet security interests. While the modalities of achieving its objectives have to some extent changed over time, one goal has remained constant: to prevent the resurgence of a strong united Germany not under Soviet influence. Today, as in the past, this is the overriding objective of Moscow's postwar policy in Europe.

While the Soviet Union did not consciously seek the current division of Germany, the division none the less serves Soviet interests. Not only does it prevent the emergence of a strong, unified German state, which would almost certainly dominate Europe, but it imposes major constraints on the freedom of maneuver of *both* German states. In addition, the GDR acts as an important glacis for Soviet military operations in Europe should war ever break out. It is also the linchpin of the Soviet security system in Eastern Europe. Among Moscow's East European allies it has the most modern and reliable armed forces in the Warsaw Pact, and spends the highest percentage of its GNP on defense (nearly 8 per cent). Economically, it is the Soviet Union's most important trading partner in the bloc and a key source of high technology. Thus the Soviet Union has a strong interest in maintaining the current territorial *status quo*, and has traditionally been suspicious of any effort to call this *status quo* into question. While not above using the desire of the two German states for greater cooperation for its own purposes, the USSR has been careful to ensure that this interaction corresponds to Soviet security interests and remains within clearly defined parameters.

At the same time the Federal Republic has been the centerpiece of Soviet policy toward Western Europe. Bonn is the strongest economic power in Europe; it has the largest army in NATO and is the United States's most important ally. In short, the Federal Republic is the linchpin of the Western alliance. Any weakening of West Germany's ties to NATO and the United States would automatically weaken the cohesion of the alliance itself. Hence the Federal Republic has been the focal point of Moscow's *Westpolitik* in Europe.

This does not mean, as some authors have suggested, that the primary Soviet goal is to eliminate the United States from Europe or to promote Bonn's withdrawal from NATO.[1] Rather, Moscow's chief goal is to promote Bonn's independence from Washington and to encourage it to pursue a more autonomous policy, one less subservient to Washington and more consistent with Soviet interests. Indeed, it is unlikely that Moscow would want to see a total withdrawal of the United States from Europe or Bonn's withdrawal from NATO. The US presence and NATO act as important constraints on Bonn's freedom of maneuver. A total withdrawal of the United States would not only eliminate these constraints but open up new pressures on the Soviet Union to withdraw its forces from the GDR and Eastern Europe generally. It is in part for this reason that the Soviet Union has regarded the recent strengthening of Franco-German military cooperation with concern and that it continues to reassert its Four-Power rights.

Yet if Soviet policy has been well served by Germany's division, it is not because the Soviet Union initially sought it. On the contrary, as noted earlier, the division of Germany occurred more by default – as a result of the breakdown of Four-Power cooperation at the end of the Second World War – than by conscious design. Indeed, for several years after the Second World War, the Soviet Union insisted on treating Germany as a unified entity, despite the breakdown in allied cooperation and the growing *de facto* division. And, as one of the four victorious powers, it continues to insist on its responsibility for 'Germany as a whole', pending a final peace treaty.

This is not to imply, however, that Soviet policy toward the German Question has been completely static. On the contrary, it has undergone a number of distinct shifts. These have largely coincided with the advent to power of different Soviet leaders. It may be useful to briefly review these shifts as a background to more recent developments under Mikhail Gorbachev.

I   STALIN'S *DEUTSCHLANDPOLITIK*

Contrary to popular belief, Joseph Stalin neither sought the division of Germany nor the full communization of it – though he probably never gave up hope for the latter. Rather, he appears to have pursued a policy of 'watchful waiting', which allowed him to keep his options open and exploit various opportunities that arose during the course of occupation. His policy evolved incrementally, if inconsistently, in response to events. Indeed, his policy was contradictory. At times he seems to have entertained the possibility of the communization of all of Germany, whereas at other moments he seems to have been ready to settle for half a loaf.

Stalin, however, never seems to have fully resigned himself to the division of Germany. One small piece of evidence is contained in his book *Economic Problems of Socialism in the USSR*, which was published shortly before his death.[2] In the book he predicted that Germany and Japan would rise again and throw off American tutelage. From the context of Stalin's remarks it is clear that Germany is a capitalist country belonging to the Western camp. Nowhere is there mention of the GDR. This suggests that, even in 1952, he expected that Germany would be reunited at some point.

Stalin's controversial notes to the Western allies in the spring of 1952, in which he suggested that the Soviet Union might be willing to accept a neutral, independent and reunified Germany, should be seen against this background. A detailed discussion of this fascinating chapter in Soviet postwar diplomacy, which has provoked much heated debate between those who see the notes as a 'missed opportunity' and those who regard them as a propaganda ploy designed to block the FRG's entry into the European Defense Community (EDC), is beyond the scope of this chapter.[3] Both views, however, seem oversimplified. Clearly the notes were designed to prevent or at least delay Bonn's entry into the EDC. But it is also conceivable that Stalin would have been willing to strike a bargain had he found some interest on the part of the Western allies, and had he been able to ensure a strong Soviet veto right over developments in a weak, reunified Germany.

Clearly, only a very urgent danger would have induced Stalin to entertain ideas of a reunified Germany. But the prospect of a million West German soldiers armed in a strong Western alliance – at a time when the Soviet Union had not fully recovered from the ravages of war and when its control in Eastern Europe, and particularly the GDR, was by no means solidified – might have been enough to counsel such a step. As the West German historian Waldemar Besson has noted, it has frequently been underestimated 'what it must have meant psychologically when seven years after the end of the war German soldiers once again appeared on European soil and this time on the side of the powerful adversary, the United States'.[4]

From Stalin's viewpoint, a 'Rapallo' policy at this point would have offered a number of advantages. First, it would have prevented the unification of Europe under US leadership. It was not just the strengthening of the Western half of Germany that Stalin wished to avoid but the consolidation of Europe as a whole. By 1952, however, it was clear that the two were closely linked and that to prevent Western integration Stalin had to prevent Germany from becoming the Western linchpin. Second, a neutral Germany could form part of a belt of neutral states which could act as a 'cordon Stalinaire' between the Soviet sphere of influence and the West. Third, a Rapallo policy offered the possibility that, once the linchpin of European unity had been removed, the United States might eventually be tempted to withdraw its troops from Europe, with the result that a weak, neutral Germany would become increasingly open to Soviet pressure and influence and perhaps even to intimidation.

Whatever Stalin's true intentions were will never be known, since the allies never sought to follow up his offer. The proposals, moreover, were made too late. Had Stalin made the proposals in 1947 – before the Cold War had intensified and Western perceptions of the Soviet threat had solidified, they undoubtedly would have fallen on fertile soil. By the time of the Soviet diplomatic offensive in the spring of 1952, however, plans for West Germany's rearmament had gained too much momentum to be halted. Too much effort had been invested in the plans to risk the possibility of their collapse while the West engaged in long, weary and frustrating negotiations to probe the ambiguities contained in the Soviet proposals.

II SHIFT TO A TWO-STATE POLICY[5]

Exactly when the Soviet Union abandoned the idea of reunification as a realistic goal of policy is difficult to say. Clearly, however, the

June 1953 uprising in East Berlin was an important watershed. The revolt significantly increased the Soviet stake in the GDR. Having decided to pay the price of intervention, the Soviet leadership was forced to ride out the storm. Thereafter, the Soviet commitment to the GDR – and to Walter Ulbricht personally – increased, and Soviet interest in reunification declined accordingly.

With the entrance of the FRG into NATO in May 1955, Soviet support for reunification was for all practical purposes dead, if not buried. While lip service continued to be paid to it in Soviet statements for some years to come, from that point on Moscow openly shifted to a two-state policy, and its diplomacy followed a two-track course aimed at (1) stabilizing the GDR and integrating it more tightly into the bloc and (2) securing Western, particularly West German, recognition of the postwar *status quo*.

Indeed, the continuity of Soviet objectives in Europe after 1955 is striking. For the next fifteen years, the main goal of the USSR's policy *vis-à-vis* the Federal Republic remained constant: to obtain Bonn's acceptance of the postwar borders and the permanent division of Germany. Khrushchev sought to do this through a policy of 'strategic bluffing' designed to exploit advances in Soviet missile and space technology in order to force a settlement of the German Question. This, in essence, was the meaning of the series of crises over Berlin between 1958 and 1962. The allies called his bluff, however, and he was forced to back down.

After the Cuban missile crisis in 1962 Khrushchev shifted gears and sought to achieve through courtship what he had failed to obtain through intimidation. Moreover, having been rebuffed by the allies he sought to open direct bilateral contacts with Bonn. His ouster in October 1964 on the eve of his planned visit to West Germany ended one of the most intriguing chapters in Soviet–West German relations. What Khrushchev had in mind we will probably never know, but there is little reason to think that the visit would have been a major breakthrough. Khrushchev's main goal, then as before, was to obtain recognition of the postwar territorial *status quo*. This neither the allies nor West Germany at this point were willing to entertain.

The continuity of objectives extended under Brezhnev. What changed after Khrushchev's removal in October 1964 was not the goals but the style and methods of Soviet policy, and above all the context in which the new Soviet leadership sought to achieve a relatively constant set of objectives. Whereas Khrushchev had tried

– and failed – to obtain Bonn's acceptance of the postwar territorial *status quo* by threats and missile diplomacy, his successors sought to exploit West European desires for both change and the breakdown of rigid Cold War boundaries in the mid-1960s in order to solve the German Problem within the wider framework of a campaign for European security.

At the time the campaign was launched at the Bucharest meeting of the Warsaw Pact in July 1966, its main aim was largely offensive: to mobilize West European public opinion against Bonn in order to force it to revise its policy and accept the territorial *status quo*. By the time of the Warsaw Pact conference in Karlovy Vary in April 1967, however, the main goals of Soviet policy, and its campaign for European security in particular, had clearly become defensive: to blunt the impact of Bonn's new *Ostpolitik* and halt the erosion of Moscow's own authority in Eastern Europe.

An important symbiotic relationship existed between the developing state of crisis in Eastern Europe in the late 1960s and the evolution of Bonn's *Ostpolitik*. While the *Ostpolitik* did not cause the ferment in Eastern Europe, which reached a climax in 1968, the changes in Bonn's policy tended to reduce the fear of West Germany on the part of its East European neighbors – a fear which had traditionally been one of the major sources of cohesion in Eastern Europe – and thus accelerated polycentrist tendencies in the area. The 1968 Prague Spring in particular reduced Moscow's room for maneuver and caused Soviet policy toward Bonn to harden. In the face of the growing instability in Eastern Europe, the German 'threat' remained one of the few cards which Moscow could play to bolster its crumbling position there. After January 1968, therefore, whatever hopes Moscow may have had of inducing Bonn to change the basic tenets of its policy were largely subordinated to an all-out campaign to discredit the *Ostpolitik* and isolate the Federal Republic.

The August 1968 Soviet invasion of Czechoslovakia marked an important turning-point in Soviet policy in Europe and toward the FRG in particular. Paradoxically, while the invasion was a reflection of the weakness of the Soviet position in Eastern Europe and a response to forces which Bonn's *Ostpolitik* had encouraged, it helped to create the very conditions of stability which allowed Moscow gradually to abandon the German bogey image and move toward a *rapprochement* with Bonn. The invasion not only halted efforts to implement change in Czechoslovakia but reversed the whole trend toward dissolution of Soviet control which had been gathering momentum during the previous two years.

At the same time the invasion underscored for Moscow the importance of achieving a settlement with the West which would recognize the legitimacy of Soviet interests in Eastern Europe, and thus reduce the prospect of another Czechoslovakia-type movement. As long as the West would not accept the postwar *status quo*, a threat to Soviet hegemony, however latent, still existed. This consideration highlighted Moscow's need to intensify efforts to achieve some sort of a settlement with Bonn. It had become increasingly clear that the Federal Republic held the keys to solving the outstanding issues of European politics – the recognition of the Oder–Niesse line and the acceptance of the GDR. Moreover, as the Federal Republic began to undertake *détente* initiatives of its own, Moscow had difficulty portraying Bonn as the seat of 'revanchism' and 'militarism'.

III *RAPPROCHEMENT* AND RECONCILIATION

In the wake of the invasion of Czechoslovakia, Soviet policy toward Bonn underwent a gradual shift, which culminated in the signing of the Bonn–Moscow Treaty in August 1970 and its ratification in May 1972. This shift began to manifest itself much earlier than is generally thought – well *before* the assumption of power by the coalition of Social Democrats and Free Democrats in the autumn of 1969 – and was influenced by a number of factors.[6] These included (1) De Gaulle's fall in early 1969 and the subsequent shift in French policy toward Atlanticism, which removed the main *raison d'être* for centering Soviet *détente* efforts on Franco-Soviet *rapprochement*; (2) the emergence of China from its isolation after the Cultural Revolution, and the beginnings of a thaw in US–PRC relations, which threatened to reduce Moscow's room for maneuver; (3) growing Soviet economic problems, which gave Moscow a new sense of urgency about expanding ties with the industrially advanced countries of the West; (4) a desire to improve relations with the United States, and particularly to stabilize the arms race; and (5) the election of the Brandt/Scheel 'small coalition' in October 1969, and the new government's willingness to sign the Non-Proliferation Treaty and abandon its claim to speak for all Germans (*Alleinvertretungsanspruch*). This was signalled by Willy Brandt in his inaugural address, when he acknowledged the existence of 'two German states in one German nation'.[7]

The change in Soviet policy toward the FRG was part of a larger Soviet reassessment of policy toward the West as a whole, particularly the United States. Moscow's interest in improving relations with the United States – particularly its desire to proceed with negotiations on a strategic arms limitation (SALT) agreement – forced Moscow to view its actions elsewhere with an eye to the impact they would have on relations with the United States, and thereby played a crucial role in influencing the shift in Soviet policy toward the Federal Republic. There was, in effect, an *implicit* linkage between European *détente* and superpower *détente*, especially SALT, and this linkage accentuated the Soviet leadership's desire to seek the resolution of the German problem, the main source of East–West tension.

The signing of the Renunciation of Force Agreement between Bonn and Moscow in August 1970 and its ratification by the West German Bundestag in May 1972 laid the basis for normalization of relations between the FRG and the USSR. In the treaty, both parties agreed to regard the borders in Europe as 'inviolable' and to settle all disputes by peaceful means.[8] From the Soviet point of view, its significance lay in the fact that it signalled Bonn's official acceptance of the postwar territorial *status quo*. Moscow, as noted earlier, had regarded this as the *sine qua non* for the stabilization of the situation in Eastern Europe.

The importance of the Bonn–Moscow treaty extended beyond its bilateral framework, however. Ratification of the treaty acted as a 'can opener' – to use Theo Sommer's apt characterization[9] – for the whole process of East–West *détente*. It cleared the way for the implementation of the Four-Power Agreement on Berlin, convocation of a Conference on Security and Cooperation in Europe, and the signing of the Basic Treaty between the GDR and the FRG.

IV DISAPPOINTMENT AND DISCORD

The ratification of the Bonn–Moscow Treaty established the basis for the normalization of relations and served to remove the German problem from the East–West agenda – at least formally. Moscow's hopes for a significant revitalization of Soviet–West German relations, however, were never fully realized. On the economic side, trade increased significantly, but it never reached the volume that Moscow initially had anticipated.[10] Moreover, after a steady increase over the past decade, it has recently witnessed a decline.

On the political side too, Moscow's early hopes have not been fulfilled. During the 1970s the Federal Republic occupied pride of place in the Soviet Union's *Westpolitik*; it was Moscow's most important economic and political partner in Western Europe. The Eastern treaties removed the most important obstacles to an expansion of relations, and for several years after the ratification of the treaties Soviet–West German relations witnessed a gradual improvement.

Toward the late 1970s, however, bilateral relations began to deteriorate. Several factors contributed to this deterioration. One was a change of leadership in the Federal Republic. The first change came in 1974 with the resignation of Willy Brandt as Chancellor and his replacement by Helmut Schmidt. Schmidt, while a Social Democrat, was a confirmed Atlanticist and never shared Brandt's passion for *Ostpolitik*. While he continued the basic outlines of Brandt's policy toward the East, he directed his major concerns toward trying to revitalize the Western alliance and advising the Americans how it should be run. As a consequence, *Ostpolitik* received a somewhat lower priority.

The collapse of the SPD–FDP coalition in 1982 and its replacement by a CDU/CSU–FDP coalition headed by Chancellor Helmut Kohl reinforced the general stagnation in relations. Kohl came to power determined to avoid the growing friction with the United States that had characterized Schmidt's last years in office and to reestablish a more solid partnership with Washington. His greater willingness to follow the American lead – especially on security issues – as well as his stronger emphasis on the 'openness' of the German Question, accentuated Soviet concerns about the general directions of West German policy and contributed to a further cooling of relations.

A second important factor contributing to the deterioration of relations between Bonn and Moscow was the lack of a strong leader in the Kremlin. After 1978 Brezhnev's health declined precipitously, and he was no longer able to give Soviet policy the strong direction which he had provided in the early 1970s. Andropov had less than six months at the helm before he became sick. He died six months later. During much of this period the Soviet leadership was preoccupied with the succession issue and Soviet foreign policy was largely characterized by vacillation and drift.

Andropov's death in February 1984 exacerbated this sense of

drift. His replacement, Konstantin Chernenko, had little experience in foreign affairs and largely deferred on foreign policy matters to Foreign Minister Andrei Gromyko. During this period Gromyko exerted a virtual monopoly over foreign affairs, and Soviet policy toward the West was characterized by increasing rigidity and defensiveness. This is particularly true in regard to relations with Bonn, which were viewed mainly through the larger prism of Moscow's competition with the United States. Moreover, Gromyko remained highly suspicious of the long-term implications of an intensification of the German–German dialogue and tried as much as possible to keep it under tight control.

A third important factor contributing to the erosion of Soviet–West German accord was the general deterioration of East–West relations after 1979. Here the INF controversy played a particularly important role. The controversy underscored the vulnerability of the Federal Republic as well as the changing psychological–political climate within the country. Bonn was the key to the implementation of the deployment decision. If the Federal Republic could have been persuaded to reject deployment – either through intimidation or enticement – then it would have been unlikely that other countries in the alliance would have gone forward with the decision. Hence Soviet policy during this period focused strongly on the Federal Republic, which was alternatively wooed and warned of the dire consequences to follow any deployment of US missiles.[11]

At the same time domestic developments in the FRG, particularly the growth of the peace movement and the erosion of the defense consensus after 1979, encouraged Moscow to believe, erroneously, that it could prevent deployment without making major concessions. In so doing, it overestimated, not for the first time, the strength of 'pressure from below' and underestimated the ability of the Western alliance to stand firm despite obvious divergences – a fact which Gorbachev's later embrace of the 'zero option' implicitly acknowledged.

The Soviet walk-out from the INF talks in November 1983 and Bonn's willingness to proceed with deployment despite Soviet threats underscored the failure of the 'Gromyko line'.[12] The confrontational policy pursued by the Soviet foreign minister neither prevented deployment nor split the NATO alliance, and left the Soviet Union with little option but to return to a confrontationalist policy. At the same time, it accentuated new fissures within the Warsaw Pact and led to growing friction between the USSR and several of its East

European allies, especially Hungary and the GDR, who both – for somewhat different reasons – resisted the Soviet effort to return to a policy of confrontation.[13] Indeed, for a period in 1984 a tacit alliance between Budapest and East Berlin seemed to be developing in an effort to convince Moscow to return to a more cooperative policy.

Perhaps most importantly, the policy of confrontation created the most serious strains in Soviet–East German relations in over a decade.[14] While Honecker on several occasions had warned that German–German relations 'could not flourish in the shadow of US missiles', after the collapse of the INF talks he embarked upon a course consciously designed to insulate German–German *détente* from the deterioration of overall East–West relations. In a key speech that set the outlines for East German policy over the ensuing months, Honecker noted at the 7th SED plenum in November 1983 that, while the start of deployment had altered the basis of inter-German relations, the prime task now was 'to limit the damage' resulting from this development.[15] Rather than deteriorating, as had been predicted, FRG–GDR relations actually improved. This growing *rapprochement* ran counter to the general trend in Soviet policy and created a growing disharmony between Moscow and Berlin.

After the collapse of the INF talks Soviet policy toward the Federal Republic shifted visibly. This shift did not manifest itself immediately, but by the time of Foreign Minister Hans-Dietrich Genscher's visit to Moscow in May 1984 the frost was clearly off the pumpkin. Soon thereafter Moscow began to initiate a campaign against West German 'revanchism' and 'neo-nazism' – charges that had largely disappeared from the Soviet press since the early 1970s.[16] The revival of the revanchism campaign was a clear signal that Soviet policy toward Bonn had shifted and that Bonn was being placed in the docks of the accused for having followed through with deployment.

The campaign, however, was as much aimed at East Berlin as at Bonn. It was designed to signal Moscow's displeasure at Honecker's continued pursuit of closer ties with Bonn, which ran contrary to Moscow's larger interests of forcing a chill in East–West relations. Initially Honecker resisted the mounting Soviet pressure, in part because it was unclear whether the attacks represented the view of the top Soviet leadership or simply Gromyko and the Foreign Ministry. By the end of the summer, however, Moscow's displeasure with the German–German *détente* was unmistakable, and Honecker felt compelled to postpone the visit. It would be wrong, however, to see his decision solely as a response to pressure from Moscow. Internal factors also played a role, particularly Honecker's desire to initiate an arms control dialogue with Bonn. Once it became clear that these goals were unlikely to be met, Honecker reluctantly decided to postpone the visit.

The discord between the GDR and the Soviet Union over the Honecker visit in the summer of 1984 should not, however, be exaggerated. The dispute was over means, not ends. It in no way implied that the GDR was about to become a second Rumania or break loose from the Warsaw Pact. Nevertheless, it does highlight the way the GDR's stake in *détente* with the Federal Republic has grown over the last decade, and the dilemmas this poses for Moscow's ability to manage its relations with Bonn.

V SOVIET POLICY UNDER GORBACHEV

Under Gorbachev, Soviet policy toward the Federal Republic has again visibly shifted. Gorbachev has abandoned the effort to isolate the Federal Republic initiated by Gromyko and embarked upon an effort to develop more cordial and cooperative relations. This change should be seen as part of a general shift in Soviet policy toward the West which began to manifest itself in the fall of 1985, and to some extent was related to internal factors, especially the removal of Gromyko as Foreign Minister and a general restructuring of the Foreign Ministry and International Department of the Central Committee, which allowed Gorbachev to put his personal stamp on foreign policy.[17]

The shift in policy toward Bonn did not manifest itself immediately. During the first year and a half after Gorbachev's assumption of power, Bonn continued to be given the cold shoulder and was the subject of constant vituperation for its 'revanchist' policy.[18] While Gorbachev made highly visible visits to Paris and London in 1985 and 1986, Bonn was consciously excluded from Moscow's *détente* efforts. Indeed Gorbachev's policy during this period bears similarities with Soviet *Westpolitik* in the late 1960s, when Moscow sought to make Paris the centerpiece of its *détente* efforts while at the same time trying to isolate Bonn.

Part of the reason for this may simply have been the Soviet

Union's mistaken assessment of the prospects for exploiting Franco-Soviet cooperation and especially Mitterrand's opposition to SDI, which encouraged Gorbachev to think that Moscow could revive the 'special relationship' with France that had flourished under De Gaulle. In addition, Kohl's more openly pro-American policy during this period, particularly his qualified support for SDI as well as his increased emphasis on the 'openness' of the German Question, irritated the Kremlin and made it less inclined to court Bonn. Internal factors also may have played a role. In the early months after Gorbachev took over, Gromyko was still in charge of foreign policy on a day-to-day basis and he had a strong vested stake in continuing the hard line toward Bonn, of which he was the chief architect. It was not until after Gromyko's removal in July 1985 – and really not until the 27th Party Congress in February 1986 – that Gorbachev was able to gain full control of the foreign policy apparatus and put his own view in place.

The first tentative signs of a reassessment began to appear in early 1986, about the time of the 27th Party Congress, with the gradual abatement of the revanchism campaign. These signs became more distinct during Foreign Minister Genscher's visit to Moscow in July 1986. Genscher and his entourage were given extremely cordial treatment and during his discussions with Genscher Gorbachev offered to 'open a new page in relations'. In addition, a long-delayed framework agreement on scientific and technological cooperation was signed and three other agreements on the peaceful uses of nuclear energy, agricultural research and health care were initiated.

The Genscher visit was an important sign that Soviet attitudes were beginning to shift. It did not, however, lead to an immediate intensification of relations. Relations went into a temporary tail-spin in the fall as a result of Chancellor Kohl's tactless comparison of Gorbachev to Nazi Propaganda Minister Josef Goebbels. The barrage of recrimination that followed suggests that support for a shift in policy was far from uniform, and that Moscow had yet to make up its mind about the long-term direction of policy toward the Federal Republic.

However the onslaught against Bonn that followed Kohl's remarks may also have been motivated by tactical considerations, particularly the approach of the national elections in January 1987. For the previous several years the Soviet Union had been consciously cultivating closer ties with the SPD, whose policy since 1983 had progressively shifted to the left, particularly on security issues.[19]

Thus Moscow may have wanted to avoid any actions that would have given a boost to the CDU's political fortunes on the eve of the election. However, once the elections – which returned the CDU to power – made clear that the Soviet Union would be confronted with a conservative government in Bonn for the next few years, Moscow quickly sought to pick up the reins of *détente* left dangling in the months prior to the election.

Since the 1987 elections relations have witnessed a significant improvement. The tone of Soviet commentaries has become more positive, and the number and frequency of high-level visits have increased markedly. The list of prominent West German politicians has included SPD leaders Johannes Rau and Hans-Jochen Vogel, Federal President Richard von Weizsaecker, Foreign Minister Genscher, and Bavarian Prime Minister Franz Josef Strauss.[20] Soviet Foreign Minister Shevardnadze also paid an important visit to Bonn in January 1988 – the first visit by a Soviet foreign minister in over five years.

Another important sign of Moscow's interest in better relations with Bonn has been the dramatic rise in the number of ethnic Germans permitted to emigrate from the Soviet Union – traditionally a key barometer of Soviet–West German relations. In 1987 14 500 ethnic German were allowed to leave the USSR as compared to only 700 in 1986.[21] In 1988, the figure is expected to reach 30 000. In addition, during Foreign Minister Genscher's discussions with Shevardnadze in New York in September 1988 the Soviet Union agreed that a joint Soviet–FRG working group on humanitarian issues should deal not only with emigration issues but also with the conditions of Germans living in the Soviet Union.[22]

Moscow has also shown a greater readiness to find practical ways to include West Berlin in bilateral agreements with the FRG.[23] This more flexible approach to the West Berlin issue paved the way for the signing of two long-delayed agreements on cultural exchanges and environmental protection during Chancellor Kohl's visit to Moscow in October 1988.

The Kohl visit was the most important sign of the thaw in Soviet–West German relations lately. The visit officially ended the quarantine imposed on Bonn in the aftermath of the collapse of the INF talks and laid the foundation for a broad improvement in bilateral ties. During the visit six new governmental agreements were signed in areas ranging from environmental protection to nuclear and maritime safety. In addition, more than 30 new contracts with West German firms were concluded, including a major deal for the sale of a high-temperature nuclear reactor.

The visit highlighted the gradual shift in Soviet policy toward Bonn that has occurred since mid-1986. The significance of this shift, however, should not be exaggerated. To a large extent it represents an effort by Moscow to bring its policy toward the FRG more in tune with its policy toward Western Europe as a whole. Given the Federal Republic's key role within the Western alliance, it became increasingly clear that any détente policy toward Europe had little chance of success if it excluded Bonn. In short, the Kohl visit signals a return to the *status quo ante* – that is, the period before the collapse of the INF negotiations, rather than a radical new departure.

The Soviet reassessment has also been influenced by several other factors, particularly the cool state of Franco–Soviet relations. As noted earlier, Gorbachev initially appears to have had hopes of reviving the special relationship with France and making France the centerpiece of Soviet policy toward Western Europe. The progressive hardening of French policy in Mitterrand's first term, however, and Paris's skeptical attitude toward arms control – particularly the INF agreement – dashed whatever hopes Moscow may have had in this regard and made a *rapprochement* with Bonn both more attractive and more necessary.

In contrast to the cool attitude displayed by France, the Federal Republic has shown a growing interest in arms control and East–West detente. Foreign Minister Genscher in particular has forcefully argued for testing Gorbachev's intentions and supporting his modernization plans.[24] At the same time, Bonn has softened (although by no means abandoned) its initial emphasis on the 'openness' of the German Question. While West German officials continue to insist that the German Question remains open over the long term, they have increasingly stressed that the issue can be resolved only as part of a larger European settlement and that any future settlement must take into consideration the interests of its European neighbors.[25]

Economic factors have also played a role. Bonn is Moscow's largest Western trading partner and an important source of high technology. If Gorbachev's modernization effort is to succeed, he will need considerable Western assistance. Bonn is the most likely source of such credits. This has given Moscow a strong incentive to improve ties to the Federal Republic. In particular, Moscow would like to enlist Bonn's assistance in the modernization of its consumer goods industry and the development of industrial projects in the oil- and gas-rich areas of western Siberia.

Bonn, moreover, seems increasingly ready to help. In October 1988 a consortium of West German banks formally granted Moscow a $1.6 billion credit for the renovation of its consumer and food processing industries – the largest Western credit to the Soviet Union since 1981. The credit is an important indication of Bonn's willingness to assist in the modernization of the Soviet economy, and is likely to presage a new push for increased economic ties between the two countries.

Finally, the shift in Moscow's policy should be seen as part of a larger effort to exploit the changing security environment in Western Europe, and particularly the erosion of the defense consensus within the FRG. While this erosion actually began at the time of the 1979 dual-track decision, recent developments, above all the Reykjavik summit (October 1986) and the signing of the INF Treaty (December 1987), have given it greater impetus. On the one hand, the INF Treaty has removed an important linchpin in the American nuclear deterrent on which Bonn is highly dependent; on the other, it has accentuated the importance in Bonn's eyes of Soviet convenitonal and chemical superiority and made the need to address these asymmetries all the more urgent.

It has also left NATO more dependent on short-range tactical nuclear weapons for its defense. This poses special problems for the Federal Republic because, if fired, these weapons would land on West German soil, killing millions of Germans. The INF agreement has therefore resurrected the fears of 'singularization' and produced new fault lines in the alliance. While Bonn wants to push ahead with negotiations to sharply reduce the number of tactical nuclear weapons, its allies, especially France and Britain, have taken a more reserved stand toward such negotiations. Moreover, whereas Paris and London favor some modernization of short-range nuclear weapons, especially the Lance missiles (most of which are stationed in the Federal Republic), Bonn's position has been more ambivalent. While not refusing modernization, the Kohl government has sought to postpone any decision, for fear it might provoke domestic unrest similar to that which occurred after the NATO dual-track decision in 1979.

The differences between Bonn and its NATO allies over short-range nuclear weapons open up new prospects for the Soviet Union to exploit fissures in the Atlantic alliance. An offer to eliminate all tactical nuclear weapons would elicit large public support in the Federal Republic. At the same time there is little public support for modernization of short-range tactical nuclear weapons. Indeed a decision by the Kohl government in favor of modernization might spark renewed public protests as well as prompt opposition within parts of the CDU itself.

At the same time, demographic pressures are likely to increase Bonn's interest in conventional arms control. Over the next decade the Bundeswehr will face a severe manpower shortage as a result of the decline in the West German birth rate, which will make it hard to man the Bundeswehr at current levels. This gives the Federal Republic a strong interest in seeing some reductions of conventional forces. In addition, many West German officials fear that budgetary and other domestic pressures are likely to compel the next US administration to make some reductions of US troops in Europe. These developments are likely to encourage Moscow to push for some reductions in the Bundeswehr – one of its prime goals in the MBFR talks on conventional arms control in Vienna.

The general erosion of the security consensus in the Federal Republic, as well as the growing divergences between Bonn and its Western allies, especially the United States, have increased Moscow's interest in courting Bonn and provided new opportunities for exploiting the fissures within the Western alliance. This is not to argue that Moscow expects, or even wishes to see, a collapse of the Western alliance. On the contrary, Gorbachev appears to have a realistic appreciation of the strengths of the alliance.[26] Nevertheless, the growing malaise within the alliance since Reykjavik, as well as the indications of greater self-assertion on the part of Washington's Western allies, appears to have convinced Gorbachev that he has more to gain by encouraging Bonn's interest in *détente* and arms control than by seeking to isolate the FRG.[27]

The recent reorganization of the Soviet foreign policy apparatus, particularly the appointment of one of Gorbachev's closest advisors in the Politburo, Alexander Yakovlev, to head a new Central Committee Commission on Foreign Affairs, is noteworthy in this regard. Yakovlev's writings display a strong streak of anti-Americanism and a concern with growing divergences between Western Europe and the United States.[28] At the same time the retirement of Anatoli Dobrynin, Ambassador in Washington for nearly two decades, as head of the International Department in the

Central Committee, removes one of the Kremlin's top Americanologists from a key advisory position. Dobrynin's replacement, Valentin Falin, served as Ambassador to West Germany from 1971 to 1978, and is one of the Soviet Union's top German experts. He will report directly to Yakovlev. These moves suggest that Western Europe, and especially the Federal Republic, may get higher priority in Soviet foreign policy considerations in the future.[29]

VI MOSCOW AND THE GERMAN – GERMAN DIALOGUE

Gorbachev has also taken a more flexible position toward relations between the two German states, allowing a greater degree of interaction and cooperation. After a period of cooling off, inter-German relations have again begun to warm, as highlighted by the Honecker visit to Bonn in September 1987. Rather than fearing this dialogue, Gorbachev appears to see a modest increase in interaction between the two German states to be in the Soviet interest, for several reasons. First, it is a useful reminder to Bonn that the keys to improved German – German relations lie in Moscow, and provides an incentive for Bonn to be more cooperative on issues of interest to Moscow, especially in the security area. Second, it provides the GDR with a number of economic advantages, especially credits, at a time when there are growing constraints on Soviet resources and Moscow's ability to supply such credits. Finally, inter-German trade is a useful source of much-needed high technology for the modernization of Soviet industry.

Gorbachev, however, has not given Honecker entirely free rein, and has continued to ensure that East German initiatives are consistent with, or at least do not contradict, Soviet foreign policy objectives. In the spring of 1986, for instance, Moscow reportedly intervened to scotch initial preparations for a Honecker visit to Bonn in the summer, presumably because it felt the timing was not right. By the fall of 1987, however, the international climate had improved sufficiently for the visit to take place. Similarly, Soviet pressure appears to have played a role in Honecker's decision to decline an invitation to attend the opening celebrations of West Berlin's commemoration of the city's 750th birthday at the end of April 1987.

On the whole, however, the GDR has been given wider latitude to pursue its own interests as long as these are consistent with, or at least do not contradict, Soviet interests. The dialogue with the SPD over a chemical-weapons-free zone provides a good example. The dialogue clearly was coordinated with Moscow and had Soviet backing. However, it also provided an opportunity for the GDR to pursue its own national interests and raise its international profile.

Yet, if Gorbachev's greater emphasis on *détente* has been widely hailed in the GDR, his 'new course' in domestic policy has provoked reservation, at times even resistance. Honecker's basic attitude has been that Gorbachev's reforms are fine for the USSR, but unnecessary in the GDR. As Kurt Hager, the SED's chief ideologist, tersely put it in an interview in the West German weekly *Stern*: 'Just because your neighbor papers his walls, doesn't mean you must do the same'. In essence, GDR spokesmen have argued that there is no one 'model' of socialism and that the conditions in the GDR differ from those in the Soviet Union.

Part of the explanation of the GDR's reluctance to embrace Gorbachev's reform program lies in the GDR's economic performance, which has been far better than that of Moscow or the other East European countries. Hence the SED has seen little reason for change. Unlike Gorbachev, moreover, Honecker cannot blame current difficulties on his predecessor. Whereas Gorbachev has portrayed the 1970s as a period of stagnation, Honecker has pictured the era in his speeches as a period of great achievements. He cannot do otherwise without calling his own policies into question.

These divergences, however, are not fundamental. They reflect the different domestic challenges with which the leaders of the two countries are confronted. To date Gorbachev has been willing to allow a certain degree of diversity within the bloc, and has not openly insisted that the Soviet reforms be replicated elsewhere. However, his calls for *perestroika* have had a certain resonance among the GDR population, and if his reforms begin to succeed, the GDR could find itself under greater pressure to introduce more far-reaching reforms and to liberalize further.

At the same time, Gorbachev is likely to be careful not to put too much pressure on the GDR to introduce reforms that could prove destabilizing. The last thing he wants or needs is instability in the GDR, especially at a time when he is facing increasing signs of unrest at home and elsewhere in Eastern Europe. He is thus likely to tread relatively cautiously in dealing with Honecker and/

or his successor.

The same is true in the arms control field. The Soviet Union maintains 19 divisions – nearly 400 000 men – in the GDR. These troops are the linchpin of Moscow's military strategy in Europe. They also play an important role in ensuring political stability in the GDR. Their removal or drastic reduction would have serious political–psychological as well as military consequences for Moscow's position in Europe. Thus Gorbachev is likely to be very reluctant to make sizeable reductions in these forces, preferring instead to make the bulk of any cuts from Soviet forces stationed in other East European countries.

VII MOSCOW AND THE 'GERMAN CARD'

The shift in Soviet policy toward the Federal Republic which has become evident recently raises a number of intriguing questions regarding Soviet policy in the future. Is the shift simply a belated tactical adjustment designed to bring Moscow's policy toward Bonn in line with Soviet policy toward Western Europe as a whole, or does it presage a more fundamental shift in the Soviet approach to the German issue? Is Moscow wedded to the permanent division of Europe or might Gorbachev be willing to reassess Soviet *Deutschlandpolitik* as part of a rethinking of policy toward Europe as a whole? What role are the two German states likely to play in Gorbachev's European policy?

These questions are of more than academic significance in the light of Gorbachev's demand for 'new thinking' in foreign affairs. On a number of important international issues, especially INF, Afghanistan and verification, Gorbachev has shown unexpected flexibility and a willingness to depart significantly from the policy of his predecessors. The question therefore arises: might he not be willing to rethink Soviet policy on the German issue as well?

Recent statements by some Soviet and West German spokesmen have given this question greater weight. In October 1987 Ottfried Hennig, the State Secretary in the Ministry for Inner-German Affairs, alluded to reports that Gorbachev had commissioned four policy experts – Valentin Falin, Georgi Arbatov, Nikolai Portugalov and Daniil Melnikov – to examine alternative ways of dealing with the German questions.[30] Several Soviet officials (for example Portugalov and Falin) have hinted that a withdrawal of foreign troops from both German states might be possible in the future and could facilitate increased cooperation between the two German states.[31] Such remarks have fuelled speculation that at some point Gorbachev might be tempted 'to play the German card', that is, make an offer for reunification or confederation as part of a comprehensive European settlement involving a sharp reduction or withdrawal of foreign troops from both German states.

Some reassessment of Moscow's *Deutschlandpolitik* is undoubtedly going on as part of Gorbachev's general effort to seize the diplomatic initiative and exploit emerging trends in Western Europe to Soviet advantage. This effort has sparked a more open debate on foreign policy and a reexamination of options. The remarks by Falin and Portugalov should be seen in that context. There is no hard evidence, however, that a fundamental shift in Moscow's German policy on reunification is in the offing. Nor is one likely. A reunified Germany would inevitably dominate Europe. It would also require Moscow to relinquish control over the GDR, which has become Moscow's most important political, economic and military partner within the Eastern bloc. Finally, it would have serious repercussions for Eastern Europe, especially Poland, creating new fears of a *Drang nach Osten* and weakening Moscow's hegemonic position in the area.

Limited reassociation, in other words, is one thing; reunification quite another. Gorbachev may be willing to allow the German occupants of his 'European house' greater freedom of maneuver and closer interaction, but the foundation of this house is the current territorial *status quo* and the existence of two sovereign and independent German states. Gorbachev made this quite clear during West German President Richard von Weizsaecker's visit to Moscow in July 1987. In response to von Weizsaecker's emphasis on the unity of the German nation, he stated that he did not want to 'theorize' about the question of the existence of a German nation. The 'reality' was that two German states with two different political and economic systems existed, and what happened in one hundred years 'would be left to history to decide'.[32] He made the same basic point even more sharply in his dinner speech during Chancellor Kohl's visit to Moscow in October 1988. The current situation, he stressed, was the result of a specific historical development and any attempt to change the situation or push 'unrealistic policies' would be 'an unpredictable and even dangerous business'.[33] These statements make clear that Moscow has no intention of significantly departing from the broad outlines of the 'two state' policy which it has pursued since the mid-1950s.

VIII PROSPECTS FOR THE FUTURE

This is not to suggest that there will be no change in Soviet *Deutschlandpolitik* in the future, but simply to highlight its limits. In the future, Moscow seems likely to give increasing priority to relations with the Federal Republic. Bonn, in fact, could once again become the centerpiece of Soviet *détente* efforts in Europe, as was the case in the early 1970s.

Economic considerations in particular point in this direction. If Gorbachev's plans to modernize the Soviet economy are to succeed, he will need help from the West. The Federal Republic is Moscow's most important trading partner in Western Europe. It is also the country in Western Europe which has both the technological capability and the greatest political interest in providing the type of economic assistance Gorbachev wants and needs. This gives Gorbachev a strong incentive to maintain, and even step up, the current effort to improve relations.

Gorbachev can also be expected to press more vigorously on arms control in the future. The elimination of long- and shorter-range INF systems has accelerated Bonn's security dilemmas, leaving it more dependent on 'self-deterring' short-range systems, which, if fired, would mostly land on German soil, killing millions of Germans. (In Volker Ruehe's pointed phrase, 'The shorter the range, the deader the Germans'.) West German public opinion strongly opposes any modernization of tactical nuclear weapons. Moreover there is growing pressure from both the left and the right to sharply reduce, if not eliminate, short-range nuclear artillery. This pressure is likely to grow and increase the difficulties of achieving and maintaining an alliance consensus in the Conventional Stability Talks (CST), expected to begin in Vienna in late 1988. At the same time the growing manpower problems facing the Bundeswehr over the next decade will place major constraints on any effort to bolster Bonn's conventional forces to compensate for the reduction of NATO's nuclear capability. Indeed, demographic pressures seem likely to force a cutback in the overall manning levels of the Bundeswehr over the next decade.

None of this is to suggest that Bonn is likely to drift toward neutralism, as some Western analysts, particularly in France, fear. But it does highlight the very real difficulties that will exist in maintaining the credibility of NATO's strategy of flexible response and the opportunities that may arise for Moscow to exploit alliance weaknesses. In particular, Moscow can be expected to try to take political advantage of the growing anti-nuclear sentiment in the Federal Republic to press for an elimination of all tactical nuclear weapons (the 'triple-zero' solution) – a position which is likely to appear increasingly attractive to a large number of the West German public – and to continue to encourage Bonn to adopt a more differentiated and independent policy on security issues from the United States. Gorbachev's emphasis on a 'common European house' should be seen in this light – as an attempt to suggest that Bonn has more to gain over the long run by closer ties with the Soviet Union, which is a European power, than with the United States, which is not.

There are, however, distinct limits to how far Moscow is likely to push this policy. A truly independent Federal Republic – one no longer constrained by ties to the United States and NATO – would raise a number of critical problems for the Soviet Union. First, without the American nuclear guarantee, the Federal Republic might be tempted to acquire its own nuclear weapons or to develop them in cooperation with another European power such as France and/or Britain. Moscow's highly critical attitude toward Franco-German military cooperation to date suggests this is not a development it favors. A neutral Federal Republic, moreover, might prove to be a more nationalistic Federal Republic. Indeed, the two parties that are most anti-nuclear – the Greens and the SPD – are also the parties that most strongly favor closer cooperation with the GDR. Once the Federal Republic had left NATO, moreover, there would be little grounds for Moscow to keep troops in the GDR – or in the rest of Eastern Europe for that matter. This might open the way for an intensification of the German–German dialogue in ways which Moscow might find hard to control and could stimulate nationalist trends in both German states inimical to Soviet interests.

In short, Soviet interests would be better served by a Federal Republic formally integrated into the Western alliance, but one less supportive of American policy and more capable and willing to pursue its own autonomous interests. A sharp reduction, not to mention an elimination, of nuclear weapons serves these goals. It not only reduces the nuclear threat to the Soviet Union, but also erodes the credibility of the US nuclear guarantee in general. This process is bound to have an impact on public opinion in the Federal Republic, and encourage a search for security alternatives and a weakening of ties with Washington.

In short, NATO remains an important constraint on German national ambitions. To be sure, at the moment these ambitions remain largely in check and pose no major threat to the Soviet Union. However, Moscow cannot be sure that this will always be the case. Over the long run, therefore, Soviet interests would probably be best served by a Federal Republic formally integrated into the Western alliance, but less supportive of American policy and more capable and willing to pursue its own interests.

This seems to be the chief Soviet goal at present. While Gorbachev has begun to move away from the Gromyko effort to isolate Bonn, he does not seem to have a well thought-out grand design for Germany or for Europe in general. The notion of a 'common European home' remains a vague concept without substance, and Gorbachev has yet to spell out concretely what he means by the idea. What is the structure of the house? What are its implications for the current security order in Europe? And most important, what role will the two German states play in this order?

The answer to these questions remains unclear. Probably the Soviets themselves have no clear answer. For all his rhetoric about a common European home, it is doubtful whether Gorbachev really wants to see a radical change of the current European order, especially at a time when he faces such daunting problems at home. As noted earlier, the division of Germany has served Soviet interests well, and any effort fundamentally to change the postwar political order would risk unleashing forces that Moscow might find difficult to control, particularly German nationalism. Thus for the foreseeable future the Soviet Union is likely to continue to seek a gradual improvement of ties with Bonn, especially in the economic area, while eschewing any grand designs which would radically alter the postwar European order.

9 American Interests and the German–German Dialogue

W. Richard Smyser

The United States has had, and will continue to have, a stake in relations between the Federal Republic of Germany and the German Democratic Republic. That stake grows out of broad US interests in Germany and in German affairs, interests that are among the most important that the United States has anywhere in the world. To examine America's role in inter-German relations, it is appropriate to review such US interests in Germany, to study their impact on inter-German relations, and to project how these questions will evolve in the future.

America has interests in three particular aspects of the German question. The first is the relationship that the United States has with the Federal Republic of Germany. The second, not of the same dimension, is the relationship that the United States has with the German Democratic Republic. The third, tied to the others but important enough to merit consideration on its own, is the continuing interest that the United States has in the future of Germany itself.

The relationship with the Federal Republic of Germany is vital to America's position in Europe and in the world at large. The Federal Republic is in many ways America's most important ally. The United States is the Federal Republic's most important ally. Some years ago I characterized the relationship as 'equivalence' because the two states had become so important to each other that neither could achieve a number of major international objectives without the support or at least the acquiescence of the other.[1] The relationship has, if anything, grown even more significant since that time.

The central element in the US–FRG relationship is the strategic collaboration that has existed since the 1950s when the Bundeswehr was established and when the FRG joined the North Atlantic Treaty Organization. German forces were, and remain, limited by rules that bound them to be part of NATO rather than a fully independent national force. Those rules also limited the Bundeswehr to a size of 500 000 and established limits on the types of equipment that it could acquire. None the less, the Bundeswehr has become a vital component of the NATO force structure in central Europe. It now numbers 486 000 men under arms. It is the largest single force on the central front and provides one half of the available manpower of NATO forces in Central Europe and the northern flank. In that same area, the Bundeswehr fields over 60 per cent of NATO's main battle tanks, one half of all ground air defenses, and one third of all combat aircraft.[2] Next to American nuclear forces, the German forces of NATO constitute the most important segment of European defense.

West German territory also offers the base on which American forces and those of other NATO allies are stationed. A quarter of a million American military personnel are on West German soil. So are US nuclear missiles of various ranges as well as thousands of nuclear warheads and the bulk of American equipment in Europe.[3] So are the other West European forces which, together with the German and the American forces, are to hold the NATO front line in the event of an attack from the East. No territory of the Western alliance is more subjected every day to the presence of foreign and national forces, their tanks and trucks, their maneuvers, their overflights, and their simple presence on the roads, streets and other public places.[4] Without that presence, the concept of a NATO defense of Western Europe, a territory vital to American security, would be virtually impossible to realize.

Mutual dependence between the United States and West Germany does not end with the NATO security relationship. The two countries constantly coordinate their political and diplomatic policies. Such coordination not only covers strategic matters like arms control agreements with the Soviet Union but a whole host of other questions such as votes at the UN General Assembly, policies toward crises that might arise anywhere, or humanitarian matters such as refugee support in Africa. The two countries do not always agree, particularly about political events that take place outside Europe. They have, for example, disagreed about American operations against Libya or developments in Central America, but the consultation itself is close, friendly and conducted in an open and cooperative spirit. Even when there are divergences, the public and private figures of the two countries speak to each other with mutual understanding, if not agreement.

The economic element also looms large in relations between the United States and West Germany. The West German economy is now the biggest in the European Community. It has the highest level of trade with the United States of any European country. Decisions on German economic policy can have a significant effect on the American economy and, therefore, directly on American prosperity and the American standard of living. This was underlined in 1986 and 1987, when the United States urged the Federal Republic to expand its own economy in order to help increase US exports to Germany and to help balance the US international trade and currency deficits. The Germans did not reflate as the United States had hoped, helping to precipitate severe international financial strains, but they have supported the US economy by heavy investment in the United States and in US government securities.

Coordination of West German and American policies became a particularly important element for the success of *détente* and inter-German talks in the 1970s. By the late 1960s, several West German leaders had already indicated their interest in improving relations with the Soviet Union and East Germany, but this policy accelerated dramatically under Chancellor Willy Brandt. West German negotiations with the East were carefully coordinated with general American *détente* negotiations conducted under President Richard Nixon and National Security Adviser Henry Kissinger. They were also coordinated with the British and French governments during the talks leading to the Quadripartite Agreement on Berlin. Much of the coordination was informal, running through a back channel message circuit between Brandt's and Nixon's advisers, Egon Bahr and Henry Kissinger, but it was none the less real and even essential.[5]

American relations with the German Democratic Republic are not of the same order of magnitude. The United States is still negotiating with East Germany about issues that have long ago been settled or that do not even exist in relations with the FRG, such as property and financial claims of American citizens, emigration and human rights policies, reunification of divided families and compensation to Jewish victims of Nazism. East German propaganda organs still engage in crude inventions about the United States. Annual US trade with the GDR is valued at about $100 million, lower even than when the two states first established relations, because the GDR does not now purchase as much American grain as it did then.

The United States has lagged behind other Western states in its ties with the GDR. The most senior U.S. officials to visit the GDR and East Berlin have been Deputy Secretary of State John Whitehead, who visited in November 1987 and June 1988, and Commerce Secretary C. William Verity, who also visited in June 1988. It was the last of the Western powers to open an embassy in East Berlin. It has made clear that its own policy is heavily influenced by West German attitudes because the FRG has the primary interest. None the less periodic consultations between East Germany and the United States do take place and the mood surrounding those consultations and even the total relationship is considerably less negative than in the 1960s. East German SED (*Sozialistische Einheitspartei Deutschlands*) Politburo member Hermann Axen visited Washington on an unofficial basis in May 1988 as the most senior GDR official to come to the United States. He spoke in a conciliatory manner during his private meetings with U.S. officials. As a further signal of improved relations with the United States, the GDR in July 1988, after a meeting between GDR leader Erich Honecker and West German as well as East German community leaders, announced that it had agreed in principle to compensate Jewish claimaints.

The United States has a major interest in GDR territory with respect to one particular security matter. Under the quadripartite occupation regime for Germany established at the end of the Second World War, the United States still maintains a Military Liaison Mission to the Commander of the Soviet Forces in East Germany, as do France and the United Kingdom (and as the Soviet Union maintains in West Germany). These missions are permitted to travel throughout much of what was formerly called the Soviet Zone of Germany although they must avoid restricted areas. They are periodically harassed by Soviet forces, and an American Mission officer was killed in an incident in 1986. They are still, however, regarded as a significant instrument for the United States to monitor the presence and level of activity of Soviet and East German forces. Those Soviet forces in East Germany are about twice as numerous in personnel, aircraft and major ground equiment as American forces stationed in West Germany. Not one of the four former Allied powers would be prepared to surrender its mission under present circumstances.

The third major American interest in Germany is the future of Germany itself. This interest is potentially the most important but it is now the least concrete. It colors all other interests and affects many day-to-day political and strategic questions, but it is not itself a specific issue. The Federal Republic speaks of 'two German states in one nation', a formula that accurately expresses the complex and even contradictory situation in which the German people find themselves.

The word 'Germany' represents many things. One is a nation, already identifiable at the time of Julius Caesar and the Roman Empire. Another is a culture, distinguished in music, literature, philosophy and science. Another is a geographic area, with often disputed boundaries that have shifted over time. Another is a strategic domain across the center of Europe, vital to all who are concerned with the fate of that continent. Last but not least, Germany also represents a concept in search of political expression, a concept that has rarely found such expression in the form of one state alone.

After the two world wars and the revelations of Nazi atrocities, the victorious allies were determined to make sure that no further threat to humanity could arise from German soil. They were equally determined to establish a Germany committed to democracy and peace. But the victors had different definitions of those terms. They each believed that the part of Germany that they occupied should live in accordance with their particular definition. The differences in those definitions, and the German people's reaction to those differences, brought about the division of Germany in the immediate postwar years and ultimately completed it in 1961, with the Berlin Wall, when the total separation of the German people from each other was grafted to the political and economic schism.

Détente diplomacy, particularly in its inter-German forum, has made it possible to ease that separation somewhat by permitting at least some visits back and forth between the FRG and the GDR as well as between the two halves of Berlin. Even then, *détente* did not – and could not – resolve the political division. The 'German Problem', therefore, remains. In addressing it, America cannot be more German than the Germans themselves, but it also cannot forget, or appear to have forgotten, that the problem is still there. The political structure that the future of Germany will take, even if not an issue immediately on the agenda, still remains in the form of an unanswered question. It also remains in part an American responsibility, just as it remains a responsibility for the other victorious allies – including the Soviets – who charged themselves with the task of rebuilding Germany after the Second World War. Berlin and the inter-German dialogue itself are symbols of the division and also of the pressures for and against unity.

American policies and attitudes toward the inter-German dialogue must continue to reflect all these US interests, as they have done in the past. Equally important, these interests, like those of the Soviets and the other victors, remain elements in the West and East German negotiations with each other. This was evident in the inter-German negotiations during the time of *détente* in the early 1970s and it is equally evident in recent contacts between West and East Germany.

When Chancellor Willy Brandt opened the door to inter-German talks in his speech before the West German Bundestag on 14 January 1970, the following points in his statement showed that the chancellor clearly understood allied and American interests in the discussions that were to follow:[6]

1. The Paris Treaties (establishing FRG participation in NATO) were not a subject for negotiation;
2. The FRG had no interest in striving for unlimited sovereignty;
3. Freedom had to be preserved in those parts of Germany where it existed;
4. The existing rights and responsibilities of the Four Powers with regard to Germany as a whole and to Berlin were to be respected;
5. Both states were obligated to maintain the unity of the German nation.

Four months later, during Brandt's second meeting with the GDR Prime Minister Willy Stoph, Brandt stressed an additional point that was also an American as well as FRG interest: the links that had developed between West Berlin and West Germany were to be maintained and respected.[7] His stress on that issue undoubtedly reflected his awareness that the allied ambassadors were presenting the same point to their Soviet counterpart in the quadripartite negotiations regarding Berlin.

Brandt's points were echoed whenever appropriate in allied statements not only within the quadripartite forum but in other meetings with the Soviets and in public. The US Ambassador to Bonn, Kenneth Rush, underlined them in a speech in 1970.[8] The West German government accepted them and even agreed with them. They were also reflected in the Quadripartite Agreement on Berlin to the degree to which they were applicable.[9]

The mutual recognition of respective West German and American interests helped make the *détente* negotiations on Germany and Berlin successful. Those talks also reflected carefully coordinated diplomacy on all sides. Although the Soviet Union and the GDR occasionally tried to circumvent the allies through direct conversations with the FRG, and although West German negotiators often appeared impatient, the collaboration worked effectively.[10]

The inter-German negotiations even helped other negotiations to succeed. The Soviet and GDR interest in securing the inter-German agreement, as well as their later interest in securing a successful outcome for the Conference on Security and Cooperation in Europe (CSCE), led the Soviets to sign the Quadripartite Agreement on Berlin and to make several important concessions on the form that inter-German relations were to take.[11]

Equally important from the standpoint of the West, general Western and Eastern policies reinforced each other at the time of these negotiations. The Soviet Union, like the West, wanted constructive talks. All wanted a change from the Cold War. Pressure for negotiation was in the air. Chancellor Brandt recognized this situation and understood its potential. His contribution lay in his awareness that the way to begin to overcome the division was to recognize it.

Relations between the German states since the *détente* period have kept their generally positive tone and have continued to make some progress despite tensions that have from time to time marked general East–West diplomacy and even Bonn–Moscow contacts. Inter-German relations appear to have been deliberately insulated, at least to some degree, from outside events. During the years between 1979 and 1983, when NATO was deploying Pershing II and cruise missiles in response to the Soviet SS-20s, when the Soviet Union discontinued the arms control negotiations with the United States, talks between the German states were not significantly disrupted. The advent of the government of Helmut Kohl, whose CDU/CSU had, while out of office, strongly opposed the inter-German accords and the whole *détente* process, did not disrupt ties. Kohl in office has sought further improvements in inter-German contacts.

The most notable sign of progress has been in personal travel. More than 2 million West German visits to the GDR have taken place every year during the 1980s. In return, there have been about 1.5 million visits of pensioners from East to West. From 1981 to

1985, there have also been between 50 000 and 65 000 visits to the FRG each year by East Germans travelling for urgent family reasons.[12] In 1986, the latter number suddenly jumped to about 575 000, a remarkable nine-fold increase.[13] Despite some questions in the press as to whether such ambitious plans could be fulfilled,[14] East German officials indicated that they hoped to reach the level of one million visits in 1987.[15] Relatively few of these visitors have over the years remained in the West, which may have increased East German confidence that they could be permitted to travel in greater numbers, but there are signs that more than before are applying for emigration to West Germany once they return to the GDR.[16] Most of them, as in the past, still must leave family members at home when they travel.

The 1980s have also been marked by continued East–West German contacts at senior levels and by some further agreements. Kohl and East German leader Erich Honecker met in Moscow at the time of the Chernenko funeral in 1985. Many West German officials have met senior East Germans on various occasions at the Leipzig Fair. Kohl sent his Minister for the Chancellery, Wolfgang Schaeuble, to call on Honecker in East Berlin in March, 1987, after Kohl had been re-elected. East German SED Politburo member Guenter Mittag called on Kohl in Bonn shortly thereafter. A cultural accord has been signed, as have agreements on youth exchanges. There have also been some mutual exchanges of persons. In June 1987, pursuant to their determination to make further progress, the two German states initialed an environmental agreement intended to help reduce air and water pollution, damage to forests, and pollution from industrial waste products.[17]

The most significant event, however, from the standpoint of the American interest in inter-German matters, was the visit to West Germany by East German chief of state Erich Honecker from 7 to 11 September 1987. Such a visit had been cancelled twice before, in 1984 and 1985, at Moscow's insistence, reportedly once to protest at West German stationing of US Pershing II missiles and once because of Soviet concern that inter-German relations were becoming too intimate. However, it was agreed for 1987 during the July visit to Moscow of West German President Richard von Weizsaecker, who also reportedly arranged for Soviet leader Mikhail Gorbachev to visit West Germany (tentatively scheduled for spring 1989).[18]

Honecker's visit concentrated for the most part on the familiar inter-German agenda. He and his West German hosts signed the environmental agreement as well as agreements on science and technology and on cooperation against hazardous radiation. He also visited his homeland in the Saar and took other small trips. Although his visit was labelled as 'official', the West German treatment of the visit in many ways resembled that for a state visit.

Aspects of Honecker's visit could, however, affect American interests in ways that inter-German relations have not done to date. Honecker took the occasion of his visit to echo Gorbachev's statement about a European house from the Atlantic to the Urals, suggesting a Europe without an American presence or role. On several occasions, he linked progress on inter-German relations with the overall East–West dialogue, a suggestion that his West German hosts might be expected to pressure Washington on political issues handled in East–West talks as a condition for progress on the inter-German agenda. This suggestion was tangentially reinforced in the joint communiqué, in which the two German states reviewed the entire status of East–West relations and committed themselves to using their influence within their respective alliances toward 'relaxing tensions and ensuring peace'.[19]

The future of inter-German relations can never be foretold with certainty, not only because of the complexity of the relations themselves but because of the fundamental unpredictability of surrounding world events. It is difficult now to forecast the likely global political atmosphere over the next decade or so. Even though no early change appears imminent in the governments of East or West Germany, or at least in their basic policies, there is a new and energetic leader in Moscow who may want to look again at some old problems. The year 1989 will also bring a new American president to the scene. Eastern Europe will see some top-level shifts as its leaders age, and perhaps some disruptions resulting from the new mood in Moscow. So many things *can* change on the global strategic, political or economic scene that it appears almost certain that at least some things *will* change. Even if it is impossible to predict what any particular change will be, at least some changes could have an impact of Germany and perhaps on inter-German affairs.

The fabric of inter-German relations need not, however, exist at the whim of outside events. As recent years have shown, those relations have acquired a logic and some interests of their own. The FRG has a lot at stake, such as employment tied to inter-German trade, appreciation for family visits, and the apparently general desire of the German people for a period of calm after so many turbulent decades.[20] The GDR probably has some similar considerations in mind as well as some interests of its own, such as greater recognition. There have been indications that the GDR is negotiating with West Germany for a major loan at the level of billions of D-marks.

Honecker's visit to West Germany did not represent the first time that inter-German relations had embraced topics of wider East–West concern. FRG Foreign Minister Hans-Dietrich Genscher had said during April 1986 that the inter-German talks might include at least some security matters.[21] There have, in fact, been inter-German discussions on some multilateral international security agenda topics such as chemical warfare, and there are periodic FRG–GDR consultations on international arms control issues without definitive or negotiated conclusions. The West German Social Democratic Party has made some joint statements with the SED about security zones in central Europe. But the general agenda for the inter-German dialogue has normally concentrated, and would normally continue to concentrate, on more practical and more achievable matters than the broad spectrum of East–West political and security affairs. The expectation that it would remain as in the past was reflected in Chancellor Kohl's new government policy statement in March 1987.[22]

The inter-German agenda for the next several years, even if concentrated on practical matters, will not be easy. Technical and economic issues can prove stubborn, lengthy and costly to resolve. Problems like autobahn repair or construction across East German territory, or possible exchanges of electrical power through grid system links in some areas, are time-consuming to negotiate. In addition, there will undoubtedly be the usual matters involving travel, human rights, exchanges of persons, details regarding the implementation of existing agreements, and some further steps to ease the more brutal effects of the Wall on families split between the two German states or the two halves of Berlin. Although these may not be issues of global import, they are important to the further progress of FRG–GDR relations and to those people directly affected. They must be carefully negotiated and can take time to conclude.

Objective realities also set limits to the breadth of the dialogue. When the inter-German agreements were signed more than a decade and a half ago, Egon Bahr spoke of *Wandel durch Annaeherung*, change to be brought about by the greater proximity of the two states to each other. If this was intended to mean internal change in the GDR toward greater political freedom, as some interpreted it, it has not taken place and can probably not be expected to take place. Some greater freedoms for residents of the GDR have come about, especially through relaxed travel restrictions and greater East–West contacts, but these do not amount to genuine political choice. The sharp East Berlin police reaction to young people who gathered near the Brandenburg Gate during the 1987 Pentecost holidays to hear a West Berlin rock concert suggested that the regime had not lost its sensitivity to the dangers of outside influence, a sensitivity only compounded by Gorbachev's commitment to a more open dialogue within socialist systems and to calls in Berlin, by such Western leaders as President Ronald Reagan and Premier Jacques Chirac, for the destruction of the Wall.[23]

Earlier Soviet vetoes on planned visits by Erich Honecker to West Germany suggest that Moscow itself will want to set some very clear limits to where the inter-German dialogue might lead, and almost certainly some guidelines. Just before coming to West Germany, Honecker had declined an invitation to participate in a West Berlin ceremony on the occasion of Berlin's 750th anniversary, most probably because the presence at that ceremony of many senior FRG officials would have been seen by the Soviet Union as well as the GDR as too much of a violation of the separate status that they claim for West Berlin. The Western allies had themselves been very concerned about a possible return visit by Berlin Governing Mayor Eberhard Diepgen to East Berlin's 750-year celebration. Diepgen finally also declined that invitation. The Western allies had not vetoed that visit and probably would not have done so if Honecker had gone to West Berlin. But they – like the Soviets – do not wish to see developments that might work to their disadvantage with respect to such sensitive matters as the status of Berlin.

Future American relations with the Federal Republic of Germany as well as with the German Democratic Republic are not cast in concrete. US relations with the FRG embrace so many subjects that, while strong, they can be disrupted in many areas by crises that may appear of overriding importance at any given moment, whether they be about economic matters or about arms control, both subjects that are at present under intense and not always unanimous discussion and that can be expected to generate attention and even disagreement for at least some time. Soviet–American relations could have an impact on relations between the United States and the FRG, as was evident in the concerns that some West German officials voiced privately about the Soviet–American agreement on the elimination of intermediate-range missiles in Europe. There also remain the concerns, long voiced if not realized, that a new generation of Germans who have no memories of the Second World War or of the Cold War may see their security interests differently, or that the United States may withdraw into its own continental shell in response to global political or economic developments or to public opinion trends at home. All these potential developments suggest that the relationship between Washington and Bonn cannot be taken for granted or regarded as an immutable constant in the background of inter-German relations.

On the other hand, there is room for modest improvement in relations between the GDR and the United States. The small steps taken during 1988, combined with general progress in East–West relations, could open the way for further progress. Resolution of claims issues and further progress on humanitarian questions could produce a more positive American attitude, especially in the U.S. Congress, towards such GDR interests as expanded trade, but the shadow of the Wall inevitably hinders the further development of bilateral ties. It is uncertain how the Soviet Union might react to improved US–GDR ties. None of these developments in US relations with the two German states need change the fundamental East–West equation, but they could create some variations within the present situation.

Inter-German ties would not need to be immediately affected by any such developments. In contrast to the situation in the late 1960s, no breakthrough in relations between East and West Germany is now necessary, and it seems unlikely that any major departures in new directions would take place unless there were major shifts in the global situation or in the European equation. Concentration on practical issues should mean that US interests should not be affected.

Yet the fundamental American interests persist and the United States would have to protest or to act if they were violated or threatened. The United States clearly would not wish anything to develop that would jeopardize West Germany's role in NATO or that would weaken the Western position in Berlin. It would also want to preserve its own consultations with the FRG on inter-German matters, whatever other issues might trouble Bonn and Washington at any given moment. It would not wish to see progress in the practical and humanitarian aspects of inter-German relations held hostage to its own policies toward the Soviet Union. Bearing in mind the purposes to which the allies dedicated themselves during and after the Second World War, the United States would also still want to maintain its ultimate commitment to a Germany united in freedom.

The above analysis indicates that the current and likely future direction of inter-German relations can be expected to remain broadly compatible with American interests as here perceived and presented. The anticipated development of inter-German relations would also reflect or at least not jeopardize the interests of other major partners in the European strategic balance on the Eastern or Western side. This appraisal would change, however, if there were a sudden upsurge in tension which would make a placid inter-German relationship clearly incompatible with global realities or if inter-German relations, raised to a new political level by Honecker's visit, were to be exploited by the Soviet Union and the GDR to weaken West German links to the United States and to the West as a whole.

To give effect to American interests, the following policies are now appropriate:

1. To synchronize West German and American political and diplomatic steps as much as possible so that they reinforce each other. This would require continuous consultations and exchanges of information, as during the *détente* era. Such synchronization would ensure that the inter-German dialogue does not depart too far from general East–West discussions, to their mutual disadvantage.
2. To make the concentration of favorable conditions for the maintenance of inter-German relations an objective in general US policies and particularly in dealings with both the FRG and the GDR. This may not be necessary, since those relations appear to have acquired a logic and momentum of their own, but it should still be kept in mind as an objective.
3. To make clear on suitable occasions what America's particular interests are and to indicate US determination to protect them. This not only provides a useful reminder that the United States retains a major stake and voice in Germany and in the ultimate arrangements regarding the future of Germany. It also helps protect the FRG from pressures to deal with issues that are more

properly allied matters.

Inter-German *détente* has a positive balance of achievement. It has helped reduce the strains existing in central Europe and has helped reduce the risk of war by miscalculation or excess levels of tension. It has served not only German but also American and other interests and wishes. It has eased many human tragedies and overcome at least some of the pain created by the war and by the Wall. In an age where significant breakthroughs on German or European matters may not be possible, an achievement on a human scale has much to commend it. It is in this spirit that inter-German relations can best be evaluated now and in the probable future, and in this spirit that the United States can welcome and support them.

The United States should, therefore, be able to follow the inter-German dialogue indirectly as a sympathetic if sometimes cautious friend. It will not, and to all appearances need not, attempt to guide the dialogue or become involved in those aspects that do not directly affect American interests, but it can and perhaps on occasion must play a role. In particular, it must remain sensitive to the impact that inter-German talks can have on East–West relations and on the future of Germany.

10 The German Problem and the Security of Europe: A Polish View

Ryszard Wojna

Public opinion in Poland believes that European security is closely linked to the state and manner of resolving the German problem. This stems both from historical premises and the goals the Federal Republic of Germany had set for itself in regard to the so-called national issue.

The Second World War began with the German aggression against Poland. Contemporary Polish historians regard this as yet another stage in the more than one-thousand-year-long conflict bearing the stamp of the German drive eastwards (*Drang nach Osten*). The losses suffered by Poland in the Second World War, in proportion to the number of inhabitants and economic resources, were higher than those of any other member of the anti-Nazi coalition. Over 6 million Polish citizens died. Only one-tenth of that number were killed in combat, while the remainder, including 2.7 million Polish Jews, perished in mass executions and extermination camps. The losses in national wealth resulting from war destruction amounted to 38 per cent. Because of the enormous magnitude of overall losses, the memory of the German occupation has become a lasting element of the contemporary Polish national consciousness, while susceptibility to every manner of potential threat from the German side continues to be the most important point of reference in approaching the issue of national security in Polish foreign policy.

Formulating a lasting indictment against the Nazi state, right from its inception, Poland rejected the notion of any collective responsibility of the German nation. On the many commemorative plaques in the streets and squares of Warsaw and other Polish cities in tribute to the victims of mass executions, the perpetrators of these crimes are not referred to as 'Germans' but as 'Hitlerites'.

This attitude, so different from the nationalistic stereotypes that

220

are so deeply rooted in European history, proved helpful in establishing initial contacts between the Polish and German peoples after the war. The signing at Zgorzelec on 6 July 1950 of the treaty between Poland and the German Democratic Republic 'on the delimitation of the established and existing Polish–German state frontier' was a turning-point in these contacts. The frontier line was defined in Chapter IX of thc Potsdam peace settlement:

> The three Heads of Government agree that, pending the final determination of Poland's Western frontier, the *former* [emphasis added] German territories east of a line running from the Baltic Sea immediately West of Swinemunde, and thence along the Oder River to the confluence of the Western Niesse River and along the Western Niesse to the Czechoslovak frontier, including that portion of East Prussia not placed under the administration of the Union of Soviet Socialist Republics in accordance with the understanding reached at this conference and including the area of the former Free City of Danzig, shall be under the administration of the Polish State and for such purposes should not be considered a part of the Soviet Zone of occupation in Germany.

The word 'former', which I underscored above, settles the ultimate character of that frontier, even though its 'final determination' was to have been included in a 'peace settlement'. No such settlement was reached; with regard to the Polish–German frontier its function was fulfilled by the treaties Poland concluded with the two successor states to the former German Reich.

The ultimate character of the Polish–German frontier was sealed, incidentally, by another Potsdam decision, namely that of Chapter XIII about the resettlement of the German population from Poland, Czechoslovakia, and Hungary and 'the distribution of these Germans in the various occupation zones'. In accordance with that decision the Western powers granted Poland assistance in carrying through the resettlement action.

The Polish position, which has its roots in the outcome of the Potsdam conference, is not shared by the Federal Republic of Germany. The FRG sees in it a unilateral verdict of the victorious powers, and therefore a verdict of revenge focusing – selectively – on the individual provisions of the Potsdam document (first and foremost those relating to a future peace settlement), elaborating its own interpretations of them, while simultaneously overlooking those provisions which are inconvenient from the perspective of the legal-state doctrine of the Federal Republic of Germany.

From the formal viewpoint, the bulk of the differences and difficulties in relations between Poland and the Federal Republic of Germany rests in the legal sphere. These legal controversies are not abstract, but rather issues which directly threaten the interests of individual citizens of Poland and the FRG and hamper cooperation between the two countries in many key areas.

The proposal to conclude an agreemeent on normalizing relations between Warsaw and Bonn was made by First Secretary of the Polish United Workers' Party Central Committee Wladyslaw Gomulka in May 1969. The Polish initiative rested on the following premises:

1. that the lack of diplomatic relations between Poland and the Federal Republic of Germany constituted a serious obstacle in the all-European dialogue on the usefulness of convening the Conference on Security and Cooperation in Europe (CSCE), which had been proposed by Poland;
2. that the refusal by the Federal Republic of Germany to recognize Poland's Western frontier along the Oder and Western Niesse Rivers, as defined in the Potsdam Agreement, was an insurmountable obstacle in the drafting of the charter of principles of European cooperation, which later took the shape of the Final Act of the CSCE;
3. that in proposing the conclusion of a normalization treaty, Poland was creating new prospects for Bonn's *Ostpolitik*, at the same time lending her support to those political forces in the Federal Republic of Germany which favored the shaping of relations with the European socialist countries on realistic grounds;
4. that in an effort to establish diplomatic relations with Bonn, the Polish government wished to create a legal framework for Polish citizens to vindicate financial claims from the Federal German government for the suffering and losses which had been committed in Germany's name and by Germans;
5. that the creation of the broadest possible system of collective European security has been the overriding goal of Poland's foreign policy from the very outset. The shaping of Warsaw–Bonn relations had to be one of the central links within that system.

Gomulka's initiative, put forward at the threshold of an election campaign to the Bundestag, was taken up by the SDP, then in a coalition with the CDU, and by the FDP. Loudly proclaiming the intention to open talks with Poland, the two parties won the support of the majority of the Federal German electorate and assumed power in Bonn. In November 1969, the author was able to convey to the Polish government his press interview with the newly elected Chancellor Willy Brandt, which contained the news of Bonn's readiness to start negotiations on a normalization treaty with Warsaw.

The talks on the matter began concurrently with related negotiations between the Federal Republic of Germany and the Soviet Union. (Gomulka's initiative of May 1969 had not been aired beforehand with Poland's allies, a fact which led to some tensions between Leonid Brezhnev and the Polish leader.) In Moscow on 12 August 1970, the Soviet Union and the Federal Republic of Germany concluded an agreement which had all the features of a treaty on peaceful co-existence and renunciation of the use of force in resolving issues in conflict. At the same time, both sides expressed the conviction that peace can be based only on the inviolability of existing frontiers in Europe, including the Oder–Niesse line and the border between the FRG and the GDR.

Several days later, the Bonn government proposed that the Polish government accept and repeat the formulations contained in the treaty with the Soviet Union; this was tantamount to suggesting that the negotiations on drafting a separate text of the treaty between Poland and the FRG be discontinued. The Polish government responded with a letter from Prime Minister Jozef Cyrankiewicz to Chancellor Willy Brandt containing a firm rejection of the proposal and declaring a lack of interest in further negotiations with Bonn if their aim was not to be a repetition, in Article 1, of the wording of the Potsdam Agreement defining Poland's Western frontier, as was the case in the treaty concluded between Poland and the German Democratic Republic in 1950. The intention of the Polish side was to conclude a treaty on normalizing relations, the foundation of which would be the recognition by the Federal Republic of Germany of Poland's existing Western frontier. Gomulka also considered it important to secure from the two German states, successors to the former Reich, signatures on almost identical texts concerning the frontier with Poland. This should be regarded as one of the ways to safeguard the future interests of the Polish state in case of a unification of Germany at some future stage.

Last but not least, Poland wished to secure the recognition of the postwar territorial *status quo* directly from a state which considered itself a legal successor to the state which had launched the 1939 aggression, and not *per procura* from Soviet hands. The stand adopted by Warsaw threatened to obstruct the whole system of treaties with the socialist countries of Eastern Europe. As a result, the Bonn government relinquished its intention to confine the treaty with Poland to a document on refraining from the use of force.

In Warsaw on 7 December 1970,, the Heads of Governments of Poland and the FRG, Cyrankiewicz and Brandt, concluded an agreement, Article I of which reads as follows:

1. The Polish People's Republic and the Federal Republic of Germany agree that the existing frontier line, which, in accordance with Chapter IX of the decisions of the Potsdam Conference of 2 August 1945, runs from the Baltic Sea immediately West of Swinoujscie along the Oder River to the point of junction with the Western Niesse River and along the Western Niesse River to the frontier with Czechoslovakia, constitutes the Western State frontier of the Polish People's Republic.
2. They confirm the inviolability of their existing frontiers, now and hereafter, and pledge absolute respect for each other's territorial integrity.
3. They declare that they have no territorial claims against each other and will advance none in the future.

To appreciate fully the significance for Poland of this document, one should realize that from the beginning of the eighteenth century the country's history had been shaped to a large extent within the sphere of German–Russian relations. Poland twice regained its independence at a time when the Germans and the Russians were in a state of war, in 1918 and 1945. The Russians drew conclusions from these two German aggressions. The pattern of mutual relationships within the triangle of Poles, Germans and Russians was torn apart by the Polish–Soviet 1945 treaty on friendship and assistance and by the agreements Poland concluded with the two German states in 1950 and 1970. Therefore a historic situation had evolved in this part of Europe.

However, from the moment Poland and the FRG put their signatures to the 1970 agreement to a substantiation of its provisions, which were designed to consolidate the Polish sense of security, the road was a long one. The provisions of the agreement in their international legal impact have yet to be embodied in the domestic law of the Federal Republic of Germany.

The course of the ratification process provided a warning signal for Warsaw. The Christian-Democratic opposition in Bonn declared itself strongly against the agreement. When it abstained in the final ratification vote on 17 May 1972, thus paving the way for the ratification of the agreement, it was only as the result of an agreement which had earlier been concluded between all the parties in the Bundestag concerning the so-called 'resolution' (*die Entschliessung*), the idea of which was, in effect, to deprive the 1970 agreement of what was, for Poland, its most important element. Point II of the Bundestag 'resolution', which became a foundation of the interpretation of the agreements with Poland and the Soviet Union binding in the FRG, reads as follows:

> The obligations which the Federal Republic of Germany took upon itself in the agreements were undertaken in its own name. The agreements accept the frontiers existing in their present shape, which precludes a unilateral change. The agreements do not preclude peace-treaty settlement for Germany and do not create any legal foundation for the frontiers existing today.

It was only after the above 'resolution' had been agreed upon that the ratification vote on the agreement with Poland took place. The result was 248 'for', 17 'against' and 231 abstentions, with a total of 496 votes cast.

The Polish government has never accepted the 'resolution', acting on the conviction that a unilateral interpretation of a document of international law can have no binding force. Regrettably, such an interpretation of the agreement casts a shadow on Polish–FRG relations and impedes their normalization in certain areas.

The argument on the side of the Federal Republic that the 'resolution' remains in an alleged logical conformity with Article IV of the 1970 agreement ('This Agreement shall be without prejudice to any bilateral or multilateral international agreements which the Parties have previously concluded or which affect them') does not take into account the letter and spirit of Article I. The Bonn interpretation, which is described in the Polish press as 'revisionist', acquired legal substance in the judicial decisions of the Federal Constitutional Tribunal in Karlsruhe in the years 1973–5. The Tribunal recognized the agreement with Poland as a political agreement, therefore having no constitutional impact; with the agreement being considered solely as the definition of a *modus vivendi*, the Court ruled that:

- the German Reich has survived the unconditional surrender of 1945 and the taking over of power by the victorious powers as the subject of international law;
- the German Reich still exists as a state as a whole (*Gesamtstaat*); it has the status of a legal entity but is unable to act in view of the lack of institutional organs;
- the Federal Republic of Germany is not a new state, but merely a newly-organized part of Germany and thus it is identical with the German Reich as a state, and partly identical with it in the territorial and national aspect;
- the Federal Republic of Germany, whose supreme authority covers the territory of the influence of the Constitution, considers itself responsible for the whole of Germany, that is, the German state within its 1937 frontiers.

On the basis of these assumptions the Bonn legislation created the concept of '*Inland*', denoting the 'internal territory', as opposed to the notion of '*Ausland*' or 'outside territory', which incorporated some one-third of the territory of the Polish state. Even though the concept does not in any way infringe upon Poland's sovereignty and security, it nevertheless constitutes a declaration of intent which, understandably enough, is interpreted by the Poles as a potentially serious territorial claim. In the Federal Republic of Germany extreme right-wing groups exist which seek the restoration of the frontier dating from 1914, that is, from a period when the Polish state was still non-existent on the political map of Europe. The effort to create effective safeguards against such threats constitutes the foundation of the Polish *raison d'être* and the country's political–military defensive doctrine.

It should also be added that concrete impediments encountered by the citizens of both countries are a consequence of what is described in Bonn as 'German legal positions'. One example involves the legal obstructions in contacts between the registry offices in the two countries.

The stand of the FRG government evokes, on the one hand, the mistrust of Polish society and, on the other, legitimizes the right-wing nationalistic forces in the Federal Republic. These are forces which are represented in government and whose aim is to retrieve, at least in part, the territorial losses sustained as the result of the defeat of the Third Reich in the Second World War. This factor is bound to exert a bearing on the Polish stand on security matters.

It would be wrong, however, to conclude from what has been said so far that the agreement on normalizing relations between Poland and the FRG has not fulfilled its task. Indeed, in numerous areas of bilateral contacts it has resulted in real breakthroughs. With no other Western country does Poland maintain such broad human contacts (hundreds of thousands of people annually in both directions), and such diverse economic, cultural and postal exchanges as with the FRG. The factors underlying this state of affairs are highly complex. Let me dwell on just one of them. By virtue of the decisions of the Potsdam Conference, Poland resettled several million Germans from its territory. At the same time, over a million former citizens of the Reich, once they had proved their ethnically Polish ancestry and wishing to remain in Poland, were allowed to do so. Then, in the years 1956–86 permission was granted by the Polish authorities to over 800 000 persons who sought to emigrate to the Federal Republic of Germany within the family-reunification scheme; in numerous cases this concerned families of mixed nationality. After many centuries of living side-by-side and a deep intermixing of the Poles and Germans on the territory between the Oder and Western Niesse and the Warta River, the web of complex human problems is not easy to disentangle. The Polish government has been guided in this respect by humanitarian principles, while at the same time opposing the demands voiced in the Federal Republic to recognize the existence of a German minority in Poland.

In fact there is no German minority in Poland today. The number of ethnic Germans holding Polish citizenship and residing in Poland does not exceed several thousand. Proclaiming the argument of the existence of the German minority in Poland (FRG estimates put the number of Germans in Poland at over a million), the Bonn government cites Article 116 of the Constitution of the Federal Republic of Germany which states that each and every person who possesses or possessed the so-called German statehood (*Staatsangehoerigkeit*) and his descendants is a German. Guided, therefore, by its internal legislation, the FRG is making an attempt to decree that the indigenous Polish population, for centuries inhabiting the western and northern lands of the present territory of the Polish state, is, despite the holding of Polish citizenship and an undisputed affiliation to the Polish ethnic group, a German population. The Federal Republic side ignores the fact that – while defining the existence of a German minority – the ethnic bond cannot be replaced by the bond of a political–legal character or, what is more, by the bond undermining the sovereignty of another state. Further, the striving of a certain group of people to emigrate from Poland to the FRG with the aim of improving their material well-being does not constitute grounds for claims about a German minority in Poland; economically motivated emigration has nothing to do with the criteria defining the existence of a national minority. Polish jurists describe this type of usurpation exercised towards a section of Polish society and a part of the territory of the Polish state as 'legal aggression'.

Recently the government of the Federal Republic has attempted to internationalize the problem, placing it, among other things, on the agenda of the CSCE Follow-Up meeting in Vienna. This does not portend a propitious climate for that meeting. As can clearly be seen, this problem, too, has its roots in the legal doctrine binding in the FRG. This is a doctrine which considers the West German state a *sui generis* provisional organism, whose self-set goal is the unification of Germany and which puts off the ultimate demarcation of the frontiers of the postulated, future German state until that state itself adopts relevant decisions on the matter. This is in fundamental contradiction with the basic premise of the security of neighboring countries, namely the security of existing frontiers, recognized in the Final Act of the CSCE as one of the foundations of peace.

Of course the Poles are aware that, in a contemporary world, matters of national security cannot be divorced from a broad international context and treated autonomously, solely in the context of bilateral controversies between Poland and the Federal Republic of Germany. Peace in Europe is found on the existing balance of forces, that is, the existence of two opposing military blocs and the special position and role played in these blocs by the two superpowers, the United States and the USSR. With this in mind, Poland closely follows and attaches great importance to the character of relations between the Federal Republic of Germany and its allies, notably the United States and France.

As regards FRG–US relations, in Poland's view they involve the co-existence and interplay of two tendencies. One is born out of the memory of the Polish–American brotherhood-in-arms in the struggle against fascist Germany in the Second World War and out of the conviction that a genuine support of unification tendencies in the FRG, particularly those which would strike at Poland's frontiers and security, cannot lie in the American interest. The other tendency underscores the community of American and West German interests in the rivalry with the Soviet Union and treats Poland instrumentally, as one of the elements in that rivalry.

The latter tendency appears in a speech to the Germans by US Secretary of State James Byrnes in Stuttgart on 6 September 1946. In that speech, the American politician called on defeated Germany to support a new American policy line towards the Soviet Union and the newly-emerged people's democracies in the 'Cold War' that was then being launched. The payment offered in return for that support was the calling in question of the finite character of the Potsdam decisions concerning Poland's frontiers and a pledge to revise them in a future peace treaty.

According to Polish historians, the Byrnes speech marks the beginning of close political and military cooperation between the United States and those German forces which were responsible for the establishment of the Federal Republic of Germany and the shaping of its character. The cornerstone of that cooperation was attachment to the capitalist economic system and Western-style democracy, a negative attitude to real socialism and to the firm establishment of the Soviet political and military presence in central Europe and, as a consequence, the joint commitment to 'overcome Yalta'. Within this broad platform of common political and strategic interests with the United States, the Federal Republic of Germany built its own national goals. Their implementation does not necessarily lie in the US interest, and would surely be at variance with the interests of the remaining NATO members. Despite that, bilateral and multilateral patterns of interrelationships do arise within the Western alliance. They conceal the contradictory nature of goals to be arrived at in the future, and sometimes mislead the West German public as to the scope of the real support granted by NATO countries to the national program of the FRG Government.

Poland is aware that the Federal Republic's NATO membership tangibly limits that country's freedom of maneuver in pursuing its autonomous national interests, while the incorporation of West German armed forces in NATO's military structure does not permit them to be used as an instrument of pressure by the Federal Republic Government. However, the declarations of support granted by successive American administrations to the policy and political goals of the FRG *vis-à-vis* the GDR and Poland – expressed, for example, at the periodic meetings of the foreign ministers of the United States, Britain, France and the FRG that usually precede the annual NATO foreign ministers' conferences – lead to the maintenance of what appears to Poland as an ambiguous American policy line toward the Bonn concept of the allegedly continued 'open' character of the 'German Question'.

It should be added that in almost all talks and contacts with the United States, the Polish side is assured of the full understanding of the Polish stand concerning the ultimate character and irreversibility of the present Polish–German frontier. The same declarations are made, incidentally, by representatives of France, Britain, Italy and all the other signatories of the Final Act of the CSCE.

The view of the Polish people on the potential threat from the German side is basically unanimous, irrespective of internal divisions. Those differences of view which do come to light relate to the assessment of the sources of those threats. Some see in them an expression of the revival of old German imperialist tendencies towards Poland, dressed in a new attire and adapted to today's realities. Others, including the author, maintain that these threats stem from a qualitatively new situation.

Imperialist Germany, which in the two world wars had sought to become the ruler of Europe and a great power on a world scale, was crushed in 1945, and its ability to re-emerge in the old shape, so dangerous to mankind, is still basically impaired by:

1. the restriction of the sphere of influence of its possible successors solely to the Federal Republic of Germany;
2. the extensive integration of the Federal Republic's economy with the countries of the 'European community';
3. the military strength of the Soviet Union, which makes it wholly impossible for the Federal Republic of Germany to pursue its policies by threatening to use force;
4. the lesson learned by the German establishment from the defeats in two world wars: no West German politician today views a Clausewitzian war as an instrument in the pursuance of political objectives.

The new situation is such that the self-proclaimed legal successor to the German Reich has become structurally tied to the rest of Western Europe, as well as with the United States and Canada, in the political, economic and military spheres. While the FRG is shaping its national goals on the foundation of Western ties, at the same time it overlooks the fact that one precludes the other. The truth is that either the FRG will become fully integrated with the other partners of the 'European community' and its functions as a national state will be basically weakened, or it will forge ahead with expansive national objectives at the cost of disturbing the integration process. At the same time, West European integration, which has already created irreversible facts, has considerably strengthened the stature of the West German state in Europe and the world.

This is also a new situation for Poland. The Federal Republic's political, economic and military ties with the West lead the West to view Poland's geopolitical situation from a different angle. The prime factor is that Poland lies along the marches of the Soviet Union and not, as was argued previously, on the other side of Germany. For some 400 years, it was that latter consideration which was the basis for the cooperation and friendship, often of alliances as well, between Poland and France – all in the understanding that the foe of my foe is my friend. Today, the lines dividing military groupings run quite differently than at any other time in Europe's history. This is largely due to the defeat suffered by German imperialism – which for the second time in a generation had brought the Eastern and Western parts of the continent into conflict in the Second World War.

The solid leaning of the FRG on the West and its related security foundation have created a new assumption for West Germany's policy toward Eastern Europe. At the same time, the new *Ostpolitik* launched by Willy Brandt in 1969 has led to a marked strengthening of Bonn's position in the Atlantic alliance by virtue of a feedback process. Through the so-called Eastern Treaties, the Federal Republic can now directly represent its national interests in Moscow, Warsaw, Berlin or Prague without having to benefit from the services of France or the United States, whose interests do not always converge with those of West Germany. The famous statement by former Chancellor Erhard that the Federal Republic is an economic giant but a political dwarf is no longer true, largely because of the Eastern Treaties.

When signing these treaties, could the Soviet Union, Poland and the GDR have anticipated the manner in which they enhanced the international standing of the FRG? Some Polish experts on German affairs believe that Bonn gained incomparably more in political terms than did Warsaw from the bilateral treaty and the other Eastern treaties. I do not share that view, believing it to be an outdated mode of stereotyped thinking. To the Poles, the treaty as such will remain a major diplomatic achievement. Moreover, the

Eastern treaties were a *conditio sine qua non* for setting into motion the future CSCE process, which has already become a major accomplishment and presents a real opportunity for the countries of Europe.

Nevertheless it is a fact that in the period which has elapsed since the signing of the Eastern treaties, the FRG has enormously expanded its trade and in part its political relations with the socialist countries of Eastern Europe. Poland is following that trend intensively, raising issues resulting from Bonn's policy towards the socialist countries at all bilateral and multilateral meetings of the Warsaw Pact members. In the foreign trade statistics of all these countries, the FRG has developed into the leading partner in the capitalist world, and second overall after the Soviet Union. If we were to also add trade with the GDR to West Germany's trade with the countries of what was previously termed central Europe, then today the two German states would have a higher volume of trade with that part of the world than the prewar Reich. It is no coincidence that the term '*Mitteleuropa*' is now appearing in West German publications. As is known, in German political terminology this is not a geographical, but a geopolitical term applying to the sphere of past German influences. Today, however, the political scope of these influences is basically restricted by the wholly new alignment of forces. In my view, the notion of middle or central Europe can today at best be considered in respect to certain civilizational differences motivated by historic factors. The fact remains, though, that the German factor has returned to the body politic of this part of the world, though not as the decisive factor it was before the Second World War. Here also the defeat of German imperialism has left a lasting imprint.

Let us return once again to the position of the FRG in the Western alliance and in Western European integration processes. Polish opinion centers most often on two consequences: first, the stature of the Bundeswehr within NATO and the way relations between Paris and Bonn affect developments within the 'European community', and, second, East–West relations.

The Bundeswehr, America's most powerful military ally, is the strongest conventional force in Western Europe. Its officers maintain a proportionately high presence in NATO's central decision-making centers and, for this reason, top officers of the Bundeswehr have a major say in shaping the alliance's strategic doctrines. The belief prevails in Poland that the Bundeswehr officer corps was highly instrumental in the evolution of the so-called *Vorwaertsverteidigung*, offensive defense, which seeks to move the frontline of battle forward; in other words, in the direction of Poland's frontiers.

The consequences of this doctrine are discussed in a recently published book by several authors, including some from the General Staff Academy, entitled *International Factors of Poland's Security* (Warsaw 1986; State Scientific Publishers), where it is stated:

> . . . even though Poland's geographic location creates a favorable defense situation, particularly in the initial war period, nevertheless because Poland acts as something of a bridge between Eastern and Western Europe, and simultaneously is a strategic area for deploying successive contingents of the Warsaw Pact's operational units, the territory of Poland can prove to be a zone of particularly intensive enemy operations already in the first days or even hours of the war. This danger results from the fact that the territory of Poland lies within the range of intercontinental and intermediate-range missiles, the strategic air force and – to a large extent – the tactical air power of the enemy.
>
> . . . In his calculations, the enemy will set the pace of the operation, which – to judge by exercises – may be between 20–30 km over a 24-hour period. Therefore, having started the war, the enemy expects its land forces to reach the line of the Bug River in 35 days [i.e., Poland's Eastern frontier].

People in Poland associate the Bundeswehr – even though West Germany is subordinated to the NATO command – with the continued existence of a threat from that side. This becomes more understandable when one considers that a part of the professional officers' corps is seeking to uphold the old traditions of German militarism in the Bundeswehr (borne out by the names of military barracks in West Germany and the choice of subjects in ideological –political instruction curricula), thus creating a breeding ground for right-wing nationalist forces in the FRG, and that the Bundeswehr constitutes a strong lobby in favor of expanding offensive armaments and curtailing the willingness of political parties to arrive at arrangements with the socialist East in matters of disarmament and *détente*. The manner in which Chancellor Kohl's government dealt with the issue of including or excluding the nuclear warheads to Pershing 1A missiles from the scope of the US–Soviet agreement highlights the links between politics and military problems. Despite the fact that, as the non-nuclear power, it has no access to the nuclear weapons, the Federal Republic of Germany achieved its objectives by becoming, to a certain extent, an independent subject joining in the American–Soviet dialogue. From the point of view of diplomatic skills it was nothing short of a '*Meisterstueck*'. Having no prospects whatsoever for keeping the Pershing 1A missiles in the Bundeswehr arsenals once the US–Soviet agreement was concluded, the Federal Republic of Germany was capable of turning the consent it had been forced to give into an argument underlining Bonn's significance and standing on what is a key international issue.

On the other hand, the expanding links between France and the FRG in the economic and political spheres, the ever closer military cooperation, as well as the idea – still theoretical – of an independent Western European defense potential resting on the Paris–Bonn axis, strengthen the conviction of the Poles that the founding of Poland's security on an alliance with the Soviet Union in 1945 was a far-sighted decision. The meaning of that decision is also becoming obvious to those in Poland who either were, or still are, guided by anti-Soviet feelings.

At this point, a few remarks are called for regarding the concepts of 'overcoming Yalta' that are currently circulating in the West. These are concepts which provide a common denominator for various political forces in Western Europe and their attitude to the socialist part of the continent. Poland cannot underestimate the threats to its security coming from such quarters.

Yalta is a code-name applied most commonly in the West not so much to the meeting of the Big Three in the Crimea and its results, but to the division of the continent, consolidated by the 'Cold War'. By seeking to 'overcome Yalta', the objective in Paris, Bonn or London is to roll back the Soviet military and political presence in the East, and to create conditions for the countries of central Europe to come under the direct influence of the West. In practice, this would amount to a complete realignment of forces on the continent, to the disadvantage of socialism and, as such, a fundamental altering of the premises of European security as well as a change in favor of the FRG and all that is associated with the 'national issue' in Bonn. Such a course of events would completely destroy the peace order shaped at Yalta and Potsdam. Whatever would emerge from the ruins of the present order would have to take into account the FRG's present position in Europe, thus tempting that country to reach once again for the status of a great power. The price of that would be dangerous to European peace and to Poland in particular.

Let us consider here a scenario for 'overcoming Yalta', which, while discussed by some, is wholly improbable. The existing alignment of forces in Europe does not allow us to expect that such a course of events would be possible without a war. Even accepting as the point of departure the views on 'Yalta' by Zbigniew Brzezinski, published several years ago in *Foreign Affairs* ('The Future of Yalta', Winter 1984–5) and *Europa Archiv* ('Die Zukunft von Jalta', 10 December 1984), that the countries of Western Europe – acting under the umbrella of America's military might – would assume the task of destabilizing such countries as Poland by actively supporting the anti-socialist opposition there in order to change the existing constellation of political forces in Eastern Europe, it would be inappropriate to overlook possible Soviet countermeasures – not necessarily of a military nature – and the need for the Soviet Union to reconsider its security on the Western flank, with all the consequences this would entail for Poland. Advocates of 'overcoming Yalta' choose not to see that the socialist establishments more fully express the national interests of their countries (something that is not questioned even by anti-Polish communists) than the bourgeois media in the West are inclined to admit. Secondly, the naive assume that a more or less conflict-free 'withdrawal' of the Soviet Union to its own borders is possible. But that – from the viewpoint of Soviet security – would imply a wiping away of the effects of the Soviet contribution to the defeat of the Nazi Reich.

The only concrete effect of successive concepts aimed at altering the 'Yalta order' can be a growing suspicion of the ruling socialist forces as to the good intentions of the West and a temporary arresting of *détente* processes in Europe.

Will the present alignment of forces, founded on the Yalta decisions with regard to Germany and their formal sealing in the Potsdam Agreement, thus continue forever? Nothing is eternal in history. The 'Viennese' order lasted close to a century, from 1815 until 1914, the 'Versailles' order a bare twenty years. The 'Yalta–Potsdam' order has now existed for over forty years, making peace in Europe so lasting and stable that it would be necessary to go back many centuries to find a similarly long period without a major war on the European continent.

This does not mean, however, that this order is the same now as in 1945. Since then, the premises of European peace have changed. This peace is not now directed against the defeated Germans. As a matter of fact, the two German states which succeeded the Reich do not perform the role of the defeated today. They have, along the way, been integrated by the rival victorious powers into their respective alliances. The remnants of restricted sovereignty, held by the four powers in regard to 'Germany as a whole', have no bearing on the policies of the FRG and the GDR. The question today is how to weaken the divisions in Europe so as to preserve and consolidate simultaneously the existing security foundations and initiate broader cooperation in order to make the continent a common home for the European nations and countries.

There is much to suggest that we are entering the prologue to an approaching new stage of European history. Pressure aimed at overcoming the division of Europe and regaining cultural and civil unity is growing both in the East and the West, albeit guided by different motives. There are two grand proposals suggesting the course of future action: one advanced by the 'European community', and the other whose foundations were defined in the CSCE Final Act. The sense of the first can be gleaned from the tone of pronouncements by West European statesmen. Essentially, they make clear the desire to consolidate Western Europe, and to make it an independent element in world politics, thereby increasing Western Europe's attractiveness in the eyes of East European societies. The norms of what is 'European' and 'common' would be defined by the West according to its own political and economic considerations.

From the viewpoint of Poland's interests, however, the foundation for turning Europe into a 'common home' can only be the principles of international behavior for countries of differing political and social systems laid down in the CSCE Final Act. Political pluralism, stressed so strongly by Western representatives in discussions with the East, must be reflected also in the area of inter-state relations. In spite of all the divisions within Polish society, the overwhelming majority of the Polish people are in favor of a socialist system of values.

The discussion on the future of Europe is inseparably linked to its security, and not only in the military context. The present-day concept of a country's and a nation's security has many components, including the political, economic and ideological. Finding a common denominator for them will be a long and complex process. Its characteristic feature is the speedy growth of all manner of interrelationships between the two parts of the continent. I dare say that the number and quality of these factors is greater than those which divide them. The policy line of Soviet General Secretary Mikhail Gorbachev has created a major opportunity for the consolidation of this trend.

In seeking to ameliorate the existing divisions in Europe, it is impossible to overlook the German Question. The FRG believes that this is still an open issue. On the other hand, the socialist countries believe that it has been resolved, in the form of the coexistence of the two German states. (Incidentally, many people forget that before the FRG became a NATO member, the GDR was the driving force in efforts to achieve the unification of Germany.)

What is the situation today? The notion of unification has been taken over by the FRG, although the wording has changed under new conditions. There are no longer voices in Bonn calling for 'absorbing' the GDR by the FRG, or for a mechanical unification of the two states into one state organism, if only in the form of a confederation. Views of this kind are a thing of the past. The ruling Christian Democrats have taken over the line of the Social Democrats and the Free Democrats, committing themselves today chiefly to maintaining a sense of national unity among the two German societies. In Poland the view largely prevails that in the past ten years this sense has grown, although this should not be identified with the unification of Germany. This joint declaration of a German identity, in spite of the emergence of a socialist society in the GDR, is a specific restoration of the situation of a century and a half ago when the German nation regarded itself as a '*Kulturnation*' (the nation in the context of culture), and not '*Staatsnation*' (a nation-state), because at that time there were German states of many sizes in coexistence, as well as states with different systems and a varying degree of feudal and democratic–bourgeois features.

A question that comes to mind in this context is whether the visit that the chairman of the State Council of the German Democratic Republic Erich Honecker paid to the Federal Republic of Germany in September 1987 will have any bearing on the future shape of relations between the two German states, and if so what sort of prospects it has opened for these relations.

In a commentary I contributed for the Polish government daily *Rzeczpospolita* on the eve of the visit I described it as the crowning of the process of the division of Germany and as the affirmation of that division by the two sides. It is significant, surely, that the organ of the Socialist Unity Party Central Committee *Neues Deutschland* considered it appropriate to reprint my article instead of publishing its own.

There is much to suggest, however, that the gradual expansion of the scope of institutionalized cooperation between the two German states will be accompanied by the broadening of the pattern of social contacts. From the point of view of restoring the sense of national unity this trend can give rise to qualitatively new phenomena, the nature of which is difficult to predict at the moment. But everything seems to indicate that the establishment in the German Democratic Republic will be doing its utmost to ensure that the processes of social contacts between the two countries, which had already been set into motion, do not get out of control.

Mention should also be made here of a truly unprecedented development: the publication on 28 July 1987 of a joint declaration between the Academy of Social Sciences at the Socialist Unity Party Central Committeee and the Programme Commission of the Social Democratic Party (*Grundwertekommission*) on the principles of political culture to be adhered to in discussing and resolving ideological conflicts and security issues. The declaration, in which the formula 'we, the German communists and social democrats' is repeated several times, contains the following formulation: 'The two sides should be ready [*einrichten*] for a long period during which they will have to co-exist and should come to terms with each other [*auskommen*]. Neither side should contest the other side's right to exist'.

The developing cooperation between the FRG and the GDR and the increasing trend towards broad two-way contacts and travel are all followed with keen interest in Poland. I do not conceal the fact that some in Poland view these processes with distrust, as if unaware that this is a direct consequence of implementing the principles of the CSCE Final Act. At the same time, both German states are stressing the very special responsibility resting on them to improve and consolidate European security, and are keenly aware that the border between them is simultaneously the border-line dividing two opposing military blocs and differing social systems.

The distrust of the Polish people is motivated by historic experience. In Poland, the argument advanced by the FRG that the Germans have the right to self-determination is countered by stressing the overriding importance of structures of peace and the existing alignment of forces. Twice in history the Germans have sought unification and hegemony, and twice this effort led – indirectly and directly – to world war. The so-called 'small Germany' (*kleindeutsch*) solution in the shape of the unification achieved by Bismarck – which was in essence the Prussification of Germany – dislodged the firm European equilibrium and laid the foundation for the First World War. On the other hand, Adolf Hitler's 'great Germany' (*grossdeutsch*) solution, in essence pan-German, was the direct cause of the Second World War. In both cases, severe losses were suffered by both the German nation and its neighbors, and for that matter the whole of Europe. It is for this reason that there is practically no one in Europe who wants to leave the decision regarding unification in German hands – even if this were feasible. The so-called German problem is an issue that directly concerns the Poles, the French and the whole of Europe. The reunification of Germany would have a significant impact on all existing alignments of forces, to the disadvantage of both East and West.

The inconsistency of Bonn's policy is reflected, on the one hand, by the striving for an understanding by the Poles of the German quest for unification, and on the other, by the staunch upholding of the view that the final delimitation of the Eastern frontier of that mystical united Germany would be determined only by negotiations it conducted as a power of greatly increased stature. Such objectives are an additional political element of Poland's alliance and friendship with the GDR. The fact that the GDR was an offspring of the Potsdam decisions and the steadfast de-Nazification and democratization in the Soviet occupation zone, as well as the GDR view of German nationalism as the common enemy of Poland and other socialist countries, enhances the image of that country in the eyes of the Poles. The Polish–GDR border has truly become a border of peace. And even though certain problems may appear from time to time resulting, for instance, from the different approach to the role of Prussia in Polish–German history or the differences of view on the issue of delimiting the sea frontier between the two countries, in no way do they bear on the core of relations: the basically unanimous stance on the West German policy directed against both GDR and Polish interests. By accepting the superior importance of differences in the political system, though not by dissociating itself from that which is common in the German heritage, the GDR enjoys the full backing of the Polish People's Republic. The words of GDR leader Erich Honecker that the unification of Germany in present-day conditions would be an attempt at mixing fire with water essentially contain the same meaning as the adage binding in the FRG from the outset: 'Freedom before unity' (*Freiheit vor Einheit*). In Bonn, freedom is synonymous with belonging to the Western world.

Today, almost half a century after the German aggression against Poland and the beginning of the Second World War, Poland's relations with the societies of the two German states have undergone a fundamental transformation. While assiduously upholding memories of the suffering of the Polish nation in the last war and the crimes committed by German Fascism, we are also facilitating wide contacts among people; we are seeking to overcome prejudices and negative stereotypes on both sides; and we are entering paths of ever closer cooperation, *rapprochement* and friendship. These are processes of historic importance to Europe. The commission for revising history and geography school textbooks in both countries, set up 15 years ago under the auspices of UNESCO has made a profound contribution to this cause. The commission brings together prominent scholars from both countries.

The Polish people welcomed the remark made by West German President Richard von Weizsaecker, who is also a Protestant church leader, on the fortieth anniversay of VE-Day as to the overriding importance of the offer of accord, and not legal claims. (Indeed, the very special role of the Protestant church in both German states should be stressed. It views the Oder–Niesse frontier as God's punishment for the Nazi crimes in Poland and lays the main emphasis on the moral aspect of German–Polish accommodation.)

Still, relations between Warsaw and Bonn are not simple or free of tension. The list of controversial issues is long. Some, in addition to those mentioned earlier, are of a bilateral nature (for example, the FRG's denial to Polish nationals of the right to claim damages for the suffering and losses caused by the criminal policy of the Third Reich, or slave labor for the Reich; damages were awarded to only a small group of persons who were subjected to pseudomedical experiments in the Nazi concentration camps). Others relate to the wide spectrum of East–West relations and the different concepts of the future shape of Europe, as well as the differing approach to the issue of collective security.

However, it would appear that the conviction is spreading on both sides that, notwithstanding the importance of matters of substance such as frontier issues, the future of Germany and certain matters of a legal nature which are irreconcilable, primary attention should be devoted to those areas in which a gradual maturing and agreement are possible. These are areas of economic cooperation and the steady widening of the framework for two-way travel, and everything that concerns the concept of European security.

The offer of good will was stated quite clearly recently by Polish leader Wojciech Jaruzelski in an interview with the *Gazeta Lubuska (Trybuna Ludu* of 24 April 1987):

> For years Poland has been steadfastly declaring its constructive will to achieve a full normalization and the development of good relations with the Federal Republic of Germany. I say this most forcefully once again. We do not wish to quarrel eternally. It is not our desire to continue squaring the accounts indefinitely, from one generation to another, for the years of the Nazi crimes.

Poland's goal is to arrive at a system of collective security embracing the entire continent as envisioned in the CSCE process. In this system the countries of the Eastern and Western parts of the continent would not organize their own separate collective security systems directed against each other, as is the case now, but work jointly toward guaranteeing mutual security for both sides. In the meantime, the conflicting views on the nature and forms of resolving the German problem amount to a clash of viewpoints on this key issue of European security.

11 France's German Problem

Anne-Marie LeGloannec

Ever since the Second World War, the Franco-German relationship has been something other than bilateral. At a minimum, it can be described as a triangle with a hidden side, the GDR; at most, it involves the European and East–West network of power relations. Bearing in mind France's long-standing conflict with the House of Austria and later with its Prussian heirs, the way in which the French view the German problem – that is, the excruciating question of Germany's stake and role in Europe – illuminates French perceptions and conceptions of France's own role on the continent. French inquiries into the German Question reveal, then, at least as much about the French themselves, both elites and the public, as about Germany. France's selective perception finds a German reality which is quite 'contrariwise', as Lewis Carroll would have put it. Both objective realities as well as subjective perceptions mirror French symbolism and politics, fears and models, aims and means. In all areas of differences and discrepancies between the two countries (social, economic, political and military), be they mythical or real, Germany plays an ambiguous dual role for France. On the one hand, Germany often acts as a model for France, what France itself is not but would like to be. On the other hand, when Germany exceeds the bounds of the role France envisages for it, France often uses Germany as a straw man, a focus for criticism. Often Germany can play the parts of model and straw man simultaneously.

Nevertheless, France's perception of the German problem has undergone a subtle yet dramatic evolution in recent years among both public opinion and elites. While the German Question played a decisive role in shaping the postwar policies of the Fourth and the Fifth Republic (as a prod to European integration, for instance), France seems to have concentrated, in the 1980s particularly, even more than before on the European continent and the German component of that continent as such. A number of factors account for this emphasis: (1) dwindling resources (and forces) have obliged France to withdraw partially from Third World countries; (2) the

242

Euromissile and post-Euromissile debates have underscored the reality of a Soviet–American condominium at least as far as decisions pertaining to the fate of Europe are concerned, while at the same time the ever-looming danger of a Euro-American decoupling undermines the credibility of France's – and Europe's – defense; and (3) an increased fluidity in central Europe, characterized by numerous interchanges between East and West and by the rise of pacifist movements, particularly in West Germany, which has underscored the possibility of subtle, incremental modifications at the core of the old continent. As a result, France's approach and attitude toward the German problem has changed. While for the past twenty years France's German problem had to be understood primarily if not solely in Franco-German terms, pointing at a complex relationship of competitive and sometimes conflictual cooperation, it has now regained in French eyes a geopolitical dimension dormant ever since the last days of the Cold War. To what appears to be a geopolitical problem, the French have tried to respond in geopolitical terms – namely, by reviving Franco-German security cooperation. Is this, however, the appropriate solution, or even a correct diagnosis? Before answering such a question, let us consider first the many facets of France's perception of the German problem, and second, its most recent evolution.

I PERCEPTIONS AND ATTITUDES

The very notion of a German problem or German question is both emotional and conceptually blurred. From geopolitics to the history of state-building, the term refers to the central position of Germany, which, at the heart of Europe, has been sometimes too weak and sometimes too strong, either prey for or a threat to its neighbors; or again to the old notion of *Deutscher Sonderweg* (special German path) of a Germany, though neither Western nor Eastern geographically, sufficiently 'Eastern' in the sense that it was hindered in its progress towards freedom to follow the path leading from authoritarianism to totalitarianism. When dealing with these issues – Germany's respect for human rights, or the role of Germany, reunified or not, in Europe – French public and elite opinion have not always coincided. Surprisingly enough, French public opinion has grown increasingly relaxed as far as German democracy or reunification is concerned. French elites meanwhile have proved more emotional, sometimes underestimating West Germany's democratic soundness or economic capabilities or, to the contrary, overrating its economic and political weight. In recent years, however, all have agreed that the role of West Germany and the strengthening of a Franco-German axis in a changing world is *the* issue.

Human Rights

Time and again French elites have been suspicious of relations between the government and the governed and respect for human rights in both German states. The GDR has long been shunned by Western public opinion, viewed from the very beginning as a mirage, a creation of the Soviet regime, deprived of both national and democratic legitimacy. Attention in the media or in academic and intellectual circles was directed at the GDR's mightier twin,[1] Western Europe's political and economic pillar, or at its Eastern neighbors, nations of long history which proved their political vitality by rebelling against the regime, Soviet *diktat*, or both. As no dramatic evolution took place in the GDR besides the violent suppression of the June 1953 revolt and the erection of the Berlin Wall in 1961, French and, generally speaking, Western public opinion quietly inferred that nothing much would happen. When political opposition or dissent was formulated in the GDR, it did not assume the drama or aura of Solidarity's fight in Poland. It was less far-reaching, less popular – the cause of individuals rather than of a movement. As a consequence, whereas France should have supported the battle for human rights in the GDR – all the more as the French had rediscovered 'anti-totalitarianism' in the late 1970s – it was the Polish fight for democracy that attracted all of its attention.

Compared with their Polish brethren, it almost seemed to the French that East Germans would remain Germans, heirs to all undemocratic traditions and *Untertanengeist* (obedience) which had taken root in the moors of Berlin. To make matters more complex, a feeling of 'the worse the better' seemed to prevail: how would the French have reacted had an East German Walesa risen and fought for freedom, possibly leading to calls for reunification? Would they have rejoiced as much as they did over Solidarity? These questions raised by Alfred Grosser in a famous article published in *Le Monde*[2] were addressed not only to the French but to others – Americans and Poles, West and East Germans – as well.

While political and ideological priorities, that is, the explicit ties with the FRG or the implicit desire to maintain the *status quo*, may have dictated France's overwhelming lack of interest in the GDR's evolution, the same applies to the few who have often displayed such interest. Whether it be the communist-affiliated Société France–RDA which supports the East German regime, or the Codene, a pacifist movement which has chosen to stand for the East German independent peace movement, ideological and political standards have dictated their choice.

The case of the FRG is even more complex. The legitimacy of the Federal Republic, a democratic regime created in the West by elder democracies, has not entirely protected it from suspicions accrued in the past. In the 1970s, the French left expressed unease at the professional restrictions (*Berufsverbote*) designed to bar communists, or suspected communists, from holding federal or local positions, including menial jobs. It also criticized sharply some aspects of the anti-terrorist campaign, such as prison conditions in the noise-proof cells of the Stammheim jail; the famous, if not infamous, writer Jean Genet even sided with the Stammheim inmates of the Baader-Meinhof gang in an extremely controversial article published by *Le Monde*.[3] The French Socialist Party, at that time in the opposition, went so far as to build a so-called defense committee for human rights. This gave the impression that party-to-party dialogue (between the opposition French Socialist Party and the governing West German SPD) would no longer be sustained and nothing short of public controversy could ever bring the West German comrades to revise their positions on and respect for human rights along French lines.

As professional interdictions were quietly eliminated, as terrorism seemed to be eradicated from West German soil – at least for a few years – and as West German democracy proved to be aware of the dangers of leviathan, Franco-German tension abated. The tension had, however, illuminated some deep-set misgivings and misunderstandings between the French and the German left, dating back to the first days of the socialist movement. The French Socialist Party had always wanted to be more radical than the German Social Democratic Party, reproaching the latter for being too respectful of state institutions and authority. This same criticism flared up again in the 1980s over the Polish question. While West Germans sent thousands of care packages to Poland, the French demonstrated in favor of Solidarity. The former favored humanitarian practicalities, the latter humanistic symbolism. Each side highlighted the other's insufficiencies; the French were blamed for indulging in ineffective rhetoric while the Germans were suspected of sacrificing freedom for the sake of reason, and human rights for the sake of improvements in everyday life (*menschliche Erleichterungen*).[4]

In France, the socialist government's shift to the right – manifested not only in a new economic policy but also by a new *Realpolitik* which induced President Mitterrand to officially greet General Jaruzelski in Paris; the replacement of a Socialist prime minister by a Conservative one; and the necessity for French and West Germans to concentrate on similar internal problems, like immigration, or to fight jointly against common terrorist foes – all have contributed to mute mutual reproaches over the past few years. More significantly, the French left has emulated its West German counterpart by launching charity campaigns in France and abroad, such as the *Restaurants du Coeur* or *Médecins sans frontières*. Is this a sign of *rapprochement* in concepts and methods; of lack of interest, with the French concentrating on internal problems; or again the expression of increased normalcy, as the West Germans cease to be the objects of scrutiny and suspicion?

While there is probably no single answer, it should not go unnoticed that sometimes French intellectuals have operated as the watchdogs of West German democracy. At the same time they encountered the impatience of West Germans and also, to some extent, the indifference of French public opinion, which after all, harbors a different image of Germany, as will be examined later.

Reunification

The question of reunification, that is, whether Germany should and could reunify and what the new *political* form would be, has long been a primary one. As such, it has often been presented as the crux of the German Question, as if the Germans and French were preoccupied by nothing but Germany's reunification, the Germans supposedly striving for it (following Gambetta's recommendation, 'Think of it always, speak of it never'), while the French allegedly opposed it. Never has a phrase been so often quoted by both peoples as François Mauriac's: 'I love Germany so much that I am happy there are two of them'. For the French, the phrase was pronounced sometimes as a confession, often in jest; for the Germans, it exemplified French opinion.

While Mauriac's phrase has become, to a certain extent, a useless, if not an irritating reminder of policies past, it remains certain that French policy *vis-à-vis* Germany's reunification has long been ambiguous, if not entirely negative in the immediate postwar era. Without going into well-known details, suffice it to say that De Gaulle had then aimed at controlling a weakened Germany, a policy pursued by his successors during the first years of the Fourth Republic. In practice it means (1) holding Germany in the Franco-Soviet pliers of the 1944 treaty; (2) fragmenting it, following the policy Richelieu had implemented with the Westphalia Treaty; and finally (3) annexing territories bordering on France. De Gaulle and his successors, however, missed these three points: the Franco-Russian treaty quickly became moribund; fragmentation could never be pursued because of the other three allies' opposition; and out of the projected annexation of the Ruhr and Saar came nothing but a special status given the latter and terminated in 1957 by a local vote following a Franco-German agreement. However, the policy of opposing the reconstruction of a German state, or at least the aim of fragmenting Germany, met with public approval. Of a representative sample of French people questioned in the summer of 1947, 78 per cent agreed with De Gaulle's concept, while only 12 per cent spoke in favor of a new German confederation and 10 per cent expressed no opinion.[5]

With the Cold War, realignment swept in. France had to decide who was the foe – Germany or the Soviet Union. France could not repeat the mistake of fighting against the wrong enemy, as it had in the nineteenth century when fighting against the Habsburgs instead of the Hohenzollerns. Having sided with the West, and hence the West Germans, France had to support the latters' claim for reunification, a *quid pro quo* without which the Franco-German alliance could not have been cemented. The Federal Republic's allies were also aware that the mistakes of the Versailles Treaty and its dramatic consequences should not be repeated: German national feelings should not be repressed for fear of provoking a new wave of revanchism. The reunification of Germany seemed, however, impossible under prevailing conditions – a repetition of the past would have been even more ominous. The recognition of Germany's eastern borders was the minimum requirement that De Gaulle put forward – quite officially – at his March 1959 press conference:

> The reunification of the separated parts into a united Germany that would be entirely free seems to us to be the normal future of the German people, provided that the present borders in the

West, East, North and South are not again called into question
and Germany tries one day to fit contractually into a pan-
European organization for cooperation, freedom and peace.[6]

A future Germany, in other words, should be free and democratic.
Its political configuration, however, remained unclear and could
only remain so. De Gaulle referred sometimes to reunification and
sometimes to confederation. He sometimes spoke of the German
people and sometimes of the Saxons and Prussians, as if to underline
the distinctiveness of the German states. As to the means, De
Gaulle clearly foresaw what would later become West Germany's
Ostpolitik:

> Until this ideal [of reunification] is reached, we still intend that
> the two separate parts of the German nation multiply their
> respective ties and relations, on all levels: transportation and
> mail, economics, literature, science, arts, the comings and goings
> of individuals, etc. . . . would be the objects of agreements that
> would bring the Germans closer together, for the sake of which
> I would like to speak of the German matter [*la chose allemande*]
> – which they have in common in spite of the difference in regime.[7]

De Gaulle would not suggest a practical step, however; the East–West
stalemate rendered all plans irrelevant.

Stanley Hoffmann, who rightly pointed out that a powerful neutral
state was unacceptable, labelled France's policy 'byzantine'.

> Paris assured the West Germans that it stood up for this ideal of
> reunification, so that the case would never happen where a
> disappointed West Germany risked entering a separate dialogue
> with Moscow. At the same time, France indicated to the other
> Western powers that she had everything under control: no
> reunification could take place, at least no reunification within a
> mighty, neutral state.[8]

As long as Adenauer and De Gaulle were pursuing similar goals,
that is, strengthening the Federal Republic's ties to the West,
suspicions were kept to a minimum. Once quiet understanding
vanished, however, these suspicions flared up. De Gaulle's immediate
successors never addressed the question of reunification. On the
one hand, Pompidou suspected that the Kiesinger and Brandt
governments were pursuing reunification under the cover of *Ostpolitik*. He viewed the Moscow treaty and Brandt's visit to the Crimea

as proof of a new Rapallo. Giscard, on the other hand, was probably less moved by defiance than by an ahistorical vision of international relations: for him, the German Question was settled once and for all. Both leaders carefully insisted on France's rights in Berlin, the former during the negotiation of the Quadripartite Agreement, the latter when he visited Berlin in 1979 and the Federal Republic in 1980 – a way to close the German Question with a French seal . . . by leaving it open.

The recent evolution of French public opinion thus appears all the more surprising. While in 1979 the French still expressed their concern at a possible reunification (36 per cent thought it would be detrimental to France and to other European countries as well),[9] five years later, in January 1984, 42 per cent thought France should not intervene in a reunification process.[10] More significantly, the following year, a remarkable majority of French people – 59 per cent – considered Germany's reunification would be fully legitimate while only 20 per cent dismissed it as undesirable.[11] Some prominent experts and analysts share this view. Jean-Marie Soutou, former secretary general at the Ministry for Foreign Affairs, recently wrote:

> I do not think that we can consider today and even that for a long time we could have considered France's uneasiness at Germany's possible reunification as an objective factor in European or Western political reality; that France would have entertained good relations with both German states in order to maintain partition, may probably have entailed some truth – though much less than is generally thought, and actually for less time than is generally admitted. . .
>
> As far as I am concerned, even after fighting all my life against the Nazis, I have always considered that Germany's partition is most terrible. . . . Political wisdom – if not morality – requires that we put an end to it.
>
> There certainly are people in Paris who do not think as I do. But they are increasingly fewer.[12]

President Mitterrand never went as far as French public opinion. Yet he expressed understanding most notably in his 1983 Bundestag speech when he underlined the tragedy of partition – while, at the same time, favoring the deployment of Pershing IIs on German soil: 'For having lived in occupied France, I deeply feel what the Germans – divided as they are – may feel. For having known a devastated Europe, I feel what dispersed people may feel.[13] Contrary to his predecessor Giscard, Mitterrand went so far as to invite Chancellor Kohl to France when he visited Berlin in October 1985, a significant symbol of Franco-German togetherness in the divided city. This does not mean, however, that all misunderstandings are forgotten and that French elites have dismissed all suspicions regarding West German policy; the debate which flared up in the FRG in May 1987 over rumors pertaining to an alleged long-term Soviet reunification plan – and which actually proved to be limited to a vocal circle of West Germans – raised some concern in Paris.

Geopolitics

This change in public mood and, to some extent, in elite attitudes may partly be accounted for by increased sympathy for France's West German neighbor, the result of years of incremental cooperation and togetherness;[14] partly and paradoxically by a sense of France's own weakness which has coincided in the late 1970s and early 1980s with a kind of opening up, of renewed interest in foreign economic, political and cultural processes and a willingness to enter cooperative ventures; and, last but not least, by a perceived weakness of the Federal Republic of Germany, a dramatic change in France's perception of that country. In the 1960s and even more so in the 1970s, France indeed had worried about the shadow West Germany cast over it. In all areas, economic, commercial, financial and even political,[15] the Federal Republic seemed to out-trump France, reviving past traumas, repeating history. After the devastation of two wars, the (West) German phoenix had risen again, while France's economy had lost its vitality once the *trente glorieuses* had passed.[16] The last days of De Gaulle's government evidenced the differences, as if to shatter the political edifice built up by the grand old man. Bonn's refusal to reevaluate the deutschmark in 1968 and France's subsequent devaluation ushered in a succession of monetary crises, repeated devaluations and widening inflation differentials for years to come. The blue line of the deutschmark became the new dividing line between West Germany and France,[17] a source of quarrels, in particular as Paris repeatedly demanded the creation of a European currency fund while Bonn procrastinated because common economic policies should, according to West German leaders, be the prerequisites to a monetary union and not the reverse.[18]

Economic policies could not, however, be attuned because of

diverging structures and dynamics. While France's trade margins were dwindling,West Germany accumulated surpluses. Wondering about the secrets of the Federal Republic's 'virtuous circle',[19] French politicians and businessmen would order analyses and studies to ponder over the German model. Meanwhile French Communists expressed fear of West Germany's structural influence: austerity, first experimented with by Prime Minister Raymond Barre to bring down inflation, was criticized as a submission to Bonn's will. Campaigning for election to the European Parliament in 1979, the PCF launched the motto: 'Non à l'Europe de Schmidt' (No to Schmidt's Europe). That under these circumstances both Pompidou and Giscard d'Estaing obviously dismissed reunification as a hypothesis was perfectly logical, and Giscard even brought forward the idea of increasing conventional troops to counterbalance West Germany's weight.

French perception, however, changed drastically at the turn of the 1980s, for two reasons. At the beginning of the 1980s, French economists (the CEPII in particular)[20] and, a little later, West Germans themselves, began to wonder – but not for long – whether the West German miracle was not fading away, a result of having concentrated since the nineteenth century on machine tools and now ignoring the third industrial revolution in the production of numerical command machines (NCM) and in other areas. The heirs of 1968, involved in the ecological movement, together with the trade unions, which were fighting unemployment, nourished opposition to technological development on the basis of its destructiveness to humanity and nature and as a source of unemployment. This new form of Luddism seemed to confirm the dramatic predictions of the Hudson Institute which, in the 1960s, had foreseen France's economic superiority and West Germany's decline. Yet this could not cause much satisfaction in France as it went along with a modification of public attitudes in the FRG as well as heated discussions between West German conservative and left parties on defense issues. While the SPD and a large part of West German public opinion opposed the stationing of Pershing IIs in Western Europe, France opposed the double Soviet threat, ideological and military – a reversal of previous stances when France had indulged in Gaullism and the Federal Republic in Atlanticism. As Jacques Huntzinger, then in charge of international relations within the Socialist Party, bluntly put it: 'Formerly, we feared German militarism, now we fear German pacifism'.[21]

In spite of this apparent reversal in attitudes and policies, the logic behind them remained constant. While previously France had feared West Germany's increased power, what the French now feared was that the West Germans might gradually become unable to fulfill their NATO commitments and that an incremental modification of West German attitudes and policies might subtly alter the balance of power in Europe. This was perceived as detrimental to both France and the Western alliance. Determined French criticism of the Soviet Union and the continued expansion of France's *force de frappe* with the *Lois de programmation militaire* (Military Program Laws), should not hide the fact that France depends on the Federal Republic for its security. An eventual decoupling of European and American security and a weakening of the Federal Republic's willingness and capabilities to defend itself and Europe threaten France's defense posture. In January 1983 Mitterrand had to plead for the deployment of Pershing IIs in front of the West German Bundestag.

The military and political security of both France and Europe as a whole is at stake. Some observers have predicted that, if the Federal Republic were to become neutral, Europe would end up as a Soviet Hong Kong.[22] Without going to these extremes, one commentator warned: 'The German question must not be isolated from its international context'.[23] As Michael Stuermer, a leading historian, political commentator and counsellor to Chancellor Kohl, likes to put it, the German Question resembles a mobile: move one element and all elements move together. Certainly all issues – social, economic, political and military – are interconnected. The German Question must be considered within an international context, but it must be remembered that the latter also influences the former. Ever since the Reykjavik summit and the resumption of Soviet–American negotiations, political fronts have been regrouping. Though officials in Paris and Bonn officially support the INF Treaty, the French right, much more so than the left, as well as German conservatives, barely conceal concern over Soviet and American schemes and the eventual weakening of Europe they might cause.

While the future of Europe looks fluid and possibly more somber than at the height of the pacifist wave, the French and West German governments have moved closer to.one another, but not the two opposition parties. The French socialist party is part and parcel of the national consensus on the necessity to defend both France and Europe against a perceived Soviet political and military threat. The

German left, however, denies the existence of such a threat and is striving for the 'demilitarization' of East–West relations. It seems that, as a result of this evolution, French public opinion has realized that France needs a stable ally, and it now advocates a hypothetical reunification of Germany for the sake of understanding with the Germans and cementing Franco-German cooperation. Some experts support the public reasoning. As Jean-Marie Soutou wrote in a leading West German newspaper, the neutralization of Europe is at stake and 'we need a German national consciousness, steady, outright, pure, asserted without inhibition and without arrogance, with a quiet transparency. We need it for all that is essential'.[24] That is, to cooperate closely in the construction of Europe, including its defense, and to assert itself *vis-à-vis* the Soviet Union.

II POLICIES: FROM THE RHINE TO THE ELBE

Dilemma as a Heritage

Since the German problem has first and foremost a geopolitical and strategic relevance which has been dramatically enhanced in the 1980s, the French have tried to tackle the problem in primarily strategic terms, that is, by trying to intensify Franco-German military cooperation. Yet past policies have hindered it. To that extent, Franco-German military cooperation epitomizes the difficulties and chances of a Paris–Bonn axis.

The first steps were made with little success when the EDC treaty was signed, later floundering on France's unwillingness to sacrifice its own army for the sake of controlling the Germans. However, only a few years later, an extremely bold policy of tripartite cooperation was agreed upon by France, Italy and the Federal Republic which provided for the 'development and co-production of modern weapons', including nuclear weapons. The agreement provided that 'none of the three powers could hold a monopoly of production; the cooperation of all three would be necessary'.[25] At the time, the French leadership did not think that France alone could afford the development of nuclear weapons; cooperation with other powers was considered necessary and the 1954 Paris agreement that denied the Federal Republic the right to produce ABC weapons on its own territory was not looked upon as an obstacle. This tripartite cooperation, about which little has been written, was part and parcel of a wider scheme, the Colomb-Bechar agreement, concluded in 1957, which provided for the development of industrial and technological cooperation between France and the Federal Republic, the first step toward what was to become an intense cooperation between the two countries in the co-production of conventional weapons.

After the fall of the Fourth Republic, De Gaulle's role was primary both in hindering and promoting Franco-German cooperation. In 1958, he assumed the policy of the previous governments, yet with his personal twist. One of his very first decisions was to put an end to the 1957 secret agreement, a decision which, according to François Puaux, Franz Josef Strauss, then West German Defense Minister, resented: as a result, the Federal Republic is said to have preferred the American Starfighter to French Mirage III jets.[26] The cancellation of the 1957 agreement came at a time when De Gaulle, in a famous memorandum to President Eisenhower, called for the transformation of NATO into a Franco-Anglo-American triumvirate which would address and decide together political and strategic questions. Deliberately excluding the Federal Republic from the suggested alliance, the proposal was met with little enthusiasm by West German public opinion, which looked upon it as an effort to reactivate the *Entente Cordiale*. Moreover, not only did France try to assign the Federal Republic a second-rank role, but is also became clearer that France was pursuing a different road. While the Federal Republic depended on NATO and US protection, ambiguously pursuing the acquisition of nuclear weapons in the framework of the Multilateral Force, France was striving towards independence, ultimately pulling its troops out of the integrated framework in 1967. On the whole, it seemed that De Gaulle's proposals and policies were to burden the Franco-German relationship for a long time.

Yet at the same time De Gaulle promoted European and Franco-German coordination. He tried to push forward European unity and coordinate rather than integrate policies, including the defense policies of European states. After the floundering of the Fouchet Plans, he suggested a Franco-German tandem. The Elysée Treaty of 1963 called for joint examination of all important questions pertaining to foreign policy, particularly East–West relations, as well as matters of concern for NATO, the integrated military network of which France had not yet left. Doctrines, strategies and tactics were to be adjusted, staff exchanges between armies promoted and common armament projects fostered from the very start. For this purpose, defense ministers and chiefs of staff were to meet on a regular basis, defense ministers at least on a trimester basis, and chiefs of staff at least once every two months. As both François Puaux and Michel Tatu underlined, De Gaulle's suggestions, as formulated by the Fouchet Plans and the 1963 Elysée Treaty, were bolder indeed than all that has been put forward since to further Franco-German defense cooperation.[27]

However, differing aims clashed. It became immediately obvious to France's partners that a common defense policy, be it within a European framework or within a 'small alliance' with the Federal Republic, could hardly be implemented when all partners were increasingly at odds over the strategy to be followed. In other words, the avowed aim to narrow tactical and strategic differences was blatantly contradicted by France's pursuit of independence at a time when its partners depended on the alliance with the United States. As a result, the significance of the Elysée Treaty was considerably diluted and its defense provisions never implemented. As Nicole Gnesotto has noted, while the Soviet threat had drawn both countries together fairly quickly, paradoxically enough, the alliance has been a point of contention between them for a number of years, though the quarrel has decreased in intensity and significance with the passage of time.[28]

On the whole, De Gaulle's role was unique. Contrary to the leaders of the Fourth Republic who had envisaged a triple (West German, Italian and French) key, he realized that the essence of deterrence implied a one-man decision: the possession of nuclear weapons could not be shared. He was, on the other hand, quite daring in suggesting common defense schemes – European or Franco-German. A man of vision, he could intellectually handle the dilemma, while his European partners prevented him from mastering it politically. His followers would never master it: withdrawing from common defense schemes, depleted by then of any sense, both Pompidou and Giscard were stuck with a narrowly interpreted version of Gaullist visions and left with the burden of Franco-German misunderstandings which stemmed from France's newly gained independence in the defense area. Dilemmas fossilized into taboos. And cooperation was sometimes laden with recrimination.

With France's withdrawal from the integrated network of NATO, French and West German political and military leaders faced a fourfold problem: the stationing and targeting of French tactical nuclear weapons was to become a major point of contention between the two countries. After 1967, France sought to replace NATO with French tactical nuclear weapons, the future 110-kilometer range Plutons. Deployed on French soil, the Plutons could hit West German territory. A dialogue of the deaf between Bonn and Paris ensued, the former requiring consultations, the latter insisting both on France's sovereignty and on uncertainty of use as prerequisites to credibility. Furthermore, the deployment of French conventional troops on West German soil and their possible role in case of war were codified by the Ailleret-Lemnitzer agreement concluded in 1967, with France strongly opposing both automatic engagement and participation in the forward defense of the Federal Republic. On both the strategic and logistical level, France's withdrawal excluded its national territory from NATO contingency planning, though agreements have been concluded to provide for France's logistical support in certain cases.[29] Last but not least, France's withdrawal from NATO's integrated framework concretized doctrinal differences. While NATO – and the Federal Republic – rallied to McNamara's 'flexible response', France elaborated the doctrine of proportional deterrence and, as a consequence, assigned to its tactical nuclear weapons a 'pre-strategic' role.

Differences and divergences, however, should not be exaggerated. Arms co-production proved to be fruitful – though the 1970s were characterized by the completion of projects which had already been agreed upon rather than by the elaboration of new plans. Still more significantly, feelers were sent out which signalled some progress towards a Franco-German *rapprochement*. First Prime Minister Jacques Chirac, then General Méry and finally President Giscard D'Estaing suggested extending the French nuclear umbrella beyond France's border. In February 1975, while presiding over the introduction of the first Plutons, Prime Minister Jacques Chirac stated that the French theater nuclear weapons could contribute to the defense of Europe. General Méry, General Chief of Staff, put forward the following year the concept of 'extended sanctuarization', implying both that France might participate in NATO's forward defense and that French tactical nuclear weapons might be assigned a kind of European mission. Finally, President Giscard D'Estaing declared in June 1976 at the Institut des Hautes Etudes de Defense Nationale that, in case of war, there would be a single battle theater: hence, there should be a single military response.[30]

All three suggestions came at a time when, within a still fairly stable security framework characterized by ongoing East–West negotiations, the dilemma between independence and integration was considered unsustainable. In other words, the pursuit of closer defense cooperation between the two major West European countries was unavoidable. The personal friendship which tied the two leaders, Giscard and Schmidt, certainly supplemented whatever willingness already existed on the part of Giscard's UDF, which has always been more prone to greater cooperation within both European and alliance frameworks than any other French political party. Since leaving office, former Chancellor Schmidt has several times hinted that both he and Giscard had been on the verge of making a dramatic step forward – namely, building a Franco-German army.

Whether true or false, the time was not ripe. President Giscard D'Estaing did not contribute to reassuring France's German neighbors when, on the one hand, he decided to thin out the first army stationed in Baden-Baden, and, on the other hand, he had to revise his position as regards the use of tactical nuclear weapons. A few months after his declaration, he admitted that they could not deter any attack on Germany. And in 1979, after General Buis and General Sanguinetti suggested in the press that West German industry might contribute to France's nuclear armament, Giscard once more severely criticized the very idea of Franco-German nuclear cooperation. The concept of 'extended sanctuarization' had indeed been met with a general outcry. The French consensus, though being built, was not yet full-fledged and French elites still resisted a Franco-German *rapprochement*.

The Rise

A Socialist president was to achieve what his predecessor had failed to do. Although Giscard had been more inclined to promote Franco-German cooperation thanks to the backing of the liberal, pro-European UDF and to his own personal connection with Schmidt, the Socialist party, ruling at first with the Communist party, actually made decisive progress toward achieving this goal. In February 1982, François Mitterrand made an agreement with Helmut Schmidt to reactivate the security and foreign policy provisions of the Elysée Treaty. It was decided that, in the future, the four defense and foreign ministers would meet regularly before each Franco-German summit. A Commission on Defense and Security, created in October 1982 and including civil servants from the four ministries, was to be convened four times a year and control three working groups on arms production, military cooperation and strategic and political matters.[31] Another political step was taken a year later: the Western European Union (WEU) was reactivated and in June 1984 discriminatory clauses which had impinged upon West Germany's sovereignty and military capabilities were discarded.

These measures were taken at a time when a twofold debate was going on, within the alliance and in France. While the Euromissile debate did not flare up in France, both French public opinion and elites displayed deep concern for the debate which rocked the alliance. The debate, particularly in the Federal Republic, and the development of an anti-missile mood led them to fear, as described above, for their security. 'The French had to face the hypothesis of a faltering of the Federal Republic as a consequence of intense external pressures and internal tensions', explained André Adrets in an article analyzing the reasons and modes of the Franco-German *rapprochement*. In a sense, by means of what was perceived as a Soviet political and military threat, that is, an attempt 'to impose a veto on the deployment of US medium-range rockets, as well as the ability to strike both front- and second-line states with emerging "smart weapons"', Moscow managed to bring the French and the Germans together.[32] As a consequence, in his famous speech to the West German Bundestag in 1983, François Mitterrand sided with the proponents of deployment and stressed the necessity to recouple European and American security. More than his predecessors, in this particular case the Socialist president was taking an Atlanticist stand.

The prerequisite had been the rallying of the two left-wing parties (the Communists in 1977 and the Socialists in 1978) to deterrence, which they had fiercely opposed previously. Henceforth, all parties agreed on a common basis: the necessity to uphold nuclear weapons as credible instruments of deterrence and the undesirability and superfluity of reintegrating France into NATO's military network were conceived of as preconditions for France's independent stand. A consensus was built, and has been a source both of wonder and fear to French politicians ever since – wonder that it exists, and the well-founded fear that it is fragile and will break down, which, as we will see, tended to be proved by post-INF developments. While independence, if not greatness, is viewed as desirable, a certain degree of realism nevertheless prevails. Wondering whether France was still a *grande nation*, a major weekly revealed at the beginning of 1984 that a majority of French thought of their country as a middle power subsequently accompanied, especially in 1987 and 1988, by concerns over putative French decadence. A majority also held that, in case of conflict, because of its weakness France would have to count on West Germany first – while the West Germans thought they would have to count on themselves.[33] Another series of polls proved that, under the socialist government, both Atlanticist and European options have progressed, the former among conservatives, the latter among socialists.[34] Last but not least, major polls showed that even in 1983 a majority of French people approved of a 'common Franco-German security'[35] and, in 1985, that 57 per cent thought that France should defend the Federal Republic.[36] Once more the public mood proved bolder than presidential policy.

So too, however, did French elites, who as early as 1983 started to promote the offering of some kind of nuclear protection to the Federal Republic. The rationale behind the offer was that France had to be consistent with its advocacy of deployment of Euromissiles on West German territory and contribute in its turn to West German security, without of course replacing American protection. In other words, because France's sanctuarization could only promote German neutralism, French elites thought their country had to go further and stop giving the impression that the Federal Republic was a mere glacis. Whereas most agreed on the premise, debate flared up on the extent and form this protection should assume.

Some advocated extreme solutions. Simone Weil, a former concentration camp inmate, former minister and a UDF representative at the European Parliament, and the philosopher André Glucksmann agreed that 'the Germans should be given the bomb' lest they drift toward neutralism. Pierre Lellouche, associate director of the French Institute for International Relations (IFRI), advocated nothing less than the stationing of French tactical nuclear weapons at the German–German border. And Michel Tatu, a renowned journalist at *Le Monde*, suggested providing the FRG with a double key, giving them a veto right over the possible use of the Hades missiles, due to replace the shorter-range Plutons. Others, however, such as Pierre Hassner, a senior researcher at the National Foundation for Political Science (FNSP), argued in favor of a symbolic declaration. 'Certain sentences', he wrote, 'decide war and peace. . .such as Kennedy's "Ich bin ein Berliner"'. French politicians were asked to tie France and Germany symbolically into a *communauté de destins (Schicksalsgemeinschaft)*.[37] Others finally saw a policy of 'small steps' as more promising. Ambassador De

Rose, for instance, suggested the creation of a Franco-German Nuclear Planning Group, following NATO's model.

Political parties took somewhat more prudent, yet, considering previous taboos, daring positions. Jacques Chirac, President of the RPR (then in opposition), was in October 1983 the first to call for France's participation in an American–European deterrence, a proposal formulated during a visit to the Federal Republic! Michel Aurillac, one of his advisers and from 1986 to 1987 a minister in his government, that same year also suggested both stronger French involvement in forward defense and a French nuclear guarantee. In its pre-electoral program published in 1985,[38] Chirac's RPR was much more modest, as its president's declarations had caused some uproar: it called for full respect of the Elysée Treaty, including consultations on the possible use of tactical nuclear weapons. Its future coalition partner and sometimes challenger, the UDF, faithful to its pro-European stand, required that steps be taken toward a European defense in which France, resorting to its tactical nuclear weapons, would take an active role in the forward defense of Europe. The UDF, it is true, had never entirely accepted the proportional doctrine, pleading more or less openly for NATO's flexible response.[39] As for the Socialist Party, it expressly called for an extension of France's nuclear deterrence to Europe, short of formal guarantees.[40]

Half Empty or Half Full?

The wide range of proposals and the extreme volatility of the debate which abated almost as quickly as it had flared up (only to resume again after the March 1986 elections) pointed less to a lack of consensus than to what leaders and elites consider the limits of feasibility. The credibility of French deterrence rests on the twin notions of capability and uncertainty, which can be summed up by two questions. First, 'Would the French die for Hamburg?', a question which echoes another famous one: 'Would the Americans die for Hamburg?' If Americans hesitate, the French might hesitate even more. Second, 'When, where and how would French nuclear weapons be employed?', a question which must remain unanswered as it lies at the very core of deterrence. 'Deterrence: that is I,' François Mitterrand once underlined. Nevertheless some French experts and politicians have at times tried to make the most of it to shun responsibilities. As Pierre Hassner put it:

The fact that deterrence entails some kind of uncertainty and that the decision to resort to nuclear weapons cannot be shared – two obvious evidences which lead us to reject both nuclear guarantees and double keys – should not be used as alibis to maintain uncertainty over the use of our conventional force in case of an attack on Germany, or to avoid identifying the security of Germany with that of France, or not to want to earnestly discuss the conditions of use of our nuclear weapons (which does not mean an obligation to use them at a definite time or in a definite place).[41]

While French arguments and proposals wavered from a boldness bordering on unreality to a subtlety verging on timidity, the West Germans have met them with polite disinterest. Certainly Helmut Schmidt advocated in his Bundestag speech of 8 June 1984 a French nuclear guarantee, a proposal which he actually watered down in subsequent speeches and interviews, stressing the primary importance of a Franco-German army. So did the unpredictable Egon Bahr, who declared a few weeks after Schmidt's speech that 'the real question is to know whether or not the French are ready to share Germany's risks. If yes, not only would Germany accept the deployment of French conventional forces at the front, she would also accept French nuclear forces on her soil'.[42] This was a remarkable proposal considering that he had asked in another context for the withdrawal of all nuclear weapons from the territory of states which do not own them.

Generally speaking, however, a lack of concern has prevailed as nuclear weapons are, if not widely criticized, at least 'out of fashion' in West German public opinion. Whereas 30 per cent of the French agreed in 1984 to the possession of nuclear weapons by the Federal Republic, only 14 per cent of the Germans shared this opinion.[43] While the MLF project had found an echo at the governmental level in the late 1950s and early 1960s, floundering not because of public opposition – which did exist – but because of differences within the alliance, public opinion has nowadays too great an influence on the decision-making process – via the opposition parties – for the government to approve of French suggestions.[44] Some of these, moreover, may have sounded too rhetorical or symbolic while the West Germans are, on the whole, concerned with practical problems in other areas. That former Chancellor Schmidt has, ever since his June 1984 speech, more or less put aside the idea of a

French nuclear guarantee, insisting rather on the necessity to build a Franco-German conventional army, is indicative of Germany's preferences. While Schmidt certainly goes further than any of his contemporaries in insisting upon a scheme which would 'envelop French military forces in an overall West European security system',[45] West German politicians and elites primarily wish, as he does, for a stronger involvement in forward defense by stronger French conventional forces. They also have persistently and consistently required some kind of consultation on planning and targeting of tactical nuclear weapons, a demand which has been high on the agenda ever since the appearance of the first Plutons. And, last but not least, they have been insisting on narrowing the gap between French and NATO strategies.

Though disappointed by West German indifference to France's efforts, Paris has tried to meet its neighbor's specific demands. Decisions in the military area followed the political ones taken at the beginning of the legislature. After a series of declarations including then Defense Minister Charles Hernu's June 1985 admission in front of his West German counterpart that France and the Federal Republic have 'common security', and the October 1987 underwriting of the WEU's most recent platform strengthening this commitment, Prime Minister Jacques Chirac went the furthest when he recognized in December 1987 that France would engage its forces 'immediately and without reservations' if an attack were launched on the Federal Republic. 'There cannot be a battle of France and a battle of Germany', he added. This indeed comes down to the solemn declaration, similar to Kennedy's 'Ich bin ein Berliner' statement, which the West Germans and some French experts had been asking for in the past years. President Mitterand later endorsed this declaration, limiting it, however, to the conventional area: the decision to resort to nuclear weapons should lie with the president, even though in January 1986 at Baden-Baden he had proposed consultations on the possible use of tactical nuclear weapons under the condition that 'rapidity of action' and 'unity of decision' be respected, an offer which was confirmed at the February 1986 summit meeting. This long-awaited suggestion was not hailed by the West German press, however, since it fell short of expectations.

Second, a number of instruments have been created or perfected over the past few years that allow France to participate in Germany's conventional defense. In 1984, the creation of the Rapid Action Force (*Force d'Action Rapide*) was agreed upon. Conceived to meet defense purposes in France, Europe and other areas, the RAF is designed, among other things, to supplement the First Army wherever needed. Highly mobile, it could play a decisive role in the forward defense of the Federal Republic if necessary – a dramatic reversal of France's previous policy. While then Defense Minister Hernu had stressed that the RAF, and particularly its 4th Airmobile Division, would 'permit us, infinitely better than today, to commit ourselves at the side of our allies, as soon as we would have taken the decision, at the time and place that we would have chosen, should the occasion arise', the September 1987 *Bold Sparrow* exercise was the first in which major units of the RAF based in particular in the south of France crossed the Rhine and penetrated into Bavaria, east of the Dortmund–Munich line, with so much material, under the 'operational control' of a West German commander. The West Germans clearly got the message even though some observers criticized the shortcomings and problems which the exercise evidenced, yet the joint exercise demonstrated shortcomings which are now known to all and can be corrected in the future . . . .The joint maneuvers as well as other measures, in particular the common brigade suggested by Chancellor Kohl and the Common Defense Council put forth by President Mitterrand, have to perform a twin function, both practical and symbolic: (1) to help evidence the problems raised by the cooperation of French and West German troops in the operational-tactical area: and (2) to evidence the Franco-German community of security-interests.[46]

That present and future governments will pursue previous efforts is more than certain; what is uncertain is in what manner they will do so. Changes in doctrines, though undesired, are not to be excluded entirely. Ever since the cohabitation, a rift has appeared in the French consensus concerning what, exactly, France's doctrine should be – a rift which actually reflects certain former differences. On the one hand, Defense Minister Hernu suggested in 1982 and 1983 that the RAF and even the First Army might be decoupled from French nuclear forces; he even put forward the idea of a special command for nuclear forces distinct from the First Army, and underlined that the 350 km-range Hades could be 'used beyond the zone of interest of the army corps and without a necessary link to their maneuver if the president so decides'. Mitterrand's ambiguous statement of October 1987 probably reflects the same position: 'Nothing', he said then, 'permits anyone to affirm that France's ultimate warning to the aggressor would be delivered on German territory. Tactics are subject to strategy. . .France's nuclear strategy is addressed to the aggressor and him alone, in order to deter him'. Whether this means dropping tactical nuclear weapons altogether or lengthening their range remains uncertain, and François Mitterrand is probably too clever to raise the issue now.

Jacques Chirac, on the other hand, stressed in fall 1986 the coupling between conventional and nuclear weapons, divorcing tactical nuclear weapons, which he dubbed *tactical* rather than *strategic*, from strategic weapons. These subtleties announced the present, important, though half-muted, debate between left and right, between socialists and conservatives, between Elysée and Matignon, between, on the one hand, those who want to raise the nuclear threshold and thus solve the problem of tactical nuclear targeting and hence come back to the purity of deterrence and the notion of massive retaliation, withdrawing on the national territory; and, on the other hand, those who stress the importance of tactical nuclear weapons as the intermediary rungs of flexible retaliation, links partly destroyed by the INF agreement and to be reconstructed together with other European allies within a broader defense scheme (consider Giraud's spokesman's declaration of July 1987, mentioning the deployment of Hades and neutron bombs on German soil). On the one hand, all or nothing, on the other a gradual European response. . .

To blur the debate further, it is to be noted again that both answers stem from the same concerns: how to build Europe, how to bind Germany. To make matters even more confusing, both correspond to diplomatic views which are precisely at odds with current military doctrines. François Mitterrand, the nuclear isolationist, has welcomed the INF Treaty and advocated further disarmament steps, which meets West German concern, while the conservative supporters of a European defense have criticized the INF agreement, and even decried it as a new Munich, thus running the risk of isolating themselves from the Germans and other Europeans. While François Mitterrand would like to delay the modernization of SNF and consider conventional negotiations primary, Jacques Chirac certainly would like a conventional agreement before an SNF one.[47]

The Reykjavik summit, continuing negotiations, the eventual partial decoupling of European and American security, as well as the US stock market crash of October 1987 and economic problems generally, have all proved the necessity for European military and economic cooperation and encouraged the French – and others as well – to go further in that direction. In a sense, a kind of competition is going on in France between left and right, between the Elysée Palace and Matignon, on how best to consolidate the Franco-German axis and get credit for it: both wish to take the ball and run with it.

Yet, while both necessity and desires are more intense than ever, problems still exist. First, though routine cooperation certainly works best, it does not exclude mutual incomprehension as in years past when complaints marred the game. The French are unhappy with the lack of interest displayed by some Germans. In particular – though the 1980s cannot be compared with the 1960s in terms of an alleged West German choice between the United States and France – Paris feels that for whatever reason, technical, financial or political, when the chips are down, the West Germans choose to 'buy American'. As far as space projects (such as Hermes) are concerned, the West Germans have shown a lack of readiness to cooperate with Paris, even disregarding the fact that the French certainly bear some responsibility for sometimes presenting projects that are suited mainly to their own needs. Second, though the French and the West Germans do have common security interests, the latter are faced with constraints the French do not have, such as the stationing of foreign short-range missiles on German soil which, with the enforcement of the double-zero solution, would, according to current West German rhetoric, 'single out' the FRG. Hence the repeated demand of mainstream West German conservatives and some social-democrats for a firm and unambiguous French commitment, or again, the lack of interest, mainly of the left, in Franco-German schemes. While the changing East–West configuration makes Franco-German cooperation all the more necessary, ambiguities and contradictions in both countries, as well as differently conceived French and West German interests, render it all the more difficult. Military cooperation between the two countries seems more firmly anchored than ever because of practical steps taken in the past. Nevertheless, looming dangers remain.

III PROSPECTS

Despite temporary setbacks or disappointments, the pursuit and intensification of Franco-German relations do not support an overall pessimistic outlook. On the one hand, the current Soviet–American configuration highlights the necessity for action. On the other hand, the common training of officers of both nationalities, the establishment of a Franco-German brigade, that is to say, some of the less dramatic decisions taken in recent years, may have incremental yet sweeping consequences in the future. Besides these expected developments one should ask, however, whether cooperation in the military and security areas is the most appropriate answer to France's German Question. Whereas the French tend to interpret the German problem more and more in geopolitical terms, geopolitics does not come down solely to the military. Certainly other measures were envisaged at the February 1982 summit meeting: not only was the reactivation of the security provisions of the Elysée Treaty suggested, but mention was also made of coordinating foreign policies as provided by the Treaty, especially policies *vis-à-vis* the East.

Policy *vis-à-vis* the East is part and parcel of the German problem. Put another way, the German problem is a European problem: because the partition of Germany epitomizes the division of Europe, the two are intimately linked. While the Soviet Union has in the past sometimes referred to alleged 'revanchist tendencies' in the Federal Republic as a pretense to reinforce its control over Eastern Europe, the relaxation of tensions between the two German states, both a condition and a result of East–West *détente*, has allowed, if not the democratization of Eastern Europe, at least the emergence of some 'free areas' which the citizens can hope to preserve. This was the very essence of *Ostpolitik* as first designed and detailed by General De Gaulle. Yet De Gaulle's *Ostpolitik* fostered suspicion beyond the Rhine: what if *détente* only cemented the *status quo* in Europe and hence the partition of Germany? While De Gaulle sought, if not to Europeanize the German question, at least to blur, in the long run, the consequence of partition within a European framework, it could not be forgotten that he had asked very early for the recognition of the Oder–Niesse border and, moreover, that at the end of the war he had conceived a policy of reassurance *vis-à-vis* Germany. Yet if De Gaulle's policy failed it was not because of cynicism; rather, it failed because his vision of Europe was inadequate for the 1960s. His version of a Europe from the Atlantic to the Urals floundered when the Soviet Union invaded Czechoslovakia, a reminder to those who had forgotten about the existence of blocs.

A few years later roles reversed. West German *Ostpolitik* aroused suspicions in France. In other words, the suspected aims of policy *vis-à-vis* the East, be it Germany's *Ostpolitik* or France's *politique envers l'Est*, has often been a matter of concern to each other's partner: Rapallo or reassurances? Short of conflict, however, competition has prevailed. In the 1970s, defiance caused the French to emulate their West German neighbor, to ask Soviets and East Europeans who was fairer in their eyes. Giscard's hastily arranged 1980 meeting with Brezhnev in Warsaw and his attempted mediation between East and West which was highly criticized in France; or again France's presence at the 1980 Olympic Games, which the Federal Republic boycotted along with the United States; and even Mitterrand's visit to Moscow or his meeting with Jaruzelski – all may be partly interpreted as attempts, if not to counterbalance the Federal Republic, at least to trump it in the East. This policy, however, encounters precise limits. On the one hand, as long as Bonn and Paris turn to the East to ask who is fairer, both capitals give up some margin of maneuver – a fact which they cannot ignore. On the other hand, France privileges its Western ally to *Ostpolitik*. Though over the years French policy *vis-à-vis* the GDR has acquired a certain dynamic – as is evidenced by the existence of the French Cultural Institute *Unter den Linden*, a very active center – the other German state remains largely *terra incognita*.[48] The first official visit of Erich Honecker, Secretary General of the SED, to Paris, from 7 January to 9 January 1988, may have paved the way, if not to better knowledge, at least to better understanding. While semi-official West German circles worried that this visit, coming just a few weeks before the celebrations of the twenty-fifth anniversary of the Elysée Treaty, might evidence a French double game, President Mitterrand stressed the necessity to develop understanding and reconciliation between France and 'all the Germans' while advocating civil liberties and individual freedom.[49]

Coordination remains difficult, however, be it on the multilateral or on the bilateral level. That divergence exists was epitomized by the Polish crisis. French and German reactions to the installation of a military regime in Poland were quite opposite, as mentioned above, and strenuous efforts were required to settle disputes both between the French Socialist Party and the West German Social Democrats within the Socialist International, and at the diplomatic level within the European Community framework. Is further integration, let alone harmonization of French and West German *Ostpolitik*, possible? While it is desirable, problems will persist.

Because of the very nature of inter-German relations, of their special quality and intensity, one may strongly doubt that efforts to coordinate policy with Bonn in this area will transcend present achievements. Additionally, this inter-German connection heavily skews relations between the Federal Republic and East European countries: another 'Polish crisis' will again precipitate divergent reactions in Bonn and Paris. Yet, if the French analysis of the German problem in its 1980s version is correct, other ways and means should be found to promote a Franco-West German *rapprochement*, on both symbolic and practical levels: the French are well aware of this, as the recent decision to establish a committee to coordinate French and West German economic and monetary policy underlines.

12 Economic Relations Between the Two German States

Gert Leptin

I INTRODUCTION

The economic relations between the Federal Republic of Germany (FRG) and the German Democratic Republic (GDR) have been strongly influenced and at times even determined by political factors since they began as interzonal trade between the three Western Zones of Occupation and the Soviet Zone of Occupation shortly after the end of the Second World War. The relative importance of either political or economic factors depends upon the different levels of East–West relations: at the level of the basic political and legal framework, the political elements clearly dominate (to be more exact, the elements of world politics, based upon the relations of the two superpowers in Europe and especially in Germany and in Berlin). These elements proved to be stable in a long-term view, as they could not be changed unilaterally by either superpower and in any case were far beyond the influence of German political decision-making. Furthermore, for West German politicians the limits for policy toward the GDR are even more restricted by the regulations of the federal constitution, which cannot be easily changed.

At the level of macroeconomic decision-making, characterized by political and economic decisions of the Federal Government and treaties and agreements between the two governments in Germany, a more balanced relationship exists between economic and political factors of influence. Owing to specific economic or political objectives, one or the other becomes more important. Analyzing the long-term development of inter–German trade creates the impression that the continuous increase in trade turnover is a clear sign of the dominance of economic interests. But if one recognizes the special political and economic conditions of this trade, then it might be the political efforts of one or both sides in particular which made this development possible. In any case, only important political

269

disturbances could negatively influence the inter-German economic relationship.

At the microeconomic level, that is, in the area of enterprises and their economic interests, economic factors are clearly decisive. Nevertheless one must not forget that these factors sometimes were created, controlled or at least influenced by political objectives. This is one of the many specialities and characteristics of inter-German trade.

This chapter primarily tries to describe and analyze the political and legal foundations of inter-German economic relations, the technical-economic problems of its realization, its development and structure, and its importance for those who are involved. Based upon the political and economic interests of the two German states and considering their persisting economic problems, some conclusions will be drawn with respect to the use of these economic relations for political objectives.

II POLITICAL AND LEGAL FOUNDATIONS

The long-term dominant influence of political factors upon the basic conditions of inter-German trade can be illustrated, for example, by the different official designations for these relations: while in West Germany the original expression 'interzonal trade', which came into use immediately following the Second World War, continued to be employed until the end of the 1960s, in the GDR the term 'Inner-German Trade' (IGT) was already established by the 1950s. By the time the Federal Republic of Germany adopted this expression, the GDR had already taken up new positions in this area, now referring to 'foreign trade with the Federal Republic of Germany and [separate] foreign trade with West Berlin'. Here the fundamentally different political positions and legal interpretations assigned by the two German states to their mutual economic relations is expressed: while the German Democratic Republic regards trade with the Federal Republic of Germany as foreign trade and, in addition, still reports its economic relations with West Berlin separately, West Germany takes a different stand. For the Federal Republic of Germany, it remains inter-German trade and not foreign trade. There is a certain similarity to the GDR's point of view: the Federal Republic also differentiates between trade with the GDR, that is the former Soviet Zone of Occupation, and the eastern part of the city of Berlin, which from the Western point of view is not regarded as a part of either the Soviet Zone or the GDR.

For West Germany, this trade for political and constitutional reasons does not fall under the regulations of its 1961 foreign trade law, the *Aussenwirtschaftsgesetz*, and therefore is not listed under 'foreign trade' in its statistical publications, but rather under 'domestic trade'. Such trade is governed by special rules and is regarded as unique – *sui generis*. This is expressed clearly in the decision of the West German Federal Constitutional Court of 31 July 1973 with regard to the Basic Treaty (*Grundlagenvertrag*): 'The GDR is part of Germany and cannot be regarded as a foreign country in its relationship to the Federal Republic of Germany. Therefore, for example, the former interzonal trade and the current Inner-German Trade which corresponds to it did not, and do not, constitute foreign trade'.

Naturally the statement ought to read: 'did not, and do not, constitute foreign trade in a legal sense'. From an economic point of view, it certainly must be treated as foreign trade, that is, trade with an area outside the economic territory of the Federal Republic of Germany, regardless of how it is described in legal terms. Nevertheless this special legal status is of considerable economic significance: if the GDR is not a foreign country, then it is also not outside the German customs frontier. Thus the West German government cannot impose import duties on goods delivered by the GDR, which also provides justification for the GDR's special position with the Federal Republic as a part of the European Community (EC).

In accordance with the legal positions of the three Western Powers against 'Germany as a whole' and especially their position in Berlin, inter-German trade is basically regulated by occupational law. Exemptions from the prohibitions on transfer and foreign exchange control regulations for the Allied Zones of Occupation after 1945 still represent the legal basis for inter-German trade. In decisions made by West Germany's Federal High Court in 1965 and by its Federal Administrative Court in both 1971 and 1978 it was established that these exemptions are still legally valid.

On 20 September 1951, the 'Berlin Agreement on the Regulation of Goods Traffic between the Currency Areas DM-West and the Currency Areas DM-East' was concluded. This agreement, as amended on 16 August 1960, is still valid today. Its special political significance is due to the fact that, by using the plural form 'currency areas' twice, it was possible to include both parts of Berlin while excluding the specific problem of recognition. This verbal solution was apparently such a success from a political point of view that it was called into play again over twenty years later when the Basic Treaty was concluded. In the supplementary protocol to the Basic Treaty it is stated with reference to Article 7, Paragraph 1, that trade between the Federal Republic of Germany and the GDR should be developed on the basis of existing agreements, including, in particular, the Berlin Agreement of 1951. Thus no further reference to the two parts of Berlin was necessary.

III TECHNICAL ASPECTS OF IMPLEMENTATION

Along with its special political aspects and the legal provisions associated with them, inter-German trade – rather like overall trade with the East (or, to employ the more neutral official formulation, the trade of the Federal Republic of Germany with state-trading nations) – is characterized by the differences between the economic systems concerned. The economic relations in question take place between a market economy based on private property and a planned economy based for the most part on state property in which, according to the constitution, foreign trade (and therefore inter-German trade as viewed by the GDR) is a state monopoly. The same applies to foreign exchange control. This means that it is not possible for just any enterprise in the GDR – not even any government enterprise – to participate independently in foreign trade, but rather only selected enterprises may do so. For a time these enterprises were directly subordinate to the Ministry of Foreign Trade and had the character of specialized trading enterprises. More recently, the foreign trade enterprises involved have been those affiliated with industrial ministries or combines; they have special authorization from the Ministry of Foreign Trade and are subject to its supervision and approval with regard to trade. It is thus possible for the state to subordinate foreign merchandise traffic to its economic and political goals. In addition to this, by employing a system of differentiated exchange rates, by exchange-rate surcharges and discounts and, if necessary, by means of price levies and subsidies, the state can ensure that the prices or price reductions considered necessary are achieved without affecting the profits of domestic producers.

The fact that the foreign trade of state-trading countries is subject to so much government control makes it necessary for the Western trading partners to organize their trade accordingly. This does not mean that Western governments must now also constantly intervene in this area of trade. On the contrary, trade has been greatly liberalized during the past years, that is to say, freed from economic[1] government controls. However, governments must retain the basic possibility of intervening to regulate trade so that, if necessary, they can ward off influences that distort competition or even cause market disturbances. The very fact that such a possibility exists tends to moderate any overly extensive attempts at control by the East European trading partner.

While West German trade with all the state-trading countries, including the GDR, takes place within this framework, that is, on the basis of general, world-wide or special import and export licenses, the payment transactions in inter-German trade involve a remarkable feature. In contrast to transactions with other state-trading countries, the payments are not made in convertible currency (such as the deutschmark, US dollar, British pound and so on), but rather by means of a bilateral clearing system employed by the two central banks participating. Via the respective commercial banks, payments are made to or received by each of the two central banks on the basis of West German prices for goods and services. Each of the central banks keeps a clearing account for its partner bank in clearing units, informs the other bank constantly about incoming and outgoing payments and coordinates payment transactions with the other bank. Since it is practically impossible for out payments and in payments to correspond exactly at any one point in time, a special agreement is necessary with regard to just how great an imbalance between the accounts may be permitted. This means that each central bank has to grant the other an overdraft credit for its clearing account which can then be used by one side or the other as required. Because this overdraft credit 'swings' back and forth between the two banks, it is usually referred to as a 'swing' credit. Thus it can be seen that such a credit is not peculiar to inter-German trade, but rather is a necessary part of any clearing arrangement. It is impossible to have a clearing agreement without a 'swing' credit. The significance of this credit in inter-German trade is that it does not, as was originally intended, 'swing' from one side to the other, but rather is consistently used by the GDR as an interest-free credit of unlimited duration. This can be corrected, but not by eliminating the 'swing' credit. If such an overdraft credit were abolished, it would mean the end of the bilateral clearing system and require a transition to payment in convertible currency. In principle, this would be possible, but both sides agree that it would not be in conformity with their respective interests in these transactions and would also violate the 'existing agreements' which form the basis for the development of trade between West Germany and the GDR.

IV DEVELOPMENT AND STRUCTURE

The development of trade agreed upon in the Basic Treaty has definitely made progress since the Treaty was signed. Compared to 1970, trade and service transactions between West Germany and the GDR had more than tripled by 1986, increasing to a volume of 14.3 billion clearing units. Even if price rises are taken into account, this still seems to be a striking increase. Compared to 1950, such transactions had increased more than twenty times by 1985, which also seems quite impressive, although these transactions account for less than half of the overall increase in West German foreign trade during this period. Accordingly, the share of inter-German trade of overall foreign trade (including IGT) dropped from 3.6 per cent in 1950 to 1.8 per cent in 1970, to 1.5 per cent in 1985. In 1950 nearly half of the trade with socialist countries was inter-German trade; in 1985 it shrank to less than one quarter. While in 1950 and even in 1960 inter-German trade exceeded West German trade with the USSR, in the 1980s it has been reduced to about 60 per cent.

The GDR statistics show basically the same trends of development. The decline of inter-German trade as a share of its foreign trade from 1950 to 1985 was from 16 per cent in 1950 to 10.2 per cent in 1970 to 8.3 per cent recently.[2] While more than half of the GDR's trade with industrialized Western countries in 1950 was inter-German trade, in 1985 it was less than 30 per cent.

The original thesis – that inter-German trade is subject to 'important' political influence – can be proved not only by pointing to the expansion of such trade after 1972, but also by examining developments before then. During the entire period this trade has existed (with the exception of the Berlin Blockade in 1948–9), only four significant decreases in trade volume can be observed: in 1951–2, 1961–2, 1967 and 1986. The causes are obvious: the decrease in 1951–2 was a reaction to the war in Korea and resulted from the embargo policy subsequently applied to the Soviet Union and Eastern Europe, which also affected inter-German trade. On the other hand, the slump in trade which occurred in 1961–2 was primarily due to developments in Germany – the construction of the Berlin Wall and the political and psychological effects this had. By contrast, the third setback to more recent trade relations which occurred in 1967 did not have a political cause. Rather, it can be explained by the economic situation in the Federal Republic at that time, with a recession affecting West German economic growth for the first time. Economic factors – the decline of oil prices – also caused a nominal setback in 1986 (in contrast to a small increase of trade in constant prices).

If we examine overall developments in trade, it becomes clear that the political climate must considerably worsen to have a lasting effect on inter-German trade (as with, for example, the Korean War and the construction of the Berlin Wall). With reference to the current situation, we might conclude from the stability of inter-German trade between 1983 and 1986 that either the political influences on this trade still exist but no longer affect trade as directly as is often assumed or that, contrary to appearances, political relations in Germany are not so bad after all.

If we examine the product groups involved, it can be seen that the commodity structure of inter-German trade has been characterized by stability for many years now, although there have been some striking shifts with regard to individual products. In 1986 most of the products delivered by West Germany to the GDR as well as most of those it received – over 55 per cent in both categories – were products of the basic materials and producer goods industries. In this connection the most important roles are played by the chemical products the West Germans send to the GDR and by the petrochemical products they receive from it (following a rapid decline in this category during the second half of the 1960s). But it is precisely in this area that a special feature of inter-German cooperation becomes evident: West Germany serves as an exporter of crude oil to the GDR and receives gasoline and fuels in return. With the help of these transactions, providing surpluses of between 0.6 and 1.1 billion deutschmarks, it has been possible to achieve a balance in goods and service transactions between West Germany and the GDR. By purchasing crude oil from West Germany, and to some extent by taking advantage of its clearing account for inter-

Table 12.1 Federal Republic of Germany: foreign trade and inner-German trade (IGT)

	1950	1960	1970	1975	1980	1982	1983	1984	1985
Foreign Trade (without IGT)	19736	90669	234882	405902	691708	804205	822473	922480	1000975
Inner-German Trade (Mill. DM)	745	2082	4412	7264	10872	13022	13825	14134	15539
Inner-German Trade (1970 = 100)	17	47	100	165	246	295	313	320	352
Foreign Trade plus IGT (Mill. DM)	20481	92751	239294	413166	702580	817227	836298	936614	1016514
Foreign Trade (1970 = 100)	9	39	100	173	294	342	349	391	425
IGT as a percentage of									
– Foreign Trade plus IGT	3.6	2.2	1.8	1.8	1.5	1.6	1.7	1.5	1.5
– Trade with socialist countries[1]	48.9	32.4	31.7	21.8	24.1	23.2	23.0	22.1	22.3
– Trade with USSR		143.5	157.6	71.3	70.3	62.7	60.0	56.2	64.3
– Trade with industrialized Western countries	5.1	3.1	2.3	2.4	2.0	2.1	2.1	1.9	1.9

[1]CMEA countries plus PR China, North Korea, Vietnam and the GDR.
Source: *Leistung in Zahlen '84*, Bonn 1984, pp. 59–67; *Leistung in Zahlen '85*, Bonn 1985, pp. 62–67.

Table 12.2   German Democratic Republic: foreign trade and inner-German trade (IGT)

	1950	1960	1970	1975	1980	1982	1983	1984	1985
Foreign Trade (Mill. VM)[1]	3677.8	18487.4	39597.4	74397.4	120100.8	145109.3	160423.7	173902.5	180191.3
Foreign Trade (1970 = 100)	9	47	100	188	303	366	405	432	455
Inner-German Trade (Mill. VM)	588.4	1911.4	4050.0	6474.6	10077.3	12527.4	13559.6	13791.6	14993.8
Inner-German Trade (1970 = 100)	15	47	100	160	249	309	335	341	370
IGT as a percentage of									
– Foreign Trade	16.0	10.3	10.2	8.7	8.4	8.6	8.5	7.9	8.3
– Trade with socialist countries	22.1	13.9	14.3	12.5	12.6	13.1	13.0	12.1	12.6
– Trade with USSR	40.3	24.2	26.2	24.4	23.7	22.7	22.3	20.6	21.4
– Trade with industrialized Western countries	58.6	49.0	41.9	33.6	30.6	30.7	28.8	26.8	28.3

[1]VM = Valuta mark – statistical foreign trade unit (4.67 VM = 1 transferable ruble)

Source: *Statistisches Jahrbuch der DDR 1971*, (Ost)Berlin 1972, pp. 228–291
 Statistisches Jahrbuch der DDR 1985, (Ost)Berlin 1985, pp. 214–242
 Statistisches Jahrbuch der DDR 1986, (Ost)Berlin 1986, pp. 240–241

Table 12.3 Federal Republic of Germany: commodity structure of inner-German trade (VE: Verrechnungseinheiten = clearing units)

| Commodity | Purchases | | | | | | | | | | | |
| | Mill. VE | | | | | | % | | | | | |
	1981	1982	1983	1984	1985	1986	1981	1982	1983	1984	1985	1986
Agricultural products	637.2	661.7	702.9	692.5	677.2	594.7	11	10	10	9	9	9
Crude oil	—	—	—	—	—	—	—	—	—	—	—	—
Gasoline and other products of oil	1634.3	1729.2	1573.3	1755.4	1689.9	888.8	29	26	23	23	23	14
Iron, steel and products thereof	252.1	231.6	322.7	335.4	320.2	330.5	4	4	5	4	4	5
Non-iron metals	—	—	247.8	354.8	342.2	326.9	—	—	4	5	5	5
Chemical products	734.2	797.2	829.3	962.5	917.5	791.8	13	12	12	13	13	12
Machinery, electrical equipment	441.5	487.9	545.5	644.8	658.1	772.7	8	7	8	9	9	12
Textiles, clothing	675.3	837.1	878.3	1008.4	1036.1	1043.5	12	13	13	13	14	16
Wood products	282.4	319.5	336.7	387.4	368.8	375.7	5	5	5	5	5	6
Others, not specified	985.4	1479.8	1258.4	1347.3	1325.5	1359.2	17	23	19	18	18	21
Total commodities	5642.4	6543.8	6694.9	7488.5	7335.3	6483.8	100	100	100	100	100	100
Services	486.4	536.0	866.6	752.3	822.3	859.8	9	8	13	10	11	13
Total inner-German trade	6128.8	7079.8	7561.5	8240.8	8157.6	7343.6	109	108	113	110	111	113

VE = Verrechnungs-Einheiten (Clearing-Units) – equals DM.

Sources: Bulletin des Bundesministeriums fuer Wirtschaft, 2 March 1983, 27 February 1985, 5 March 1986 and 4 March 1987.

Commodity	Deliveries											
	Mill, VE						%					
	1981	1982	1983	1984	1985	1986	1981	1982	1983	1984	1985	1986
Agricultural products	459.5	792.6	960.3	820.3	868.2	601.0	9	14	15	14	12	9
Crude oil	689.0	692.6	675.8	660.5	706.1	279.2	13	12	10	11	10	4
Gasoline and other products of oil	—	—	—	—	—	—	—	—	—	—	—	—
Iron, steel and products thereof	326.4	641.9	1037.7	741.8	756.5	674.2	6	11	16	12	10	10
Non-iron metals	268.3	461.4	518.6	539.3	638.8	481.5	5	8	8	9	9	7
Chemical products	930.5	1203.5	1212.0	1279.6	1413.2	1187.1	18	21	19	22	19	18
Machinery, electrical equipment	1188.0	1057.3	1021.9	905.0	1250.3	1765.4	22	18	16	15	17	27
Textiles, clothing	277.6	364.7	386.8	362.1	451.7	503.6	5	6	6	6	6	8
Wood products	—	—	—	—	—	—	—	—	—	—	—	—
Others, not specified	1172.5	636.7	658.9	642.6	1228.0	1147.5	22	11	10	11	17	17
Total commodities	5311.8	5850.7	6472.0	5951.2	7312.8	6639.5	100	100	100	100	100	100
Services	1037.7	1137.5	1208.7	1299.6	1272.7	1197.3	20	19	19	22	17	18
Total inner-German trade	6349.5	6988.2	7680.7	7250.8	8585.5	7836.8	120	119	119	122	117	118

German trade, the GDR is able to ease its strained currency situation.

Agricultural products, as well as the food, beverages and tobacco industry, account for 9 per cent and 14 per cent of trade turnover, respectively. On the other hand, a long-term and characteristic difference exists with regard to capital and consumer goods: West Germany supplies primarily capital goods, which account for between 16 and 29 per cent of its deliveries to the GDR while consumer goods have never represented a share greater than 10 per cent. The reverse is true for the goods West Germany receives from the GDR, with consumer goods representing a 20 to 30 per cent share, while capital goods almost never account for more than 12 to 13 per cent. Along with the GDR's problems with technical competitiveness, its difficulties in providing spare parts and service probably represent another reason it has had only limited success in selling capital goods to West Germany despite its efforts in this area.

IV   THE SIGNIFICANCE OF INTER-GERMAN TRADE

The conceptual difficulties posed by an attempt to assess the significance of inter-German trade for the national economies participating in it are greater than any statistical problems. Quantitative assessments can be based on a number of more or less meaningful comparative statistics. Thus, in 1986 per capita trade turnover for trade between the GDR and West Germany was 3.5 times greater in the GDR – 858 clearing units (that is, deutschmarks) – than in West Germany, where it was 234 clearing units, due to the numbers of the population. Inter-German trade appears to be even more significant for the GDR if it is seen in relation to overall foreign trade. The share of inter-German trade is five times greater for the GDR, accounting for (officially) 8.3 per cent of total GDR foreign trade, compared to only 1.5 per cent for West Germany. The ranking of each German state among the other's most important foreign trading partners corresponds to this: West Germany is the GDR's second-most important trading partner, following the Soviet Union. By contrast, the GDR ranks only thirteenth among West Germany's trading partners, after countries like Spain, Iran, Sweden and Denmark. However, these results are not very surprising. Based simply on the sizes of the national economies concerned and their different degrees of involvement in foreign trade in general, it could be expected that inter-German trade would be of much greater quantitative significance for the GDR than for West Germany.

However, a very long-term quantitative examination reveals that, despite the rapid growth which has taken place during recent years, inter-German trade is of only marginal significance today compared to the strong economic integration of the unified German national economy prior to the Second World War. In 1985 the nominal value of commodity exchange was 2.5 times greater than in 1936 but, if price increases since 1936 are taken into account, then actual trade now amounts to less than 40 per cent of what it was then. Furthermore, if we consider the real increase in the West German national product since then, we find that the significance of inter-German trade for overall economic activity has shrunk to about 6 per cent compared to before the Second World War.

Nevertheless, the significance of inter-German trade can hardly be assessed by making reference to these figures. What does it mean when we talk about the 'significance' of trade? Basically, the significance of trade can only be measured in terms of how hard it would be for one of the trading partners to do without it. Thus the real measure of the significance of such trade is represented by the political or economic costs created by doing without its advantages. To some extent, these costs can probably be calculated exactly, but sometimes – especially when the political objectives of inter-German trade are involved – only a rough estimate can be made, or even only a subjective guess about them. If the political or economic costs are too high – because there is no economic alternative or because political objectives can only be pursued by means of trade – then a state of dependence exists. Thus the significance of inter-German trade can only be determined by analyzing the interests associated with it.

VI POLITICAL AND ECONOMIC INTERESTS

Political interests are pursued primarily by the Federal Republic of Germany, or, to be more precise, by the West German government. For the most part, the FRG links its concessions in inter-German trade or other economic advantages for the GDR with improved access to Berlin, ensuring adequate supplies for this city, and maintaining what are usually called 'human contacts'. Since the West German government has very few other means of pursuing these objectives, in this case at least it is rather dependent on inter-German trade. Therefore it is necessarily interested in expanding this trade as much as possible and in doing all it can to promote it.

The GDR hardly tries to realize any political objectives through inter-German trade, and it is therefore politically independent of inter-German trade. But the situation tends to be reversed on the economic front. Here the direct economic interest of the West German government is limited. There are nevertheless strong West German economic interests associated with inter-German trade. These are the interests of persons and enterprises who want to realize profits by making purchases or selling their products. And such interests are neither less important nor less legitimate than the political interests of the West German government, especially since they provide the economic foundation for such trade.

However the situation is different with regard to the GDR's economic interests. For the GDR, inter-German trade not only represents about 28 per cent of its foreign trade with Western industrial nations, but it also is characterized by a number of advantages with regard to both sales and purchases. Thus procuring products from West Germany generally makes it possible to take advantage of the high level of technology in West Germany, particularly in the areas of machine building, electrical engineering and electronics, and in some areas of the chemical industry. 'Completing deliveries' play an important role for industrial machinery and equipment in the GDR which, as is common in the entire Council for Mutual Economic Assistance (CMEA) area, suffer from poorly organized service. Naturally the sale of large-scale industrial units is also of certain significance for inter-German trade, but precisely in this area the deals made with Italian and Austrian companies show that West Germany can by no means regard the GDR market as an uncontested domain.

In connection with the GDR's indebtedness to the West, there have been some official statements in the GDR calling for export surpluses and the necessity of gaining more economic independence to avoid the possibility of being blackmailed by Western countries. To a certain degree these statements are understandable, in spite of the fact that they represent a call for autarky. On the other hand, it still cannot be expected that the GDR would be any more successful today than it was some twenty years ago, if it tried again to institute a policy of *Stoerfreimachung*, that is, freeing itself from the 'disruption' caused by the failure of West German deliveries. In

1961, following the shock caused by the West German government's cancellation of the Berlin Agreement in 1960 (even though an extension was agreed upon later), the GDR leadership tried to make the GDR independent of West German deliveries. However, this policy of *Stoerfreimachung* failed, because attempts by the GDR to produce for itself what had formerly been purchased from West Germany, or to find substitutes in the CMEA area or in other Western markets, proved to be too expensive or impossible to realize because equivalent products could not be located or hard currency was not available to pay for them.

The possibly greater significance of West Germany as a major market area for the GDR is based on its special political status: for West Germany, the GDR is not a foreign country and is therefore not outside German customs territory. Thus no customs duties can be charged for GDR goods imported directly into West Germany, neither national nor supranational external tariffs of the European Community (EC).[3] EC marketing regulations and EC import adjustment levies also do not apply. On the contrary, in order to encourage imports from the GDR, West German importers are allowed to take the usual pre-tax deduction from their value-added tax liability because these goods have already been subject to 'German' – that is, East German – taxes.

However, the most important economic reasons for the significance of the West German market apply to both purchases and sales: these are the advantages of a currency-free clearing system (some of it on credit), the close geographical proximity and the low transport costs associated with it, traditional business relations and the resulting knowledge of the market concerned and, last but not least, the advantage of having a common language.

VII ECONOMIC PROBLEMS

Nevertheless, along with the political problems caused by the fluctuating political situation, there are also a number of economic problems associated with inter-German trade. Even if it is not possible to examine them in detail, the most important of these problems should at least be mentioned here.

The discrepancy existing between the GDR's almost unlimited desire to import and its limited ability to pay for its imports or to export is usually considered the most important of these economic problems. However, this so-called problem should not be taken too seriously, especially since the GDR shares it with many countries – and many individuals. It frequently happens that the desire and the ability to purchase something do not harmonize.

The common reaction of individuals in such a situation is also possible for governments – going into debt! The GDR has taken this path during the past eight to ten years and has thus let foreign sources finance a good part of its 'socio-political program'. There are no official figures; however, it is estimated that the GDR's indebtedness to the West amounted to $15.4 billion at the end of 1986:[4] $12 billion bank-to-bank credits, the rest suppliers' credits and state credits ('swing' and so on). At least $5.8 billion is owed to Eastern Europe, that is, to the Soviet Union. The GDR's payments on interest[5] and principal to Western countries in 1985 amounted to about $4.4 billion and in 1986 to at least $3 billion. This means that without new credits its scope for importing is correspondingly reduced – which also applies to inter-German trade – even if the GDR's annual DM revenues are taken into account. These are official West German payments for a wide variety of purposes which can be estimated at over one billion deutschmarks annually – including so-called 'humanitarian measures' – plus the same amount in DM revenues from other sources (the minimum currency exchange requirement for visitors to the GDR, Intershop purchases in hard currency, purchases from the GDR's 'Genex' gift service and so on).

To a large extent this indebtedness has resulted from increased prices in raw materials and the drastic worsening of GDR terms of trade associated with them. It took a long time for GDR economic policy to react to this situation by making corresponding adjustments in its domestic oil policy, such as by converting its heating plants to use brown coal instead of fuel oil.

The unfavorable structure of the goods sold by the GDR in inter-German trade – specifically, the small and declining share represented by mechanical engineering products (also in comparison with GDR sales to the CMEA and OECD areas) – has been criticized in both the GDR and West Germany as a constant economic problem. Since West Germany is a leading international competitor in this area, the GDR's small market share is often explained by the exceptionally harsh competition for the West German market. However, this could also be due to the limited capacity of GDR industry and the demands made on it by the USSR and other East European trading partners. Furthermore, the GDR has opportunities to sell goods in West Germany which it can hardly sell anywhere else, so that it is not as necessary for the GDR to sell machinery in West Germany as it is in other OECD countries. Instead, the GDR can sell 'soft', that is, internationally less competitive, products there.

To some extent the GDR compels purchases of these goods by insisting, when it places orders in West Germany and especially in the case of large-scale transactions, that the West German suppliers accept certain goods as (at least partial) payment. Such compensation transactions are prohibited by the Berlin Agreement, but it is easy to circumvent such a prohibition. Economically, the GDR forces its suppliers to assume responsibility for the sale of its products. There can hardly be any objection to this practice in so far as the suppliers are capable of assuming this function and they can arrange to be paid for their efforts by setting correspondingly higher prices for their goods. The real economic problem lies in the negative structural effect: smaller West German firms which neither need such GDR products nor have appropriate trading organs to sell them are thus excluded from doing business with the GDR. Only the emergence of specialized dealers for compensation transactions who have become more common during recent years offer a way out for these firms.

Another type of problem is related to the advantages the GDR enjoys in connection with its special status in inter-German trade and its special position in the European Community (EC). This is not intended as a reference to the controversial, but defensible, argument about subsidies to the GDR which are worth 'thousands of millions'. Rather, we refer here to the opportunities for abuse associated with wide-ranging EC administrative regulations.[6]

The special position the GDR enjoys in relation to the EC is threatened by the GDR's repeated demands for 'modernization' of procedures in inter-German trade. This refers to the demand, which sometimes also finds support in West Germany, that the legal basis of the Berlin Agreement, Military Government Law No. 53 of 1949, be repealed. The purpose of this demand is to eliminate the system of import quotas which places limits on the volume or value of certain GDR deliveries. Apart from the fact that it is not possible to apply West Germany's foreign trade law to inter-German trade for political and constitutional reasons, even if this were to be attempted, considering the fact that the West German government would have to introduce a special law on inter-German trade in its lower house of parliament (which also could not be politically desirable for the GDR), the West German government would be more likely to expose itself to new risks – internal and in relation to the EC – than to achieve the result it desires. If inter-German trade were to be placed on a new legal basis, then neither the preferential EC status of the GDR nor the clearing system – regarded by many as outmoded – and the 'swing' provisions would remain unchanged. Furthermore, no West German government can afford to do without the instruments necessary to put an end to government-directed mass exports at extremely low prices which could ruin entire branches of West German industry.[7]

VIII CONCLUSIONS

As in the past, so in the future the development of economic relations between the Federal Republic of Germany and the GDR will be determined as much by the overall political conditions in Europe as by economic and political interests and economic problems. In this connection it is interesting to note that the economic problems on the one hand limit the possibilities for economic development, while on the other hand they open additional starting points for economic support, which could be used by the West German government for economic–political agreements. It is obvious from the viewpoint of internal political concerns that in most cases both sides will disavow any connections between political and economic concessions and insist on their formal autonomy.[8]

Within the framework of inter-German trade, the possibilities for the Federal Government to achieve certain political objectives are rather limited. In this respect some of the advantages the GDR enjoys, for legal or other reasons, cannot be changed and therefore cannot be used for concrete political goals. For example, the exemption of GDR commodities from German customs duties cannot be made dependent on the GDR's political behavior. It is just the same for the relationship of the GDR to the Federal Republic as a major member of the EC. These regulations also could not be varied as easily as would be necessary for their political use. In this respect the Federal Government, only by the degree of intensity with which it opposes the attempts of the partner countries to terminate the special position the GDR enjoys in relation to the EC, can make clear how much it values its political–economic relations with the GDR. On the other hand, one may easily assume that the special status the GDR enjoys with respect to the EC does not remain unquestioned between the GDR's partners in the CMEA. In relation to the smaller CMEA partners the GDR enjoys a remarkable advantage of competition, especially in the field of agricultural goods. In relation to the Soviet Union this cannot be regarded as a major problem, owing to the special structure of the Soviet exports (that is, mainly energy raw materials). The Soviet Union seems to be less affected by competition problems and benefits from the GDR's access to West German markets and technology.[9]

More opportunities for the political use of economic relations are at the disposal of the Federal Government and can be found in the instrument of taxation, of securing credit and, last but not least, of regulating the overdraft credit of the clearing agreement. In relation to taxation regulations, goods purchased in the GDR are treated more favorably, that is, are eased from certain taxes, than goods imported from abroad.[10] These regulations are formulated in special taxation laws and therefore can be changed if deemed necessary. Almost the same is true for the system of federal guarantees for investment goods deliveries to the GDR and for the special credit insurance company founded in 1967, because the German export credit insurance company Hermes only works in the field of foreign trade and was not allowed to deal with inter-German trade problems.

At the center of all discussions concerning the inter-German policy instruments at the disposal of the Federal Government has been the overdraft credit, the so-called 'swing'. These discussions have often overlooked the fact that it was not the amount, in which range imbalances of payments are allowed, but rather the autonomous renunciation (by the Federal Government) of the agreed annual repayments in DM cash of existing imbalances that really affected things. By this renunciation – as pertains to its intended meaning – the misuse[11] of the swing as an interest-free permanent credit became possible. Contrary to widespread opinion, this change in the original functioning of the swing did not promote inter-German trade but hampered it: trade turnover could be extended only once by credit-financed purchases, while the permanent range for short-term imbalances in trade was reduced accordingly. On the one hand, to promote trade more favorably a regulation rendering the swing more dynamic would be helpful (relatively generous and related to trade turnover as it had been between 1969 and 1975), while on the other hand both partners could stick to the Berlin Agreement and its regulation of annual cash payments for existing imbalances on 30 June of each year. Then it would always be possible to decide whether a new balance should be provided by payments in cash or by special credits. Credit conditions, whether public or private, with or without public guarantees, obviously have to be agreed upon in mutual negotiations. Besides the economic advantages in the further development of inter-German trade, the political advantage of having a new instrument for negotiations is evident.

The economic strength of the Federal Republic for promoting and influencing inter-German relations has in the past been used much more outside the range of inter-German trade. Lump-sum payments for the use of the transit roads to and from Berlin, for the use of GDR roads by West German visitors to the GDR and for the services of the GDR postal system, payments for so-called 'humanitarian measures' (that is, payments for getting GDR prisoners to the West), and West Germany's financial participation in traffic investments of the GDR (highways from West Berlin to Helmstedt and to Hamburg) furnished the GDR with very important hard-currency income. An almost equally important source of hard currency is the visa fees and the obligatory minimum currency exchange for Western visitors to the GDR. Also, money gifts given by West German visitors to their friends and relatives form a considerable part of state income, because this money flows – with some delay – via special hard-currency shops (Intershop) to the State Bank of the GDR and therefore to the government. All in all, the deutschmark earnings of the GDR during the first half of the 1980s can be estimated to be about 2.5 billion DM annually. Since the conclusion of the Basic Treaty in 1972, it is estimated to total more than 20 billion DM. If one adds the transfers in goods, represented by the stream of parcels flowing from West Germany into the GDR, on the basis of 50 DM per parcel, the annual value amounts to additional ·85 billion DM, and for the fourteen years since 1972 their value totals about 10 billion DM. Together with the accumulated indebtedness both to the West and East the overall foreign contribution to the internal consumption of the GDR can be estimated to be about US $25 billion – the largest part of which comes from the Federal Republic of Germany.

In recent years the so-called 'theory of the Soviet umbrella', or loan guarantee, has been discussed in Western countries. Developments since then have proved that a Soviet umbrella for

Table 12.4 Federal Republic of Germany: inter-German trade (Mill. Clearing Units = Verrechnungs-Einheiten VE = DM)

Year	Purchases A	Purchases B	Deliveries A	Deliveries B	Turnover A	Turnover B
1948	124.1[1]	—	155.0[1]	—	279.1	280
1949	205.8[1]	—	221.7[1]	—	427.5	—
1950	414.6[1]	451	330.0[1]	359	744.6	810
1951	145.3[1]	158	141.4[1]	155	286.7	313
1952	220.3	119	178.4	153	398.7	272
1953	306.9	295	271.3	261	578.2	556
1954	449.7	434	454.4	450	904.1	885
1955	587.9	583	562.6	576	1 150.5	1 160
1956	653.4	657	699.2	671	1 352.6	1 328
1957	817.3	845	845.9	838	1 663.2	1 683
1958	858.2	880	800.4	873	1 658.6	1 753
1959	891.7	935	1 078.6	1 063	1 970.3	1 998
1960	1 122.4	1 007	959.5	1 030	2 081.9	2 037
1961	940.9	917	872.9	911	1 813.8	1 828
1962	914.4	899	852.7	902	1 767.1	1 801
1963	1 022.3	1 029	859.6	907	1 881.9	1 936
1964	1 027.4	1 112	1 151.0	1 193	2 178.4	2 305
1965	1 260.4	1 249	1 206.1	1 225	2 466.5	2 474
1966	1 345.4	1 323	1 625.3	1 681	2 970.7	3 004
1967	1 263.9	1 255	1 483.0	1 490	2 746.9	2 745
1968	1 439.5	1 451	1 422.2	1 458	2 861.7	2 909
1969	1 656.3	1 656	2 271.8	2 078	3 928.1	3 734
1970	1 996.0	2 064	2 415.5	2 484	4 411.5	4 548
1971	2 318.7	2 582	2 498.6	2 652	4 817.3	5 234
1972	2 380.9	2 395	2 927.4	2 960	5 308.3	5 355
1973	2 659.5	2 688	2 998.4	2 938	5 657.9	5 626
1974	3 252.5	3 256	3 670.9	3 662	6 923.4	6 918
1975	3 342.3	3 391	3 921.5	4 028	7 263.8	7 419
1976	3 876.7	3 938	4 268.7	4 470	8 145.4	8 408
1977	3 961.0	4 071	4 409.4	4 663	8 370.4	8 734
1978	3 899.9	4 066	4 574.9	4 755	8 474.8	8 821
1979	4 588.9	4 792	4 719.6	5 093	9 308.5	9 884
1980	5 579.0	5 855	5 293.2	5 875	10 872.2	11 730
1981	6 050.6	6 350	5 575.1	6 129	11 625.7	12 478
1982	6 639.3	6 988	6 382.3	7 080	13 021.6	14 068
1983	6 878	7 562	6 947	7 681	13 825	15 243
1984	7 744	8 241	6 408	7 251	14 134	15 492
1985	7 636	8 158	7 903	8 586	15 539	16 744
1986	6 831	7 344	7 454	7 837	14 285	15 180

A Commodity transport statistics of the Federal Statistical Office
B Payment statistics of the Federal Ministry of the Economy
[1]Federal Republic of Germany, without Berlin

Year	Balance		Accumulated Balance		Indebtedness of the GDR
	A	B	A	B	
1948	30.9	—	30.9	—	
1949	15.9	—	46.8	—	
1950	− 84.6	− 92	− 37.8	− 92	
1951	− 3.9	− 3	− 41.7	− 95	
1952	− 41.9	34	− 83.6	− 61	
1953	− 35.6	− 34	−119.2	− 95	
1954	4.7	16	−114.5	− 79	
1955	− 25.3	− 7	−139.8	− 86	
1956	45.8	14	− 94.0	− 72	
1957	28.6	− 7	− 65.4	− 79	
1958	− 57.8	− 7	−123.2	− 86	
1959	186.9	128	63.7	42	
1960	−162.9	23	− 99.2	65	
1961	− 68.0	− 6	−167.2	59	
1962	− 61.7	3	−228.9	62	
1963	−162.7	−122	−391.6	− 60	
1964	123.6	81	−268.0	21	
1965	− 54.3	− 24	−322.3	− 3	
1966	279.9	358	− 42.4	355	
1967	219.1	235	176.7	590	
1968	− 17.3	7	159.4	597	
1969	615.5	422	774.9	1 019	
1970	419.5	420	1 194.4	1 439	
1971	179.9	70	1 374.3	1 509	
1972	546.5	565	1 920.8	2 074	
1973	338.9	250	2 259.7	2 324	
1974	418.4	406	2 678.1	2 730	1 900
1975	579.2	637	3 257.3	3 367	2 400
1976	392.0	532	3 649.3	3 899	2 600
1977	448.4	592	4 097.7	4 491	3 000
1978	675.0	689	4 772.7	5 180	3 700
1979	130.7	301	4 903.4	5 481	3 900
1980	−285.8	20	4 617.6	5 501	3 900
1981	−475.5	−221	4 142.1	5 280	3 650
1982	−257.0	92	3 885.2	5 372	3 700
1983	69	119	3 954	5 491	4 100
1984	−1329	−990	2 625	4 501	3 100
1985	267	428	2 892	4 929	3 500
1986	623	493	3 515	5 433	4 100

the CMEA countries never existed. But a different credit umbrella most certainly has had positive effects: the contribution that the Federal Government made to the credit standing of the GDR in recent years and still continues to make. That does not mean public credits or public interest subsidies for private loans, but the possibility of using money transfers from the Federal Republic for payments of interest and principal of loans granted to the GDR. Further, it includes the guarantee, which the Federal Government in July 1984 granted to a private loan of 1 billion DM to the GDR, and finally it means support of government statements and scientific analyses in favor of the credit standing of the GDR. In addition to the numerous efforts of the GDR itself, all this greatly contributed to achieving the GDR's primary foreign policy objective in the last several years: to avoid at almost any cost the necessity to ask for a credit moratorium in the West. The new loans given to the GDR in 1984 and 1985 in spite of its precarious balance-of-payments situation (which had been kept secret for this very reason) make clear that that objective was achieved.

Certain conditions which influenced the development of inter-German economic relations and especially inter-German trade will exist in the future as they have in the past. On the one hand there are factors that limit economic relations: the legal and technical conditions of trade and the economic problems described above; and on the other hand there is the political will to intensify and develop inter-German contacts and meetings. The GDR government regards those private contacts as the political price it has to pay for economic and political concessions granted by the Federal Government, and it tries to minimize this price, in spite of the clear improvements in recent years. In this connection, in the future as in the past, it will be the unilateral economic contributions of the Federal Government ('transfers') which are most important. With regard to the political contacts between the Federal Republic and the GDR, which were supported by both the government and the opposition, inter-German trade will continue to be of central importance despite the fact that other fields of discussion, concerning environmental problems, security problems and disarmament, are being developed in the meantime. Nevertheless, the special position that inter-German trade enjoys, even in relation to new fields of discussion, is rooted in the long-standing positive experience which both sides have enjoyed in different ways, and in the material interests which are connected with it on both sides of the inter-

German border. The present and the future governments of the Federal Republic, therefore, will do what they can to develop and extend inter-German trade. Inter-German economic relations, besides satisfying concrete economic and political objectives, will always be regarded as a symbol of the unsolved problems of a divided country and the last element binding together both parts of Germany.

Thus, on the one hand, the peculiarities of inter-German economic relations, which are based on the political contradictions between the superpowers in Europe and Germany and reflected in the complicated legal framework of this trade, are a clear sign of existing tensions and therefore must be considered as a source of uncertainty and insecurity. But on the other hand, besides the problems related to the division of Germany, the development of inter-German economic relations, the agreements and procedures which regulate these relations, and finally the economic and political interests which are involved – all lead to a state of stability in inter-German political relations far greater than anyone had ever expected. This stability greatly contributes to security not only in Germany but in Europe as a whole. In this view, not only both parts of Germany, but all countries in Europe, in the West and in the East, must be interested in the effects of inter-German economic relations.

13 GDR–FRG Economic Relations: Determinants, Trends and Problems

Juergen Nitz

Representatives of the two German states signed the so-called Berlin Agreement in 1951 in order to provide a contractual basis for trade between the German Democratic Republic and the Federal Republic of Germany. The foundations in terms of international law for reciprocal economic relations were developed further in 1972 by the Treaty on Basic Principles of Relations between the German Democratic Republic and the Federal Republic of Germany. Important commitments of both governments are laid down in that Treaty, including the following clause in Article 7: 'The German Democratic Republic and the Federal Republic of Germany shall conclude conventions on the basis of this Treaty for the purpose of developing and promoting for reciprocal benefit cooperation in the fields of economy, science and technology, transport, legal affairs, post and telecommunication, health, culture, sport, protection of the environment, and other areas. Details are formulated in the Supplemental Protocol to this Treaty'.[1]

Article 7/II in the Supplemental Protocol reads as follows:

1. Trade between the German Democratic Republic and the Federal Republic of Germany shall be developed on the basis of existing agreements.

   The German Democratic Republic and the Federal Republic of Germany shall enter into long-term conventions, with the view of stimulating high-continuity development of economic relations and to readjusting outdated settlements and to improving the structure of trade.
2. The German Democratic Republic and the Federal Republic of Germany proclaim their determination to develop to reciprocal benefit cooperation in the fields of science and

technology and to enter into agreements hereto required.[2]

These legal settlements and explicitly formulated political intentions have greatly helped to further economic relations between both German states. Substantial headway has been made, especially since the 1970s. Exchange of commodities, for example, worth 4 500 million DM in 1970, grew to 11 700 million by 1980 and to 16 500 million in 1985, and has yet to reach its potential upper limit.[3] Expansion of economic relations was and continues to be characterized and affected by a wide variety of factors, some reflecting considerable continuity and others reflecting extremely contradictory features.

These major trends largely conform to overall trends in economic relations between socialist and capitalist countries. This is not meant to rule out the sizeable impact on trade and cooperation between both German states of their own specific political and economic interests. Nevertheless, in discussing economic relations between the two German states, it is first necessary to consider the complicated background of world politics and the world economy. Economic relations are closely associated with a number of basic political and economic laws of our time, as well as with the strategic approaches of each side, and attention should be given to these factors as well.[4]

I THE IMPACT OF BASIC PROCESSES IN THE WORLD ECONOMY AND WORLD POLITICS UPON GDR–FRG TRADE

A major point of departure for any consideration of economic relations is the recognition that the world economy today is characterized by numerous relations between different partners. While this *single* world economy should be defined as a contradictory unity of different socio-economic systems – capitalism and socialism – in which the international division of labor undergoes an increasing process of differentiation, trade and cooperation at many levels have given rise to a complex mosaic of interrelations and interdependences. Increasing utilization of the international division of labor by all countries – lesser developed or advanced, socialist or capitalist – has become a characteristic feature of economic policy today. For a nation to neglect it would gravely harm its economic effectiveness. The GDR, like all socialist countries, endeavors to expand international economic cooperation with all nations, including the FRG, on the basis of equality and mutual benefit.

The world economy should not be perceived as a static variable. The GDR's own analysis of the issue is based on general trends in the advancing internationalization of economic life in all major facets of global economic relations, including those between the two German states, despite the fundamental divergence between the two major world systems. Several of the general characteristics of these trends deserve particular attention.

Trends toward stronger internationalization are evident in the spheres of production, including research and development and circulation (production, trade, transport, science, research). At the same time independent trends toward the internationalization of scientific–technological activities are intensifying, and new dimensions of technology transfer are developing. Activities involving mineral and power resources, such as exploration of deposits, extraction of minerals, processing and substitution, are becoming internationalized, and closer cooperation on environmental issues, including environmental engineering and safety, is developing. In the area of finance, there are growing trends toward internationalization in currency and credit. Finally, institutionalization is increasing with the establishment of new mechanisms (for example, integrated groupings such as the EEC or CMEA, or multilateral programs, such as Eureka and the CMEA Complex Program of Scientific and Technological Progress to the Year 2000). Both German states are associated with such institutions, their orientations and goals, and the resulting economic policies and practices.

Such developments take place in close relation to politics and economic policies and consequently are based on the close correlation between economics and politics. There can be no doubt that under the conditions of different social systems priority has to be accorded to politics in the context of international economic relations.

None the less there is no automatic mechanism to regulate inter-system developments, neither world-wide nor between the two German states. Economic processes and political developments are not necessarily reflected in the same direct fashion in similar areas. In other words, favorable political relations will not automatically and directly lead to better economic relations, and an aggravation of the world's political situation will not necessarily have an adverse impact upon economic relations between the two German states. In the long run, however, a deterioration in the climate of cooperation under such conditions will be unavoidable, and have damaging effects on the dynamics of economic relations. Politics and economics are thus *relatively* independent of each other. True, politics is and will continue to be the concentrated expression of the economic interests of the GDR and FRG and, consequently, the determining element in strategic concepts and their interaction. Nevertheless economic interests certainly play an independent role within that framework, in so far as they ultimately result from trends that lead toward the further internationalization of society. The relations of economics to politics is qualified by the processes of economic internationalization, and economic cooperation tends to assume a position of relative independence, which is more clearly borne out under conditions of the scientific–technological revolution and against the background of numerous global problems.

The 1980s have brought about a situation in which it has become absolutely essential to struggle for the preservation and expansion of mutually beneficial relations. The stakes are high and call for the strongest possible containment of the negative effects of political tension and an aggravated international situation on overall relations, including economic links. Aggravation of the East–West political situation would, in the long run, have unavoidable effects on GDR–FRG relations, and economic relations would then gradually cease to play their role in stabilizing overall relations. A favorable international climate between East and West (the two German states included) is, in the final analysis, a prerequisite for the positive development of economic cooperation.

The GDR and FRG today face a world filled with controversy. On the one hand this world is shaped by the need for peaceful competition between the existing social systems, which is the only acceptable alternative when it comes to handling divergences between systems, since political objectives can no longer be attained by military means. On the other hand, there is a growing range of interdependences between various areas and levels of the world economy as well as between states and their national economies. In this context, one should bear in mind not only the great political and military issues touching on the very existence of mankind; their world-wide dimensions and their relevance to war and peace are no longer questioned by anyone. Rather, one should recognize the growing globalization of fundamental economic problems which has become increasingly apparent in recent years, demonstrating that all the different parts and elements are parts of one integral whole. The progress of science and technology, the protection of the environment and its thoughtful, careful utilization, prudent solutions to transport problems, power, minerals and other resources — all underscore the growing trend toward the interdependence of states. The policies of the two German states cannot fail to be affected by this fact.

Inter-German economic relations are also influenced by general trends in the capitalist world economy. Periodic slumps, for example, throughout Western economies, including that of the FRG, have impaired GDR product sales in FRG markets. The cyclical economic crisis of 1980 to 1982 demonstrated this. Sales of GDR capital goods became quite difficult, owing to a decline in plant investment or the flattening of the investment curve in the FRG.

Structural weaknesses in large sectors of the FRG economy have had additional adverse effects, for example, in construction, textiles, shipyards, wood-processing and several consumer goods industries. Serious sales problems also exist in the structurally weak regions of the FRG close to the borders of the GDR and Czechoslovakia.

While a certain amount of economic growth has continued to be recorded in the FRG and other Western industrial countries, economic developments in large parts of the capitalist world economy, including to some extent within the FRG itself, have remained unstable and contradictory. At best, a somewhat flattened level of growth can be envisaged for the late 1980s, as compared to the 1950s, 1960s and early 1970s. Sales opportunities in a number of industries today are certainly better than those in the rock-bottom years of the early 1980s recession. However, according to estimates made by research institutions in several Western countries, it is only a question of time until the incipient deceleration of growth will again affect the economy of the FRG. Hence chances for trade and other economic cooperation remain uncertain and even unpredictable for the GDR.

Additional problems in East–West trade and thus in GDR–FRG trade have emanated from recent price fluctuations, primarily for fuels and raw materials. Price indices from 1980 to 1986 dropped from 100 to 90.6 for fuels; to 73.2 for industrial raw materials; and to 80.1 for raw materials for the food and beverage industries. Such a decline in the prices of fuels and other resources has created major problems for East–West trade. All fuel and raw material exporters and those selling products on the basis of these raw materials have suffered losses in foreign exchange earnings. For example, the barrel price of crude oil dropped from over US $40 to approximately

US $8–12 and even lower, which also affected semi-finished and finished products using petroleum. It is generally known that the oil product trade played a substantial role in exchange between the two German states. As a result, problems have developed that ought to have been minimized. Furthermore the situation in international monetary markets remains unstable. General uncertainty regarding exchange and interest rates has resulted in serious problems which have had an effect on economic relations. In short, economic cooperation between countries of different social systems continues to be accompanied by complications, given the specific political and economic conditions under which both systems operate. These complications will certainly continue to exist for some time to come.

II THE LONG-TERM STRATEGY OF THE GDR

The GDR, taking into due consideration the basic determinants of the processes of the world economy and inter-system economic cooperation, has adopted a constructive approach to economic relations with Western industrial countries, including the Federal Republic of Germany. With a keen interest in the activation of economic and scientific–technological relations, the GDR works for its own constructive involvement in the international division of labor. These concepts were reaffirmed by the resolutions adopted at the XIth Congress of the Socialist Unity Party of Germany (SED) in April 1986.[5]

The GDR, like other Council for Mutual Economic Assistance (CMEA) countries, is committed to building such relations primarily to preserve and consolidate peaceful relations among all states and to utilize advantages resulting from economic cooperation for the development of the GDR national economy.

It is in this spirit that the GDR – along with the other CMEA countries – is working toward the long-term expansion of fruitful commercial and other economic links as well as scientific–technological relations with Western industrial countries at practically all levels: trade; science; technology; finance; credits; differentiated modes of mutually beneficial cooperation, including joint action on the construction and completion of projects; industrial cooperation; buy-back business; joint treatment of technical-economic problems; and East–West cooperation in third markets in line with the interests of all countries involved.[6]

The national economies of both German states are characterized by high foreign trade intensity. In 1986, roughly 40 per cent of the GDR's earned national income resulted from foreign trade. Both German states are primarily involved in the international division of labor within the framework of their respective social systems. For the GDR, CMEA cooperation is a long-term strategy which accounts for about two-thirds of its foreign trade, a strategy which will continue in the future. About one-third of GDR foreign trade is carried out with Western and developing countries. At present, this one-third has the following regional structure: about 20 per cent with developing countries, approximately 30 per cent with the FRG and West Berlin, and roughly 50 per cent with other developed Western industrial countries.

The GDR, like all CMEA countries, has begun developing commercial cooperation with Western governments, as well as corporations, firms, and banks. It is continually looking for new forms of scientific–technological cooperation, including cooperation with the FRG.

In all activities the GDR is generally guided by the principle of mutual benefit. Exchange of commodities is developed on the basis of equality, free of political pressures, embargo, boycott and sanctions and in full compliance with the generally established and recognized principles of international law and of reciprocal consideration of each other's legitimate interests. The GDR thereby makes a concrete contribution toward a policy of peace and international *détente*,[7] and it goes without saying that an equivalent attitude is expected from its partners. The GDR takes into due consideration the political and economic goals and strategies of the FRG. In this context, reference must be made to the fact that the FRG has continued to insist on damaging positions with regard to a number of issues of relevance to the normalization of inter-state relations (see Chapter 5, by Max Schmidt).

III   TRENDS IN ECONOMIC RELATIONS

A closer look at present trends in GDR–FRG economic relations supports a number of conclusions. GDR–FRG trade, overall, has grown more than two and a half times throughout the 1970s and by a factor of about 3.5 from 1970 to 1985. Trade reached a peak of more than 16 billion DM in 1985. These developments deserve a favorable assessment, despite the fact that other problems remain. Marginal drops in trade of goods did occur in 1986, but these were due to several factors in the world economy rather than to action by trade partners in the two German states. (Price fluctuations for crude oil and other commodities and unstable currency exchange rates were among the causes.)

In addition, GDR–FRG trade is at present highly balanced, in accordance with one of the goals of GDR economic policy, as well as in compliance with the interests of the FRG. GDR purchases in Western industrial countries, including the FRG, were characterized by high growth rates in the second half of the 1970s, which corresponded to a general trend in the overwhelming majority of countries, including most countries in the OECD area. GDR imports from industrial capitalist countries in the 1970s considerably exceeded its exports to those countries, which resulted in a somewhat extended period of negative trade balances. This, together with credit restrictions imposed upon the GDR, necessitated long-term efforts to re-establish a balanced export–import situation. An export surplus was eventually achieved by the GDR in the early 1980s, including a period of surplus toward the FRG. Debts to Western industrial countries were thus considerably reduced. Debts to the FRG, according to international statistics, declined from over 4 billion DM to about 3.3 billion.

The GDR's favorable balance of payments situation, and the size of its trade surplus (more than $6 billion) have given it greater economic flexibility with regard to the FRG. Furthermore this more favorable balance provides better opportunities to satisfy the GDR's own interests in the future by importing under more favorable conditions. Nevertheless, the GDR should work for a higher export surplus in order to achieve deficit reductions and greater stability in the balance of trade.

Mutual trade is clearly relevant to both German states and is a priority in inter-system economic relations. FRG–GDR trade accounted for an average of 25 per cent of all FRG trade with CMEA countries in the 1970s. That percentage has made the GDR the FRG's second largest CMEA trade partner; the USSR, with percentages of 21.2 in 1970, 32.7 in 1975, 35.4 in 1980, and over 45.0 in 1985, is the FRG's leading CMEA trade partner. Trade with the FRG is an important item in GDR foreign trade, as international statistics demonstrate. Yet other economic partners, such as Japan, France, Austria, Italy, the United Kingdom, Netherlands, Belgium,

Table 13.1 The GDR's top twelve industrial trading partners (percentage of total GDR trade with capitalist industrial countries)

	1970	1980	1984
FRG	35.5	22.2	20.2
Austria	2.6	5.9	9.1
Switzerland/Liechtenstein	6.0	7.7	8.3
Belgium/Luxembourg	2.9	4.8	7.3
West Berlin	6.4	8.4	6.6
United Kingdom	5.7	5.3	4.9
France	4.8	6.6	4.5
Netherlands	5.8	5.3	4.0
Sweden	4.2	4.5	3.8
Japan	1.5	3.2	3.0
Italy	3.5	3.0	1.8
Canada	0.4	0.1	1.4

Source: Statistical Yearbook of the GDR.

Finland and Sweden, have also assumed greater importance in GDR foreign trade in recent years (see Table 13.1).

Generally positive developments in the sale of goods have been accompanied by differentiated developments for certain categories of goods. The structure of foreign trade between the GDR and FRG is similar to that of East–West trade in general, in that it obviously does not yet correspond to either side's scientific–technological potential and, consequently, has much room for further expansion. Import and export patterns have clearly shown that the commodity structure of trade between both states requires substantial qualitative improvement.

The FRG has been buying large amounts of petroleum products, textiles, chemicals and agricultural produce from the GDR, but at the same time it has purchased much fewer products from the GDR's metal-working industries. The GDR has purchased mineral fuels (primarily crude oil), products of the chemical industry and, until the early 1980s, agricultural products from the FRG. Declining trends were noted for products of mechanical engineering, including electrical equipment. By contrast, consumer goods purchases increased. As Otto Wolff von Amerongen remarked: 'Both of us are highly industrialized countries of high technological standards.

Yet the amount of investment goods still falls short of that level'.[8]

Small and medium-size enterprises are very much a part of GDR–FRG economic relations. Approximately 6 000 to 7 000 small and medium-sized FRG firms are at present engaged in business with the GDR, and approximately 25 000 to 27 000 contracts are signed annually with GDR partners. This accounts for about 40 per cent of all GDR–FRG trade.

The GDR has insisted on the principle of having small and medium-sized FRG enterprises involved in economic relations now and in the foreseeable future. The investment priorities laid down in the 1986–1990 Five-Year Plan call for large-scale modernization and renewal of various sectors of the GDR national economy. This provides a good opportunity for many specialized small and medium-sized companies in the FRG to establish or intensify business relations with the GDR, particularly in the areas of capital goods, labor-saving aids for rationalization of production, environmental engineering, software and 'tailored-to-measure' projects. This policy of the GDR is in full accordance with the CSCE Final Act of Helsinki and the 1983 recommendations made by the Madrid Follow-Up Conference.

More intensive forms of East–West trade, such as industrial cooperation and joint ventures, still play a minor role in GDR–FRG trade, although the GDR has repeatedly underscored its willingness to develop economic cooperation with the FRG, within the framework of the GDR's economic cooperation with the CMEA states and Western industrial countries. As Erich Honecker, Chairman of the GDR State Council, noted in an interview with the *Saarbruecker Zeitung*, 'We are in favor of expanded relations of cooperation. There is no factual reason not to do it. Cooperation between GDR and FRG firms, too, serves mutual interests'.[9]

The GDR has repeatedly declared its willingness to cooperate with FRG firms at various levels, including engineering equipment and completion of projects (on a buy-back basis and in third markets) and production, industrial cooperation or joint development of scientific–technological projects. The GDR wishes to stimulate various aspects of commercial cooperation with a diversity of corporations, individual firms and banks, with some emphasis being laid on small and medium-size enterprises.

In addition to direct industrial cooperation, joint action is also possible in such areas as the protection of the environment, protection of forests from airborne pollutants, the emission control of hydrocarbons, plant safety and nuclear engineering, as well as the efficient use and protection of natural resources. An important role can be played by cooperation in various fields of science and technology. Examples of closer economic cooperation include collaboration between Volkswagen and Peine-Salzgitter AG (metallurgy) and completion of chemical installations on the premises of Leuna and Buna. In addition, there are numerous examples of economic cooperation in third countries, such as Elektrotechnik GDR with Mannesmann FRG and Technopromex USSR on power station construction in Greece; Unitechna-Textimaprojekt with Krupp Stahlexport on the construction of a cotton-spinning mill in Ethiopia; VEB Kombinat Textima with CCC Hamburg on the construction of a cotton-spinning mill in Port Sudan; and Schwermaschinenbau Kombinat Ernst Thalmann Import with Mannesmann and DEMAG on conveying equipment in Bulgaria.

Nonetheless, the GDR is absolutely convinced that formal cooperation between the two German states can flourish only when it is mutually beneficial and on an equal footing. The GDR simply will not act as an extended workbench for the FRG; nor will it participate in unprofitable projects. Joint ventures must also be based on the principle of reciprocity.

IV CONDITIONS AND PROBLEMS IN ECONOMIC RELATIONS

Due consideration should be given to some objective conditions for economic relations between the GDR and the FRG in order to illustrate some of the underlying determinants of the volume, trends and structure of GDR–FRG trade. There are many aspects, no doubt, that might favorably affect economic relations or even stimulate them, but there still are a significant number of inhibiting factors.

It should be absolutely clear that the factors which are conducive to the development of economic relations between the GDR and the FRG result not from preferential treatment of the GDR by the FRG but rather from objective conditions that prove to be favorable for economic relations between the two states.

There are a number of factors which could have a favorable impact upon GDR–FRG economic relations. For example, both sides are highly advanced industrial countries with economic and industrial structures that provide good prerequisites for a mutually beneficial division of labor, particularly under the conditions of scientific–technological progress. In addition, the markets of these two highly industrialized countries are close to each other geographically. This is particularly favorable for chemical products, construction materials and other items which are voluminous and require high transport efforts and, therefore, are generally subject to site-related limitations. The structure of exchange is thus affected, since higher amounts of bulk goods can be moved.

The historical factor also plays a role. For almost 70 years the territories of the two German states formed one common state with one national economy and domestic market, before new and different social systems emerged. This has fostered certain traditional economic links which are still felt today (for example, export and import of textiles or agricultural produce), and extends in some instances to a congruence between industrial standards and codes of practice. What in the past had been a division of labor within one domestic market has continued to be relevant for today's different social systems as an element of the international division of labor between sovereign states. (Similar aspects can be noted in international trade relations elsewhere, for example between Austria and Hungary or the USSR and Finland.)

Specific elements relating to the modes of commercial exchange between the two German states – such as customs regulations, the trade-encouraging 'swing' financing which improves chances for FRG exporters in trade with the GDR, and certain tax preferences granted by the FRG – are additional stimulating factors. These are not the subject of this paper, but their favorable effects are generally known. However, these specific elements apply only to GDR – FRG economic relations and not to economic relations the GDR maintains with third countries. It is false to claim that the GDR is a 'clandestine member of the EEC' or should be envied by others for having 'one leg in the EEC'. On the contrary, should not such an economically stimulating commercial regime (or some of its elements) be appreciated for its compliance with the spirit and letter of the CSCE Final Act and with the concept of Most-Favored-Nation treatment? In this sense GDR–FRG economic ties could provide an example for future contractual settlements between the EEC and the CMEA, which is preferable to high customs barriers and other restrictions.

Political intentions on both sides to develop trade can also have a positive effect. Such intentions have been repeatedly expressed by the GDR. In the FRG, statements to the same effect were made by leading industrialists, including Berthold Beitz, Chairman of the Board of Directors of Friedrich Krupp AG, and Otto Wolff von Amerongen, President of the (West) German Federation of Industries. They defined the economic relationship as an element that stabilizes overall relations, and they called for that relationship to continue to grow.[10]

The effectiveness of these objective factors conducive to reciprocal economic relations is diminished, however, by a number of economically and politically inhibiting factors. First of all, economic warfare was waged against the GDR for decades. It actually began right after the end of the Second World War and continued intensively throughout the Cold War period, reaching a climax when the GDR was established as the first socialist state on German soil. Those policies had long-lasting consequences. Ranging from futile embargo attempts in the 1950s to a broad variety of methods employed at present, various efforts have been made to inhibit exchange, dependent on the prevailing political requirements and concepts. This has naturally had an impact on the structure of trade. In addition, the export restrictions mandated by COCOM, including embargo lists which cover industrial robots, computers, scientific instruments, equipment and material for the production of semiconductors and microprocessors, have an adverse impact on technology trade. Application of the COCOM restrictions to trade with the GDR has seriously threatened reciprocal economic relations.

The entire package of tender and permit procedures imposed on GDR export products is an obstacle to free trade, giving FRG agencies power to play with the quantity, value and structure of GDR imports and exports. These procedures have continued to be applied according to a 'Decree on Interzonal Trade' dated 18 July 1951 (BGB1, I, p.463, Amendment to Rules on Interzonal Trade, dated 22 May 1968, *Federal Gazette*, No. 97, 25 May 1968). These bureaucratic procedures are difficult for company managers to follow and are not at all conducive to an improvement in economic relations and structures. Restrictions in various forms continue to be applied to about two-thirds of all deliveries from the GDR.

A large number of GDR products are affected by restrictions in quantity and value. Delivery quotas granted by the FRG to the GDR for certain products equal only one-third of quotas granted to other countries not subject to restrictions. The volume of GDR products affected is several hundred million accounting units. The imposition of such restrictions is rising, as is the trend toward protectionism. For example, quantity and value limitations on many important traditional GDR export products do not at all accord with changes in general economic conditions, such as international trends toward an expansion of commodity flows, the growing efficiency and export performance of the GDR, and price rises in the FRG market (amendments to quotas lagging behind rates of inflation).

A certain amount of responsibility for pricing in the domestic market of the FRG is shared by associations of industrialists. They have quite often taken action against GDR products for purely protectionist reasons, for example, by initiating price control cases with the Federal Agency of Industries. Cases against a variety of GDR products have been filed with growing intensity since the beginning of 1980. The volume of GDR products affected is roughly 500 million accounting units. Most of the measures taken have eventually proved to be absolutely unwarranted, nothing but attempts to reduce the marketability and image of GDR products and to persuade suppliers to take restrictive action.

The idea and goal of using trade for political pressure on the GDR is to some extent backed by certain political circles in the Federal Republic. They do not have the slightest chance of success and do not at all fit in with the political and economic landscape.

V CONCLUSIONS

In the context of GDR–FRG relations, trade is of substantial importance and benefits both countries and their national economies and citizens. This situation is a result of clear economic interests on both sides. For example, Berthold Beitz has told Erich Honecker that the dynamism of trade with the GDR was of substantial importance to many FRG enterprises, both big corporations and specialized small and medium-sized companies. Trade plays an important role in the development of overall political relations between the two states. That insight is shared by many leading industrialists in the FRG. This favorable situation has resulted from the opposition of important political and economic forces in the FRG to efforts to conduct economic warfare and attempts to use East–West trade as an instrument of political confrontation.

Taking into account the world economy and its direction at present, there is cause for dissatisfaction with what has been achieved so far in economic relations. We are still far from exhausting the potential of bilateral economic relations. There is room for expansion, measured by the capability and structure of both national economies. Removal of restrictions, application of more intensive forms of cooperation, and exploration of new areas for cooperation could have a positive impact on trade. Efforts should be made to improve the structures of trade.

Owing to its own long-term political and economic concepts and goals, the GDR is interested in the positive development of economic relations with the FRG. The GDR considers such economic relations an integral component of overall relations and, consequently, a highly stable element conducive to a favorable overall atmosphere and to the continuation of a policy of result-oriented dialogue. The GDR has repeatedly declared its resolute determination to do its best now and in the future to help improve the conditions for expanding relations. The same attitude should be exhibited by the FRG if its stated interests are to be achieved. An improvement of political conditions will give added momentum to the development of trade between the two German states.

Notes and References

1 From Reunification to Reassociation (F. Stephen Larrabee)

1. Fritz Stern, *Dreams and Delusions* (New York: Alfred A. Knopf, 1987), p.230.
2. For a good discussion of the origins of the unofficial peace movement in the GDR, see Ronald D. Asmus, 'Is there a Peace Movement in the GDR?' *Orbis* (Summer 1983), pp.301–41; also Pedro Ramet, 'Church and Peace in East Germany', *Problems of Communism* (July–August 1984), pp.44–57.
3. Peter Brandt and Herbert Ammon, 'Patriotismus von Links', in Wolfgang Venohr (ed.), *Die deutsche Einheit Kommt bestimmt* (Bergish Gladbach: Gustav Luebbe Verlag, 1982), p.159. See also their *Die Linke und die Nationale Frage* (Reinbeck bei Hamburg: Rowohlt Verlag, 1981).
4. For the text of the Havemann letter see *Frankfurter Rundschau*, October 1987.
5. For the text of Eppelmann's appeal see *Sueddeutsche Zeitung*, 9 February 1982.
6. Kurt Sontheimer, 'Ein deutscher Sonderweg', in Werner Weidenfeld (ed.), *Die Identitaet der Deutschen* (Munich: Carl Hanser Verlag, 1983), pp.322–33. See also Karl Dietrich Bracher, 'Identitaets frage und Entspannungsdenken in der neueren Deutschlanddiscussion', *Politik und Kultur* (June 1987) pp.19–35.
7. Peter Bender, *Das Ende des ideologischen Zeitalters. Die Europaeisierung Europas* (Berlin: Severin und Siedler, 1981).
8. See in particular the essays in Weidenfeld (ed.), *Die Identitaet der Deutschen*.
9. Josef Joffe, 'All Quiet on the Eastern Front', *Foreign Policy* (Winter 1979–80), p.164.
10. Richard Lowenthal, 'The German Question Transformed', *Foreign Affairs* (Winter 1984–5), p.304.
11. For a good discussion of this process of historical revisionism see Johannes Kuppe, 'Die Geschichtesschreibung der SED im Umbruck', *Deutschland Archiv* (March 1985), pp.1278–94; also Ronald Asmus, 'The GDR and the German Nation: Sole Heir or Socialist Sibling?', *International Affairs* (Summer 1984), pp.403–18.
12. See in particular the biography of Bismarck by the East German historian Ernst Engelberg, *Bismarck: Urpreusse und Reichsgruender* (West Berlin: Seidler Verlag, 1985).
13. See also the data in Gerd Langruth, 'Wie Steht die junge Generation zur deutscher Teilung', *Politische Studien* (September–October 1986),

pp.504–42.

14. Cited in Walter Leisler-Kiep, 'The New Deutschlandpolitik', *Foreign Affairs* (Winter 1984–5), p.320.

15. 'Unsere Verantwortung in der Welt: Christliche-demokratische Perspektiven zur Aussen-, Sicherheits-, Europa- und Deutschlandpolitik', Diskussionsentwurf (Bonn: CDU-Bundesgeschaeftsstelle, 18 February 1988).

16. Hans-Dieter Jacobson, 'Security Implications of Inter-German Economic Relations', Working Paper 77 (Washington, DC: The Wilson Center, 27 August 1986), p.35.

17. For the text of the paper see *Deutschland Archiv* No. 1, January 1988, pp.86–91.

18. Kurt Hager, 'Friedenssicherung und Ideologischen Streit', *Neues Deutschland*, 28 October 1987. See also the somewhat more differentiated reaction by Otto Rheinhold, Rector of the Central Committee's Academy of Social Science and one of the authors of the paper, 'Antwort auf Fragen zum Streit der Ideologen und zur gemeinsamen Sicherheit', *Neues Deutschland*, 11 November 1987.

19. See Stephen Szabo, 'The New Generation in Germany: Protest and Post-Materialism', in Robert Gerald Livingston, (ed.), *The Federal Republic of Germany in the 1980s* (New York: German Information Center, 1983) pp.31–41; also his 'Brandt's Children: The West German Successor Generation', *The Washington Quarterly* (Winter 1984), pp . 50–9.

20. For a discussion of the problem of the counterculture in the GDR, see Wolfgang Buscher and Peter Wiensierski, *Null Bock Deutschland. Aussteiger Jugend in der anderen Deutschland* (Reinbeck bei Hamburg: Rowalt Taschenbuch, 1984). Also Antonia Grunenberg, 'Jugend in der GDR: Zwischen Resignation und Aussteigertum', *Aus Politik und Zeitgeschichte*, B 27/86, 5 July 1986, pp.3–19.

21. James Markham, 'Germans' Defense Pledged by Paris', *The New York Times*, 21 December 1987. For the text of Chirac's statement, see *Le Monde*, 13–14 December 1987. See also 'Mitterrand expose les principes de la dissuasion française', *Le Monde*, 19 December 1987.

2 The Changing Nature of the German Question (Renata Frisch-Bournazel)

1. Rudolf Bahro, *Wahnsinn mit Methode* (Berlin: Olle & Wolter, 1982), p.69.

2. Gert Bastian, *Atomtod oder Europaeische Sicherheitsgemeinschaft* (Cologne: Pahl-Rugenstein, 1982), p.75.

3. Quoted in Wilfried von Bredow, 'Friedensbewegung und Deutschlandpolitik', *Aus Politik und Zeitgeschichte*, no. 46, 1983, p. 43.

4. Karl Jaspers, *Wohin treibt die Bundesrepublik? Tatsachen, Gefahren, Chancen* (Munich: Piper, 1966), p. 177.

5. Eberhard Schulz and Peter Danylow, *Bewegung in der deutschen Frage? Die auslaendischen Besorgnisse ueber die Entwicklung in den beiden deutschen Staaten* (Bonn: Europa Union Verlag, 1985, 2nd edn), p. 6.

6. Carlos de Sarego, 'Géographie: Centre-Europe', *Libération*, 7 March 1983.
7. Werner Weidenfeld (ed.), *Die Identitaet der Deutschen* (Munich: Hanser, 1983), p. 42–3.
8. Pierre Hassner, 'Was geht in Deutschland vor? Wiederbelebung der deutschen Frage durch Friedensbewegung und alternative Gruppen', *Europa Archiv* 37, no. 17, 1982, p. 524.
9. Helmut Wagner, 'Europagesinnung und Europapolitik', in Eckhard Jesse (ed.), *Bundesrepublik Deutschland und Deutsche Demokratische Republik. Die beiden deutschen Staaten im Vergleich* (Bonn: Bundeszentrale fuer politische Bildung, 1980), p.149–50.
10. Wolfgang Schollwer, 'Der politische Handlungsspielraum der Bundesrepublik und der DDR im Zeichen internationaler Spannungen', *Liberal*, July–August 1981, pp.484–93.
11. Heinrich Windelen, 'Die Grundfragen der Deutschlandpolitik der Bundesegierung. Vortrag auf einem deutsch-amerikanischen Seminar der Konrad-Adenauer-Stiftung in Washington am 7. 2. 1984', *Bulletin des Presse- und Informationsamtes der Bundesregierung* no. 15, 1984, p. 133.
12. Jonathan Dean, 'How to Lose Germany', *Foreign Policy* 55 (Summer 1984), p. 70.
13. Erich Honecker, 'Diskussion auf der 7. Plenarsitzung des ZK der SED in Ost-Berlin am 25. 11. 1983', *Neues Deutschland*, 26–27 November 1983.
14. *Pravda*, 2 August 1984.
15. Rudolf von Thadden, 'Thesen zum Geschichtsverstaendnis und seiner Rolle in den Gesellschaftsordnungen der Bundesrepublik Deutschland und der Deutschen Demokratischen Republik' in *Deutsche Geschichte und politische Bildung. Oeffentliche Anhoerung des Ausschusses fuer innerdeutsche Beziehungen des Deutschen Bundestages* (Bonn: Deutscher Bundestag, 1981), p. 19.
16. *Neues Deutschland*, 10 November 1983.
17. Siegfried Kupper, 'Festhalten an der Entspannung. Das Verhaeltnis der beiden deutschen Staaten nach Afghanistan', *Deutschland Archiv* 16, no. 10 (1983), p. 1065.
18. *Pravda*, 21 June 1985.
19. Richard von Weizsaecker, 'Probleme der Deutschland- und Europapolitik. Interview im Deutschlandfunk vom 19.8.1984', *Informationen, Bundesminister fuer innerdeutsche Beziehungen*, no. 17, 1984.
20. Wolf Jobst Siedler, 'Was im Mai 1945 wirklich geschah. Laengst bevor Europa seine Welt verspielte, verlor es seine Vernunft', *Frankfurter Allgemeine Zeitung*, 5 May 1985.
21. François Bondy, 'Selbstbesinnung, Selbstbestimmung: Kultur und Integration', in Werner Weidenfeld (ed.) *Die Identitaet Europas* (Bonn: Bundeszentrale fuer politische Bildung, 1985), p.76.
22. Henri Froment-Meurice, 'L'Allemagne entre l'Est et l'Ouest', *Géopolitique* no. 6, 1984, p.78.
23. Konrad Adenauer, 'Grundsatzerklaerung in Moskau vom 9.9.1955', quoted in Boris Meissner (ed.), *Moskau–Bonn. Die Beziehungen*

zwischen der Sowjetunion und der Bundesrepublik Deutschland 1955–1973. Dokumentation (Cologne: Wissenschaft und Politik, 1975), p.85.
24. Kurt Georg Kiesinger, 'Rede anlaesslich des Staatsakts zum Tag der deutschen Einheit am 17. 6. 1967', quoted in Boris Meissner (ed.), *Die deutsche Ostpolitik 1961–1970. Kontinuitaet und Wandel* (Koeln: Wissenschaft und Politik, 1970), p.206.

3 The Origins of a New Inter-German Relationship (A. James McAdams)

1. See A. James McAdams, *East Germany and Detente: Building Authority After the Wall* (Cambridge: Cambridge University Press, 1985) Chapter 6.
2. For an illuminating exposition of exactly this problem, see Robert Axelrod, *The Evolution of Cooperation* (New York: Basic Books, 1984), especially Chapter 4, on the 'live-and-let-live system' in trench warfare in the First World War.

4 German Questions or the Shrinking of Germany (Gebhard Schweigler)

1. See the letter by Erich Honecker, General Secretary of the GDR's Socialist Unity Party, to Chancellor Helmut Kohl, 5 October 1983, in Bundesministerium fuer Innerdeutsche Beziehungen (ed.), *Innerdeutsche Beziehungen. Die Entwicklung der Beziehungen zwischen der Bundesrepublik Deutschland und der Deutschen Demokratischen Republik 1980–1986. Eine Dokumentation* (Bonn: Bundesministerium fuer Innerdeutsche Beziehungen, September 1986), p.154.
2. For an analysis of foreign reactions to the noise emanating from the two German states see Eberhard Schulz and Peter Danylow, *Bewegung in der deutschen Frage? Die auslaendischen Besorgnisse ueber die Entwicklung in den beiden deutschen Staaten* (Bonn: DGAP, Arbeitspapiere zur Internationalen Politik, No. 33, 1985).
3. Joseph Kraft in a column ironically titled 'The German Realities', *The Washington Post*, 2 May 1985, p.A23.
4. For a useful early and authoritative analysis of the Kohl government's thinking in regard to *Ostpolitik* and the German Question, see 'Kohls Beharren auf dem Wiedervereinigungs-Ziel ist nur ein neues Stueck einer alten Linie', *Frankfurter Allgemeine Zeitung*, 14 July 1983, p.5.
5. For a review of Andreotti's remarks and West German reactions see 'Genscher: Andreotti hat die Bundesrepublik gekraenkt', *Frankfurter Allgemeine Zeitung*, 17 September 1984, p.1.
6. For exhaustive reviews of the immense amounts of literature produced during this debate see Juergen C. Hess, 'Die Bundesrepublik Deutschland auf dem Wege zur Nation?', *Neue Politische Literatur*, Fall 1981, pp.292–324; Hess, 'Westdeutsche Suche nach nationaler Identitaet', and Eckhard Jesse, 'Die (Pseudo)-Aktualitaet der deutschen Frage – ein

publizistisches, kein politisches Phaenomen', both in *Die Deutsche Frage in der Weltpolitik, Beiheft 3* of *Neue Politische Literatur* (Wiesbaden: Steiner, 1986) pp.9–68.

7. This phrase, first enunciated in the 'Letter on German Unity' that the West German government presented to the Soviet government in the context of concluding the Moscow Treaty of 1970, has since become the standard formula for describing the West German goal in regard to the reunification of Germany.

8. See Karl Feldmeyer, 'Beharren auf Deutschland', *Frankfurter Allgemeine Zeitung*, 4 May 1985, p.1.

9. Helmut Kohl, 'State of the Nation in Divided Germany', speech to the *Bundestag*, 27 February 1985, as provided by German Information Center (GIC), *Statements & Speeches*, 5 March 1985, pp.4–6.

10. The argument that 'German history will continue' (some may wonder whether that should evoke hopes or fears) has been advanced by, among others, Richard von Weizsaecker, now the Federal Republic's president. See his collection of pre-presidency speeches, *Die deutsche Geschichte geht weiter* (Berlin: Siedler, 1983).

11. Chancellor Kohl in his 'State of the Nation' message of 14 March 1986, quoted according to *Bulletin*, 15 March 1986, p.202. The chancellor may have realized that he was walking on thin ice when he argued that the continued division of Germany was a threat to peace (who would go to war to overcome it?), for he also claimed: 'We remain conscious of the fact that the inviolability of borders and respect for the territorial integrity and sovereignty of all states in Europe in their present borders are a fundamental requirement for peace'. Such contradictions in official statements are the source of consternation among those observers who seek to understand events in Germany today.

12. The idea that the Soviet Union – pressed economically and under challenge politically – might some day offer the Germans reunification in exchange for economic concessions and political and military neutrality is the source of many dreams – or nightmares – among certain observers of the German scene. Neglecting the extreme unlikelihood that the Soviet Union would actually extend such an offer, would the Germans themselves accept it? In theory, yes; in practice, considering the multitude of problems involved in reunification today, probably not. And would the Western powers, still formally in charge of matters pertaining to Germany as a whole, let the West Germans go ahead and upset the *status quo* in Europe while enlarging the reach of the Soviet empire? It is certainly difficult to imagine that they would.

13. For a review of generally diffuse Green positions regarding the German Question see Wilfried von Bredow and Rudolf H. Brocke, 'Dreimal Deutschlandpolitik. Deutschlandpolitische Ansaetze der Partei der Gruenen', *Deutschland Archiv*, January 1986, pp.52–61.

14. 'Ein Traum, der vorueber ist, wenn man aufwacht', *Frankfurter Allgemeine Zeitung*, 19 November 1984, p.2. Brandt's speech was part of a series of lectures by prominent West Germans about the German Question, published as *Reden ueber das eigene Land: Deutschland* (Munich: Bertelsmann, 1984). For a thorough review of SPD thinking

about the German Question see Wilfried von Bredow and Rudolf Horst Brocke, *Das deutschlandpolitische Konzept der SPD Darstellung, Hintergruende und Problembereiche der Deutschlandpolitik der SPD Mitte der achtziger Jahre* (Erlangen: Deutsche Gesellschaft fuer zeitgeschichtliche Fragen, 1986).

15. Klaus Boelling, 'Die offene deutsche Frage', *Der Spiegel*, 18/1985, pp.52–3.

16. The SPD's reluctance to engage in a debate about changes of the Basic Law may have been influenced by public opinion polls showing that up to 80 per cent of all West Germans stand opposed to such changes.

17. 'Mit den Sprechblasen ist es aus', *Frankfurter Allgemeine Zeitung*, 22 October 1984, p.2.

18. The 1984 *Spiegel* survey (which included the poll quoted in Table 4.1) also asked a question about the most important political problems of the day. Among the seventeen problem-areas mentioned by the pollster or quoted by the respondents, not one referred to the German Question; 'improvement of relations with the GDR' ranked thirteenth.

19. Zbigniew Brzezinski, 'The Future of Yalta', *Foreign Affairs* (Fall 1984), p.292 (emphasis added).

20. Kraft in 'The German Realities' (see note 3).

21. It may not be entirely accidental that historical studies attributing the ills of German history to its *Mittellage* (its position in the center of Europe) have recently enjoyed a certain renaissance. Currently the most prominent proponent of this approach is historian Michael Stuermer, author of *Das ruhelose Reich. Deutschland 1866–1918*, Volume 3 of *Die Deutschen und ihre Nation* (Berlin: Siedler, 1983), who is also known as one of Chancellor Kohl's advisers on matters pertaining to the German Question. Stuermer is among those who insist on holding on to the 'German nation' while pleading for an unqualified recognition of the postwar *status quo* in Europe in order to prevent Germany from once again becoming the victim of its *Mittellage*. See his articles 'Kein Eigentum der Deutschen: Die deutsche Frage', in Werner Weidenfeld (ed.), *Die Identitaet der Deutschen* (Bonn: Bundeszentrale fuer politische Bildung, 1983), pp.83–101, and 'Die deutsche Frage in der europaeischen Geschichte', in Klaus Lange (ed.), *Aspekte der deutschen Frage* (Herford: Buss & Seewald, 1986), pp.21–34.

   The opposite argument is most prominently put forward by Wolfgang Venohr. See, among others, his article about 'Deutschlands Mittellage. Betrachtungen zur ungeloesten deutschen Frage', *Deutschland Archiv*, August 1984, pp.820–9, where he typically claims that it was an 'unnatural, indeed anti-natural situation that the Germans for years and decades did not want to have anything to do with their fatherland' (p.825).

22. Klaus Boelling has sought to explain the resilience of this argument in political terms:

> We could not discount leading articles about the dangers of German nationalism in *Le Monde* and *The Times* as mere journalistic opinions. Leadership circles [*Fuehrungszirkel*] in Western capitals found that

it paid to revive fears of an overmighty, reunified Germany in order the better to discipline us. Who would be surprised that a man like Carter's Security Adviser Brzezinski, being of Polish origin, helped to spread these rumors – for which he then found a grateful audience in certain floors of Foreign Offices.

Klaus Boelling, *Die fernen Nachbarn: Erfahrungen in der DDR* (Hamburg: Stern-Buch, 1984), quoted in Timothy Garton Ash, 'Which Way Will Germany Go?' *The New York Review of Books*, 31 January 1985, p.33.

23. The classical formulation of the 'social model' is in Karl W. Deutsch, *Nationalism and Social Communication: An Inquiry into the Foundations of Nationality* (Cambridge, Mass.: MIT Press, 1966). For an application of this approach to the German Question see Gebhard Schweigler, *National Consciousness in Divided Germany* (London/Beverly Hills: SAGE, 1975).

24. For a more comprehensive treatment see Schweigler, *National Consciousness*, and, by the same author, *West German Foreign Policy: The Domestic Setting. The Washington Papers: 106* (New York: Praeger, 1984). The German version of the latter study contains additional material: *Grundlagen der aussenpolitischen Orientierung der Bundesrepublik Deutschland* (Baden-Baden: Nomos, 1985).

25. The erosion of public support for a policy of not recognizing the Oder–Niesse Line is documented in detail in Schweigler, *National Consciousness*, pp.146–55.

26. For some arguments in favor of a peace treaty see Theodor Schweisfurth, 'Keineswegs obsolet: Der deutsche Friedensvertrag', *Deutschland Archiv*, July 1985, pp.711–15.

27. Kohl, 1985 'State of the Nation' message, p.5.

28. Quoted according to GIC *Statements & Speeches*, 9 May 1985, p.6.

29. The increasing political irrelevance of the expellee organizations and their representatives is highlighted by the fact that Herbert Hupka (responsible for the Silesia affair) was not renominated by the CDU as a candidate for the January 1987 elections. Herbert Czaja, president of the federation of expellee organizations (and also a CDU representative), complained in November 1986 that 'a majority in the CDU has accepted as final the present Eastern borders, and threatened to found a new party dedicated to the pursuit of reunification within the 1937 borders after the January 1987 elections – a sure-fire recipe for political irrelevance in the Federal Republic. See 'Vertriebene denken an die Gruendung einer eigenen Partei', *Sueddeutsche Zeitung*, 8 November 1986, p.6.

30. For summaries of the GDR's evolution of thought regarding the national question see Schweigler, *National Consciousness*, pp.89–106; Ronald Asmus, 'The GDR and the German Nation: Sole Heir or Socialist Sibling?', *International Affairs* (Summer 1984), pp.403–18; and Roland W. Schweizer, 'Wandlungen im Selbstverstaendnis der DDR – Aspekte der nationalen Frage 1961–1969', *Deutschland Archiv*, October 1985, pp.1071–83.

31. For an analysis of the effects of the treaties on cross-border contacts see Margit Roth, *Zwei Staaten in Deutschland. Die sozialliberale Deutschlandpolitik und ihre Auswirkungen 1969–1978* (Opladen: Westdeutscher Verlag, 1981).

32. For a highly interesting and still relevant analysis of this development see Norbert Elias, *Ueber den Prozess der Zivilisation*, Vol. 1, *Wandlungen des Verhaltens in den weltlichen Oberschichten des Abendlandes* (Bern/Munich: Francke, 1969, 2nd edn), Chapter 1: 'Zur Soziogenese der Begriffe "Zivilisation" und "Kultur"', pp.1–64.

33. For a representative exposition of this point of view see the article by historian Wolfgang J. Mommsen, 'Wandlungen der nationalen Identitaet', in Weidenfeld (ed.), *Die Identitaet der Deutschen*, pp.170–92.

34. See the reminiscences by Guenter Gaus about his time in East Berlin, *Wo Deutschland liegt: Eine Ortsbestimmung* (Hamburg: Hoffmann & Campe, 1983).

35. For a summary of earlier analyses of this problem see Schweigler, *National Consciousness*, pp.46ff. It reappeared with particular vehemence after the influx of some 35 000 refugees in the spring of 1984. One survey among the new refugees showed that half of them felt that people in the Federal Republic were different from people in the GDR. Many West Germans themselves were lukewarm in welcoming the refugees. See Volker Ronge, *Von drueben nach hueben* (Wuppertal: Verlag 84 Hartmann Petit, 1985), and Anne Koehler/Richard Hilmer, 'Ein Jahr danach. Wie sehen die Bundesdeutschen die Uebersiedlerfrage heute?', *Deutschland Archiv* (January 1986), pp.41–6.

36. The GDR as a country is held to be unlikeable by almost half of the West Germans and likeable by only four per cent; apparently the West Germans draw a distinction between the GDR as a political system and the people who live there. See Elisabeth Noelle-Neumann, 'Im Wartesaal der Geschichte. Bleibt das Bewusstsein der deutschen Einheit lebendig?', in Werner Weidenfeld (ed.), *Nachdenken ueber Deutschland. Materialien zur politischen Kultur der Deutschen Frage* (Cologne: Verlag Wissenschaft und Politik, 1985), pp.145–6.

37. Of course, relatively few West Germans – at most some 30 per cent – actually know East Germans (just as they generally know very little about the GDR). The perception of the cultural estrangement is therefore not necessarily based on first-hand experiences. In the light of this fact, the low esteem accorded East Germans by West Germans seems all the more surprising and thus politically relevant. For a review of West German attitudes about the GDR see Anne Koehler, 'Wiedervereinigung – Wunsch und Wirklichkeit. Empirische Beitraege zur Frage der nationalen Orientierung unter innerdeutschen Aspekten', in Weidenfeld (ed.), *Nachdenken ueber Deutschland*, pp.147–63.

38. For a review of such literature see Arno Klonne, *Zurueck zur Nation? Kontroversen zu deutschen Fragen* (Cologne: Diederichs, 1984).

39. There is yet another reason why the concept of the *Kulturnation* is, for the time being in any case, not a viable one: an injunction by West Germany's Supreme Constitutional Court against its application. The Court was asked in 1972 to rule on the constitutionality of the Treaty

on the Basis of Relations between the GDR and the Federal Republic of Germany. The claimant – the state government of Bavaria – argued that the Treaty violated the Basic Law's demand that the federal government seek the reunification of Germany.

The Court ruled that the treaty was indeed not unconstitutional, on the grounds that any government was free to choose its means of pursuing the goal of reunification. It did, in the process, reaffirm the goal of reunification as constitutionally mandated and claimed once again that Germany as a nation-state still existed. (One prominent legal scholar termed the Court's reasoning in this respect 'unpalatable definitional mush'.) At the same time, the Court stated specifically that no government shall attempt to avoid the goal of national unity by taking recourse to the construct of *Kulturnation*.

40. See on this point the excellent review by Eckhard Jesse, 'Die deutsche Frage rediviva. Eine Auseinandersetzung mit der neueren Literatur', *Deutschland Archiv* (April 1984), pp.397–414.

41. When asked whether they thought the East and West Germans belong to one *Volk* (that near-mythical German term only inadequately rendered as 'people'), 73 per cent of all West Germans in 1984 said 'yes', but only 58 per cent of the 14–29 age group. The affirmative responses among West Germans to the question whether, for them, the 'other part of Germany' was *Ausland* (another term only inadequately translatable as 'foreign country'), increased from 22 per cent in 1973 to 33 per cent in 1984, at which time, however, almost half of the 14–29 group felt that the GDR was *Ausland*. See Koehler, 'Wiedervereinigung–Wunsch und Wirklichkeit', pp.150–3.

42. For a summary of earlier polls on this question see Schweigler, *National Consciousness*, p.169.

43. Until the mid-1960s, between 65 per cent and 70 per cent of all West Germans expressed their agreement with the statement that it would make sense to keep demanding the reunification of Germany, whereas some 25 per cent thought it would be better to let time take care of the problem. By 1983, the public's attitude had become almost reversed: now 33 per cent were for constant demands, 55 per cent for the effects of time. Similarly, until the mid-1960s some 40 per cent named reunification as the most important political issue; during the last 20 years less than 1 per cent did so. See Noelle-Neumann, 'Wartesaal der Geschichte', p.134.

44. A large minority of West Germans consistently supports a posture of neutrality when asked in public opinion polls. In reality, however, they are not prepared to endorse a meaningful policy of neutralism, as support for remaining in NATO, for instance, or for continued allied troop stationing in Germany has similarly stayed on a consistently high level. Apparently the idea of neutrality implies an understandable desire for not getting involved in dangerous superpower conflicts and not an outspoken willingness to leave the Western alliance. See on this point Schweigler, *Grundlagen der aussenpolitischen Orientierung*, pp.113–16.

45. See Schweigler, *National Consciousness*, pp.162–6.

46. Heinrich Windelen, 'Basic aspects of German reunification. Policy on

Germany pursued by the Government of the Federal Republic of Germany under Chancellor Kohl' (Bonn: Bundesministerium fuer innerdeutsche Beziehungen, 1984), pp.12–13.

47. See 'Windelen baut auf die "Idee der Freiheit"', *Frankfurter Allgemeine Zeitung*, 26 June 1985, p.6.

48. For a critical assessment of this debate see Werner Weidenfeld, 'Mitteleuropa – ein alter Mythos stiftet Unruhe', *Rheinischer Merkur/ Christ und Welt*, 3 October 1986, p.3.

49. Typical for the lack of clarity often found in this kind of argument is the following statement by former President Walter Scheel in his 1986 *Bundestag* speech commemorating 17 June 1953: '. . .the creation of a European peace order would itself amount to the realization of the goal of German unity. In such a peace order the borders that so painfully cut apart Berlin, Germany, Europe, would lose their importance. Then every German could go to any place in Germany. In that case the division itself would dissolve with the pain of the division'. (Quoted according to the documentation *Informationen*, published by the Bundesministerium fuer innerdeutsche Beziehungen, 4 July 1986, p.17.) What does it mean that 'Every German can go to any place in Germany'? Can he just visit or can he actually relocate his home? Freely or under restraining conditions that apply even within Western Europe? And what is Germany: just East and West Germany or also formerly German territories beyond the Oder–Niesse Line? Scheel's simplistic formula hides a host of difficult questions.

50. For an analysis of such observations until the early 1970s, see Schweigler, *National Consciousness*, pp.106–11.

51. Rudolf Bahro, *From Red to Green: Interviews with New Left Review* (New York: Verso, 1984), quoted according to Ash, 'Which Way Will Germany Go?' p.34. Ash attests the GDR citizens a 'qualified loyalty'.

52. Hermann Rudolph, 'Wie sieht das Selbstverstaendnis der DDR-Gesellschaft aus?', in Weidenfeld (ed.), *Die Identitaet der Deutschen*, p.201.

53. Rudolph, 'Selbstverstaendnis der DDR-Gesellschaft', p.208. *Selbstbewusstsein* can mean both consciousness of self and self-confidence (but decidedly not self-consciousness).

54. Only recently, for instance, did the German TV networks decide to end their daily broadcasts with a rendering of the national anthem. The relative lack of pride in being a German, revealed in many a public opinion poll, has led Noelle-Neumann, among others, to point to the dangers inherent in such a low level of national identification and plead for a more deliberate use of national symbols. See *Jahrbuch 1983*, pp.198–207.

55. The SPD, fifteen years later finally in power, to some extent repudiated its own previous arguments when it claimed that its new *Ostpolitik* would protect the possibility of reunification. Similarly, the CDU/CSU repudiated its arguments against Brandt's *Ostpolitik* (which mirrored the SPD's previous claims that reunification was being given away), when it in effect continued *Ostpolitik* after October 1982. Apparently

318 *Notes and References to pp. 100–103*

arguments made when in opposition do not count for much, even though they may eventually turn out to have been correct.

56. See, for instance, Manfred Haettich, 'Nationalbewusstsein im geteilten Deutschland', and Kurt Sontheimer, 'Ein deutscher Sonderweg?', both in Weidenfeld (ed.), *Die Identitaet der Deutschen*.

57. For a review of recent studies documenting support for the political institutions of the Federal Republic, see Schweigler, *West German Foreign Policy: The Domestic Setting*, pp.29–34.

58. For an earlier analysis of this phenomenon, based on content analyses of sports reports in East and West German newspapers, see Gebhard Schweigler, 'Sport und Staatsbewusstsein im geteilten Deutschland', *Politische Studien*, September/October 1972, pp.462–77.

59. It might be worth noting that the term 'East German' is itself not used by the GDR and only infrequently in West Germany. The East German regime went to great length to push the term 'GDR' as the proper way of identifying itself, whereas in the Federal Republic the term 'East German' was officially reserved for the formerly German territories beyond the Oder–Neisse Line ('Middle Germany' being the officially correct term for the GDR). By now the term 'GDR', however, has gained common usage in West Germany as well.

60. West German President Richard von Weizsaecker felt it necessary to admonish his countrymen in this regard (in all likelihood a futile admonition):

> Some of the things we do are hardly likely to be appreciated in the other part of Germany. For instance, when here in the Federal Republic someone keeps talking about reunification but at the same time shouts 'Germany, Germany' when supporting a team from the Federal Republic playing against a team from the GDR. There is of course nothing wrong with encouraging your own team, but one should also be pleased with the truly impressive performances of GDR sportsmen. After all, sporting events should help rather than hamper us in our efforts to recognize and retain our position as Germans.

> From a speech to the Convention of the Evangelical church in Dusseldorf, 8 June 1985, quoted according to SCI *Statements & Speeches*, 25 June 1985, p.3.

61. In the age of nationalism, 'state' and 'nation' appear as inseparable, both cognitively and affectively; that is, almost everywhere else the German (intellectual and scholarly) attempt to draw a distinction between the two in regard to a people's sense of identity would meet with outright rejection or, more often perhaps, with a baffling lack of understanding.

The empirical and definitional problems faced by German scholars are typified in an article by Karl Dietrich Bracher about 'Das Modewort Identitaet und die deutsche Frage' (*Frankfurter Allgemeine Zeitung*, 9 August 1986, section 'Bilder und Zeiten'). Bracher at first attests to the fact that the current debate is highly artificial in nature, then goes on to state that 'the *political* criterion of a nation, besides the language and cultural criteria, is now, forty years after the "hour zero", becoming a historical criterion as well and tends to separate the question about German identity from the expectation of reunification', but at the end reaches a surprising conclusion: it is, he argues, the Federal Republic's unique challenge 'to live as a post-national democracy among nation-states'.

62. See, for instance, the articles by Johannes Kuppe, 'Die Geschichts-schreibung der SED im Umbruch', *Deutschland Archiv* (March 1985), pp.278–94, and 'Kontinuitaet und Wandel in der Geschichtsschreibung der DDR. Das Beispiel Preussen', *Aus Politik und Zeitgeschichte*, 17 May 1986, pp.17–26. For an earlier, different, interpretation see Gebhard Schweigler, 'Zum Nationalbewustsein in der DDR', *Politik und Kultur*, 1/1977, pp.61–8.

63. Strangely enough, as Juergen C. Hess has repeatedly pointed out (see note 6), West German scholars have done almost no empirical work regarding the question of a separate West German and East German identity.

5 The Two German States and European Security (Max Schmidt)

1. *Bayrisches Volksecho*, Munich, 8 March 1952.
2. *Quick*, Munich, No.34, 1986, p.34.
3. *Neues Deutschland*, 13 March 1985.
4. Ronald D. Asmus, 'Bonn and East Berlin: The "New" German Question?', *The Washington Quarterly* 9, No.1 (Winter 1986), p.56.
5. Wolfgang Schaeuble, 'Die deutsche Frage im europaeischen und weltpolitischen Rahmen', *Europa Archiv*, No.12 (1986), p.341.
6. *Die Zeit*, Hamburg, 15 August 1986, pp.9–10.

6 The GDR's Deutschlandpolitik in the Early 1980s (Gerd Meyer)

1. See Gerd Meyer, *Buerokratischer Sozialismus* (Stuttgart: 1977), *Sozialis-tische Systeme* (Opladen: 1979) and *Das Politische System der DDR* (Frankfurt/Main: 1984), edited version in English by Eberhard Schulz: *GDR Foreign Policy* (Armonk, NY: M.E. Sharpe, 1982).
2. For a systematic overview of the GDR's foreign policy see Hans Adolph Jacobsen *et al.*(eds), *Drei Jahrzehnte Aussenpolitik der DDR* (Munich/ Vienna: 1979); Wilhelm Bruns, *Die Aussenpolitik der DDR* (West Berlin, 1985). In June 1987, the Twentieth DDR-Forschertagung dealt with 'Das Profil der DDR in der sozialistischen Staatengemeinschaft'. Papers presented, for example, by S. Kupper, B.v. Plate and W. Pfeiler analyzed the relations between GDR, the USSR and Eastern Europe. For excellent accounts of the press dispute on the GDR's foreign policy in 1984, especially toward the FRG, see Ronald D. Asmus, 'East Berlin and Moscow: The Documentation of a Dispute' (RFE-RL/RAD Background Report 158) (25 August 1984) and William E. Griffith, 'Superpower Problems in Europe: A Comparative Assessment, *Orbis* 29, No. 4 (1986).

3. *New York Times*, 5 September 1987.
4. See, for example, *Der Spiegel* 39/1984, p.19.
5. *New York Times*, 15 September 1984.
6. Ilse Spittmann, 'Die deutsche Option', *Deutschland Archiv* 5 (1984) p.453.
7. Christian Schmidt-Haeuer, *Die Zeit* 38, 21 September 1984, p.83; *Der Spiegel* 32 (1984) pp.35–8; and *Der Spiegel* 37 (1984), pp.17–32. See also Griffith, 'Superpower Problems in Europe: A Comparative Assessment'.
8. *Neues Deutschland*, 26–7 November, 1983.
9. For a good overview of the period 1982–4 see Ronald D. Asmus, 'East and West Germany: Continuity and Change', *The World Today* 4 (1984) pp.142–51. For an overview of the preceding period see Wilhelm Bruns, *Deutsch-deutsche Beziehungen* (Opladen: 1984).
10. For a very clear and detailed analysis of the years 1984–6 see Griffith, 'Superpower Problems in Europe: A Comparative Assessment', who also gives a quite complete overview of original sources and recent literature.
11. *Frankfurter Rundschau*, 7 August 1984.
12. See *Der Spiegel* 37 (1984) pp.17–32.
13. See the article by 'Vladimirov', a pseudonym for CPSU Central Committee member O. Rachmanin, who in effect argued against greater autonomy for the East European states in the Warsaw Pact. *Pravda*, 21 June 1985.
14. See Griffith, 'Superpower Problems in Europe: A Comparative Assessment', (for more details and documentary references); also Gerhard Wettig 'Die kleineren Warschauer-Pakt-Staaten in den Ost-West-Beziehungen. Berichte des Bundesinstituts fuer ostwissensch-aftliche und internationale Studien', Cologne, No. 39/1985.
15. Asmus, 'East and West Germany: Continuity and Change', p.145.
16. For further details and analysis see Hans-Joachim Spanger, 'Initiativen der DDR zur Vertrauensbildung und Ruestungskontrolle', (paper presented at the Twentieth DDR-Forschertagung, June 1987).
17. See, for example, *Neues Deutschland*, 22–3 November 1986, p.3; or Honecker's 'Address to the First District Secretaries [1. Kreissekretaere] of the SED', given on 6 February 1987, printed in *Neues Deutschland*, 7 February 1987.
18. See W. Pfeiler, 'Die DDR als Bruderstaat' (paper presented at the Twentieth DDR-Forschertagung, June 1987).

7 Changing Security Dimensions of the Inter-German Relationship (Jonathan Dean)

1. For this earlier period of the inter-German relationship, see Peter Bender, 'Interessen in Mitteleuropa', in *Merkur*, Stuttgart, #8, 1987; Christian Hacke, 'Von Adenauer zu Kohl: Zur Ost-und Deutschland-Politik der Bundesrepublik, 1949–1985' in *Das Parlament*, Bonn, B 51–52/85, 21 December 1985; Hans-Adolf Jacobsen *et al.*, *Drei Jahrzehnte Aussenpolitik der DDR* (Munich: R. Oldenbourg Verlag,

1979); and Jonathan Dean, 'Directions in Inner-German Relations', *Orbis* 29, No. 3 (Fall 1985).

2. Text in *Dokumentation zur Entspannungspolitik der Bundesregierung-Deutschlandpolitik*, Press and Information Office of the Federal German Government, 9th edn. 1981, p.66.

3. Helmut Kohl, 'Report of the FRG Government on the State of the Nation in a Separated Germany', Bundestag, 15 October 1987 (excerpts), *Europa Archiv* 22 (25 November 1987), pp. D603–12.

4. Sources: Foreign Broadcast Information Service (FBIS), *Soviet Union*, 7 July 1987, Page H7; FBIS-WEU-87-200, 16 October 1987, p.6; *Statements and Speeches*, German Information Center, New York, vol. X, no. 15, 9 Sept. 1987, p.9.

5. 'Joint Statement of Helmut Kohl and Erich Honecker', *Deutschland Archiv* 18 (April 1985), p.446.

6. 'Speech of French President François Mitterrand in Bonn, January 20, 1983', *Europa Archiv* 5 (10 March 1983), pp.D145–55.

7. Press and Information Office of the Federal German Government, *Jahresbericht der Bundesregierung 1986*, Bonn, p.283.

8. For further discussion of gains and losses from extending the inter-German dialogue to security issues, see Wilhelm Bruns, *Der Beitrag der beiden deutschen Staaten zur Sicherheits und Entspannungspolitik* (Bonn: Friedrich-Ebert-Stiftung, January 1986); and Jonathan Dean, *Watershed in Europe* (Lexington, MA: Lexington Books), pp.250–6.

9. Text in Pressemitteilung 38/85; 3 December 1985, Bundesministerium fuer innerdeutsche Beziehungen.

10. For details, see Bruns, *Der Beitrag der beiden deutschen Staaten*, pp.6–8.

11. Wilhelm Bruns, 'Die deutsch-deutschen Beziehungen in der zweiten Haelfte der achtziger Jahre', in *Das Parlament*, Bonn B 51–52/85, 21 December 1985.

12. Author's own notes.

13. The Independent Commission of Disarmament and Security Issues, *Common Security* (New York: Simon and Schuster, 1982), pp.15–151.

14. See articles by Hermann Scheer and Karsten Voigt in *Aus Friedenssehnsucht praktische Friedenspolitik machen* (Munich: Rolfe Seeliger Verlag, 1986).

15. 'Pressenkonferenz Mit Egon Bahr und Hermann Axen', SPD Bundestagsfraktion Tagesdienst, 21 October 1986.

16. Karsten Voigt, 'On the SPD/SED Proposal for a Nuclear Weapon Free Corridor', *Deutschland Archiv*, February 1987.

17. *Frankfurter Allgemeine Zeitung*, 19 February 1988.

18. For summaries of proposals on non-provocative or alternate defense, see David Gates, 'Area Defense Concepts: The West German Debate', in *Survival* (July–August 1987); and Jonathan Dean, 'Alternative Defense: Answer to NATO's Central Front Problems', *International Affairs* 64, No.1 (Winter 1987/8).

19. See Wilhelm Bruns, 'Nach dem Honecker-Besuch – und wie weiter?' *Aussenpolitik*, No.4, 1987.

20. Joint Communiqué on the Honecker visit to the FRG, *Europa Archiv* 19 (10 October 1987), pp. D538–43.

21. Text of the Kohl–Honecker communiqué is in *Statements and Speeches*, vol. X, No. 15, 9 Sept. 1987, distributed by the German Information Center, New York.
22. Text of the letter is in FBIS-EEU-88-02, 5 January 1988, pp.10–11.
23. New Year's Speech of Erich Honecker, *Neues Deutschland*, 31 December 1987.
24. Reported in the *Frankfurter Allgemeine Zeitung*, 8 October 1987.
25. Reported in *Frankfurter Allgemeine Zeitung*, 9 July 1987.
26. 'US Envoy Rebukes Pentagon Aides', *The New York Times*, 17 December 1986.

8   The View from Moscow (F. Stephen Larrabee)

1. See Gerhard Wettig, 'The Soviet View', in Edwina Moreton (ed), *Germany Between East and West* (Cambridge: Cambridge University Press, 1987) p. 39.
2. Joseph Stalin, *Economic Problems of Socialism in the USSR* (New York: International Publishers, 1952) pp.28–9.
3. For a balanced discussion see Boris Meissner, 'Die deutsch-sowjetischen Beziehungen seit dem Zweiten Weltkrieg', *Osteuropa* 9/85, pp.631–52. For the argument that Stalin's offer represented a 'missed opportunity' see Paul Sethe, *Zwischen Bonn und Moskau* (Frankfurt: Verlag H. Scheffler, 1956). For a more recent interpretation of this view, see Rolf Steininger, *Die vertane Chance. Die Stalin Note vom 10 Maerz 1952 und die Wiedervereinigung* (Berlin: Verlag J.H.W. Dietz Machf, 1985).
4. Waldemar Besson, *Die Aussenpolitik der Bundesrepublik* (Munich: R. Piper Verlag, 1970) p.125.
5. This section draws heavily on the author's article, 'Moscow and the German Question: Continuities and Changes', *Problems of Communism*, (March–April 1981) pp.68–75.
6. It is impossible to date the change precisely. However, preparations for it seem to have been undertaken some time between mid-October 1968 and the beginning of 1969. For a detailed discussion, see F. Stephen Larrabee, 'The Politics of Reconciliation: Soviet Policy Toward West Germany 1964–1972', unpublished Ph.D. dissertation, Columbia University, 1978, pp.180–218.
7. Brandt insisted, however, that the Federal Republic could not recognize the GDR under international law – one of the major preconditions postulated by the East German leadership for the normalization of relations – because the GDR was 'not a foreign country'. For the text of Brandt's address, see *Europa Archiv*, No.21, 1969, D 499–506.
8. For the provisions of the treaty, see *Der Vertrag vom 12. August 1970 zwischen der Bundesrepublik Deutschland und der Union Sozialistischer Sowjetrepubliken* (The Treaty of 12 August 1970 Between the Federal Republic of Germany and the Union of Soviet Socialist Republics) Bonn, Presse- und Informationsamt der Bundesregierung, 1970, pp.7–9. The Russian text is in *Pravda*, 16 May 1972.
9. *Die Zeit* (Hamburg) 25 October 1974.
10. A detailed analysis of Soviet–West German economic relations is

beyond the scope of this essay. For a comprehensive discussion, see Angela Stent, *From Embargo to Ostpolitik* (Cambridge: Cambridge University Press, 1981).

11. For a detailed discussion of Soviet policy and West German reactions to the missile crisis at this time, see Elizabeth Pond, 'Andropov, Kohl and East–West Issues', *Problems of Communism* (July–August 1983) pp.35–45.

12. Gromyko (along with Ustinov) is largely credited with being the architect of the confrontational policy pursued by Moscow after the collapse of the INF talks in November 1983. As noted below, his removal as foreign minister was an important prerequisite for the shift in Soviet policy on INF as well as relations with Bonn.

13. For a good discussion of the East European reaction see Charles Gati, 'The Soviet Empire: Alive But Not Well', *Problems of Communism* (March–April 1985) pp.73–86, especially pp. 77–81. Also Ronald D. Asmus, 'The Dialectics of Détente and Discord', *Orbis* (Winter 1985) pp.753–7.

14. For a detailed discussion of the dynamics of the dispute see Asmus, 'The Dialectics of Détente and Discord', pp.743–74. Also see Gerd Meyer's chapter in this volume.

15. For Honecker's speech see *Neues Deutschland*, 26–7 November 1983.

16. For background, see Ronald D. Asmus, *East Berlin and Moscow: The Documentation of a Dispute*, Radio Free Europe Research, Background Report/158, 25 August 1984.

17. For details see F. Stephen Larrabee and Allen Lynch, 'Gorbachev: the Road to Reykjavik', *Foreign Policy* (Winter 1986–7) pp.3–28.

18. See Fred Oldenburg, 'Das Verhaeltnis Moskau-Bonn unter Gorbatschow, *Osteuropa* (August/September 1986) pp.774–86.

19. The Soviet preference for the SPD was made clear in particular by the unusual publicity accorded former Chancellor Willy Brandt, a Soviet favorite since the early days of the *Ostpolitik*, during his visit to Moscow in May 1985 as well as the cordial treatment given the SPD's Chancellor candidate Johannes Rau during his visit to the USSR in September 1985. This favorable treatment contrasted markedly to the cold shoulder which Moscow accorded Kohl during this period. For a good discussion of Soviet attitudes and policy toward the European left at this time see John van Oudenaren, 'The Soviet Union and the Socialist and Social Democratic Parties of Western Europe', N-2400-AF (Santa Monica: The Rand Corporation, February 1985).

20. The invitation of Strauss is an indication of the increasing sophistication of Soviet policy lately. It appears to have been designed to exploit Strauss's increasing disenchantment with US policy as well as his barely disguised nationalism. If this was the Soviet calculation, it clearly worked. Strauss, who had never visited Moscow in his entire political career, was warmly received by Gorbachev and returned with lavish praise for the Soviet leader, announcing that a 'new era had begun' and that Bonn should begin to deal directly with Moscow. See 'Gorbachev hofft auf bessere Kontakte, Strauss: Eine neue Seite aufgeschlagen', *Frankfurter Allgemeine Zeitung*, 31 December 1987;

also 'Lob von Strauss fuer Moskaus Abruestungspolitik', *Neue Zuercher Zeitung*, 1 January 1988, and Karl-Christian Kaiser, 'Spaete Entdeckung', *Die Zeit* Nr.2, 8 January 1988.

21. David Marsh, 'Moscow Eases Curbs on German Emigration', *Financial Times*, 12 January 1988.

22. 'Genscher and Schewardnadse erzielen Fortschritte fuer West-Berlin in "praktischen Bereich"', *Frankfurter Allgemeine Zeitung*, 29 September 1988.

23. Claus Gennrich, 'Stockungen in der Beziehungen zu Bonn passen nicht in das Bild der Moskauer Aussenpolitik', *Frankfurter Allgemeine Zeitung*, 29 September 1988. Also 'Genscher und Schewardnadse erzielen Fortschritte fuer West-Berlin in "praktischen Bereich"'.

24. See in particular Genscher's speech in Davos, Switzerland, in February 1987, 'Nehmen wir Gorbatschow's "Neue Politik" beim Wort' (Bonn: Auswaertiges Amt und Presse- und Informationsamt der Bundesregierung, March 1987); and his speech at the Institute for East–West Security Studies conference in St. Paul, Minnesota, in October 1987, 'Towards a Strategy for Progress', *Implications of Soviet New Thinking* (New York: Institute for East–West Security Studies, 1987), pp.33–47.

25. See in particular Minister for the Federal Chancellery Dr Wolfgang Schaeuble, 'Die Deutsche Frage in Europa', *Europa Archiv* No. 19, pp.414–20, especially p.420. See also the speech by Bundesminister for Inner-German Relations Dr Dorothee Wilms, 'Europaeische Integration und deutsche Einheit', *Bulletin des Presse- und Informationsamt der Bundesregierung* No. 75, 8 June 1988, pp. 726–8.

26. In his speech to the 27th Party Congress, for instance, Gorbachev noted that 'the existing complement of economic, politico-military and other common interests of the three centers of power [that is, the United States, Japan and Western Europe – FSL] can hardly be expected to break up in the present-day world'. See *Pravda*, 23 February 1986.

27. The growing divergence of interests between the United States and its West European allies has been a common theme in Soviet analyses over the last few years. See in particular Yu. P. Davydov, 'SShA-Zapadnaia Evropa: vremia partnerstva', *SShA: ekonomika, politika, ideologiia*, no.5 (May 1987) pp.3–14; Yu. Shistko, 'Inter-imperialist Rivalry Escalates', *International Affairs* (Moscow), no.5 (May 1986) pp. 28–36; and A. Knyazyn, 'Militarization and Inter-imperialist Rivalry', Ibid., no. 4 (April 1986), pp.47–54. Also the important articles by Alexander Yakovlev, one of Gorbachev's closest advisors and now a member of the Politburo. 'Mezhimperialisticheskiie protivorechiia–sovremennyi kontekst', *Kommunist* no.17 (November 1986) pp.3–17, and 'Opasnaia os' amerikano-zapadno-germanskogo militarizma', *SShA*, no.7 (July 1985) pp.3–15. For a good Western discussion see Harry Gelman, 'Gorbachev's Policies Toward Western Europe: A Balance Sheet', R-3588-AF (Santa Monica: The Rand Corporation, October 1987).

28. For a good discussion of Yakovlev's views see Gelman, *Gorbachev's Policies Toward Western Europe: A Balance Sheet*, pp. 49–51.

29. This is *not* to suggest that Western Europe will replace the United

States as the main focus of Soviet attention, as some analysts have suggested, but rather that Soviet policy toward Western Europe is likely to become more active and sophisticated. The creation of the new Institute on Europe, headed by Vitali Zhurkin, the former Deputy Director of the Institute for the Study of the USA and Canada, also points in this direction.

30. 'Hennig vermutet deutschlandpolitische Planspiele', *Frankfurter Allgemeine Zeitung*, 26 September 1988; *Der Spiegel* no.41, 5 October 1987, p.14.
31. See N. Portugalov, 'Die Bonner Torwarte oder die Angst der CDU/CSU vor der Abruestung', *Neue Zeit* no.22, 29 May 1987, p.12. Falin's remarks came in an interview on German television on 23 September 1987. For a detailed discussion see Fred Oldenburg, 'Neues Denken in der sowjetischen Deutschlandpolitik?', *Deutschland Archiv* no.11 (November 1987) pp.1154–60.
32. *Pravda*, 8 July 1987. For discussion see Dettmar Cramer, 'Der Bundespraesident in der Sowjetunion', *Deutschland Archiv* no.8 (August 1987) pp.792–4. Gorbachev's remarks are repeated almost verbatim in his book *Perestroika* (New York: Harper and Row, 1987), p.200.
33. For Gorbachev's speech, see *Izvestia*, 26 October 1988.

9 American Interests and the German–German Dialogue (W. Richard Smyser)

1. W. R. Smyser, *German–American Relations* (Beverly Hills: Sage, 1980), p.12.
2. International Institute for Strategic Studies (IISS), *The Military Balance, 1986–1987* (London: IISS, 1986), pp.67–9.
3. Ibid., pp.28–9.
4. FRG Defense Ministry, *The German Contribution to the Common Defense* (Bonn: FRG Press and Information Office, 1986), pp.18–24.
5. Henry A. Kissinger, *White House Years* (Boston: Little Brown, 1979), pp.821–5.
6. *Documents on Germany, 1944–1985* (Washington: US Department of State, 1986), pp.1059–64.
7. Ibid., p.1088.
8. Address by Ambassador Kenneth Rush before the Foreign Policy Society of Munich, 20 October 1970, Ibid., p.1110.
9. Ibid., pp.1135–43.
10. Kissinger, *White House Years*.
11. *U.S. Foreign Policy for the 1970's: Shaping a Durable Peace* (Washington: US Government Printing Office, 3 May 1973) p.28.
12. *Innerdeutsche Beziehungen: Die Entwicklung der Beziehungen zwischen der Bundesrepublik Deutschland und der Deutschen Demokratischen Republik 1980–1986* (Bonn: Bundesministerium fuer innerdeutsche Beziehungen, 1986), pp.26–37.
13. *Frankfurter Allgemeine Zeitung*, 11 April 1987.
14. *Der Spiegel*, 27 April 1987, p.133.
15. *Frankfurter Allgemeine Zeitung*, 7 July 1987. It should be emphasized

that the number refers, like past figures, to number of *visits*, not *visitors*, as calculated in East German statistics. Persons may, and indeed do, visit more than once, so that there are somewhat fewer visitors than visits.

16. *Der Spiegel*, 27 April 1987, p.133.
17. *Frankfurter Allgemeine Zeitung*, 10 June 1987.
18. For background of the discussions leading to these visits, see *Frankfurter Allgemeine Zeitung*, 3 and 17 July 1987; *New York Times*, 11 and 19 July 1987; and *Washington Times*, 9 July 1987.
19. The Honecker visit was extensively covered in the East and West German press, and information on it can be obtained from either *Neues Deutschland* or such West German newspapers as *Frankfurter Allgemeine Zeitung* during the week beginning 7 September 1987. The official West German record, containing principal speeches, agreements and the final communiqué, is in the FRG *Bulletin*, Nr. 83/S.705, 10 September 1987.
20. For consideration of some of these factors, see Lawrence L. Whetten, *Germany East and West* (New York: New York University Press, 1980) pp.81–6; Edwina Moreton, 'The German Factor', Moreton and Gerald Segal(eds), *Soviet Strategy Toward Western Europe* (London: George Allen & Unwin, 1984) p.131.
21. Wilhelm Bruns, 'Foreign Policy at the 11th SED Party Congress', *Aussenpolitik* (March 1986) p.305.
22. German Information Center, New York, *Statements and Speeches*, 23 March 1987, pp.3–5.
23. *Frankfurter Allgemeine Zeitung*, 9–13 June and 3 July 1987.

11   France's German Problem (Anne-Marie LeGloannec)

1. In the Federal Republic, however, for obvious reasons interest in research on the GDR developed soon – even if it was permanently biased.
2. Alfred Grosser, 'L'Interdit', *Le Monde*, 20 January 1982, p.2.
3. Jean Genet, 'A propos de la Rote Armee Fraktion. Violence et Brutalité', *Le Monde*, 2 September 1977, pp.1–2.
4. See A.-M. LeGloannec, 'Les réactions allemandes à la crise polonaise', *Documents* 37, no.1 (March 1982), pp.3–13.
5. See Wilfried Loth, 'Die Franzosen und die deutsche Frage 1945–1949', in Claus Scharf and Hans-Juergen Schroder (eds), *Die Deutschlandpolitik Frankreichs und die franzoesiche Zone 1945–1949* (Wiesbaden: Franz Steiner Verlag), quoted in Ernst Weisenfeld, *Welches Deutschland soll es sein? Frankreich und die deutsche Einheit seit 1945* (Munich: Beck Verlag, 1986) p.30.
6. See De Gaulle's press conference, March 1959, in Charles De Gaulle *Discours et Messages: Avec le renouveau: 1958–1962* (Paris: Plon, 1970).
7. Ibid.
8. Stanley Hoffmann, 'Verlobt, doch nicht verheiratet. Frankreich zwischen dem Wunsch nach Einbindung der Bundesregierung und eigener Unabhaengigkeit?' *Die Zeit*, 29 March 1985, as quoted by Ernst Weisenfeld, *Welches Deutschland soll es sein?*, p.112.

9. Thirty-one per cent considered it would foster peace in Europe and 33 per cent remained undecided. *L'Express* 17–23 March 1979, pp.84–5.
10. Twenty-eight per cent favored an active French policy in this respect and 15 per cent an active opposition. *Le Nouvel Observateur*, 10–16 February 1984, pp.41–3.
11. Claire Trean, 'La France doit garantir la sécurité de la RFA', *Le Monde*, 28 June 1985, pp.1–2.
12. Jean-Marie Soutou, 'Eine Stimme zur Frage der deutschen Einheit', *Dokumente*, No. 2, April 1986, p.140.
13. François Mitterrand, *Réflexions sur la politique extérieure de la France. Introduction à vingt-cinq discourses, 1981–1985* (Paris: Fayard, 1986), p.208.
14. According to polls, the French look increasingly favorably upon their German neighbors.
15. As the Guadeloupe summit evidenced.
16. 'The glorious thirty years. . .', as the 1940s, 1950s and 1960s were called in France. The keys to prosperity were both internal (reconstruction, the baby boom, new needs and new products, domestic in particular) and external (the creation of the Common Market and the liberalization of exchanges).
17. Coming half a century after the 'blue line of the Vosges'.
18. This debate is still going on.
19. In spite of subsequent re-evaluations of the West Germany currency resulting from increasing trade surpluses, West German goods would find even more customers and the trade surpluses would boom.
20. CEPII is the Centre d'Etudes Prospectives et d'Informations Internationales.
21. Quoted by the weekly *Stern*, 26 April 1984.
22. See Alain Minc, *Le Syndrome Finlandais* (Paris: Seuil, 1986) p.223.
23. See Jean-Marie Soutou in *Frankfurter Allgemeine Zeitung*, 6 May 1985, p.5.
24. Ibid.
25. Giuseppe Walter Maccotta, 'Alcune Considerazione sulla Force de Frappe', *Revista Marittima* (April 1982) quoted in François Puaux, 'La France, l'Allemagne et l'atome: discord improbable, accord impossible', *Defense Nationale* (December 1985). See also Walter Schutze: *Frankreichs Verteidigungspolitik, 1958–1983* (Frankfurt am Main: Haag Herchen, 1983).
26. François Puaux, 'La France, l'Allemagne et l'atome', p.12.
27. Michel Tatu, *Eux et Nous: Les Relations Est–Ouest entre Deux Détentes* (Paris: Fayard, 1985), p.240.
28. See Nicole Gnesotto in a detailed article on Franco-German military cooperation: 'Le Dialogue franco-allemand depuis 1954: patience et longueur de temps', in Pierre Lellouche and Karl Kaise (eds); *Le Couple franco-allemand et la défense de l'Europe* (Paris: IFRI, Economica, 1986), pp.59–66.
29. These agreements are still classified.
30. *Défense Nationale*, June 1976.
31. See the details in André Adrets (pseudonym), 'Les relations franco-

allemandes et le fait nucléaire dans une Europe divisée', in *Politique Etrangère* 31/1984, p.651, as well as Pascal Boniface and François Heisbourg, *La Puce, Les Hommes, et La Bombe: l'Europe face aux nouveaux défis technologiques et militaires* (Paris: Hachette, 1986) p.242.

32. See Adrets, 'Les relations franco-allemandes'.
33. Sixty-four per cent of the French thought of france as a middle power and 23 per cent as a great power. Jérome Dumoulin and Yves Guihannec, 'La France – est elle encore une grande puissance?', *L'Express*, 27 January–2 February 1984, pp.12–19.
34. See, on this poll and generally speaking on the consensus in France, Michel Dobry: 'Le jeu du consensus', in the issue of *Pouvoirs* devoted to 'L'Armée', 38 (1986) pp.47–66.
35. See Sofres, *Le Figaro-Magazine*, 9 July 1983, pp.46–7.
36. IFOP, *Le Monde*, 28 June 1985.
37. See Pierre Hassner, 'Les limites du pragmatisme', *Politique Etrangère*, no.4, 1984, p.941.
38. RPR, *La défense de la France. 4 ans de gestion socialiste, propositions pour le renouveau* (Paris, July 1985).
39. UDF, *Redresser la défense de la France* (Paris, November 1985).
40. PS, *La sécurité de l'Europe* (Paris, July 1985).
41. Pierre Hassner, 'La cooperation franco-allemande: Achille immobile à grands pas!' in Pierre Lellouche and Karl Kaiser (eds), *Le Couple franco-allemand*, pp.171–4. See also the evolution of François Heisbourg, who is now pleading much more daringly than he used to in favor of a French nuclear responsibility. A former counsellor to Charles Hernu, Heisbourg is now director of the International Institute for Strategic Studies in London.
42. Interview with Pierre Lellouche, *Le Point*, 9 July 1984, p.46.
43. Quoted by André Fontaine, *Le Monde*, 31 March 1984.
44. For a detailed account of German reactions to French propositions, see my paper 'Les Allemands et la dissuasion française ou: les ambiguîtés franco-allemandes', in Lellouche and Kaiser, *Le Couple franco-allemand*, pp.91–101.
45. See Helmut Schmidt's recent advocacy in the weekly magazine which he co-edits, *Die Zeit*, 21 November 1986, p.3 and the reply of Rudolf Augstein, director of *Der Spiegel*, in *Der Spiegel*, 1 December 1986, pp.20–1.
46. David S. Yost, 'Franco-German Defense Cooperation', *The Washington Quarterly* 11, no.2 (Spring 1988), pp.173–95.
47. Pierre Hassner, 'Un chef d'oeuvre en péril. La consensus françoise sur la défense', in *La France en Politique* (Paris: Editions du Seuil/Esprit, 1988), pp.71–82.
48. As former Prime Minister Fabius's visit in 1984 proved, when he made a blunder, accepting at his dinner table a general whose presence should have been barred from Berlin.
49. *Le Monde*, 9 January 1983.

12 Economic Relations between the Two German States (Gert Leptin)

1. There is non-economic control of exports to the GDR as to all other East European countries owing to COCOM regulations.
2. This share is calculated with figures from the statistical yearbook of the GDR, in which 'Intra-German Trade' is included on the basis of currency unit = 1 Valutamark (1VE = 1VM). If it is recalculated like other Western currencies via US$/transferable ruble-relations into Valutamark (4.67 VM = 1 tr.Rbl.), the share of inter-German trade would be about 11.5 per cent.
3. The additional protocol to the treaty on the European Economic Community of 1957 declares that in relation to the Federal Republic of Germany the German areas outside the validity of the basic law of the Federal Republic as inter-German trade are not affected by the regulations of the treaty.
4. Reported by Bank for International Settlements, Basel, April 1987; GDR bank assets, about $7.5 billion.
5. Interest payments alone amounted to nearly $900 million.
6. There has been an uninterrupted series of illegal or semi-legal deals over the years which can be traced to GDR state enterprises, from the prohibited indirect deliveries of Cuban sugar in 1968–9, to the attempt to defraud by providing subsidies in connection with Hamburg butter exports to Rostock in 1970, to the imports from such low-wage countries as Hong Kong and South Korea via the GDR in 1979.
7. One need only remember the GDR clothing prices made public by the West German government only a few years ago: suits for DM 7.50 and shirts for less than one Deutschmark, at DM 0.65 apiece. It was only by making these prices public (especially to the East German population) that the West German government was able to influence the GDR to hold back its deliveries without reducing import quotas.
8. There are no formal connections between the new swing agreement of 1985 and the limitation of the inflow of Tamil refugees via the GDR (Schoenefeld airport) to West Berlin, imposed by the GDR government.
9. In this respect it has to be repeated that deliveries to the GDR are subject to the same COCOM inspections as deliveries to all communist countries of Eastern Europe, including the Soviet Union.
10. This was internationally acknowledged in 1951 when the Federal Republic of Germany entered into the General Agreement on Tariffs and Trade (GATT).
11. 'Misuse' only in economic terms.

13   GDR-FRG Economic Relations (Juergen Nitz)

1. Treaty on Basic Principles of Relations between the German Democratic Republic and the Federal Republic of Germany, 21 December 1972, in *Vertraege im Dienste der europaeischen Sicherheit*, Berlin, 1979 p.103ff.
2. Ibid.
3. All numerical data given according to clearing mode under 1951 Agreement, including services and statistical calculations, unless stated otherwise.
4. Juergen Nitz, 'Probleme der Wirtschaftsbeziehungen zwischen Sozialismus und Kapitalismus', *IPW-Forschungshefte*, 2/1977, Berlin; and Juergen Nitz and Paul Freiberg, 'Probleme und Perspektiven der Ost-West-Wirtschaftsbeziehungen', *IPW-Forschungshefte*, 3/1984, Berlin.
5. *Report of the Central Committee of the Socialist Unity Party of Germany to the XIth Congress of SED*, given by Erich Honecker; *Directive of XIth SED Congress on the Five Year Plan for the Development of the GDR National Economy, 1986 to 1990* (Berlin, 1986).
6. *Documents and Proceedings of the CMEA Summit*, Moscow, 12–14 June 1984 (Moscow ADN Publishers, 1984).
7. See note 5.
8. *General-Anzeiger*, Bonn, 17–18 November 1984.
9. *Neues Deutschland*, 13 November 1985.
10. *Neues Deutschland*, 19 September 1985, p.2 and 24 September 1985, p.1.